Craig Calhoun

The Question of Class Struggle

Social Foundations of Popular Radicalism during the Industrial Revolution

The University of Chicago Press

The University of Chicago Press, Chicago 60637
Basil Blackwell Publisher Limited
108 Cowley Road, Oxford OX4 1JF

Library of Congress Cataloging in Publication Data

Calhoun, Craig J., 1952–
  The Question of Class Struggle

  Bibliography: p.
  Includes index.
  1. Labor and laboring classes—England—History.
2. Populism—England—History.   3. Radicalism—England—History.   I. Title.
HD8399.E52C34   305.5′6   81-2018
ISBN 0–226–09090–6   AACR2

Craig Calhoun is assistant professor of sociology at the
University of North Carolina, Chapel Hill.

Contents

Preface

The most widespread, powerful, and radical social movements in the modern world have been of a type we may call "populist." They have been born and nurtured of attachments to tradition and community; they have seen an intimate connection between the immediate and local motivations of their actions and the less clear but larger and more lasting results at which they aimed. These movements have been consistently misunderstood by contemporary commentators, historians, and social theorists. Most such thinkers have, where they were sympathetic enough to treat seriously of the populists at all, assimilated their movements to either or both of the great modern tendencies in high culture: rationalism and romanticism.

This pattern of error began in earnest during the British industrial revolution. A great many of the "common people" of Britain protested against and resisted the social, economic, and political changes which were disrupting their traditional way of life and depriving them of such few improvements in it as they had recently won. They were joined in a growing chorus of protest by liberals deriving their lineage from Locke and by several of the protagonists in the fledgling romantic movement. In the Jacobinism of the early 1790s the rationalists who upheld and ultimately transformed the eighteenth-century intellectual heritage joined cause with some of the earlier devotées of the singular dramatic act, the sentient nation, and the purity of force. The theoretical commonality of the two tendencies was almost wholly a matter of "individualism," and it soon became apparent that each understood the nature and obligations of individuals in a very different way. Of enduring philosophies only Marxism managed any sort of synthesis of rationalism and romanticism. It did this largely by the invention of the proletariat as a singularly rational yet romantically unified individual historical actor.

This synthesis is remarkable for its intellectual quality but still more so for the power with which it has held sway over later thinkers. It has been accepted and rejected for reasons of varying seriousness and acuity, but the problems stemming from this initial synthesis have never been fully understood, let alone worked out. This has meant, among other things, that Marxists (and most of their opponents, who have been greatly influenced by their enemy) have been unable to understand populism and thus have not understood the motivations of the bulk of social movements during transitions to industrialism and many of those in the advanced industrial countries themselves.

This problem is particularly apparent in historical studies of the early modern popular movements (those in the late eighteenth and, especially, nineteenth centuries), for two reasons. First, these have occurred in countries where a wide range of ideological positions was in fairly clear evidence and not complicated by the addition of anticolonial sentiments. Second, the empirical investigations of historians have been extremely thorough and have benefited from generations of scholarly debate. Especially with the development of the "new" social history during the last twenty years, a tremendous wealth of historical information has become available to readers, especially in English and French. No comparable theoretical treatment has yet been made. The new information continues to be understood through the old—especially Marxist—categories. Indeed, debates which are essentially theoretical have often been carried out with the problematic tools of "facts." Only on rare occasions has the new wealth of information pushed thinkers to reformulate relatively general theories, and in these few instances the attempts have been unsystematic.

The present work is something of a prolegomenon to such a rethinking of our theories of community, class, and collective action, of revolution and popular protest. It is an attempt to explore systematically and in some detail the problem as it appears in one historical instance. The instance is that of Britain between Jacobinism and Chartism, from the 1790s to the 1840s. This is a critical instance for two reasons. First, it provided the empirical and experiential basis for the original development of the theory of working-class radicalism. Second, it has been a central focus of later empirical research shaped by the general theory. In order to elucidate the problems of using the theory in empirical analysis, I have focused a good deal of attention on a single work. This is E. P. Thompson's *The Making of the English Working Class*, one of the masterpieces of social history. Surprisingly, in the nearly twenty years since its publication, *The Making* (as I shall cite it throughout) has never been subjected to a full-scale analysis. It has been of great influence in the study not only of British history but also that of America, France, Germany, and lately, parts of the Third World. It is therefore of interest not only for its own sake but as a key exemplar in a widespread style of inquiry. It is a densely empirical book, though not without theoretical intentions, the efficacy of which its subsequent influence illustrates.

The Making is, in the first place, a response to the neglect of certain historical actors—the workers of England—in favor of seemingly greater trends and issues. A bit paradoxically, its own title reveals Thompson's intention to pose, perhaps often implicitly, an argument about a general developmental tendency, one which I shall dispute. In the second place, the book is a polemic against economistic interpretations of working-class history and, relatedly, against dehumanized, depersonalized accounts of the industrial revolution. Thirdly, The Making is full of arguments against the too-rigid application of Marxist categories and against the degradation of Marxism into a scholastic discipline more characterized by arcane debates than by sympathetic understanding.

Thompson succeeds to an admirable degree in all of these undertakings (which are only three of the most important among many issues taken up in The Making). He succeeds most of all in the first, in the recreation and reanalysis of a tremendous range of events, situations, and actions, and the people who lived them. His sensitivity in such specific accounts is remarkable. It is unfortunately not matched by an equal quality of overall argument. The Making is somewhat chaotic in organization, though not without its consistent points. Thompson's disdain for abstract argument occasionally weakens his well-aimed responses to problems in theory and conceptualization. More importantly, though, Thompson marshalls a considerable weight of evidence which he does not follow to its logical conclusions but instead assimilates to somewhat idiosyncratically and unclearly formulated Marxist categories which do not fit it very well. In particular, Thompson struggles to find a single pattern of development from Jacobinism to the "made" working class of early Chartism, a pattern which incorporates rationalism and romanticism in a stable admixture. With his conceptual tools drawn from Marxism, and from the early rationalists and romantics, Thompson fails to confront the community-based, populist movement which he has, in part, empirically described.

The fundamental theoretical problem is of much broader scope than Thompson's studies of eighteenth- and nineteenth-century English workers. General problems in the theory of working-class radicalism, however, stem in large part from misapprehensions or misusages of correct understandings of the circumstances, organization, and movements of those English workers. In the present work, I shall not for the most part engage in purely abstract theoretical argument. Rather, I shall attempt to show the theory's effect on analyses of the events of the early nineteenth century; it has led into blind alleys, the formulation of insoluble problems, and, occasionally, the abuse of empirical evidence in argument. I shall suggest that the roots of the theory in the period of the industrial revolution continue in unexamined ways to shape its conceptualizations and arguments. Anticipations of and hopes for historical developments—such as class solidarity and revolutionary collective action—have led to the posing of questions in misleading or unanswerable forms and to the empirical and theoretical neglect of the bases on which better analyses could be built. These last, I argue, are most importantly to be found in the study of the social foundations of collective action, and the largely traditional premises which may make it radical.

The first chapter introduces my argument by examining problems in the way the theory of working-class radicalism has been used by modern historians to analyze popular protest during the industrial revolution. Most of the discussion is devoted to Thompson. I see his Marxism—at least in his practice of historical analysis—as primarily "culturalist," although in his work *The Poverty of Theory* he has repudiated such a label. That is, he focuses the bulk of his attention and the weight of his argument on the ideas, consciousness, and self-expressions of workers, and proportionately neglects material issues, including the social bases of collective action. My treatment of Thompson attempts to disentangle the theoretical arguments which he generally leaves implicit. I do not discuss all of Thompson's work, only that which bears specifically on the present argument. For example, I have little to say about his treatment of Methodism, a subject which has occupied a disproportionate amount of space in previous discussion. In the last part of the first chapter, I criticize the recent and widely respected—if controversial—analysis of *Class Struggle and the Industrial Revolution* by John Foster. I show, I think, that though it is radically different in its orthodox Leninism from Thompson's argument, Foster's book gives equal primacy to consciousness. It is more rationalistic and less culturalistic than Thompson's view. Consciousness appears as the correct line rather than as what people in fact thought or felt. Foster's argument is also much less subtle and generally less tenable than Thompson's.

In the second, third, and fourth chapters, I develop the narrative of popular protest from Jacobinism through the 1820s, making a few suggestions beyond that decade. Though the narrative is important as background to the argument, it is not the primary concern. Rather, I hope to show why I consider it empirically and theoretically misleading to describe the radicals of this period as the working class. They were, as I show, deeply rooted in many cases in traditional communities of both craft and locality. They acted on this social basis, not on the wider one of class; they thought in these terms, not in the rationalistic ones of class exploitation. In the early parts of this section, especially, I reanalyze Thompson's empirical argument concerning early nineteenth-century workers. Thompson suggests that we can usefully extend the language and conceptual apparatus of class—especially class struggle—back to a time before class structuration was definite or mature. He takes quite seriously Marx's suggestion that the working class was present at its own birth, looking at the consciousness which gave the workers the "agency" to create their own class, largely in political struggle. This dialectical treatment presents analytical problems, however, in considering class action. In particular, it contributes to Thompson's tendency to minimize the important divergences among different parts of what he considers a single class. These divergences include distinctions between workers in different times and places, tied to different modes of production and seeking different ends. Chapter 3 is focused on two movements of the 1810s—Luddism and the parliamentary reform agitation which culminated in the Peterloo Massacre—that illustrate the problems in analyzing the "prehistory" of the English working class as though it were its history. The two movements more resemble those which elsewhere have been called populist than they do class struggle in Marx's sense.

Traditional values and identities remained of great importance to English workers, shaping their political attitudes and activity well into the period of industrialization; indeed, those values did not vanish with Chartism. They underpinned it, and were especially strong and radical in some craft communities. But to assimilate the traditional symbols, which lent cultural unity to workers, into the rationalistic Marxist model of class is to do violence to both. This is nowhere clearer than in the case of the agitation in behalf of Caroline of Brunswick, the spurned consort of George IV. In Chapter 4 I take up this widespread and largely overlooked popular rebellion in the context of a more general examination of the ways in which English workers struggled to defend traditional values. Important symbols stressed the proper behavior of kings (and other lords), the virtues of family life and good relations between the sexes, and the duties of citizens to local communities and the nation.

The fifth chapter concludes the narrative part of the book with a brief look beyond populism. The artisan struggle for autonomy combined with other intellectual currents to develop, eventually, a critique not only of political oppression but also of exploitation. Although there was a time when the two found a common audience, they must be kept analytically distinct. The critique of exploitation within captialist industry appealed much more fully and properly to the new working class which only began to emerge in the 1820s. The artisan struggle for autonomy carried on for generations, guided in large part by traditional notions of a moral economy.

With the sixth chapter, my method of argument changes. The latter part of the book is organized topically and attempts to examine the social foundations of collective action in a less narrative and more conceptual structure. First, Chapter 6 is on the radicalism of traditional communities. In it, I consider the dynamics of authority in traditional England and the way eighteenth- and early nineteenth-century local authorities responded to industrialization. I also look at the communities into which workers were knit, seeking to understand how these influenced their accommodation to, or struggle against, various changes. In general, I argue that traditional communities were the crucial social foundation for radical collective action. This position is tested, within the range of very limited evidence, in Chapter 7. There, the Lancashire mill towns around Manchester are compared, with attention focused on the relationship between (mostly indirect) measures of community and variations in collective action. Arguments concerning weakened family structure and other manifestations of social disintegration as explanations of protest are examined and generally refuted.

In the last chapter I ask why the existing theories of popular collective action are unable to account for the reactionary radicals considered throughout most of this book. Various approaches are reviewed: explanations in terms of psychological debility and in terms of rational interests are in particular faulted. I attempt, admittedly in a condensed fashion, to give my own argument. It builds on what has sometimes been called resource mobilization theory to account for concertedness of action, and develops a cognitive as well as sociological analysis of how tradition and community bonds may make such action radical.

The arguments posed in this work are developed out of an analysis of industrializing England, but they are, I think, of much broader import. I have attempted to challenge the Marxist position that revolutionary collective action is the probable or necessary product of a process of maturation and rationalization accompanying the development of capitalism. The challenge is put not from the standpoint of liberal individualism, however, but from that of the social foundations of collective action. The divergence in early nineteenth-century England between the populists or "reactionary radicals" on the one hand and the emerging, more reformist working-class on the other has analogues throughout the world. Recent studies in American and French social history show much the same pattern later in the nineteenth century. It was significant in the Russian revolutions of both 1905 and 1917. It helps us to see how peasants might be treated in a broadly Marxian theory in a better way than by assimilating them into an increasingly vague revolutionary working class. These general ideas, helping us to understand why revolutions have tended to occur at the beginning of capitalist industrialization and not in its advanced stages, are outlined in comparative perspective in the last chapter.

Although frequent reference is made to primary sources, the present work is not mainly concerned with adducing facts to settle purely empirical questions. It is, rather, concerned with what we are to make of facts which are, in large part, widely known and not in contest. This is an essay in and on historical interpretation, and few topics for interpretation are more hotly contested than the question of class struggle during the industrial revolution. Work of this kind requires, more than does empirical description, I think, the stimulation and criticism of others. During the several years of researching, thinking about, and writing this book, I have been privileged to benefit from the comments of many teachers and colleagues. I would especially like to thank Peter Blau, Pamela DeLargy, the late Max Gluckman, R. M. Hartwell, Lynn Hunt, Morris Janowitz, Thomas Laqueur, Roderick Martin, Peter Mathias, Michael Passi, Peter Rushton, and Harrison White, all of whom read and commented most helpfully on sections of the work in progress, or on related essays. E. P. Thompson not only offered some advice in the early stages of my work but bought his young questioner lunch. I hope he sees the respect in my reconsideration of his analysis, for that respect, like my debt to him, is great. J. Clyde Mitchell supportively supervised the development of the thesis on which this book is based, and offered insight-provoking criticism. Comments by Michael Anderson and Frank Parkin, examiners of the version submitted as an Oxford D.Phil. thesis, helped considerably to improve the final product. The members of St. Antony's College contributed much, both formally and informally, as have my colleagues and students in Chapel Hill. Bruce Geyer offered fine editorial advice above and beyond his excellent typing. Carol Pickard and the staff of the Institute for Research in Social Sciences also assisted. I am indebted to the University of North Carolina for such supporting services as well as for a grant from the University Research Council's Pogue Fund. I am also grateful for opportunities to present some of the work and receive helpful criticism from audiences at the Social Science History Association, the Social History Workshop in Chapel Hill, the seminar on topics in sociology and history at Oxford, and the Universities of Kansas, Massachusetts, and California at San Diego. Parts of chapter 6 of this work appeared in *Social History* 5, no. 1, and part of chapter 7 in *Social History* 4, no. 4; I am grateful to both journals. Of course, the final version of the book is my responsibility.

Intellectual activity is not, however, everything. This book would never have been written without the unstinting support of many friends; of my uncle and aunt, Ronald and Naomi Osborn; and of my parents, Jay and Audrey Calhoun. To them I dedicate it.

Part One

One

Class Struggle in the Industrial Revolution?

On the night of June 9, 1817, two or perhaps, at most, three hundred men from Pentridge and the other villages at the foot of Derby Peak gathered to march to Nottingham in what they thought was the beginning of the "Levelution." They expected their fellows to rise not just in Nottingham but nationally. A few others did so. But this was not a revolution, except, perhaps, in intention. The men from Pentridge and many of their fellows had been misled, largely by the efforts of the notorious spy Oliver.[1] Their own isolation had made this possible. Styling themselves the "Regenerators," these village craftsmen and laborers rose in whole communities both to restore a golden age and to effect a forward-looking reform of English society. Though Oliver may have helped as an instigator and provider of misinformation, the Pentridge rebels acted in an attempt to realize their own values. Some of these were inherited from the Jacobin agitation, of which Nottingham had been an important center, some from the myth and history of the seventeenth-century revolution, and others from the traditions of their own communities. They acted, further, on the social basis of their own tightly knit communities; many of the marchers were kinsmen.

A bit like the Lancashire Blanketeers, who marched later the same summer, the Pentridge rebels fell between two major popular agitations. They differed from the Luddites of a few years before in their national political ambitions, though they resembled them in their local community solidarity. They differed from the Parliamentary Reformers who followed them in their naive expectation that a revolution could succeed, and (perhaps paradoxically but not unrelatedly) in the simplicity of their political and economic goals and analyses.[2] Yet these rebellions were of a piece with the agitations immediately before and after them. All were essentially movements of those who would fight against the coming of industrial society, who had traditional communities to preserve. The very name assumed by the Pentridge men—"Regenerators"—is indicative of their orientation to social change. The period from Luddism to the Queen Caroline agitation (1811–21) marks the ascendancy of an English populism.

This populism was radical; it rejected the very foundations on which capitalist society was being built in England. At the same time, however, the movements of early nineteenth-century workers were reactions to disruptions in a traditional way of life, a resistance to new pressures working against the realization of old aspirations. The workers who made these movements were primarily artisans, outworkers, and others who were affected by the emergence of capitalist industry but were not really a part of the social system it was creating. Their radicalism was intrinsically connected to their particular situations in the midst of social and economic transition. To treat these workers and their reactions as an advanced stage in the relatively continuous process of the making of the English working class is to obscure the most distinctive features of their movements. They strove neither for accommodation alone nor for a rationalistic utopia.

For generations the radicalism of these populist workers has either been assimilated to the Marxist notion of working-class radicalism or denied altogether. In the 1960s, E. P. Thompson struggled with a thousand empirical descriptions against this misapprehension, yet failed conceptually and theoretically to escape it.

> Nevertheless, when every caution has been made, the outstanding fact of the period between 1790 and 1830 is the formation of "the working class." This is revealed, first, in the growth of class consciousness: the consciousness of an identity of interests as between all these diverse groups of working people and as against the interests of other classes. And, second, in the growth of corresponding forms of political and industrial organization.[3]

Thompson's Marxism was both his inspiration and his conceptual prison. Let us reexamine the theoretical and empirical basis of Thompson's great work along with a much broader modern understanding of community, class, tradition, and collective action.

Edward Thompson has been called a "populist socialist" by Perry Anderson and Tom Nairn.[4] Thompson, with some justice, believes that his critics use that phrase to refer to an idealization of chauvinistically English and atheoretically popular values; he has replied with some justified indigation that he is no such animal but rather is a "socialist internationalist."[5] While I have no quibble with Thompson's chosen self-designation, I am sorry that he has chosen to accept the derisory usage of the adjective "populist."

The opposition between populism and all that is theoretically sound and practically effective in Marxism has a long pedigree. It can claim Marx and Engels only ambiguously in its lineage, but, ever since Lenin's attacks on the *narodniki,* one stem of the Marxist polemics has been unequivocal in its condemnation of populism. This condemnation is unfortunate, for it has been of a piece with the relegation of common people to the status of mere "supports" of an idealistically developing true Marxist consciousness, embodied in the Communist party(ies). More specifically, in historical scholarship and political practice alike, this position has led many Marxists to draw such strong boundaries around their concepts of class that most people are denied admission; at the same time, this concept of class has been given a transcendental theoretical importance. The values for which ordinary people have struggled and the communities which have given shape to their collective activity have been either excluded from or devalued in the theoretical discourse of these Marxists. For them, class consciousness has come to be of such overwhelming value, it plays such a critical role on the world-historical stage, that it could hardly be left to the common mass of people—who, in any case, would be intellectually unlikely to develop it. The result of this has been radically to devalue any study of what people actually want or have historically sought, and only slightly less to devalue any study of how people are knit to each other in social relations and what they have been sociologically able to do.

It was perhaps unlikely that Marx, with his acute ability to see just what different sorts of people sought in crucial social transactions, should become the paterfamilias to a tradition neglecting such considerations.[6] It is probably the case that non-Marxist historians, especially those caught up in the excitement of new quantitative techniques, or committed to the history of the rich and famous alone, have been even more guilty. Thompson wrote *The Making* to counter this neglect, especially directing his attention against the right and the supposedly value-free academics.

Ironically, Thompson later described the year of the publication of his enormously influential masterpiece as a turning point in the fragmentation of the first New Left and in the development of his own sense of isolation from its successors, as well as in his general political alienation;[7] it was the year in which the founders left the editorial board of the *New Left Review.* Since 1963, more of Thompson's critical writing has been turned against the inhumanities of other self-proclaimed Marxists. The particular historical and personal circumstances of its writing, however, left their inevitable marks on *The Making*, perhaps most of all on its implicit conceptual framework and theoretical argument. Rather than abandon the problematic usage of "class" in the Marxist tradition, Thompson sought subtly to modify it from within. Just as he presently rejects the label "populist socialist," he attempted then to extend the Marxian model of class to include the wide variety of activities of pre- and early industrial artisans, intellectuals, workers, agricultural laborers, and even small businessmen. Though this attempt was not inherently erroneous, it led Thompson to fail to appreciate fully the theoretical implications of his own historical researches. The model of class obscured more of the contributions of his book than it clarified. This was an especially easy problem for Thompson to get into because his notion of class was (and I think is) based almost entirely on cultural considerations; it is almost exclusively a matter of class consciousness and, as such, neglects the important sociological dimensions of class which led Marx to see it as a potential collective actor (and which I argue should lead to revisions in the Marxian model).

Marx and Engels did not have the same reasons to doubt the intrinsic radicalism of the working class in capitalist society which history has given us. Their analyses were shaped by attention to what once seemed possible. Capitalist and more broadly industrial society got off to many starts in many directions during the period of the industrial revolution. Within this emerging social formation, and even more narrowly within the England in which it first gained the clear attention of observers, the working class was born not once but a thousand times, not with a single identity by nature but with a thousand genetic inheritances and a nearly infinite capacity to respond to nurturance. The concept of class took shape amid this complexity of possibility and actuality. At first it was a term of minimal theoretical content and great plasticity of application. Writers in the early nineteenth century spoke, for example, of the "laboring classes" without doubting that there were several. Only gradually, and with some political and theoretical intent, did the working class come to be seen as a singular entity. Just after mid-century, Marx's disciple, the Chartist leader Ernest Jones, pleaded in his *Notes to the People* for workers

> to purge the movement of middle-class leaders, who were trying to play it into the hands of their class-selfishness. . . . The middle-classes called meetings, and misused the people's name. The first thing was to prevent the old dodge from being played once more, and the working-classes being made the cat's-paw of the rich.[8]

Though Jones was in the vanguard of English Marxism, his usage was still ambiguous. From markedly vague beginnings, however, the process of conceptualization crystallized a portion, not the totality, of the early identities and activities of workers.[9] The less precise usages always had the merit of accurately representing the diversity and disunity of the workers.

The Reactionary Radicals

In the early part of the industrial revolution, community was the crucial social bond unifying workers for collective action. Only gradually were either formal or informal patterns of organization extended to unify the class subjected to capitalist exploitation. Furthermore, traditional values, not a new analysis of exploitation, guided the workers in their radicalism. To interpret the collective actions of British workers before the 1830s as class actions is to use the concept so broadly that it loses all distinctive meaning. Even for the later years, caution is very much indicated. Community and tradition underpinned the movements and struggles of groupings whose members I will call the radical reactionaries, the mainstays of the populist agitations of the first two decades of the nineteenth century.

The reactionary radicals were, for the most part, artisans, skilled craftsmen, privileged outworkers, and, less often, small tradespeople. As a distinct force in British politics and as bearers of a distinct ideology, they were important only in the first third of the nineteenth century. They stand temporally between the Jacobins and the "modern" working class as part of the history of popular opposition in Britain. What connection there is on a causal level, however, is a more complex question. It is clear that the radical reactionaries were a quite different population from that found in most of the new industrial cities and that they provided the foundation for the new, essentially reformist, movements of the working class. They were involved in Chartism but were never dominant. They had the considerable advantage, during the period of their activity, to be able to build on the basis of strong extant community ties, while others had to turn their attention to the creation of community itself. Their communities were not threatened by social mobility but by oppression and poverty which could be experienced collectively. The rights for which they demanded recognition and protection were largely collective rights.

Because there was no way to defend the community without coming into conflict with the forces of capitalist industrialization, and with the state which sheltered and sometimes encouraged those forces, the communal solidarity of the radical reactionaries was never in a simple sense conservative. Even when they defended past practices, they called for changes in present ones. In this they were similar to many of the traditional authority figures of rural England, landed magistrates who had no desire to see their social world upset by the intrusions of capitalist middlemen or industrialists.[10] The magistrates, however, were bound to defend the rights of property and thus, in the end, of capital. Moreover, the magistrates could hardly countenance the independent collective action of the common people. These craftsmen, subsistence farmers, small shopkeepers, and on occasion small manufacturing employers were, however, powerless as individuals against the organized invasion of capitalist industry backed by state power. When the old authorities failed to maintain traditional rights, the radical reactionaries resorted to direct collective action.

Reading Jacobin literature and listening to oral traditions through the filters of their own attachments to communities and trade groups, these people created a new and important position in the firmament of political ideologies and practices. To call them radical reactionaries is perhaps infelicitous, but descriptive. They were acting in response to changes going on about them that were largely beyond their control; they were not attempting for purely ideological reasons to initiate changes. At the same time, their orientation was not simply conservative, or even restorationist, but was aimed at the creation of a radically different social order from that in which they lived, one in which traditional values would better be realized.

The reactionary radicals were able to base a good deal of collective action on the social foundations which their local and craft communities gave them. From the beginning of the nineteenth century through Luddism and the parlimentary reform agitation of the 1810s these personal bonds among kin, neighbors, friends and co-workers provided the primary basis for mobilization. The Queen Caroline affair of 1820–21 revealed the strength of traditional sentiments and the ambiguous nature of the ideology of England's popular rebels, but in Chartism the popular reactionaries were again turned in a more clearly radical direction. By the 1830s, however, a significant beginning was being made in developing national organizations to provide the basis for collective action. The informal bonds of local communities were still important, especially where congruent with formal organization, but they were no longer predominant. Similarly, in the 1820s ideology had begun to emphasize the concept of class and the economic analysis of exploitation which provided the theoretical underpinning for the solidarity of all workers against capital. This was a long time in developing, though, and longer still in penetrating the popular consciousness. The new ideology of class made its most rapid and substantial gains among the new population of urban industrial workers; village craftsmen and laborers and some urban artisans held most tenaciously to populism. The two were not diametrically opposed; as Chartist writings reveal, they could be mixed with little sense of contradiction. The critical discrimination between them came not as an abstract ideological choice but as a concrete shift in the social lives of workers.

Many craftsmen and village laborers continued long traditions of rebellion against an economic and social dislocation which had been going on for five hundred years. There had been jacqueries, revolts by urban and semiurban craftsmen, and political and economic struggles fought out in the name of religion. These revolts were on each occasion initially hard to suppress, but they could seldom maintain concerted strength for long. They overran the capital occasionally, exacted vengeance against particular villains and gained promises (that were seldom kept) of concessions; then the rebels returned home. Repeatedly, middle-class supporters encouraged rebellions only to grow alarmed at their violence and their "communistic" ideologies. Already in the fourteenth century, members of the urban middle classes occupied something of the unstable swing position that Trotsky was to analyze with particular brilliance half a millennium later in his study of the Russian Revolution. Weavers too were long in the forefront of action. For centuries they had had a slight material advantage over, and greater prestige than, landless laborers; they were more likely to be literate, organized among themselves, and yet vulnerable to immediate economic pressures. The weavers of Norfolk were no less prominent in the partially religious insurrection of the fourteenth century than they were in the Jacobin agitation of the eighteenth.

Proletarian strength was thus long in developing and had deep roots in local and craft communities. Further, within these communities, workers had the material, social, and personal resources with which to wage a resistance movement, and a strong enough sense of a better past to lend something of a vision to that movement. Their ideology was influenced by Jacobinism, by the legacy of the Revolution of the seventeenth century, and by broader traditions of enlightenment. It was also at least as importantly shaped by the communities in which they lived and the concrete demands of their immediate situations— economic and social. The fact that the communities in which people lived provided much of the basis of their action was one reason why Marx could hope for the direct continuity of popular radicalism, trade action, revolution, and socialist society. This was the sociation of the proletariat which Marx thought urbanization and factories would only enhance. By depending on it, he relieved himself of the need to deal with the problem of how the revolutionary party and postrevolutionary state apparatus could be expected to fade away. There was to be a readily available substitute in the direct social relations of the people.

A party acting independently of the mass of workers implies a problem of means in conflict with the end the means are designed to serve. Marx neglected this problem not through an act of wilful theoretical blindness but because the history of English popular radicalism was one of action based on direct social bonds. Marx could therefore plausibly imagine a class mobilized in communities rather than a class of individuals with a party substituting itself for direct class action. The radical reactionaries had, thus, a profound influence on Marx, which his students have since neglected. What Marx failed to assimilate from the lessons of practical struggles in England was the divergence between these radical reactionaries and the trade unionists and other members of the new working class which his economic and political analysis invested with historical power. The greatest social strength and radical traditions and the most extreme structural contradictions characterized that part of the "objective" working class which was being displaced by capitalism. The part of the class which capitalism was creating needed formal organizations to compensate for its weakened community strength, and needed to build community before it could readily attack more global issues. The radical reactionaries frequently resisted the attempt to remove their struggle from the informal foundations of their local communities and entrust it to larger, more bureaucratically formal organizations—just as in the eighteenth century their forebears had resisted the nationalization of religion away from its foundations in the local congregation and church.

If some workers in the industrial revolution built a political and economic ideology and practice on the foundations of fairly stable communities, others built visions of community out of the rapid changes in their social worlds. The most significant of these were the Owenite socialists.[11] It was no accident that they came to their greatest prominence in the period after the prime of the reactionary radicals, as new population centers came to the foreground of activism. Although the ideologies of the various popular movements overlap considerably, and are very fuzzy at the edges, one can draw a distinction among them. The Owenites rather consistently took an incorporative view of the transformation of society. That is, they attempted to spread the good word of cooperation out from their own ranks to those of the capitalists and aristocrats. It is true that the Owenite trade unionists were less adamant than Owen himself concerning the virtues of transforming society by example rather than by conflict, but they did share his view of relatively unlimited goods. In this they diverged from those trade unionists and more political radicals who held that the division of a more limited supply of goods was necessarily problematic, whether or not these radicals opted for "distributive socialism" or for a more basic reorganization of the relations of production.

Owen's program called for a fundamental social change but not for the mobilization of specific collectivities for collective action aimed at achieving that change. Least of all were workers to form a subjectively structured class aimed at transforming society through class conflict. In general, Owen hoped that as much of the population as possible would unite in order to seek ends which ought to be equally desired by each member of society. This view was modified by a number of Owen's followers, as they noticed who did and did not respond to their preachings and considered what structural reasons there might be for this. As they did so, though they might adopt the term "working classes" and emphasize the autonomous action, they did not emphasize a view of limited goods—the labor theory of value notwithstanding. They focused attention, appropriately, on issues like unemployment, the wastage of potentially productive forces. They held that the workers by themselves had sufficient labor power to bring about, through cooperation, at least a large first step in the direction of the millennium. Such an ideology appealed to craftsmen in search of a means of regaining lost independence but not to workers in large factories or village migrants smarting under the yoke of deference and possessing a clearer vision of opposition to another active power. The latter were more likely to enter Chartism and to develop what we may, in a very general sense, term "class consciousness."

These new urbanites, dominated by traditions of deference and by active power relations in the workplace (not simply in the marketplace) were much like the recruits to syndicalism (and to a lesser extent radical socialism) in late nineteenth-century France. Where, and when, they did escape the confines of their cultural and social circumstances, it was often in the direction of a radical (sometimes revolutionary) rejection of the existing structure of both authority and opportunity. They were likely to develop a class analysis, because the identification of counterposed classes came readily; the distinctions were manifest and the memories bitter and persistent. Neither village craftsmen nor urban artisans of longer standing experienced this particular juxtaposition of circumstances. Where they were dominated, even oppressed, it was in particular communities, not as a class. Among themselves, the artisans were extensively stratified, leading them to speak only, in the plural, of working *classes*. Yet, in many cases, they were radicals.

A Culturalist Marxism

In *The Making* Thompson describes a "working-class presence" beginning with Luddism (1811–12), and concludes that by the early 1830s something which can reasonably be considered the English working class had in fact been "made." Further, he argues that this was the result of a largely continuous process dating from the late eighteenth century.[12] There is some truth in both propositions, but the amount of untruth in them makes them misleading. Thompson's own evidence and some of his very acute analyses of narrower questions show this to be so. In addition, the theoretical background to his argument and conceptualizations is not very clear.[13] I shall attempt to sort out the elements in this background in the remainder of this chapter, and to some extent in the next.

At the beginning of his 125-page final chapter on "Class Consciousness," Thompson points out that quiet on the surface of social or political life does not mean stagnation beneath that surface.[14] Indeed this is true, and the 1820s to which Thompson refers can hardly be interpreted as an irrelevant decade. There was more activity, both political and economic, than we tend to think with our vision blinded by the explosions of the decades before and after. Moreover, there was a deep shift in the social organization of the groups in which workers struggled to live and to change the conditions of their lives. Before the 1820s artisans had dominated the popular radicalism of England. They felt the industrial revolution largely negatively, as a disruption of or threat to their ways of life and their livelihoods. By the 1830s the predominance of the artisans had passed. Factory workers and others who were the products of the industrial revolution, not its victims, were the mainstay of Chartism.[15] The older half of these men and women had been only children in the romantic 1790s. They inherited the cultural traditions which Thompson so brilliantly describes, but not the experiences. Not only was their political consciousness shaped in a different world, but the differences in social structure changed the whole calculus of interests, possibilities, and pressures for them.

Thompson clouds this change, writing of a timeless working-class "they" who reappear in slightly shifting guise from decade to decade:

> One direction of the great agitations of the artisans and outworkers, continued over fifty years, was to resist being turned into a proletariat. When they knew that this cause was lost, yet they reached out again, in the Thirties and Forties, and sought to achieve new and only imagined forms of social control. During all this time they were, as a class, repressed and segregated in their own communities.[16]

Significantly, Thompson closes his book with a discussion of culture. He sadly notes that the radical artisans and the romantic literary and artistic figures never reached a full union in the criticism they both carried out of what society was becoming around them.[17] These people fought on the losing side of the industrial revolution. They left, in various cultural forms, a legacy which would help to shape the dreams

of future generations. But culture is not society, and even the significance of the dreams changed. At the beginning of his book, Thompson
had defined class as "something which in fact happens . . . in human
relationships."[18] At the close of the book he has forgotten the human
relationships in his concern for the ideas which sprang from them.
Often, in between, he lumps workers together as a category (the working class) despite his statement to the contrary. We must look to see
what had happened to the bonds of community and the networks of
social relations if we want to evaluate the claim that the English working class had been made, and if we want to know what this "class" was
like and what it was capable of doing.

Thompson begins *The Making* by pointing out that it is "a group of
studies, on related themes, rather than a consecutive narrative."[19] He
tells us that his aim is largely one of rescue or recovery. Prevailing
orthodoxies, while not always incorrect, have nonetheless tended to
read history backwards, in terms of subsequent preoccupations.
Further, they have denied the agency of working people in various
ways; they have focused excessively on elites or on "objective" conditions. It is with the concrete, particular social actors of the time that
Thompson is concerned. He wishes, he says, to make his argument in
their terms and to evaluate their actions not by what later happened but
rather by what could then be known.[20]

> I am seeking to rescue the poor stockinger, the Luddite cropper, the
> "obsolete" hand-loom weaver, the "utopian" artisan, and even the
> deluded follower of Joanna Southcott, from the enormous con-
> descension of posterity. Their crafts and traditions may have been
> dying. Their hostility to the new industrialism may have been
> backward-looking. Their communitarian ideals may have been fan-
> tasies. Their insurrectionary conspiracies may have been foolhardy.
> But they lived through these times of acute social disturbance, and
> we did not. Their aspirations were valid in terms of their own ex-
> perience; and, if they were casualties of history, they remain, con-
> demned in their own lives, as casualties.[21]

Stockingers, croppers, weavers and others, all are brought back lov-
ingly and admirably, but this is no simple quest for the "blind alleys,
the lost causes, and the losers" of history.[22] Thompson is making an
important argument for a process of development, despite his claim
that he is merely digging up the cultural ruins of the past.

He dwells at length on a point made by Marx but characteristically
minimized by Marxists: that the working class was present at and active in its own making. This is a most difficult proposition with which
to deal. It asserts at once that an embryonic working class was extant at
some relatively early point in time, and that a more fully developed one

existed later, in large part due to the efforts of its predecessor.[23] Even the term "predecessor" is tricky, for Thompson wishes dialectically to show one class developing itself, not a succession of classes. This leaves him simultaneously attempting to demonstrate that there was class early, and both quantitatively more and qualitatively different class later. This view is a difficult, though not necessarily impossible, one to demonstrate empirically.[24] It is one of the key ideas leading Thompson away from the analysis of social structure to a greater focus on culture.

Much of Thompson's book is involved in the effort of bringing artisan culture back to life. Even when he considers politics, his focus is definitely cultural, not social-structural. He is concerned with people's ideas, perceptions, evaluations, and, in general, means and manners of viewing the world. This cultural emphasis and Thompson's dominant concern for artisans reinforce each other, since artisans left a much more articulate record of their existence than did early factory workers. It is frequently unclear, however, to what extent Thompson wishes us to see the connection between the artisan movement and that of the factory-dominated working class as primarily cultural. The relationship between artisans, outworkers, and factory workers is in general problematic. Did the artisans merely leave the workers an ideological legacy, or did they join together in struggle? When, and for how long? These queries are not aimed as much at Thompson's specific analyses as at the connection between those and his overall arguments and summary statements. Most significant is his assertion of the fundamental commonality of the artisan and working-class traditions of "class struggle."[25] It is perhaps for this reason that Thompson chooses to begin his story with Jacobinism, and with the London Corresponding Society in particular.

The 1790s were perhaps the highest point of both radical and artisan cultures in England, and the point at which they made their most lively intersection. The early 1830s also marked a high point, this time of relatively strong class-conscious political activity. Thus Thompson both begins and ends on the crests of social, political, and cultural waves. He isolates a fairly well-demarcated period. This partially vitiates the suggestion, implicit even in his title, that he describes a more or less continuous and long-term process of political development. There is a real and problematical sense in which he chronicles not the making of the English working class but the rise and fall of the radical English artisanate.[26] This was a social grouping which had risen to new heights of affluence and cultural achievement during the early years of the industrial revolution but which then found itself being increasingly displaced, both economically and politically. As processes of production changed, the artisans lost their individual and organizational grip on particular industries. And they lost their collective foothold in political society (tenuous as it had always been) as new and eventually more powerful class alignments arose. Victorian workers were indeed in many ways their heirs, but only a minority were their direct descendants. To stress the connections between the culture and experience of the new working class and that of the old artisanate too much would be to overlook one of the key reasons why the life of the latter has had to be so imaginatively and brilliantly reconstructed by Edward Thompson.

"The starting-point of traditionalist and Jacobin," Thompson says, "was the same."[27] That starting point was the notion of a stable and good traditional England, in which each Englishman was entitled to a share as his birthright, and which provided for both independence and social harmony. This represents Jacobinism as more traditional than, in its theoretical developments, it was. Rather, the popular appeal of traditionalism and Jacobinism had the same foundation. Traditionalists and Jacobins touched a responsive chord among workers because the concrete aspirations of the latter in and for their local communities were set on a similar foundation of "rights." Individualism and economism, key features of liberal or bourgeois ideology, offered a national analysis which could be of little benefit to workers at a local level.[28] Individualism meant not independence but common subjection to capital or, more crudely, to "the masters." It meant the loss of traditional forms of mutual aid and support. Economism meant that notions of just price and fair share must be sacrificed before the abstract demands of a national economy which no one on the local scene could hope to understand, let alone control.

Class fits neither of these two positions neatly. Class, as an ideal, shows more similarity to the abstract notions of liberalism than to the complex rootedness of both traditionalism and popular Jacobinism (or what we might call the radical/reactionary synthesis). It holds out the suggestion of a myriad of individuals in common circumstances, trying to organize for collective action and being ultimately dependent on each other, as a group, for success. Conversely, notions of class can be rooted in community and in concrete conflicts. Such notions can derive from the local observation of particular similarities of circumstance and shared interests in opposition to local embodiments of capital and political power. It is this second dimension which Thompson is mainly concerned to bring out. He shows how class can be seen not as an ideal but as an experience, a very concrete reality. Unfortunately, he does not make it clear that, by using the term this way, he deals with a theoretical construct that is quite distinct from that assumed in the first use of "class."[29]

Though Thompson attempts to touch all bases, his focus is always on ideas, culture, and experience. Indeed, for all his insistence that class "happens" in human relationships, he treats it primarily as a matter of common experience, not relationships. In this way he takes up both similar experiences and shared experiences. He gives little direct attention to the dynamics of turning the former into the latter. Some of the cultural events to which he gives the greatest attention, though, are precisely means for sharing perceptions and conceptions: rituals. These events are only occasionally distinguished from the more general symbolic culture on which they drew for cognitive and emotional significance. This symbolic culture was vital and wide-reaching; it drew in part on older English traditions but was also creative and able to adopt such newer symbols as the French tricolor. One simple, but typical, symbol was the white hat made famous by Henry Hunt but worn as well by Thelwall a generation before.[30] By such means the people represented both their solidarity and a vague and ill-formulated complex of sentiments and opinions.

Symbols have their primary significance as vehicles of meaning. Such meanings are seldom clear and explicit: the more important symbols are multivocal.[31] They are subject to conscious interpretation and also to less conscious assimilation. In any case, they convey or evoke references to something outside of the act of communication of which they are a part. Rituals generally include a wide variety of symbolic content, and are also communicative activities. But one of the key features of rituals is collective participation. Rituals establish a sentient group; symbols do not necessarily do so. Thus, whatever the content, however radical the interpretations of symbols, they do not produce a group prepared for collective activity. They certainly may help to arouse a predilection for certain forms of activity, but when the members of a collectivity have been subjected to a set of symbols, even to a similarly interpreted set of symbols, they are left with only similar individual experiences. From these, individual actions may well follow, but collective actions require a different sort of unity.[32] It is for this reason that initiation and other rituals were so important to the nascent organizations of political and industrial radicals.[33]

Ritual finds a key place in Thompson's framework of class analysis because it is a means of establishing the distinctiveness and solidarity of a collectivity without recourse to rational intent. In other words, through rituals people become aware of their relations within a social field. These relations are first and foremost among direct participants in the ritual event, and by implication or extension include others who are a part of the same complex of social relations.[34] It is not necessary for people to have this affirmation of collective solidarity in mind as their reason for participating in rituals for the effect to be present.[35]

Through such mechanisms of cultural differentiation and collective integration, Thompson argues, class may exist before a vocabulary or analysis of class exists or is popular. This approach informs *The Making*, but is most evident in Thompson's argument for the applicability of class analysis to the eighteenth century.

In the seventeenth and nineteenth centuries, he tells us, resistance to the ruling ideas and institutions of English society was highly articulate; in the eighteenth century it was much less so. Nonetheless, he argues, it did exist. It is to be found by "decoding the evidence of behaviour" and by inverting the conceptualizations current among elites. Class is to be seen in the struggle—behavioral and conceptual—between classes. It is based on the "polarization of antagonistic interests" and it is worked out in a "corresponding dialectic of culture."[36] What Thompson seems to mean by the "dialectic of culture" is the two-way symbolic interchange between patrician elite and plebian populace (not so much the unfolding or historical development discussed below under the same rubric).[37] In such symbolic acts, sometimes raised to the level of "social theatre," an inarticulate and often inchoate "class" proclaimed both what it thought of its "betters" and their actions, and its own existence. Further, it not only proclaimed this to the elites; it convinced itself gradually, and at the same time, of its own distinct existence.[38] It lacked a general conception of itself, but it did not lack specific, symbolically articulated conflicts with another cultural and social group that it *did* understand to be distinct, cohesive, and in opposition to its own (individually or communally understood) interests.[39] Thompson decides, therefore, that he is justified in employing "the terminology of class conflict while resisting the attribution of identity to *a* class." People were caught up in a "field-of-force" in which society divided into collective antagonists.[40] There were both centripetal and centrifugal forces, deference and obedience as well as resentment and riot.

The status of concepts of class remains problematic in analysis of the more articulate early nineteenth century. A great deal of what Thompson chooses to call class-conscious activity in *The Making* is not ordered by concepts of class but by far more concrete relations and diffuse symbols. The ambiguities, Thompson would say, appear in analysis in no small part because they appear in reality.[41] A precise theoretical conceptualization is possible only at the expense of abstraction from concrete complexities of history. We have, then, a suggestion of an ideal-type construct: class has a formalized existence as a tool for analysis; this idealization may be imposed for convenience on reality, and deviations from it duly noted. This seems to be opposed, however, to Thompson's aim to save the people whose struggles were real but sometimes misguided and often futile from being dismissed as mere sideshows of history or complications to the true (and implicitly developmental) picture.[42]

A simple question arises: why introduce the vocabulary of class unless (1) it can be meaningfully described as quantitatively or qualitatively variable, (2) it is the self-description of the actors that one wishes to describe and analyze, or (3) it is an ideal-type? The vocabulary appears for all three reasons in Thompson's work. It is employed most usefully in the first sense but very inexplicitly. It is employed somewhat misleadingly in the second sense because (a) the distinction between self-identification and analytic identification is not always clearly made, (b) the meanings that actors themselves assigned to the term vary widely and are not always clear (nor are the variations always noted), and (c) the vocabulary grew in popularity through the period but was used by actors to refer to earlier phenomena. The third or ideal-type usage is most problematic. Either the ideal type is a purely abstract construction (which Thompson seems to deny and certainly does not state) or it is drawn from some concrete instance and applied with qualifications or deviations to others. In the present case it would seem that Thompson uses the term "class" in part because of its later (including present) significance. Although this significance is largely connotative and inexplicit, it is read backwards into his historical analysis.[43]

Perhaps this can be more sympathetically stated. Thompson uses the vocabulary of class because later history has given it meaning—although this meaning cannot be wholly specified. It designates a variety of characteristics none of which is always present in a class. This helps to explain but does not resolve the vagaries. Further, Thompson is attempting to be rather more explicit. He wishes to argue for the singular existence of "the working class," not for "the working classes." The latter, he says, is "a descriptive term which evades as much as it defines."[44] This brings us back, however, to the question of the specific nature of the process of "making" and its result. I posed earlier the problem of arguing that something already existed, and yet had to be made. There is a simple, traditional way out of this; it is to posit a base/superstructure model.

There have been many varieties of such models put into use by Marxists over the years.[45] Their key common feature is the assertion of the relative independence of different aspects of a social formation from each other, and, in particular, the primary significance of the economic.[46] The relevance of this assertion to Thompson's usage is simple: if there is a relative autonomy of spheres or domains (e.g., economics, politics, culture) then any more specific phenomenon, like class, may reach its full development in different spheres at different times. More to the point, if the economic is determinant, the economic existence of a class will be likely to precede its social and cultural development. Thus, the growth of capitalism changes the structure of resources and collective interests of workers, subjecting them to common pressures which produce certain common responses. Over time, workers develop a greater consciousness of what is happening to them, and a more effective collective organization for dealing with it. Thus, we move in Marx's terms from class in itself (an sich) to class for itself (für sich). Weber's, and most economistic writers', usage of the term fits the former meaning, and Thompson's dominant usage remains that usually tied to the phrases "class consciousness" or "class struggle." To use the same term in two such differing senses is to make a statement of connection, for the link is not obvious but depends on additional factors.

Thompson does frequently distinguish stages of development as involving passage from external conditions as identifiers to internal characteristics. Part of the argument is about workers' recognition of collective interests, thus implying the prior existence of those interests.[47] Thus Thompson, like the London Corresponding Society leader Thelwall, sees "every 'manufactory' as a potential centre of political rebellion."[48] First came the factories, then the class of factory workers. But what about the artisans, who were there first? The factory workers came into the political world as the heirs to an activist tradition; they were only partially "new." And, it is important to remember, they came into the world only gradually. Even in 1830, as Thompson points out:

> The characteristic industrial worker worked not in a mill or factory but (as an artisan or "mechanic") in a small workshop or in his own home, or (as a laborer) in a more-or-less casual employment in the streets, on building-sites, on the docks.[49]

Furthermore, the outworkers and artisans remained disproportionately influential in radical organizations through the period of Chartism. The textile industry produced the only large body of factory workers of the period (though in many senses workers in the extractive industries also filled the bill as part of the modern "proletariat"). So what are the criteria for membership in the newly made working class? Were the factory employees', artisans', casual laborers' and outworkers' interests really common, or were they divergent? The outworkers were to all but die out in a decade from the end of Thompson's account; if they were disproportionately important before, then this structural weakness is not a trivial matter.

There are two main paths to membership in Thompson's working class. One is to be a worker; the other is to be part of the struggle. The book is devoted to arguing that the single term "working class" can reasonably be employed for the many different kinds of working people. And the book argues that these people had one struggle. It is in this that it is most misleading. The struggle of artisans against the industrial revolution's disruption of their relative prosperity and (initially) for a purely political liberty held little for the factory worker for whom wages and working conditions were matters of immediate concern. Thompson implicitly acknowledges as much. When he talks of political activity he talks of romantics and artisans. When he speaks of factory workers he talks more of their suffering and exploitation. Radical organizations and radical ideology attempted at times to accommodate the diverse natures and needs of these populations. But the different social groups were in many ways incompatible. Where they had the most cohesion was in their rejection of the rule of the vested authorities and the economic and social elites in general.

This is not to say that they had any clear idea who these elites and rulers were. On the contrary, they were able to maintain their unity of opposition in part by not recognizing the changes within the ruling elite of Britain. The artisan tradition bequeathed a radical culture to the factory workers, but it was not one uniformly suited to their circumstances. It left them unduly sympathetic to the sort of liberalism the political economists and bourgeoisie offered; it left them attacking an aristocratic privilege which had long since ceased to dominate English exploitation. Well into the Chartist period Blanquist notions were prevalent. "They" were the object of a widespread hostility; there was, before mid-century, only the most rudimentary analysis of who "they" might be, and how exactly "they" might be exploiting the many different kinds of workers. This is not an isolated historical phenomenon. In many countries at many times and into the present day, workers have been hostile to a nameless "they"; this lack of focus has impeded concerted activity but not always prevented radical mobilization.

Thompson, it will be remembered, asserted that class was a happening.[50] It happened in attitudes as well as organizations, in rituals as well as in rational discourse. But most of all, it happened in opposition. One of the things which most convinces Thompson that the several generations of folk who appear in his pages were part of a common phenomenon of class is that they were all, in varying ways and inconsistently, opposed to the powers that be, however much the composition of those powers may have shifted. They were, at the crudest level, "have nots" who fought with "haves" and, when they could not fight openly, complained quietly and organized on the sly. But this simplification will not quite do. If not-having were the main radicalizing characteristic of class, then common as classes formed in this way would be, they would never be active. If cultural distinctiveness were the key characteristic of class, then colonized populations would be its archetypical constituents.[51] If political oppression made a class, then native Americans could be the model. It is remarkable that in Thompson's usage "classness" appears to supersede consideration of the determinant features of specific classes.

It is exploitation which makes the modern *working* class, said Marx, not oppression, or poverty, or any cultural or ethnic or other distinctiveness.[52] Further, it is exploitation through wage labor, and exploitation through cooperation in the workplace, that forms this class, so that workers are drawn together in collective action. There might be other classes (*an sich*) than modern workers, but only modern workers have the opportunity (or compulsion?) to become a class for themselves and to mobilize to take control of society. What prepares a class for collective action? Its consciousness of itself and its internal social organization do.[53]

If the last paragraph gives the bare essence of Marx's position, let us see how Thompson's treatment departs from it. Thompson adds in political oppression. He maximizes the variable of consciousness, minimizes the variable of social organization. In relation to the latter he virtually ignores the Marxian focus on the social relations established in the workplace by the advent of cooperative labor. Marx makes class an economic category and a social category, in that order;[54] Thompson makes class a cultural category and political category, in that order. Thompson does pay some largely secondary attention to economic conditions and social solidarity; Marx does pay some largely secondary attention to political ideology. May one perhaps read Thompson as a corrective to the dominant tradition, and attempt in turn to balance his overstatements and omissions?

In *The Making*, Thompson shows throughout the "microprocesses" of class, the ways in which particular individuals and groups were affected in their day-to-day activity, and in their struggles with other individuals and groups, by their membership in the working class (which appears at first to be defined externally). He is less thorough with regard to the macroprocesses of class development. He does not much examine structural positions of workers within the economy as a whole, nor does he analyze the relationships which bound them to each other in communities. The only "macroprocesses" to which Thompson gives his attention are cultural ones. He emphasizes the gradual, episodic growth of an awareness of membership in the category of class, and of tools for understanding what that membership might mean.

Thompson is at pains to point out that this cultural aspect of class is not intended to be a denial of human volition but an affirmation of it. He is suggesting not simply that workers recognized the way in which class affected their lives, but that the nature of their recognition helped to constitute the nature of class and the way in which it affected them. As he later restates his position:

> When we speak of a class we are thinking of a very loosely defined body of people who share the same categories of interests, social experiences, traditions and value-system, who have a *disposition* to *behave* as a class, to define themselves in their actions and in their consciousness in relation to other groups of people in class ways.[55]

Experience is the crux joining external conditions to voluntary action:

> What we mean is that changes take place within social being, which give rise to changed *experience*: and this experience is *determining*, in the sense that it exerts pressures upon existent social consciousness, proposes new questions, and affords much of the material which the more elaborated intellectual exercises are about.[56]

In Thompson's work, as these passages imply, class consciousness becomes the central manifestation of class. Social being matters because it shapes experience, it helps to determine people's consciousness.

As a corrective to accounts which have neglected consciousness in general or, more often, the variability and volitional quality of experience, Thompson's argument is reasonable. But it is at least as incapable of standing on its own as is the argument to which it is counterposed. In Thompson's framework, class matters because it can be a crucial premise determining the sort of action which people will take (apparently, indeed, either individually or collectively).[57] But what is neglected in Thompson's analysis is the fact that action depends not only on the premises in people's minds but also on the objective circumstances in which they find themselves and the immediate social relations which bind them to each other. Thompson's rejection of the mechanical Marxism which stresses the determination of social structure and which treats history as a process without a subject, is too complete.

When class is identified solely with what goes on in people's minds, rather than with determinant historical social formations, it becomes a much less helpful analytic category. Most importantly, it becomes a dubiously historical one. If we see class equally among Jacobins and Luddites, parliamentary reformers and romantic artists—not to mention Chartists and trade unionists—then finding it does not give us much help in explaining what went on, what changed, between 1790 and 1834. Yet that is what Thompson's conceptualization, as used in

The Making, appears to do; it shows an existence of class (as culture or consciousness), not the making or development of the English working class as a historical actor. Indeed, Thompson's recent work on the eighteenth century exacerbates the confusion between his declared intentions and conclusions on the one hand, and his empirical analyses and demonstrations on the other. The more recent essays find class struggle taking place before the appearance of class as such. Class, in its modern (nineteenth-century) sense, "is no more than a special case of the historical formations which arise out of class struggle."[58] In a usage which borrows partly from Gramsci, Thompson, in common with other Marxist humanists, has given class struggle, as well as class consciousness, priority over class as a social-structural category.

Within the specific context of *The Making,* we find that Thompson has argued at least as much of a case for the continuity of class as he has done for its development. This is not accident. Rather, it is part and parcel of Thompson's purpose of showing that the working class made itself. In order to reinstate volition, and to give what he considers due appreciation to English popular culture, he has moved radically away from the notion of class structure. Of course, Marxism has never been preeminently a theory of class structure but rather one of class struggle. Nonetheless, the shift in priority which Thompson introduces is important. It moves Thompson to the opposite extreme from the Leninist mode of class analysis. In the latter, the correct, scientific analysis of objective structures is seen as precisely constituent of class consciousness. Traditional culture, mere volition or opinion, and immediate social relations are not to stand in its way.

Class Structure and Class Consciousness

Two separate notions have been packed into the concept of class structure. On the one hand there is structure determined by the relations of production, a class structure as broad as the expansion of the capitalist system and one that makes of class a category of individual persons. On the other hand, there is the structure of social relations among individuals and groups, which may be so stratified as to produce two or more classes, each of which has far more dense relations within than across its boundaries. The former dictates interests, the latter capabilities for collective action. Marx argued that the two were convergent—to whatever extent, and whenever, he did distinguish them. Capitalism created the class of workers as objects of the relations of production, but it also created the proletariat as a single (and ultimately transforming) subject. For Marx there was no question of the working class appearing on a local basis, and struggling with a more widely ramified capitalism. The working class was necessarily of the same extent as the capitalist system of production relations. Further, the proletariat as a transforming subject could hardly appear at a level inadequate to the transformation of capitalism; by definition it was the most radical, the most unifying historical negation. In this sense the notion of class was dictated by what the proletariat must, according to Marx, accomplish as an historical actor: it was a teleological notion.

This is too dense a packing of the concept of class structure. It is possible in Marxian theory because of the implicit assumption that the political-economic (relations of production) and sociological (interpersonal relations) dimensions would be coincident. If one is unwilling to make that assumption in advance, one must separate out the component notions. Some writers have done this implicitly by introducing the separate concept of "social being" to indicate the sociological dimension of class, while letting structure refer very loosely, to the other. The fit becomes loose in the latter case, because class structure tends for these writers, including the "Marxists" among them, to become explicitly or implicitly a matter of economic stratification, not a matter of position within relations of production. John Foster does precisely this; he makes "class" refer to the common position of people in the marketplace.[59] This removes both the dialectical reasons for classes to appear in ever more polarized opposition and the necessity for this opposition to be coterminous with the capitalist system. It becomes possible to talk about class struggle as contingent, not necessary, and possibly local, not national. There is nothing intrinsically wrong with this conceptualization, but problems arise when authors refuse to acknowledge the theoretical import of the alteration of meanings, and when they fail to note that they are no longer referring to class in the same sense that Marx did.

If "class" refers to a purely objective, economically defined aggregate of people, then there is no intrinsic reason for there to be any class action. While class dictates interests, these are only some among many for the individual members of that class. Though they are similar interests, they are not even necessarily common ones, as are many of the interests dictated by the relations of production, to say nothing of mutual interests. Furthermore, there is no intrinsic dynamic to promote collective action on the part of the class; neither the social foundations nor the individually rational motivations will necessarily develop. Either one wishes to know when, if ever, there will be class action, in which case one turns one's attention to the intervening organizational and consciousness variables which might help a class to mobilize, or one wishes to explain a particular series of events. In the latter case, with regard to the nineteenth century, one ought to be prepared to answer why one wishes to do so with the vocabulary and analytic apparatus of class in the first place. There would seem to be, barring the ideal-typical usage suggested by Thompson in his eighteenth-century essays, only two good reasons. Either the people one is studying themselves claimed to be acting on the basis of class, or one wishes to term any action by members of a class, class action. In the latter case one must be prepared to acknowledge that the Conservative-voting members of the English working class are engaged in class action. In the former case, one must admit that one is reporting the ideology of a group of people, not analyzing it in terms of Marx's or any other theory.

This problem is rendered more difficult by confusion concerning the relationship between the consciousness of actors and the social foundations on which they act. When Lenin opposed trade-union to class consciousness, and introduced the vanguard party in the place of Marx's and Engels's notion of the association of the workers themselves as the foundation for revolutionary action, this issue became deeply problematic within Marxism.[60] In the place of Marx's contention that the social development of the proletariat must be such as to transform the capitalist world, a new teleological argument is introduced. Consciousness becomes the key issue: whoever has the correct line can be held to be engaging in class struggle, class action, whatever the objective basis from which he acts, and however much or little of the class joins in his action. Thus, terrorism must be eschewed because it will fail, not because it is the action of an isolated minority. This theory offers no way to verify what is and is not class-conscious action (and thus by implication, class struggle), other than the correctness of the ideology of the actors, presumably as measured by their success or likelihood of success in seizing power on behalf of the working class. Let us look now at the way in which Foster uses this sort of conceptual apparatus in his discussion of "the development and decline of a revolutionary class consciousness in the second quarter of the [nineteenth] century.[61]

Foster suggests that capitalism as an economic and social system creates classes defined in terms of external conditions that impinge on people's lives. These conditions cause the classes of people affected by them to respond and to develop common patterns of culture. These cultural patterns may dictate, for workers, either active or passive relations with capitalism and its ruling class. An active relationship is the result of class consciousness. [62] Through class consciousness itself, and the demands of the active relationship (i.e., class struggle) community cohesion may be developed. This is one of the factors which will help determine the success or failure of the workers' movement. Another is whether a similar sequence is followed throughout the country (or the relevant economic and political system) or whether consciousness, movement, and community are isolated.

The first class-creating characteristic of capitalism is alienation. Foster defines this as the denial of people's control over their social development, of their full humanity as social beings. He does not proceed to base his analysis on this definition, as, for example, by considering the ways in which people are social and struggle to realize their full humanity as social beings.[63] Instead, he moves immediately to people's accommodation to alienation, which, he asserts tends "to limit their social contact to those possessing roughly the same purchasing power as themselves."[64] This he sees as the normal, stable accommodation to capitalist alienation. It produces fragmentation of the working class by dividing it into sectional groupings on the basis of income. In this way, it works to maintain the overall structure of capitalist alienation. It is "false consciousness."[65] True or correct consciousness emerges when, in times of crisis, the normal mechanisms by which the ruling elites of capitalism maintain this structure break down. At such times a vanguard is able to establish itself and potentially merge the various sectional identities into a collective class identity. This will be revolutionary if it is "developed around slogans incompatible with the existing order."[66] Alternatively, it may be reformist.

A great deal of Foster's analysis concerns the movement from passive response to alienation, through trade union or sectional consciousness, to class consciousness. Examining three towns, he finds completed political development only in one, Oldham. He assumes that the structural characteristics of capitalism define the lines of potential class consciousness by defining a collectivity of noncontrollers of relations of production. The first major step came during the 1790s and continued after the Napoleonic wars, when there was a major rupturing of capitalism's authority systems. By the agitations of the 1810s, workers had developed a "very special form of trade union consciousness."[67] Thus began a long period of radical control or near control over Oldham's local politics. The radicals at various points succeeded in controlling the constable's office, the poor-relief expenditures, and a host of other pieces of officialdom.[68]

Foster's book presents a detailed but remarkably isolated picture. One would never know that radicalism in Oldham was part of or related to a national movement or movements; even the rest of industrial Lancashire gets only occasional mention. The entire development through to class consciousness is portrayed as though it could happen in Oldham alone. Even fights to send working-class representatives to Parliament appear in his account to be a matter of local autonomy, not national involvement—and yet William Cobbett of Botley was one of the first elected. Thus while a great deal of attention is put on the process of getting workers in Oldham to see themselves as a class, very little consideration is given to the efforts to make this class a national actor.[69] There is only the casual comment that "if the authorities eventually won, it was because Oldham was only a smallish town in a country which remained throughout under bourgeois control."[70]

Foster, in good Leninist fashion, focuses a good deal of his argument on the transition from trade-union consciousness to class consciousness. Trade-union consciousness is seen less in its own right than as the negative side of an opposition. It is the false consciousness of workers which leads them, in the Leninist theory Foster adopts, to pursue their sectional instead of their general ends. Trade-union consciousness is held to emerge immediately from the struggles between workers and their employers. It does not require, as does class consciousness, the intervention of a vanguard of intellectuals to point out "true," but otherwise hidden, interests.[71] Such an account, however, underestimates the extent of struggles involved in the formation of trade-union consciousness. Far from being an "immediate product," this was developed in a long struggle, and, like class consciousness, was difficult to extend across community boundaries at least until the 1830s (and then it was not immediately successful).

The agitations of the 1810s reveal themselves to Foster, like all agitations before the 1830s, to be non-class-conscious in the absence of a widespread and enduring radical intellectual conviction. The radicals had, at each juncture, to reestablish control over the masses. They had to reconvince them of the need for political activity.[72] The defining characteristics of class consciousness, then, are the overcoming of sectional or trade identities and the presence of intellectual conviction (as opposed to mere desperation).[73] It is the last which, in Foster's opinion was primarily responsible for Oldham's ability in the 1830s to break free from the previous dependence of mass radicalism on economic cycles.[74]

In discussions of the new political activity we find some examples of the inexplicable analyses which follow on Foster's exclusive attention to local politics. He comments on an 1842 Chartist strike, for instance, which was intellectually thought out and transcended the sectional loyalties of various trades: "It was clearly a political one to gain what amounted to state power."[75] Yet, exactly how was a strike in Oldham going to gain state power?

In truth, though Foster doesn't take it up very much, the strike was not just in Oldham but involved extensive cooperation throughout southeast Lancashire, acting through grass-roots Chartist organization. It was not national, and this is one of the reasons that it failed. But it was an interesting event, because it was largely through this strike that the politically oriented Chartists who were concentrated in the outlying towns around Manchester forced the hand of the national executive in Manchester. Unity had been achieved by focusing Chartism's official attention on more immediate goals. Through this strike (sparked by workers from Ashton marching into Oldham) the "rank and file" were making known that they were taking their affairs and their movement into their own hands. Foster notes the strike only as an "object-lesson," focusing on the fact that it was clearly political. Its populist character is at least as interesting. It is important that the local communities could, and would, still move into action on their own.

The insurgent character of the strike—it was, after all, a wildcat political strike and therefore implicitly against the Chartist organization itself—slips past Foster. So, even more, does the involvement in the strike of the Anti-Corn Law League, and in general of Manchester Liberals who were fighting their own battles with a Tory government. The workers fit, for a moment, into their plans. Some employers actually encouraged the strike. The national Chartist executive was all but irrelevant to it. The debates involved insurgents within Chartism and liberals from without. The insurgents were, among other things, complaining that their executive had lost the initiative.[76] They showed a remarkable abiltiy to discriminate between the occasions when they were being used by their employers and those which were their own. It was not long before the dragoons were called in to quell the crowds which gathered outside of mills, calling out their fellows and doing minor damage. After considerable argument, they had voted to hold out for all six points of the Charter (including manhood suffrage, annual parliaments and free universal education) rather than to seek more immediate economic goals. The national leader, Harney, was present and in opposition. Yet all was not changed from the world of twenty years before. The meeting of 16 August was a fateful anniversary, and the original cause of the meeting was to unveil a monument to the memory of Henry Hunt, that least harmed of Peterloo martyrs.[77] And 1842 was, however political the ambition of the majority, still the fourth year in one of the worst troughs for laborers' standard of living in the postwar period. Action had not escaped the motivation of desperation.[78]

Indeed, after the government intervened with repressive force in late August, only part of the working population continued to hold out, and they made it clear that wage increases were their prime demand.[79] It is interesting to note the populations involved in the 1842 disturbances. There was some national participation, but mostly of a grass-roots variety, not mediated through Chartist organizations but rather fueled by personal relationships and rumors. After the government intervention, the southeast Lancashire region was almost the only area to continue its strike. Further, it was industrial populations and organizations of skilled workers which were most important within that region. Weavers were by 1842 no longer an important part of the work force. The advantage in craft skill and organization had shifted to the spinners. Of the communities examined in more detail below, Ashton, Bolton, and Oldham were all active; Stockport, together with other communities to the south and southwest of Manchester, was not. While Stockport had been the scene of three of the eight most important meetings held outside of Manchester itself but within the region during the 1818–20 events, none of the main meetings of 1842 took place there.[80] Foster's contention that the strike was clearly political is at least contentious; while an effort was made to turn it to political ends, it is not clear that this succeeded in supplanting purely economic goals, even in Oldham.[81] It certainly did not make the event the action of a class in any but the most industry-specific and locality-specific terms.

I have, now, to consider one of the most remarkable features of Foster's argument. This is his connection between class consciousness and community strength. He makes a great deal of the connection, for it is his "test" of the notion that Oldham moved from trade union to class consciousness while Shields remained stuck in the former stage and Northampton was even less advanced.[82] Using statistics from 1846–56, none of which allow a time-series analysis, Foster embarks on his test. He considers the extent of neighboring and intermarriage.[83] These he relates to the distribution of income.[84] He also indicates that both craft and labor families are best-off in Oldham, next in Shields, and least in Northampton.[85] He then declares himself quite surprised. Shields has the greatest income overlap and the least intermarriage or neighboring; conversely, Oldham had the least income overlap and the most intermarriage. "To this extent," he summarizes, "the evidence supplies fairly striking confirmation for the overall argument."[86]

Does it? Foster gets the results indicated in table 1.1.

The overall argument, it will be remembered, was that class consciousness leads to community solidarity. Oldham, Shields, and Northampton rank in that order in Foster's qualitative assessment of class consciousness. I offer two quibbles, two moderate protests, and one major objection. First quibble: the percentages on intermarriage are not supported by any test of the significance of variance between communities; they are not a very substantial base for argument as they stand. Second quibble: the trend is rapidly downward for neighboring in Oldham. This hardly seems to fit with the argument that growing class consciousness is creating community solidarity. First

TABLE 1.1
Foster's Test of Class Consciousness, with Communal Variables

	Northampton	Oldham		Shields
Income				
Overlap craft & labor families	17%		9%	55%
Housing				
Craft next door to	104%	108%	88%	80%
labor*	(1851)	(1841)	(1851)	(1851)
Marriage				
Craft family marrying into labor*	77%		80%	70%

*These figures are actual as percentages
of expected incidence, assuming random
distribution.

moderate protest: we know that the proportion of craft workers in Oldham was decreasing from 1841–1851 with technological obsolescence and the growth of factories. This will alter the significance of these figures. Not only the 1841–51 trend is affected, but more important, Foster's attempt to extend these statistics back in time. It is not 1851 with which he is concerned but the 1830s and 40s. Income overlap ought to have been considerably higher in Oldham while handloom weavers were numerous but impoverished.[87] The fact that there were more of them ought to have increased the chances of neighboring and intermarriage, although we can only guess what its effect would be on actual rates.[88] Second moderate protest: the figures are not interpreted by a consistent argument. If they were, the Northampton results ought to lead one to assume great class consciousness. Having already concluded that Northampton was backwards on this dimension, Foster argues that trade-union consciousness is responsible for Shields' comparatively poor showing. By implication this means that either alienation does not mean more fragmentation than trade-union consciousness, or Northampton was not suffering from alienation in the same degree. If it were not alienated in the same degree, then we must assume it was not capitalist in the same degree, and comparability becomes all the more problematic. On the other hand, if trade-union consciousness increases fragmentation relative to simple, passively received alienation, what are we to make of Foster's earlier statement that it is alienation which produces fragmentation of social structure?[89] Foster does not consider any of these problems at all.

Major objection: Foster *assumes* the order of relationship between his two main variables, class consciousness and community solidarity. He never *shows* this, though he implies that this relationship is somehow tested by the statistics cited. Foster is aware of this limitation to possible inference from his statistics, but he indicates this awareness only in a casual aside:

> [these statistics] cannot rule out the possibility (admittedly a small one) that the exceptional social cohesion of Oldham's working population was a cause—not a consequence—of radical political consciousness.[90]

Indeed they cannot. I shall attempt to show below that a great deal of the argument and information for the period covered by (and often cited in) The Making calls for the opposite view. I may add to this fact that Oldham was dominated by weavers as early as the first quarter of the eighteenth century. This dominance continued uninterrupted to the end of the century and the coming of factories. It provided the basis for a strong occupational community. Indeed this community was involved in trade organization as early as 1758. It was a community which had long known and adapted itself to the kind of struggles in which it was to be involved in the early nineteenth century.[91]

This stress on consciousness is important not only to Foster's book but to the general debate on the question of class struggle in the industrial revolution. Foster certainly puts a tremendous weight on ideas, on consciousness. His key differentiation of class struggle from other activity is "the winning of mass leadership" by the revolutionary vanguard, which happened in Oldham alone.[92] The vanguard "realized its ideas" by securing mass leadership and thus access to labor as a whole, and then using that leadership to convince people of the need for a total change in the social system. The question of who the vanguard was convincing falls into the background of the argument. By assuming the importance of a vanguard, Foster puts the actual working population in a peculiarly determined position, almost external to its own fate. The consequences of this are apparent in his treatment of the 1842 Chartist strike. The issues were never as clear as they seem in Foster's retrospect. His analysis turns on the simple antimony of trade union reformism and revolutionary class consciousness taken from Lenin's debatable analysis of politics in another country sixty years later. The proof, though, is not in the recipe but the pudding.

The ingredients of the pudding separate instead of blending. Foster treats the distinction between political and industrial demands as though it were clear, and equivalent to that between revolutionary class consciousness and reformist trade unionism. As Gareth Stedman Jones has commented:

> The fact that the industrial struggle in Oldham does not fit Lenin's conception of trade-union consciousness does not necessarily

establish it as a form of revolutionary class consciousness. That could only be established by an analysis of the political and social aims of the Oldham workers.[93]

Jones goes on to point out that Foster's concentration on the form, rather than the content, of class consciousness makes such a task difficult. As I have shown, Foster's way of establishing class consciousness is by means of flawed statistical inference in an argument which turns on an arbitrary assumption of order.

Summary

The analysis of "consciousness" occupies a prominent place in both Thompson's and Foster's theoretical schemata. Yet each makes something quite different of it. Thompson is concerned to assimilate the particularities of the culture and opinions of myriads of actual English men and women to the Marxist notion of class. He wishes to show that, despite the rootedness of their actions in an older culture, these people were a part of the rational, historically progressive creation of the modern working class. Foster, on the other hand, cares little for such particularities. "Consciousness," in his book, refers to the degree of objective, "scientific" understanding achieved by popular leaders during a period of mobilization. It is class consciousness not because it is widely shared but because it correctly interprets the interests of the working class. It is necessary only that the members of the vanguard be able to mobilize the masses through the use of appropriate slogans. "Consciousness" tends to great generality in Thompson, becoming nearly the equivalent of "culture." For Foster, "consciousness" is narrowed to very specialized manifestations of political ideology.

Conversely, Thompson tends often to lose sight of the importance of material social structure. Foster puts it in the center of his argument. Still, Foster is not much better able to make the linkage between social structure and consciousness, not only for the empirical reasons we have seen but also for theoretical ones. His expectation is always that there will be an "objective" consciousness appropriate to a given structure and discoverable by rational, positivistic, empirical anlaysis. Instead of being the object of sustained attention, therefore, consciousness comes to be taken for granted as nonproblematic. Class struggle becomes, not a phenomenon for which one finds evidence, but an overarching framework in which one explains everything.

Thompson's attention to culture is appropriate, and his description of it generally sound. The problem with his argument is in the weakness of his usage of the notion of class. Drawn in such broad strokes as it is, and so nearly equated to popular culture, it ceases to be either Marx's concept or a very discriminating tool for analysis. Had Thompson focused more on the actual social relations in which the radicals of early nineteenth-century England were embedded, some of the difficulties of seeing their mobilizations as class struggle, some of the differences between them and their often reformist successors, might have been clearer. Had Foster looked as much at social foundations of mobilizations as at the material and ideological reasons for them, his argument might have been less mechanistic, and his conclusions less surprising than the location of Leninist class struggle in relative isolation in a smallish Lancashire town.

It is my contention that we need to look at objective social structure in its large, supra-individual sense; at culture even in its most traditional manifestations; and at the immediate social relationships which make up the daily lives of individuals, knit them sometimes together in communities, and provide the basis for both collective action and collective understanding. Only when all three aspects are kept in the analysis can we hope to understand radical mobilizations.

In order to flesh out the narrative background for my contention that traditional culture and local and craft communities were the source of the early "reactionary radicalism" which preceded Chartism and class consciousness, I shall turn to look in the next two chapters at the culture which occupies so much of Thompson's attention, and at the two great mobilizations of the 1810s, Luddism and the parliamentary reform agitation.

Two

Radical Culture and the Moral Economy

For E. P. Thompson, the second decade of the nineteenth century marks the beginning of "the working class presence." By this is meant specifically an active political presence, inheriting the mantle of Radical Westminster politics and the Jacobins, but synthesizing this radical heritage with the traditions of the moral economy. It was a period in which the country, not London, dominated radical activity, though there was still an active London press. From 1815, the working-class presence is to be felt in "the heroic age of popular Radicalism," ending conveniently with 1819, and thus avoiding the difficulty of dealing with the Caroline agitation within the notion of continuous development of class. There were many discontinuities, however, not least of all that between the different populations involved in the "populist" agitation of the 1810s and the increasingly industrial agitations of the late 1820s and after. There is no clean break, of course, but there is a shift in the constituency of the movements and in the emphases of their ideologies. It is my continuing argument that the essential foundation of these movements was in local communities and that the vocabulary of class action is stretched unduly if one attempts to account for them within it.

It is too often implied that we must choose between an analysis of radicalism based on class, and one which denies radicalism altogether. I am suggesting both that class in capitalist society may be characteristically reformist and not revolutionary, and that more "populist" pre-class movements may in many ways be more radical.[1] In the specific case of early nineteenth-century England, the social and economic strength of the partisans of "the heroic age of popular Radicalism" was in danger throughout their ascendancy, and was rapidly undercut from the beginning of the third decade of the century. Further, this social basis itself limited the development of these movements in the direction of revolutionary class activity.

The Jacobin Legacy

Thompson never really analyzes the relationship between artisans and factory workers as social collectivities; he only partially distinguishes between their respective communities and the parts of the radical movements which were dominated by each. Even in his discussion of the London Corresponding Society (1790s) he refers to Wapping, Spitalfields, and Southwark as "older working class communities."[2] This is part of a well-taken point that radical London was always a more heterogeneous and socially complex community than the industrial towns and regions of the Midlands and North. It is unclear, however, in what sense we are to see the southern and eastern sections of London as "working class." Is it in contrast to the more centrally located artisan communities? Certainly the silk weavers and waterside workers were poorer for the most part than the journeymen, shopkeepers, and members of the printing trades. They had less education and less effective organizations for promoting their collective welfare. But by Thompson's own key description (we can hardly call it a definition) of class as "something which in fact happens in human relationships,"[3] the East End and south of the river were less a part of the "happening" than the Strand and Picadilly. The artisans of the latter districts had dense and multiplex social relationships with each other, communicated amongst themselves, established considerable self-consciousness, and engaged in collective action. The main justification for including the poorer districts in the class seems to be that they were indeed peopled by workers. But this is exactly the usage of "class" to denote a category that Thompson disavows in his preface.[4] It is also insufficient in its indication of the connection between the two elements of the class. The poorer districts had, in many cases, been swollen in the preceding decades by a great influx of immigrants. They had shown little ability to organize themselves for collective benefit. The artisans of the L.C.S. decided to include in their number some from among the more "common" workers, but it was the artisans who had the community, the organization, and the choice.

Thompson's opening point about the L.C.S. is that it chose to invite "members unlimited." It was an inclusive, not an exclusive, organization. Thompson's perception is accurate: being inclusive is a crucial distinction for a "working-class" organization as opposed to many other organizations which workers may form.[5] But "populism" is perhaps even more inclusive. It is the fact (or occasionally anticipation) of being in the majority that most influences the class claims of workers throughout modern political history. Marx and his colleagues (including on this point Owen and most of the early theorists of cooperation) worked hard to show the commonality of those who labor, hoping that the laborers might recognize that the interests of each lay with those of the rest. Particular and sectional interests were held most often to be spurious or at best in conflict with those of the class. The relatively elite artisans who formed the core of the L.C.S. were excluded from the main corridors of political power. The artisans called for the opening of these corridors to all sane, noncriminal men. They did not call for an abolition of the particular privileges which they enjoyed. A generation later it would be unthinkable for common workers to collaborate with elite groups which did not include at least a semblance of an appeal for economic reform and equality in their programs. But in the 1790s, political liberties, not fundamental social reforms, were the key to the popular program. In London, politics and economics were separate enough for workers (of the better sort) to be invited into a political union of "members unlimited" without economistic cavil.

In no small part this was due to the social context of the discourse. London was a city of coffeehouses and taverns where working men of all ranks and even a few gentlemen could not only brush shoulders but discuss the issues of the day. There was a public realm for such discourse which did not require a sense of community or commonality among the participants.[6] Such transactions across social ranks were never as common outside London and were all but nonexistent in the newer industrial districts.[7] There public houses were the public places and these were tied to particular crafts and residential communities, therefore to far more homogeneous populations.

In discussing the late eighteenth century Thompson has two main points. The first is that Jacobinism was a truly radical movement with deep roots in popular consciousness, even though its active participants were only an elite minority. The second is that this was the beginning of the last intensive struggle to preserve the traditional moral economy.[8]

In treating of the first theme, Thompson is establishing the existence and describing the nature of the radical ideology available for nineteenth-century popular radicals and workers to build on. It was in some ways a new intellectual creation, in other ways borrowed from other countries (most particularly revolutionary France). Most of all, for Thompson, Jacobinism involved the articulation of values and attitudes which grew directly out of widespread popular beliefs and ideologies at home in England. Thus the people hated and despised the laws before the organs of popular culture began to relate the new intellectual justifications for resistance, arguments of illegitimacy.[9] The religious struggles of Puritanism and dissent had prefigured secularism and paved a road for appeals to individual conscience and freedom of thought.[10] The "freeborn Englishman" needed little intellectual justification for his deep-seated desire to be left alone, to be independent.[11] But to turn this desire toward coherent political ideology was the role of Jacobinism.[12] Further, Jacobinism asserted these values occasionally outside the realm of parliamentary politics.[13] Though after 1796 the values became again the province of Foxite Whigs more than of Jacobin artisans and authors, a different kind of popular action, one which did not only follow, had flared on the national scene.[14] Thus it is that: "In the 1790s something like an 'English Revolution' took place of profound importance in shaping the consciousness of the post-war working class."[15] This was the result of a limited juncture between groups whose interests, experiences, and circumstances were not fully compatible. "The unity between intellectual and plebian reformers of 1792 was never to be regained."[16] Persecution set in with a vengeance; disorganization made resistance fragmentary at best.[17]

It would seem that Jacobinism gave birth to a short-lived political infant. This, Thompson suggests, is not the case. In the countryside, many a village and town had its "Old Jacks" to keep the embers hot for each new accession of flammable material.[18] While some underground organizations withered rapidly, others struck new roots in industrial contexts which changed their significance but not their essence. Jacobinism marked a cultural high point and a political turning point. Values and analyses with long histories achieved clarity of expression (though just as the socioeconomic context of their development was being radically transformed). This clear ideological statement of deeply held but generally inarticulate cultural values provided a definition of the terms of action to which workers and others could later refer. This meant that the development of popular, and eventually working-class, ideology could begin to be cumulative. As long as it had remained largely inarticulate, it was either caught in the bonds of immediate situations and reactions, or was in need of being continuously recreated.

There were, of course, problems attendant on the fact that the ideology had been tailored to fit different circumstances than those which faced nineteenth-century workers, and the fact that much of it was borrowed from a libertarian morality perhaps more suited to those with property than those without. Nonetheless, the ideology had an existence in the minds of artisans, outworkers, craftsmen, shopkeepers, journalists, and what we might now call "intellectuals." It was the product and the property of a distinct and disenfranchised population. In their minds and in certain crucial writings, it could be held on to for later application.[19]

One way in which Jacobinism contributed to the making of the English working class, then, was that it gave the workers of the early nineteenth century an ideology with which to interpret their experience in independent terms. Whether these terms were adequate or not, whether they gave the nascent class a clear conception of itself or not, they helped to make the workers capable of action rather than mere reaction. It was not directly to the "modern" working class that this legacy was given, but to a transitional population dominated by artisans and others who worked outside the factories, for themselves or small masters.[20]

If Jacobinism was a new and radical synthesis, most of its crucial elements had histories. These elements included the civil-libertarian values and the goal of economic independence long seen as characteristic of Englishmen. They also included notions of social responsibility and what Thompson describes as a moral economy, in which deference and paternalism, services from above and below, were exchanged at a traditionally sanctioned, if not always equable, rate.[21] To these Jacobinism added somewhat more sophisticated and alien (to popular culture) notions of natural rights. Such notions were both imported from abroad and borrowed from more elite thinkers at home. Thus the French Revolution and the theorists of the social contract and utilitarianism made their distinctive contributions to the growing radical synthesis. But these never had the popular roots that the traditional notions had. So when Jacobinism moved into new contexts in later years, these contributions were apt occasionally to be lost, from the synthesis, or lost from all but its rhetoric. The staying power of notions of the rights of man often came, paradoxically enough, from a linkage made with constitutionalism. The natural rights were claimed on a totally separate and contradictory philosophical basis from that used for the traditionalist claims of the historic constitution. But if these rights made their appearance in such radical philosophical garb in the 1790s, in the nineteenth century they often wore more traditional clothes. We have, then, a connection made outside the realm of logic, between natural, or human, and social, or civil, rights, which became of the utmost importance in popular ideology.[22] The older values took over the newer ideas and made them their own. These traditional attitudes and values were perhaps less "rational," but even where Jacobinism itself never had any influence they continued to operate and often to lay the basis for acceptance of a radical critique which shared some of their view of the world and interpretative assumptions and language.[23]

Workers' struggles continued through periods when their public political action was held to a minimum. This is one of the central arguments of The Making, developed especially in the opening sections of the third part of the book. The argument has two major parts. The first is that there was a radical underground linking Jacobinism to the popular rebellions of Luddism and the political reform campaigns of the late 1810s.[24] The second is that there was a largely autonomous working-class culture and society in which this underground was sheltered and in which the seeds it planted could take root. In short, conscious rebellion continued, and unconsciously workers prepared themselves for both defensive and offensive action against capitalism and political oppression. "In the heartlands of the Industrial Revolution, new institutions, new attitudes, new community-patterns, were emerging which were, consciously and unconsciously, designed to resist the intrusion of the magistrate, the employer, the parson or the spy."[25] Despite his assertion of continuity, Thompson is forced to admit that much was lost in the passing of francophile Jacobinism before it had the chance to strike deeper roots or build lasting bridges between classes. The early Jacobins had begun to unite artisans and middle-class intellectuals.[26] "The First Empire struck a blow at English republicanism from which it never fully recovered."[27] To grasp the full significance of this statement it is necessary to recall that republicanism remained an important part of the ideology of popular radicalism for a hundred years or more, until some reasonably full semblance of representation was achieved. The blow was not struck at an obsolescent ideology.

The nineteenth century started with the repression of popular politics in full swing. Much of the populace must be held party to this repression. Church-and-king mobs and obedient recruits were among its most important agents. As Cobbett remarked in response to a number of clergymen who were stirring up fears of popish insurrection in 1807:

> There has been no savage, no mischief-doing mobs, in this country for many years, except those who have been led by the cry of "church" or "king" or both together. . . . "Church and King" mobs have assaulted and killed many people; have rescued prisoners from jail; have burnt and otherwise destroyed houses and goods; and many acts of violence, including one breaking open of a jail, have been committed by "loyal volunteers." But, amongst all the assemblages of the people, the cause of which has been their attach-

ment, real or expressed, to the cause of freedom, not a single act of violence, that I remember, has ever been committed.[28]

The government was well aware that while it could command little support from urban artisans, they could command little brotherhood from the rural and village poor. It was more often the village elite who were Jacobins.[29]

At the same time, however, Cobbett made his celebrated turnaround of 1804, claiming it (with considerable justification) to be no turnaround at all.[30] He was not alone among old Tories who found the second Pitt ministry a menace to English liberties and fiscal well-being. Similarly (although with important ideological disjunctures) Middlesex politics remained rebellious. Burdett's near election in 1804 showed a restiveness among the middle classes, the artisans, the shopkeepers, and the small gentry, approximately half of whom voted for Sir Francis.[31] Among the key dynamics in their discontent was the centralization of economic power in the hands of large firms which could gain government contracts and use their increased assets to force their terms of competition on the smaller masters and tradesmen. This was a classic period of the centralization of capital in Marxian terms. The blow fell upon those who had something to lose. The terms of their defense were confused, however; these terms were compounded of respectable radicalism, Jacobinism (now occasionally held in disrepute even in radical circles), constitutionalism, and blunt reaction to the immediate economic circumstances. It was not until 1806–7 that the cause of reform even began to gain the expression that it had been given in 1790s. The *menu peuple* of Westminster, as Thompson analogously terms them, became an active political force, but not in the conventional terms of politics. They could elect few representatives but could loudly voice their opinions in public. Thompson points out that their movement could not be considered a "populist" or still less a "working-class" one.[32] In this connection it is curious that he dubs the Westminster electorate "plebian."[33] They clearly were not. But Westminster at this point did constitute something of a halfway mark between traditional reformism from above (the politics of Wilkes and others who mobilized an inarticulate crowd) and a more broadly democratic movement. Perhaps most of all it marked a shift in the direction of greater independence of reform and radical movements from conventional politics. Nonetheless, and this Thompson clearly points out, however much Middlesex radicalism kept the cause alive and offered new inspiration, it could never become a workers' movement. The Benthamite radicals, and in general the middle-class intellectuals, gained ascendancy, moved away from the Jacobinism which some of them and many of their colleagues had once espoused, and formed an autonomous "General Committee" which was not responsive or responsible to popular sentiment.[34]

When Thompson suggests that the political activity of Radical Westminster cannot be considered "populist," he distinguishes it from the "members unlimited" policy of the London Corresponding Society; it derived its tone and ideological content from the specific interests of small masters and tradesmen. These increasingly gained control of the local politics, and their respectable radicalism grew away from the at once more radical and more traditional politics of the independent craftsmen and artisans. The radicalism of these latter, the radicalism which survived in the communities of workers and some of the menu peuple can properly be described as populist.[35] This is one of the important reasons why it was able to make gradual headway in the countryside and merge with the many local movements of artisans, laborers, and outworkers.

At the turn of the century, Jacobinism was still alive in its old form, and even extending itself into the countryside in a few places. It had clearly passed its prime, however, and government repression was severe. Food riots were, for the duration of the Napoleonic wars, the most common public face of popular discontent.[36] Still, Thompson is able to assemble scattered evidence of radical organization in defiance of Pitt's Two Acts and the Anti-Combination Acts.[37] Just after the turn of the century, the worst trouble centers were, as they were to stay, Nottingham, industrial Lancashire, and the West Riding.[38] These of course were to be the scenes of Luddism within a decade. A rash of meetings was called on the expiration of the Two Acts (March 1801); the United Irishmen and United Englishmen were reputed to be active in Lancashire; in the West Riding, the partisans of the "Black Lamp" drilled at night.[39] For the most part the strategy was not unlike that of Colonel Despard, who was unfortunate enough to be caught in London; according to Thompson, the drillers and meeters thought in terms of a coup d'etat.[40]

Whatever their political strategy, these groups clearly depended on strong community support. Like the Luddites after them, they really were communities mobilized for political ends as much or more than they were separate organizations. These communities were losing their faith in government as they were oppressed by acts of various kinds, and they were losing their vertical connections to their richer neighbors. Magistrates were greeted as hostile aliens within a few miles of their seats.[41] Communities became more distinctively communities of workers, and members were reinforced in holding such a view of themselves by the divisions oppressive laws imposed. While there may have been a "less political, more apathetic majority,"[42] these people were still part of the same community. They could not aspire to exchange their communal links to plebian radicals for equivalent links to magisterial squires.

The Moral Economy

Thompson suggests that in the late eighteenth century a long struggle to maintain a traditional system of social and economic relations (and certain privileges associated with that system) entered the phase of its final dissolution: "Hence the final years of the eighteenth century saw a last desperate effort by the people to reimpose the older moral economy as against the economy of the free market."[43] This was an important source and direction of popular struggle well into the nineteenth century. Thompson's introduction of the traditional notion of a moral economy into the modern debates of economic and social historians has been of great value, but even in its original context the concept poses certain inadequately explored problems.[44]

The most important of these for our present consideration is Thompson's use of this cultural explanation of popular action with only the most fleeting attention to its sociological underpinnings, to the foundation of such action in the concrete sets of people for whom the moral economy had a powerful significance. These distinct sets included small farmers and agricultural laborers (insofar as the latter had memories of more independence in their recent background), skilled artisans with traditional claims to a "respectable" station in life, and domestic outworkers of differing heritages and degrees of degradation. It is apparent that the notion of the moral economy applied differently to these three groups. Even more obviously, it did not apply to those groups of people who were positioned to gain economic benefits within the capitalist organization of industry—either factory workers or those in the new skilled trades (some of whom, "new" artisans, worked within factories).

That the notion of moral economy can be said to be the central element in a partially autonomous ideology is demonstrated by the common appeal of certain of its main advocates to all three groups. Cobbett, for example, spoke as a small farmer and, initially, primarily for those with rural interests. Hunt also claimed a status within the traditional agricultural hierarchy, although his political pronouncements were never as preoccupied with rural matters as Cobbett's. Both men extended their base, however, to include some urban artisans and a great many domestic outworkers. Both men were spokesmen for the moral economy.

Three themes have been interwoven in claims directed to notions of a moral economy: the degradation of craft labor within the process of production; the subjection of producers to market forces; and the subjection of consumers to market forces.[45] Obviously, just as consumers, producers, and craftsmen are not mutually exclusive categories, so the three themes were frequently combined in ideological pronouncements. Nonetheless, they can be differentiated. At different points, defense of traditional crafts, wage demands, and concern over high prices have each dominated popular protest; all three were important during the industrial revolution. Thus the same community might be mobilized for machine-breaking, strikes, and food riots seriatim. The conception of a moral economy to which somewhat differently focused appeals were made did not come directly from any prior state of virtuous relations among men. Rather, it was the result of integrating the three different kinds of disruptive pressures which faced the members of rural and craft communities during the industrial revolution. From trying to make common sense of their communal experiences, they created their idealized vision of the moral past. It is because tradition was shaped in this way, by present experience as well as by "real" history, that populations of workers whose prosperity was of recent origin and dependent on industrialization and/or intensified capitalist commercialization could interpret their grievances in terms of the disruption of a traditional way of life. Most outworkers and some artisans fall into this category. Many kinds of artisans, indeed, had struggled for generations to achieve their level of respectability and remuneration; this did not prevent them from responding to new crises as challenges to a moral economy and to a standard of living which was theirs as a matter of traditional right.

Rural populations had been fighting all three of the battles which involved the ideology of the moral economy for a very long time. An early version of the ideology appears with Winstanley and the Diggers. More broadly, we may see the notion of the moral economy as very close to the economic ideology of most peasant and craft rebellions in late medieval and early modern Europe. East Anglian weavers, for example, had been active for at least four hundred years by the time of the industrial revolution—and their successes in fighting it helped cause the transfer of much of the textile industry to the Northwest. As a traditional inheritance, the notion of a moral economy does not so much distinguish the rebels of the late eighteenth and early nineteenth centuries from their forebears, as it sets them apart from the "modern" working class, which began in the 1820s to fight under a different sort of ideology.

By the period of the industrial revolution, the rural battle to preserve old agricultural relations of production—specifically small holdings—was all but over. The contest centered on people's sense of themselves as consumers. This is a large part of what differentiates the protest of the rural populations from that of village and urban craftworkers. Up to and including the Swing incendiaries of the early 1830s, rural rebels did not have the economic edge to their ideology which Luddites, for example, gained from the production focus of their rebellion.[46] The older mobilizations in defense of the moral economy made middlemen their chief enemies. This was as true of consumer agitation against forestallers and engrossers as of production agitation of outworkers against mercantile agents who handled the putting-out trade. While some village craftsmen, such as framework knitters, were concerned with the degradation of craft skills, the focus which unified the widest segment of this population during the industrial revolution (and particularly in the 1810s) was concern over the effects of unbridled competition for work on the standard of living of the craftsman.

In his discussion of the moral economy, Thompson focuses most of all on food riots.[47] He suggests that "Not wages, but the cost of bread, was the most sensitive indicator of popular discontent."[48] In other words, fluctuations in real wages appeared to the people in question to be determined more by fluctuations in prices than in nominal wages. These people thus saw themselves being exploited less by their employers than by merchant interests (to the extent that these were distinct). The emphasis laid by Cobbett on the contribution of taxation to high food prices also becomes explicable when viewed in this way.[49] But, Cobbett's stress of this interpretation should be a clue to the special context in which it was most important, where people saw themselves threatened more as consumers than as workers. This context is evident in Thompson's choice of examples but is never made explicit in his argument. Almost all his examples are drawn from agriculture or the extractive industries.[50] The situation of urban artisans was very different; indeed at points they benefited from the exploitation of the countryside by the towns. Because they were generally better-off, they were not equally subject to the swings of the market or the machinations of engrossers and forestallers. The village craftsmen and outworkers were for the most part initially closer to the artisans, and only fell into the vulnerable position of the rural population as their production position deteriorated. Their crises appeared to them as the result of destruction of a moral economy of production relations by the market, more than as the product of machinations directed against consumers who remained in essentially the same production relations throughout.

Perhaps paradoxically, the new population of factory workers was in this respect more like the agricultural population than like the artisans. In the first place, many of the factory workers had ties to the agricultural population and were often recent migrants from districts with a surplus of landless labor. More important than a simple continuity of perspective, however, was the fact that for many of them factory work meant an improvement in material standards of living; the most important issues were getting and keeping a job in the highly unstable textile industries. They too experienced crises in the early years as consumers more than as producers. They were not traditionally skilled workers under a new attack on their position in the labor market or on control over their craft. To whatever degree factory workers were exploited, they could hardly interpret their situation as a worsening of traditionally moral factory relations. They could draw on the ideology of the moral economy only as consumers. It is because of Thompson's completely cultural treatment of the moral economy, his neglect of the social foundations on which it, and claims to it, rested, that we are left uncertain in *The Making* where the food riot leaves off and "collective bargaining by riot" begins.[51] It was almost entirely in the case of the outworkers that the two overlapped.

Thompson did not invoke the notion of the moral economy primarily to deal with the skilled artisans who otherwise dominate *The Making*. Nonetheless, we can see the themes of struggle against degradation of crafts and the reductions of the position of producers to a matter of mere market relations in the battles of urban artisans to maintain their "respectable" position in society. As Prothero has recently put it:

> The artisans' basic attitude was unchanged—wages should be just and fair, sufficient for them to live in the customary style. It was custom and status differentials, not supply and demand, which they thought should determine wage rates, and they had no real conception of *improving* their standards of living through higher wages.[52]

The artisans consistently focused on wage and craft control issues, even in periods where high inflation made consumerist action plausible.

Just as Lancashire radicalism was disproportionately the activity of handloom weavers, so London radicalism was overwhelmingly dominated by artisans. Their most sustained campaigns were in defense of their privileged status. They were not only opposed to the free play of market forces, they were opposed to all forces which had the prospects of destroying the particular virtues of their trades. This meant that, at least initially, they were opposed to levelling and equalitarian drives and could hardly support an economic rationalism which threatened their identities, privileges, and livelihoods.[53] Eventually, as "conservative" solutions failed, the artisans turned to cooperation and other more drastic alternatives, but these were always ways of trying to achieve traditional values.[54] One of the most important of the early "conservative" efforts was the defense of apprenticeship. Utilitarians like Francis Place could hardly support such a strongly anti-free-trade effort on the part of the artisans, and there was not much in the defense of apprenticeship for the mass of the working population. "Though apprenticeship was an important concern in the marked trade union consciousness of these years, it also emphasized how this consciousness was still exclusive and concerned with the interests only of the respectable section of the working population."[55]

The defense of a moral economy is always bound to be particularistic, for it is in part a defense of the material web of social relations which situates individuals in their communities and in the world at large. The strength of these movements came from the same source as their limitations. Kinship bonds, informal meetings in public houses, the ability of many artisans to conduct conversations at work, indeed, the very fact of work in stable small groups or on a "gang" system all gave an enduring basis to collective action which did not have to be formally defined or mobilized on each new occasion. "Unions were very often episodic formalizations of the much more important continuous informal practices."[56] One result of this "episodic formalization," however, was to keep the formal union activity bound to the informal social base and to the ideas which united or at least were congruent with that social base. Ideology should not be seen as free-floating.

The artisans' defense of a moral economy was overwhelmingly focused on their role as producers; it was only secondarily, and through the organizations focused on production, that they fought on consumer issues.[57] We can see some of the critical differences between the London artisans and the domestic craftsmen of the Midlands and Northwest by focusing on the differences in their positions as producers. Urban artisans in general and London artisans in particular were relatively privileged (to the extent that we may generalize about them) well into the nineteenth century and in some cases into the twentieth. Throughout our period, most of the artisans worked in their trades in a relatively continuous fashion; they saw their market position deteriorate, but they did not see the trade itself destroyed. Most of these trades were too difficult to learn to be flooded by any mass of new labor. At the extreme of this position of power were tradesmen—like clockmakers and jewellers—who seldom if ever participated in activities uniting various trades. Moving along the continuum, we see those trades which met specific problems from time to time—as shipwrights did with foreign competition—but were not radically changed in domestic composition; those which remained relatively traditional but were not so highly skilled, and so suffered from market pressures; and lastly those which were fundamentally degraded by a flood of new entrants or replaced by machinery, or both. The handloom weavers are the preeminent example of this other extreme.

Handloom weavers, like better-off artisans, valued respectability, that complex of positional virtues vis-à-vis other men, self-sufficiency with a certain standard of living, and pride in one's productive contributions to society. Unlike the artisans, they were no longer concerned with protecting craft skills. They could not feel a pride in their work which set them apart from others, but they could continue to be proud that they were independent, pleased that they could control their own pace and conditions of work. These were values to be upheld; handloom weavers did not think it would be the same to work amid the din of factory machinery, under the discipline of masters or their intermediaries, and separate from their families. They wished to sell their products, not simply their labor, but by the middle of the first third of the nineteenth century the degradation of the craft had so devalued both that handloom weavers sought to rescue some of the moral economy only by protecting themselves against the ravages of the market, against unbridled competition. They could be more readily egalitarian because they were reduced to the lowest common denominator of subsistence.[58] Further, they were grouped together in villages and small towns, not dispersed through much of London and its environs. It is my suggestion that they lived in more closely knit communities.[59] Certainly they lived in smaller, more homogeneous villages and towns. In such localities, people were all weavers together, not members of one trade living scattered among the practitioners of three dozen others. The degradation of handloom weaving also meant that for the most part no one could aspire to a higher status within the trade than anyone else. There were not the hopes of becoming a foreman or a master in one's own right which sometimes encouraged divisions among the London artisans.

None of the three themes in the defense of the moral economy involved an analysis of capitalist exploitation, as Marx would locate it, within the production process. This is not to say that we, as outsiders, cannot accurately see exploitation of these workers in Marx's sense. Rather, it is to suggest that that is not how they saw their situation; the pressures which aroused them were issues of the marketplace or of the quality of work itself. Both of these issues, of course, infringed directly on the nature of their lives with each other in communities, and thus on such other traditional values as being able to support one's family.

The defense of the moral economy was economic where Jacobinism was political. To the extent that they considered economic matters, the Jacobins tended to see aristocratic theft, sinecures, paper money, and the like as the source of every economic evil; the notion of the moral economy provided an important counterweight. The evil with which the upholders of the moral economy were concerned was present in concrete relations of production and exchange. Some elements of Jacobinism, including its emphasis on political democracy, were to prove better suited to the new industrial working class than they were to those who struggled to defend a traditional way of life. These elements of the ideology would be of importance to people who could battle for participation in industrialization and for some of its benefits. Before that working class would come to dominate political action, however, there would be a good deal more struggle *against* the industrial revolution. Some of the old Jacobins themselves were prominent in this mobilization, often hoping (never, I think, very realistically) to turn it to revolution.[60] Jacobin ideology also remained important, especially among the urban artisans for whom Paine would always be a sort of patron saint. The defensive posture which was central to the notion of the moral economy was not limited to rural populations but included domestic outworkers and urban artisans as well. It is important to realize the extent of the defensive or resistance activities during the early years of industrialization; these dominated the struggles studied by Thompson in *The Making of the English Working Class*. The social composition of the populations involved in these struggles rather belies the title of that book.

"Culture" and "Not Culture"

Thompson's attitude toward these romantic (and more specifically Romantic) defenders of the moral economy and of the culture of liberty is curious. These are the heroes of his book, these two largely separate populations of rural and semirural village residents and intellectually oriented urban artisans. They are the starting point for his story of the making of the English working class. Yet, they are not quite of that class, even, in large part, in Thompson's account, though he sometimes implies otherwise. These heroes are rather in the process of giving the nascent working class a cultural heritage. This interpretation renders this part of Thompson's argument clear, but makes it seem dubiously Marxist and shows the primacy of attention to culture which allows the expectation of a class action that is quite unlikely on material, social-structural grounds.[61] In this Thompson proceeds, as Raymond Williams has suggested was the case for a general strain of English Marxists, to argue a position on culture which comes directly from the romantics through Arnold, Morris, and others, and is only supplemented by certain phrases, emphases, recognitions, and aspects of Marx's analyses. It is a treatment in which "culture can be in advance of economic and social organization, ideally embodying the future."[62] This is not a very remarkable position in itself; on the contrary, it fits with a broad modern sense of the relationship of culture to action. This very sense, however, was one of the chief objects of Marx's criticism. Practical action and cultural conceptions are both, Marx suggested, ultimately determined by the stage of social and economic development of humankind. More narrowly, the activity of particular people is determined by their actual experiences and resources. Marx did not, certainly, suggest that culture is unilaterally dominated by economic and social conditions. He did hold that culture does not constitute the font of the human creative process, generating the push toward the future or even acting as a model for it. Culture is not autonomous; it is part of a broader social formation, all parts of which influence each other, the whole being ultimately determined by the stage of social and economic development. As we have seen, Thompson's argument depends considerably on the notion of the unequal development of different aspects of this social formation, so that class could develop culturally in advance of social or economic definition.[63] This position, whether held generally or with reference to a specific historical instance, makes the bearers of "culture" the just leaders of the "masses" and the agents of class consciousness. Class consciousness ceases to be a development out of the experience of a class of people and becomes rather a theory of development about or for those people.

Thompson, to be sure, does not argue an extreme version of this position, and at several points in *The Making* he argues something close to its opposite. Nonetheless, the theoretical grounding of his argument, as distinct from the purposes to which he puts it, brings him close to Lenin's emphasis on the leadership of the intellectual vanguard, and to such statements as this by Orwell's Winston Smith:

> If there was hope, it lay in the proles. . . . everywhere stood the same solid unconquerable figure, made monstrous by work and childbearing, toiling from birth to death and still singing. Out of those mighty loins a race of conscious beings must one day come. You were dead; theirs was the future. But you could share in that future if you kept alive the mind as they kept alive the body, and passed on the secret doctrine that two plus two make four.[64]

A doctrine of false consciousness, with its extreme version of unconsciousness, produces problems at the very core of any theory of action. It not only deprives some people of valid agency but also suggests itself as the crucial explanation for inactivity. By implication, a "correct consciousness" will produce appropriate action; furthermore, a correct consciousness is a true consciousness, not simply any one which will produce the appropriate action. As I shall argue, however, collective action is not simply a rational result of recognition of collective interests. This is not to deny that people frequently fail to act in their own interests out of ignorance or poor interpretations of evidence. It is to suggest that their tendency to do so is not an independent part of the realm of culture, which can be changed without changing the whole social being of the population in question.[65] Similarly, cultural elements which are maintained as social existence is altered are themselves changed in significance.

That this line of implied argument in The Making does not embody the whole of Thompson's thinking on the subject is clear from some of his later work. In his critique of and polemic against Althusser, for example, he stresses

> the dialogue between social being and social consciousness. . . . It had been habitual among Marxists—indeed, it had once been thought to be a distinguishing methodological priority of Marxism—to stress the determining pressures of being upon consciousness; although in recent years much "Western Marxism" has tilted the dialogue heavily back towards ideological domination.[66]

But while Thompson is rightly opposed to the rigid ideological terms in which some Marxists cast the discussion of class, his alternative is to treat not social being itself but complex popular customs. While these may be preferable to the more rarified versions of class consciousness, they are still cultural categories. Thompson takes the discussion out of the realm of high rationalistic culture (if the dogmatics of the Communist parties may be called that) and removes it to that of popular culture. He does not give the sociological dimension of social being its due.[67]

Thompson's most consistent suggestion of the importance of the ideological legacy of the late eighteenth-century artisan and romantic cultures is that one segment of the working class, and some nonworkers, shaped the development of the working class. It is not that the working class made itself. He presents his view, however, as though it were the latter, and as a result tends to obscure the differences among the populations he considers. Relatedly, Thompson sometimes loses track of the change in the social foundations of workers' actions and attitudes over time, both within each different population, and especially as their relative significance changed. None of this suggests that

Thompson's argument as to the connection between late eighteenth-century radicalism and workers' movements of the 1830s is false. It does deny that that connection was essentially a continuity of tradition among the members of *a* class.

The intellectual inheritance which was left, from varied sources, to the workers of the early nineteenth century was indeed important. This inheritance had a wide range of components: radical and conservative, bourgeois democratic and utilitarian, dissenting (in matters including and going beyond religious dissent) and evangelically (that is to say soberly) enthusiastic. It included both a political ideology and a sub-political "sense."[68] Beyond any specific contributions of content which this dual heritage may have made, it was of vital importance as the basis on which future ideology and social and political analysis could be built. Popular thought could, after the 1790s, be to some extent autonomous and cumulative.

This was the great contribution of the 1790s; in a sense it was less that a seed was planted than that a seed was created which could be preserved for two decades and then planted where it might have greater growth. It was, further, a mutant seed. It had escaped the cyclical repetition in which popular rebellion had largely been caught since the English Revolution. It is because he is dealing with the creation of this seed, and its nature, that Thompson can plausibly if not wholly justifiably let social being and social structure fall into the background of his analysis of political consciousness and culture. The real dialectical interaction of the two is left to be examined, and there minimally, in another part of the book, dealing with a later part of history. It was the social being of workers in the 1810s through 1830s which was crucially interactive with a many-faceted culture to shape the English working class as it emerged from the industrial revolution to remain more or less consistent into the present day.

In the second part of *The Making*, Thompson turns "from subjective to objective influences."[69] That is, he turns from a focus on the more or less organized political and "subpolitical" activities which form part of the "making" process to the experiences of the workers. Thompson concerns himself less with enumerating objective influences, however, than with debunking the emphasis other authors have placed on them. His emphasis in Part Two is on experience, and on the suggestion that what is sometimes considered "objective evidence" is not adequate to an understanding of how people felt about what was happening to them as objects.[70] We might expect this emphasis to lead to an analysis of the social being of workers; that happens, however, only partially. Thompson does indeed take up questions of economic conditions and social relations. But he tends to look at these as they shaped ideas, culture. Thus he takes up the sufferings of the poor, the chiliasm of the despairing, and the growing awareness of exploitation, but he does this before, and in greater detail than, he examines the bonds of community, the nature of social life. It is not that he totally fails to acknowledge the importance of community; quite the contrary. But his weight of emphasis still falls on the consciousness side of the duality. By focusing on a duality between consciousness and structure, he only implicitly examines their joint constitution of communities.[71]

Part Two of *The Making* is more heterogeneous than Part One.[72] It begins by discussing exploitation, goes on to take up particular cases (field laborers, weavers, artisans, and craftsmen), offers a polemic on the standards and experiences by which early industrial workers and their contemporaries judged what was happening to them materially and morally, considers again the role of Methodism, particularly in connection with work discipline and "the chiliasm of despair," and lastly looks at the relations of working people with each other and the traditional and occasionally new pursuits which they took up when not under the direct control of employers. The message of the section can be summed up, if in exaggerated tone, by one of Thompson's more contentious statements, coming near the end:

> The process of industrialization is necessarily painful. It must involve the erosion of traditional patterns of life. But it was carried through with exceptional violence in Britain. It was unrelieved by any sense of national participation in communal effort, such as is found in countries undergoing a national revolution. Its ideology was that of the masters alone.[73]

It would seem impossible to support this statement as it stands. In any "objective" measure of violence the experience of Britain must lag behind that of India, Africa (both in the cruelly racist south and in the more specifically economically exploitative copper belt and west), the Soviet Union, and the United States. Where are the mass shootings, for physical violence, and the prison camps and utter defeats, for psychic violence?[74] Britain would seem comparable only if one held that subjectively such violence is always infinite; in that case, however, comparison would become meaningless.

Thompson works up to his assertion of the "exceptional violence" of industrialization in England through a number of more specific criticisms of assertions that industrialization in England was essentially peaceful, beneficial, and voluntary. He shows most emphatically that it was not voluntary, and shows that whether or not it was materially beneficial to a majority of people, in short or long term, the industrial revolution was experienced by many as harmful and unpleasant.[75] He is more concerned elsewhere in the book to demonstrate the lack of peace, but in his consideration of industrial relations he does point out the resentment constantly below the surface and the many instances in which confrontations grew out of specifically industrial conditions.[76] One might summarize by saying that Thompson attempts to show first that workers had motivations for class-conscious collective action and, second, that they had the social cohesiveness necessary to support at least some such collective action. At best, only some of them had the latter.

Thompson begins his chapter on exploitation in a characteristically ambiguous manner. He first points out the great significance which contemporaries and later researchers alike placed on the new contexts of industrial work—factories. He notes how many activists and analysts, from Thelwall through Marx and Engels and beyond, saw the factory as the paradigmatic shaping institution of the working class. Then he suggests that one ought not to get carried away with the newness of the cotton mills, for that might lead to an underestimation of political and cultural traditions. But we ought not to be like Francis Place, either, and assume that the diversity of workers and their cultural and social contexts means that they were not united as a class. The reader's opinion wavers: "there was a class; there was no class...." Thompson's answer, of course, is that the formation of "the working class" (not "classes") is "the outstanding fact of the period between 1790 and 1830."[77] All this would be a minor confusion of presentation, not a matter of serious concern, were it not for the fact that this is almost the whole of Thompson's consideration of the place that the growth of factories occupies in socializing the working class! This key Marxist notion is neither systematically rejected nor explicitly accepted.[78]

Factories were important to Marx and Engels as symbols and sources of the socialization of production:

> The advance of industry, whose involuntary promoter is the bourgeoisie, replaces the isolation of the workers, due to the competition, with their revolutionary combination, due to association.[79]

and again:

> The contradiction between socialized production and capitalistic appropriation now presents itself as *an antagonism between the organization of production in the individual workshop and the anarchy of production in society generally.*[80]

Outside the factories, they thought, the workers lacked both the concentration and the commonality of condition for effective class action.

The workers would neither be reduced to the same level of uniformity of circumstances nor be aware of the extent to which they were in the same situation as a class. Further, their collective organization would be impeded by problems of communication. In short, the domestic industries presented relative isolation in comparison with the factory industries. It is my suggestion that, though he never explicitly sets out to do so and never clearly indicates that he has done so, Thompson marshalls evidence which shows Marx and Engels to have been mistaken, though not hopelessly lost.[81]

Domestic industries were not as isolated as has sometimes been thought, and neither were they controlled by a fragmented capitalist class.[82] On the contrary, small masters gave way to larger employers in domestic industry as well as in factories.[83] Moreover, in many instances, the simplest tasks (not the most complex) were relegated to domestic workers in outlying villages.[84] Marx's and Engels's assertion of the relative disunity of domestic workers in contrast to factory workers would seem to be accurate only if one is concerned with the *unity of a national class*. In their own communities, outworkers were able to produce a social cohesiveness which factory workers could seldom rival.[85]

Artisans' communal ties were also strong, and most artisans had far greater intercommunity bonds than their unfortunate brethren in the textile industries. By the early nineteenth century, textile work was not only degraded but highly localized. Tramping was much more of an asset to other trades,[86] and the network of ties among various artisanal communities considerably enhanced their strength. It gave them more of an approach to national trades unity than factory workers would have for some time; it underpinned coordinated political action; not least of all, it helped individual artisans to weather crises which hit harder in some local centers than in others. Further, for most of the artisans, the dominant forms of the organization of work were small workshops, gangs, and self-employment.[87] It was these artisans, most of all, who had the (sometimes dubious) benefit of elaborate rituals developed over the years. Later, they were the principals in the organization of benefit societies and other communal self-help bodies.[88] In the course of the struggles of the 1790s and early 1800s, the artisans began to complement their long-standing awareness of themselves as an "order" with an increasing solidarity and development of the social organization (formal and informal) which enabled them to take collective action.

Thompson is not unaware of the extent to which *The Making* focuses on craft, rather than factory work, and defends it to some extent. He notes, for example, that outworkers, far from being the remnants of an earlier age, as Marx and many historians had seen them, were in fact largely products of industrialization.[89] Their number expanded rapidly between 1780 and 1830 in order to supply increased demand in other stages of the work process.[90] Thus Thompson makes a case for turning attention partially away from factory workers to artisans, outworkers, and rural laborers.[91] He does not, however, give this case much theoretical weight.

It is not a negligible observation, however, to point out that, until well into the Chartist period, radical activity was not the result of the congregation of workers in factories but of the resistance of workers in older trades to being subjected to the discipline of factory work and having craft production itself subjected to the competition of factory (and more generally capitalist) industry. Throughout the early phase of struggle, therefore, workers were not fighting for control of the industrial revolution as much as against that revolution itself. They were fighting for local communities, for "independence," for what they considered a fair share of the goods produced. They were fighting not only against factories and work discipline but against a whole pattern of exploitation of which factories were only a convenient symbol. The pattern included increasing routinization of work, distance between the worker and the market for which he produced, a smaller share of the product, complete subjugation of consumers and producers to market forces, loss of autonomy, centralization of control over the whole system of production, and disruption of personal social relations.

The primacy of artisans and outworkers in Thompson's account is of the utmost importance in understanding what he means by the making of the English working class.[92] The material circumstances which shaped the development of the class, its ideology and analysis, its sentiments and ambitions were not from the start those of factory workers. Since by mid-century the factory workers were fast outstripping the artisans and outworkers in number, some sort of transmission of the original class-nature, or else its loss, was inevitable. Such a transmission would have had to be cultural—hence perhaps Thompson's emphasis. But perhaps the explanation of the failure of the transmission can better be seen in the disjunction of social groups and organizations. This fact may be as important as the oft-cited labor aristocracy in an understanding of why the working class was not the revolutionary force Marx expected.[93] Thompson, partly through his choice of narrative end-point, sidesteps the problem of establishing the connections between the "working class" which went into Chartism and that which came out of it. The crucial lines of differentiation were apparent by the 1820s, however, as the proportion of workers in the "modern" branches of industry began to increase dramatically.

In passing Thompson attributes the decline of Chartism to the pulling apart of factory and weaving communities.[94] This was, of course, largely a result of internal change in the two populations as much as of the external circumstances of either. Among other things, their respective proportions of the total laboring population shifted considerably, and the economic status of each along with them. In 1820, at the conclusion of Thompson's first great wave of agitation ("the heroic age of popular radicalism"), there were nearly twice as many handloom weavers as factory workers. Parity was reached in 1833–34 during the second peak of agitation and in the early years of Chartism. By 1840, factory workers outnumbered handloom weavers by a margin of greater than two to one.[95] The weavers' decline, though more dramatic than most, is symptomatic of the general fate of outworkers. By the waning years of Chartism, factory workers were an immense and internally complex and differentiated population. They were also oriented primarily to industrial agitation, especially for the reduction of working hours.[96] Further, as Thompson has noted, few of the handloom weavers or other outworkers were able themselves to make the transition to factory work, and fewer still to the better-paid of the factory occupations.[97]

Despite all this, it must be remembered that handloom weavers and other outworkers were still workers under early capitalism. Their communities might be characterized by a "unique blend of social conservatism, local pride, and cultural attainment,"[98] but they were still dependent on and subject to the machinations of capital:

> Along with the development of the factory system and of the revolution in agriculture that accompanies it, production in all the other branches of industry not only extends, but alters its character. . . . This modern so-called domestic industry has nothing, except the name, in common with the old-fashioned domestic industry, the existence of which pre-supposes independent urban handicrafts, independent peasant farming, and above all, a dwelling-house for the labourer and his family. . . . Besides the factory operatives, the manufacturing workmen and the handicraftsmen, whom it concentrates in large masses at one spot, and directly commands, capital also sets in motion, by means of invisible threads, another army; that of the workers in the domestic industries, who dwell in the towns and are also scattered over the face of the country.[99]

They have, therefore, to be treated as a key part of any "working class" in the early nineteenth century. That one of its chief components was "obsolescent" in the terms of the new industrial capitalist economy did not make that component any less significant at the time. But this fact did hold important implications for the future of a class which drew much of its strength from the artisans and outworkers.[100]

This split in the ranks of the workers was of considerable immediate significance in that it gave different segments of the "class" different experiences, expectations, goals, interests, and resources.[101] Skilled workers, as Thompson points out, were in competition not only with their employers but also with unskilled workers.[102] In each industry there was an elite (or "labor aristocracy") of skilled artisans to whom the progress of industrialization was a threat and a degradation. It was no less a threat if it helped their poorer unskilled brethren. It has to be borne in mind that in most places most of the time factory workers and those who worked out-of-doors, in small workshops, or in their own homes constituted distinct populations. The latter had traditional communities and privileged positions which were threatened by the new industrial developments which gave work—however unpleasant it often was—to the former.[103] The factory workers had in their early years to *build* communities. They were often migrants, not infrequently ex-rural, and only gradually built up the formal and informal organization to maintain their day-to-day lives and to seek larger political, social, and economic ends.

It should be further recognized that artisans possessed of unchallenged skills and strong organization fared far better than domestic workers, like weavers, whose trade was overrun by outsiders, beaten down by wage cutting and by the breakdown of both customary bonds and more formal unions.[104] The urban artisans in Lancashire enjoyed a relative prosperity, for the most part, even into the 1830s.[105] Through strong collective organization (and because their trades were often less directly in competition with machinery or were more skilled than weaving) they were able to keep both weavers and ex-factory lads out.[106] The latter, in particular, suffered from both the factory system (which wanted them only as children) and the artisan culture which looked down on them as a "poorer sort" and a potential threat. As adults they were likely to find employment only as casual laborers.[107] If we keep these considerations in mind, the periods of collaboration among the varying ranks of artisans, outworkers, and factory workers appear more remarkable achievements. They were made possible in part by the very strong radical (largely Jacobin) consciousness of the artisans, which during the early part of the century encouraged a broader view of social problems and a deeper analysis of the sources of economic ills. Without this strong heritage, the artisans might never have chosen to pursue working-class objectives but stuck instead to their more particular and defensive postures.

It was not, according to Thompson, how well-off artisans were that was the prime factor influencing how radical they were; it was not their absolute standard of living which mattered so much as the extent of threat they felt, for example, during the late eighteenth century and the years after the Napoleonic wars.[108] It was in the latter period that the debasement of artisan trades was most rapid and extreme, though it continued throughout the century. The attack on the craft skills, which constituted a main part of the artisans' "property" in their view, coincided with high food prices and a fluctuating economy.[109] The artisans and outworkers were also among the prime victims (along with the many varieties of casual laborer) of the habitual insecurity of employment characteristic of the period of industrial revolution.[110] This was particularly characteristic of the outworkers in gradually mechanizing industries, who picked up the slack in good times but had no work in bad, since their employers would first keep their expensive machinery working.[111] The textile industries, with their dependence on imported materials and export markets, also fluctuated more dramatically than the home trades in which most artisans worked.[112] There were, in short, pressures pushing different parts of the laboring population in different directions. The standard of living of paupers declined; that of outworkers, artisans, and factory workers fluctuated in partial synchronization and followed differing secular trends.[113] While one sector of the population battled unemployment, another suffered from exploitative and injurious employment. As an 1823 author put it: "It is obvious that the reason why there is no work for one half of our people is, that the other half work twice as much as they ought."[114]

Of course there was more to the story: there was capital; there was exploitation. And workers were already, in their varying contexts, developing analyses of these. The fact that the poor could not store their labor but must sell it constantly to the rich convinced a Manchester silk weaver that it was meaningless to hold that capital and labor were subject to the same laws.[115] Exploitation grew more transparent with the rapidity of gain that was characteristic of new industrial growth.[116] Perhaps at least as important, such exploitation lost any pretenses of paternalism and personal relationship it had once had (and still maintained in some as yet traditional trades).[117] This not only allowed workers to develop a firmer sense of themselves in opposition, and as victims; it allowed the bulk of the wealthier elites and capitalists to ignore (to retain a certain studied ignorance of) the workers. This was characteristic of the workplace, which came increasingly under the control of intermediaries, and even more of the distribution of housing.[118] While many were rather voluntarily ignorant, and a few were concerned about the state of the poor and the workers, an active minority, supported generally by Parliament, tried ruthlessly to implement the principles of political economy and to prohibit any securing of collective goods by the poorer of the workers.[119]

By the 1830s, factory workers were organizing to defend their particular interests.[120] By this period too there was a concerted neopaternalist agitation underway about factory conditions (and, emerging more gradually, urban living conditions). Thompson argues that this "humanitarian" movement cannot be attributed to any general spirit of the age; it was rather a complex conscience which the rich developed, and was in no small part a reaction to the pressure from below produced by the factory workers themselves.[121] Indeed, he suggests that some, at least, of the official inquiries into factory and urban conditions, far from being humantiarian in motivation, were procrastinations and appeasement tactics.[122] When the self-conscious activity of factory workers did become influential, its concerns were with such local and reformist issues as working and living conditions and with the threats posed by child and female labor to the industrial position of men and ideals of family life.[123]

Three

The Reactionary Radicals

What sorts of actual movements could grow out of the defense of the moral economy? What material obstacles confronted, what strengths aided, those who would mobilize for such a defense? The two great waves of agitation in the 1810s—Luddism and Parliamentary Reform agitation—give us an idea. The movements embodying an ideology of a moral economy were at their strongest locally and at their weakest nationally; they were limited by the communities which gave them their social foundation. It was the effort of these populists to act directly as the people, to avoid dependence on formal organizations or mediation from "outside." They were reactionary because they mobilized in response to external pressures, not out of an autonomous political program. They were radical because what they sought could not be granted except by fundamentally altering the structure of power and rewards in English society. In the next chapter I will look somewhat more broadly at the populist ideology of the period: In this, I focus on the two great movements as social events.

Luddism

The Luddite phenomenon was a movement which grew directly out of local community roots. It may have been political (as Thompson argues) as well as economic, but in neither of these orientations did it overstep the bounds of community. It was never political as opposed to economic, or class-oriented as opposed to communal.[1] This is not to say that everyone in a community was equally involved. That is never the case with anything. Rather, it is to suggest that those who were involved were linked communally to each other, and to the rest of the local population within which they lived. It is this which makes the Luddite movement so "opaque," in Thompson's term.[2] Midnight meetings and drilling were a feature of Midlands radicalism for forty years, without the authorities ever becoming much more effectively aware than they were at the outset. Only Spence among the London radicals had anything approaching a coherent policy of diffused agitation.[3] Rather, Luddism was a development out of the practical circumstances of the discontented throughout the country. Paine's works were saved, but, more importantly, the indeferential tone of his polemic was remembered. The Painites were not scholars or disciples, however, prone to worry over the extent to which their ideas followed those of the founder. On the contrary, as Jacobinism collapsed and its adherents withdrew into their local communities, their thinking was shaped as much or more by local problems. The older radicalism was recalled to support analyses of these problems, not in the abstract for its own sake. In periods of great crisis, as at the end of the Napoleonic wars, these village Jacobins (generally speaking, a literate elite) could once again become spokesmen for their fellows and participants in agitations which at least weakly linked village to village.[4]

While the focus of concern was local, it was all the more likely to be industrial and economic. Petitions to Parliament on behalf of the respectable elements of a trade (like the stockingers of Nottingham) were as close to national action as these mobilizations came. Trade organizations were forced to act in secrecy, with the Combination Acts declaring their very existence illegal. This was rendered practicable by the very small size of most shops in the traditional or respectable branches of the trades, and by the close-knit village communities.[5] Only assembly in order to petition Parliament (and that problematically) was preserved of the traditional collective rights of Englishmen. Even combinations of people for charitable purposes, like friendly societies, fell afoul of the Acts.[6] Employers were of course more readily able to circumvent the laws and act in concert. They were aided not only by their ties to those in authority but by their smaller number and greater capacity for staging private gatherings with incidental political and economic aspects.[7] In this connection, however, it is important to differentiate small employers from large. The former were continually being displaced or threatened by the latter; they were apt often to side with the journeymen in traditional trades in support of "respectable" work.[8]

There were occasional attempts by the respectable Radicals to ameliorate the oppression of the Combination Acts or to rehabilitate the traditional organization of certain trades.[9] All failed. It was not until the 1820s that Hume's exceedingly mild bill passed, offering a small concession to the by then actively mobilized trade unionists.[10] In the crises of the second decade of the century the government and the leaders of industry gave little if any ground, and often took a repressive and reactionary tack, as Lord Byron suggested in his famous maiden speech to the House of Lords:

> When a proposal is made to emancipate or relieve, you hesitate, you deliberate for years, you temporise and tamper with the minds of men; but a death bill must be passed off hand, without a thought of the consequences![11]

Amelioration of the plight of workers in the traditional industries, those who formed the most important population of Luddites, would in any case have been difficult. At the same time, the agitation and nascent trades organization of the traditional crafts was to many minds less threatening, and certainly more able to command sympathy, than that of the newer populations of factory workers.[12] The latter were more of a threat, economically, to the progress of capitalist industrialization than were the craft workers, for they were what made it possible for industry to bypass the craftsmen.

These industrial workers fought for benefits from a stronger position in the economic structure. They did not fight from a similar position of social strength, however, and their battles had not really begun to take off in the 1810s. This period of trade-union development shows a paradoxical relationship between the radicalism of older trades and the growing importance of newer ones. In the older trades a more educated working population, and one with a fairly clear and continuous connection with radicalism, joined with often radical small masters (and sometimes tradespeople) to mount an agitation which was at once remarkably constitutionalist and prone to direct action. Petition after petition was sent to Parliament without the slightest hint of support from the parliamentary elite or any kind of ameliorative action. At the same time, threats and machine-breaking provided a practical incentive to capitalists to offer material concessions.[13]

The very illegality of the trade organizations inclined them especially to direct action rather than negotiation or legal remedies.[14] Direct action had a long history, moreover, as an important means of expressing popular sentiment regarding unfair labor and marketing practices.[15] It not only had the advantage of not depending on the good offices of one's "betters," but it could be organized with some rapidity and ease on a community basis. Traditionally, any form of national political action had to go through aristocratic, or at the very least "respectable," connections. It could not be the province of the people alone. Within the local community, the people, the workers, could act as an independent force. Further, they acted with regard to employers (or merchants) who, according to traditional values, should have seen themselves as part of that same community. The very fact that these were growing apart from, more prosperous than, their fellows, and were leaving their traditional positions, was part of the change the Luddites were attacking. They were supported in this by a good many of the smaller masters and some tradespeople.[16] Their sympathy for and common interests with the artisans provided both an undefined area of toleration for trade-union activity, and a source of material support, including insurance against the blacklisting of activist workers. This is not to say that small masters would tolerate any form of artisan action, or that they identified totally with their employees, but rather that a workable accommodation had been reached, and that the split between small masters and large was at least as great as that between the former and their journeymen. The relationship between master and journeyman was in any case a part of the traditional communal organization of degrees and ranks; the large masters were moving outside of, and upsetting, this traditional organization.[17] The ambivalent role of the small masters allowed a much stronger development of trade organizations and a much greater experience of success.

The situation was quite different in the newer industries and in the more capitalistically organized sections of the old. As Thompson sums up:

> Wherever we find outwork, factory, or large workshop industry, the repression of trade unionism was very much more severe. The larger the industrial unit or the greater the specialization of skills involved, the sharper were the animosities between capital and labour, and the greater the likelihood of a common understanding among the employers.[18]

The summation is only partly accurate. It implies that there was a similar trade unionism in each case, facing different problems. But as we have seen, trade organization meant different things in a Luddite community and in large factory towns. Further, the relation of size of workplace to collective action is not a simple positive correlation.[19] On the contrary, increases in size introduce new problems of organization at the same time that concentration intensifies the structural opposition between capital and labor. In brief, the greater separation of workers from their employers is not likely to bring a new revolutionary organization of the workers (as in Marx's vision) if these are also more weakly sociated amongst themselves. The population involved in the newer trades and nonapprenticed sections of the older ones was different. It was less cohesive, had less involvement in the radical traditions, less attachment to the trade, and, as much as one can tell, less education. The emergent "new" working class was not only faced, as Thompson suggests, with a stronger enemy; it was intrinsically easier to repress.[20] Further, it was the enemy of the radical artisans. An appeal to hungry factory workers, or to those weavers who manned the wide frames, who did cut-up weaving, or who worked the new cropping machines, to desist from weakening their journeymen brothers was hardly a useful tool. In short the working "class" was pulled apart by the dynamics of its own development, both economic and social. The socially stronger and more radical workers were those whose economic position was, collectively if not necessarily individually, least tenable. That is, while artisans and skilled outworkers may have been better off than the factory workers, they were unable to maintain the industrial organization which kept them better-off.[21]

Thompson devotes himself for the most part to the more radical artisans and the journeymen in established trades. Secondarily, he takes up the growing radicalism of the less skilled (but still often initially privileged) outworkers. Least of all does he integrate the factory workers into his discussion of the "army of redressers." The reason is obvious; they were not in fact a part of the radical army of the early 1810s (and only very weakly a part later in the decade). It is important to bear in mind that Thompson's considerable success in showing the continuities between Jacobinism and Luddism, and the (not necessarily ideologically elaborate) radicalism of the Luddites, establishes a connection only to one part of an increasingly split, socially and economically, working population. It was not the Manchester operatives who were involved in the illegal activities of the would-be revolutionary followers of King Ludd. It was their cousins the domestic workers and artisans. No matter how zealous Colonel Fletcher and his spies were in tracking down those who administered illegal oaths, these were not as common in the Bolton factories (if they were there at all for political purposes) as they were a few miles out in the country. The traditions of which these oaths were a part survived more strongly in the villages.[22] When they were maintained in cities it was most often in the elite craft groups like the building trades.[23]

All this is not to suggest that the Luddites were simply a colorful, backward-looking bunch of local yokels. Their illegal labors, as Thompson points out, were not entirely romantic even in retrospect.[24] Their opposition to new machinery was thoughtful, not absolute.[25] It was also an opposition in times of crisis; the machinery frequently preceded the major protests (though not the grumblings and attempts at negotiation) by several years.[26] The manufacturers responded with an attitude which rendered sarcasm fair:

Manufacturers everywhere were availing themselves of the many wonderful inventions that were being brought out for cheapening labour, and as the new machinery threw thousands out of employment when extensively introduced, the poor, misguided wretches, who could not understand how that could be a benefit which deprived them of the means of earning a livelihood and reduced them to beggary, met in secret conclaves, and resolved in their ignorance to destroy them. Had they been better instructed, they would have known that it was their duty to lie down in the nearest ditch and die.[27]

The Luddites, whether considered strictly in reference to the years 1811–12 or more broadly, were concerned with more than machinery. They campaigned for the right of craft control over trade, the right to a decent livelihood, for local autonomy, and for the application of improved technology to the common good. Machinery was at issue because it was used in ways which specifically interfered with these values. Thus croppers, for example, proposed gradual introduction of machinery for dressing cloth, alternative employment, a tax on the machinery the proceeds from which could be used to help the displaced seek work, and so forth. Elsewhere a limitation on the number of looms a master could employ was a similarly moderate demand.

In short, the artisans were prepared to negotiate, as they had done before.[28] But this time they met with a new intransigence on the part of the larger masters. These were no longer vulnerable (as all masters had traditionally been) to community pressure. They were not so much a part of the same set of moral relations, and they had the economic resources to withstand direct action. Because of the high rate of capital investment and the prospects for enormous returns, they also had a greater interest in the changes than was the case with masters in an earlier stage of capitalist development. This aspect of the conflict also reveals why small masters played a pivotal role in it. For them as well as their employees, the domestic system itself seemed to be at stake.[29] This was part of a traditional organization of work and trade which protected its participants and was virtually coterminous with the community.[30] The separation of trade from tradition and community, from the control of anything but ownership with its fundamental impetus of capitalist efficiency was what was truly at issue. Luddism cannot be understood, as Thompson rightly points out, as a temporarily bounded movement. It was a battle in the war by which capitalism achieved social and economic dominance.

Luddism must be seen as arising at the crisis-point in the abrogation of paternalist legislation, and in the imposition of the political economy of *laissez-faire* upon, and against the will and conscience of, the working people. It is the last chapter of a story which begins in the fourteenth and fifteenth centuries. . . .[31]

We may legitimately question only whether Luddism was *the* rather than *a* crisis point, and whether it was the last chapter of the story.

Luddism was, according to Thompson, a "quasi-insurrectionary movement." It was both organized and politicized, although the two aspects were not closely correlated. The most politically oriented Luddism was in Lancashire; that of Nottingham was most specifically tied to the trade but was also the most disciplined and organized.[32] To the extent that it was an organized movement, and did "tremble on the edge of ulterior revolutionary objectives," Luddism in the second decade of the nineteenth century must be distinguished from previous and succeeding episodes of violent direct action directed against property, even specifically capital. But what was this extent? Thompson argues that it was great; I am more dubious. It is clear, and he amply shows, that there was some political content to Luddite claims and certainly to the authorities' fears. It is much less clear that there was anything resembling a Luddite organization. This was the issue which most vexed the authorities, but then any time they observed working men acting in concert, they saw an organization of the disaffected. Despite the stories of delegate visits, there is little evidence that the Luddites actually acted in concert beyond the range of local communities and small districts. On the contrary, as Darvall observes:

> One of the things, indeed, which made Luddism so difficult to suppress, made it also ineffective as the basis for a general revolutionary movement. The aims of the rioters were so limited and so local. . . . Disturbances in Regency England, though very widespread and serious and calling for all the effort of the Government for their suppression, were not directed against the Government.[33]

The government was involved, intentionally or not, primarily as a partisan of the employers. The national government, in fact, was skeptical of the alarm raised by local magistrates, though it did in the end respond.[34] The focus of Luddism was enduringly on industrial issues, and against employers. Revolutionary talk appeared only at the end and in desperation.

If the Luddites were organized, it was, as I have suggested, on the basis of local affiliations. Thus, when the peak force of the movement subsided, it left behind no organizational structures or institutions by which to carry on its battles. These battles in any case did not arise as part of a long-term project of greater mobilization or more advanced revolutionary goals. When Luddism passed, it became simply a memory, for it was neither ideologically nor organizationally part of a cumulative progress of radicalism. As Hobsbawm has suggested, speaking to the broader issue:

> "The poor," or indeed any subaltern group, become a subject rather than an object of history only through formalized collectivities, however structured. Everybody always has families, social relations, attitudes toward sexuality, childhood and death, and all the other things that keep social historians usefully employed. But, until the past two centuries, as traditional historiography shows, "the poor" could be neglected most of the time by their "betters," and therefore remained largely invisible to them, precisely because their active impact on events was occasional, scattered, and impermanent. If this has not been so since the end of the eighteenth century, it is because they have become an institutionally organized force. Even the most dictatorial regimes today learn sooner or later what ancient rulers knew, how to make concessions to unorganized and spontaneous pressure from the masses, if necessarily underlining their continued authority by face-saving punishment for "agitators." It is *organized* popular action they seek to prevent.[35]

The Luddites fit Hobsbawm's "before" category more closely than his "after" one of institutionally organized force. They had made some progress from invisibility, impotence, and total diffuseness of rebellion. They were, indeed, in the position of being able to wage a partially external, and thus threatening, critique of the dominant system of social and economic organization only because they were defending an older conception of social order. Their rebellion was not purely ritual, it did not reaffirm the hierarchy or the rest of the organization of the land, because it could no longer be readily incorporated.[36] Social relations of the older sort had grown too fragile, and those of the newer sort, dictated by capitalism, offered no possible ameliorative concessions to the Luddites.[37] By failing to distinguish between the mobilization of community relationships for political ends, and the creation of explicitly political organization, Thompson clouds the issue.

The very fact that it was the Nottingham workers who were the most organized and disciplined ought to have been a hint of the problem. For these were also the workers with the most exclusively economic aims and the most narrowly local definition of the economic issues. There was perhaps a very rudimentary beginning to the development of sustaining organization in Lancashire and Yorkshire. Certainly Luddism was able to stand up longer under pressure in these counties.[38] In Lancashire there was a combination of spontaneous rioting, reform agitation, provocateurs, and genuine insurrection.[39] It is, of course, the proportions which are at issue. Most of the information regarding the supposedly formal organization of the Lancashire Luddites comes from the depositions of prisoners, a source Thompson rightly questions in some instances, though for the most part he accepts it in this one.[40] At least, he accepts it at the outset: while he starts his account by suggesting that Luddism was both organized and insurrectionary, he devotes most of his discussion to the latter aspect and concludes that Luddism was like a peasants' revolt, lacking in national organization.[41] Part of Thompson's problem is that he sees no other way to rescue the Luddites from the suggestion that they were primitive rebels, engaged in some form of blind protest.[42] He is right that they were not primitive people; he shows them to have been intelligent and often acutely perceptive. Certainly they were right about the short-term effects of capitalist industrialization on their lives and livelihoods. And, as I have agreed above, Luddite aims were not confined to immediate economic welfare but extended in some instances to more general features of socioeconomic organization.[43] But the sophistication of the people is a distinct issue from the extent of organization which they are able to develop. Perhaps more important than extent is nature. Only a few Luddites, relatively late in the movement, and then inadequately, were going about the business of building politico-economic organizations which could sustain action beyond immediate crises. Neither the politicization of economic agitation nor the disciplined nature of protest or insurrection indicate the existence of a purposive coordinating organization.[44]

The reasons for believing that Luddites (and their communities) were generally insurrectionary in thought, mood, and even place are more convincing.[45] Certainly with the economic crisis of 1811 coming on the heels of political repression and deafness to legalist industrial complaints the Luddites had ample reason to be.[46] Further, the solidarity of the Luddite communities with the active participants in insurrectionary activities is beyond reasonable doubt. The authorities found it all but impossible to ascertain who leaders were, or, where they were fairly certain, to obtain any evidence or witnesses with which to convict them.[47] The government found it convenient to stick to prosecutions for overtly illegal acts, finding it unwise to proceed too far with political prosecutions.[48] The authorities faced the closed ranks of solidary villages. Even local magistrates who were sympathetic to the craftsmen were likely to feel uncomfortably isolated.[49] This, of course, had the unfortunate side-effect, for the Luddites, of uniting their opposition, the millowners, with the squires. This was symbolized when employers felt confident in opening fire on riotous crowds, as at Rawfolds.[50] It is also important to note, in connection with the community basis of this insurrectionism, that while rejoicing greeted the assassination of Perceval, the rather distant prime minister, revulsion was apt to greet more local manifestations of revolutionary (terrorist?) violence such as the shooting of Horsfall in Yorkshire.[51] All this said, it does not seem unreasonable for Thompson to assert that "sheer insurrectionary fury has rarely been more widespread in English history."[52] It is only unreasonable to equate this insurrectionary fury with stable revolutionary organization.

The community solidarity which gave its sanction to Luddism was all the stronger because the Luddites were primarily residents of small industrial villages. This was especially the case in Nottingham and the West Riding. Even in southeast Lancashire, however, where the average municipality was much larger, Luddism was focused in the outlying villages and smaller industrial towns. In a complaint to be all too familiar to Lancashire radicals in the early nineteenth century, an April 1812 meeting was finding it necessary to spread the word that Manchester could not be expected to act in concert with Bolton, Stockport, Oldham, Failsworth, Saddleworth, Ashton, and other towns and villages.[53] Thompson, late in his discussion of Luddism, gives much the argument of the present book when he suggests that those who place too much emphasis on agents provocateurs fail "to imagine Luddism in the context of the community. In Nottingham and the West Riding in particular, the strength of the Luddites was in small industrial villages where every man was known to his neighbours and bound in the same close kinship-network."[54] But Thompson goes on to suggest that because this community was sealed off from the eyes and control of the authorities, and because it took insurrectionary action, it can be considered in terms of "class solidarity."[55] If this is what the community solidarity was, then it was a constricted and weakly self-conscious class. The links between Luddite villages more than a mile or two apart were tenuous and fragile at best. The links between Luddites and other workers ranged from sympathetic and mildly cooperative to nonexistent.[56] It is reasonable to call this a class but not to simultaneously argue that there was a polarity of two classes, rather than several in more diffuse relationship.

Least of all was Luddism a national movement, let alone a national threat. It was very much confined to certain disturbed areas. Occasionally local authorities in other parts of the country, for example Glasgow in January 1812, feared that it would extend to their own distressed workers.[57] It seldom did, remaining almost exclusively in Nottingham, Yorkshire, Derbyshire, Lancashire, and Leicester. Although framebreaking in the Nottingham area began in March, it only attracted the regular attention of the *Times* in November 1811. At no point did the reporting of Luddite activities gain much pride of place in the "respectable" London press, even in an opposition newspaper such as the *Times*.[58] Parliament gave little attention to the disturbances, and that primarily when the government forced it to, by presenting a bill. Attendance was low on such occasions, and members seemed inclined to think the Luddite villages nearly as foreign as the scenes of the Peninsular wars.[59] Only in February 1812 did fairly regular attention begin to be devoted to the Luddites.[60] The Home Office was not a great deal more excited about the whole affair; certainly it felt no fear of immediate revolution, as much as the local magistrates writing to it might fear the most dire consequences of insurrection and disrespect for authority and property.

I suggested earlier that one of the ways in which Jacobinism may be held to have contributed to the making of the English working class was by the provision of an ideological foundation on which workers' thought could begin to be cumulative. There was little advance in this ideological foundation by the time of Luddism, but there was diffusion, with much of the core intact, albeit in changed context. This, together with the fact that on occasion the same people were involved, is the primarily link between the two agitations. Thus, a "constitution" and "oath," together with flowery libertarian addresses were associated (by somewhat dubious connection) with the Luddites involved in an attack on a West Riding mill. The former two items were identical with those found on an associate of Despard nearly a decade before.[61] Here is a connection with one of the last of the "first generation" radicals. But bear in mind that it is a *cultural* connection. Politically, it is hard to show much else.[62] As an economic or trade agitation, Luddism built on strong foundations and grew directly out of tradition. That tradition did not provide equally for political mobilization. Jacobin ideas had been preserved, but they commanded no organization save the personal network of informal acquaintanceships and kinship. The rhetoric of Luddism mattered little if at all beyond its contributions to working-class culture. The Luddite movement was determined by its community foundation. Generally, in fact, the rhetoric shows this.

Thompson suggests that "by May 1812 Luddism in both Lancashire and Yorkshire had largely given way to revolutionary organization."[63] What he does not at the same point emphasize is that by May 1812 Luddism was fast fading. It is not at all clear whether the "serious conspiratorial organization" Thompson sees emerging is the activity of the core or the rump.[64] In general, I might suggest that as the more moderate supporters of any movement abandon it, for whatever reasons, the most extreme are left. Are we to judge Chartism by the 1830s and 1840s, or by the ideological heights to which it climbed just before its 1850s demise? The most important legacy of Luddism would seem not to be in its most extreme adherents but in the more moderate, who, if not revolutionaries in 1812, had at least become more open to the preachings of Major Cartwright and Cobbett and the parliamentary reform movement in general. For if Luddism came at the end of twenty years of government repression of press and public meeting, it was followed by a veritable flowering of ideological dissemination and discussion. But the key question, perhaps, is not what would have happened had the Luddites had the benefit of national leadership or sophisticated ideology. They would, of course, have been a different movement. More interesting is the question of what would have happened could Luddite community sense have been preserved (or recreated) and extended to other populations and generations of workers.

As a movement of the people's own, Thompson indicates, Luddism strikes one not so much by its backwardness as by its growing maturity.[65] His polemical intent is clear, and probably well aimed. He goes on to draw a contrast, which his own more recent work suggests should be phrased less starkly, with the immaturity of the eighteenth-century populace.[66] Luddism indeed marked a maturation, but not only its own. It marked the development of the countryside into an autonomous political force, in part out of the necessity of responding to oppression. Never again would London so dominate national organization (unless in the twentieth century, perhaps) as it did before the turn of the nineteenth century. The communities of weavers, croppers, lacemakers, stockingers, and such were caught up with the London artisans and would henceforth lead as much as follow—for as long as they existed.[67] Luddism was an insurrection in a classical sense: the craftsmen aimed at creating a disturbance and making life uncomfortable for their masters. They wished England to be ungovernable because the government was enforcing the disruption of their trades by "free enterprise." They had no coherent plan for governing themselves, and only vague and occasional notions that they ought to do so. Thompson, it seems to me, exaggerates when he calls Luddism revolutionary. At the end of his account he suggests that delegate meetings were the weakest feature of Luddism, prone to penetration by spies and "frothy talk" of great risings with the aid of the French, Irish, or Scots.[68] Yet these were part of its ideological heritage from Jacobinism, and its most "revolutionary" manifestations. As Luddism matured, it grew into something else: the movement for parliamentary reform.[69]

Part of the shift in movements was allied to a secularization of British radicalism. Thompson has accurately emphasized the extent to which Christian eschatology and communal traditions were welded to the emerging cause of the workers.[70] As he comments on Luddism: "The fervour of the Old Testament had become assimilated to a class sol-

idarity which not even Jabez Bunting could penetrate."[71] Religion offered sanction to workers' righteous anger, and it fit their local struggles into a more global frame of reference. It provided a language for
thinking about the contradictions within everyday life and between its
deeply held values and limited possibilities. It had great power of
commonality for the working population, but it was limited in analytic
capability. While it could oppose good and bad, it was limited in its
ability to develop a deeper understanding of the dynamics of a social or
economic system.[72] Whether such an understanding makes workers
revolutionary, as opposed to reformist, is another question. The point is
that such an understanding was intermediate in range; it could not be
adequately developed with the context of the insular local community—for capitalism was more than that; and it could not be read in
ultimate teleology—for capitalism was less than that. This is part of
Hobsbawm's acute observation:

> What made modern mass organization apparently irrelevant to, say,
> Andalusian anarchist *pueblos* or highly skilled pre-industrial
> craftsmen was the informally or traditionally structured cohesion of
> their communities or occupations, and their (increasingly unreal)
> belief that the decisions which determined their lives were either
> cosmic or purely local.[73]

Workers become a truly revolutionary threat when, still acting on the
basis of their cohesive local communities, they begin to organize nationally and focus their attention on the effective sources of political
and economic power. This unstable transitional period began in England with the end of Luddism. It lasted, perhaps, for the duration of the
Parliamentary Reform agitation, and into the reaction against the
cooptation of the latter movement which had left workers with too
limited gains. By the time of the movement against the Poor Law of
1834 it was ebbing. English political, social, and economic life was
becoming stable.

The Great Populist Movement: Parliamentary Reform, 1816–20

The four years after 1815 were, according to Thompson, "the heroic age
of popular Radicalism."[74] No longer was radicalism such a minority
propaganda as it had been in the age of Jacobinism.[75] The "objective"
circumstances in which people found themselves contributed to the
difference in political orientation. In 1792 England had been governed
primarily by consent and deference. In 1816, the government was
maintained with the aid of much greater show of force.[76] Postwar

radicalism was a response of the whole community, according to Thompson, though we may append that it was less that all participated than that few opposed. The London crowd had grown somewhat more sophisticated, though what more impresses Thompson is a shift in the "sub-political" attitudes of the provincial masses.[77] The "church and king" loyalist mob all but disappeared; there were ebb tides of radicalism to be sure, but counterrevolution had ceased to be a popular ideology. When the agents of authority set out to "maintain order" or arrest popular figures, they encountered bodily resistance and, perhaps more alarming to them, a widespread network of communication that warned of their activities.[78] The people shared not only subpolitical attitudes but at least some will and capability to resist. Popular attitudes were becoming consistent, though perhaps this consistency was less of internal logic than of distribution and endurance over time. Nonetheless, it was of vital importance to the renascent radical movement. It offered only occasional support for radical activities and organizations; it offered continuous protection to the radicals and their sympathizers.

Major Cartwright, the veteran constitutionalist reformer, had renewed his campaign for equal laws in 1811–12. His was a fairly old-fashioned and respectable pitch by that year. His "radical reform" was to save "the vessel of the State . . . now threatened with shipwreck" through "a courageous and inflexible adherence to the constitution." Offering no attack on property or the organization of the economy (other than taxation), he called for:

> 1st, Representation, co-extensive with direct taxation in the books of the collectors; 2dly, A fair distribution of that common right; and 3dly, Parliaments of a constitutional duration, that is, not exceeding one year. . . . The constitution, the whole constitution and nothing but the constitution.[79]

His appeal was directly to the middle and lower classes together, and to such members of the upper classes as were not hopelessly enmeshed in corruption. He wrote to a respectable Nottingham framework knitter hoping that he would urge his fellows to consider the wickedness, folly, and impolicy of destroying the property of others. He referred to the Luddites as "the deluded and the criminal" in a letter to Lord Holland.[80] His constitutionalist appeal was a strong one, however, and it was difficult to tell just what might be claimed in the name of the constitution. His organizational vehicle was the Hampden clubs. Despite the elitism of some of their initial membership and the paternalist tone of much of their propaganda, these were open to all ranks of society.

In 1812 Cartwright had contact with "persons connected with the disturbed districts": "For turning the discontents into a legal channel favourable to Parliamentary Reform, they are anxious to have the advice and countenance of our Society."[81] He found the workers responsive, feeling "a very general sense of wrong and misery, and a very general disposition to petition for a reform of that house, the corruption of which was generally supposed to be the cause."[82] In early 1813 he took a month's tour, as a "travelling reformist," "itinerant apostle" (both labels were taunts which he turned to his own advantage) through the West Country, Midlands, and Northwest.[83] This was only one of the longer of a number of excursions on which he urged reformers to organize their own clubs to push for parliamentary reform. His ideas of "old England" and the Norman yoke could still command adherence, and his criticism of the growing authoritarian evil of which the present government was heir fit in easily after twenty years of repression.

Before his campaign, provincial reformers and radicals were without any national leadership or effective center of communications. Burdett and the Westminster Committee provided only a very little and did not really speak to the popular consciousness and concerns. Cobbett was emerging as a truly major figure, but he was (and remained) purely a journalist, advocating, as we shall see, not organizational but individual action.[84] The importance of the *Political Register* cannot be overstated, but the Hampden clubs similarly should not be underestimated as one of the first efforts of the kind of organization which would eventually grow into the characteristic modern mass organization. The Hampden clubs took off slowly, at first dependent almost entirely on the Major's personal attention and appearances on his tours. But by 1816 they took root in Lancashire, began to develop on their own and often beyond Cartwright's major tactic of petition for parliamentary reform.[85]

Leadership and organization were to remain problems for the reformers until well into the Chartist era. Personalities came and went and spent a great deal of their energy on quarrels with each other. This was especially characteristic of the London center, the home base of Thompson's problematic demagogues.[86] In villages and small towns the leadership remained remarkably stable.[87] Thompson remarks merely that from 1815 through Chartism, the movement was always strongest at its local base. [88] This is an important and telling fact, however, which suggests the extent to which we observe not class action as such, but the action of many communities of workers. Demagogic and charismatic leadership become more important in a context where social relations are weak or unstable and there is little or no formal organization. They are ways of making up partially for the deficiencies of social organization. Such deficiency exists either where a social organization is internally weak (having been disrupted, say, by social change) or where it is ill-suited to a particular set of demands (as when tribal populations face colonial powers). Both aspects were present in the workers' movements of this period in England. Instead of working at peak efficiency on its own social strengths, the movement too often adopted a stance of depending on external leadership.[89]

There were varying amounts of cooperation between middle-class and popular (artisan and worker) reformers. Lancashire was the one region which showed a very substantial independence of workers from would-be middle-class collaborators.[90] The London radicals ran the gamut from conspirators to elitist constitutionalists, with Cartwright, Hunt, and Cobbett taking up various positions in the middle. Support for the movement in London was the most diverse and, as a result scattered. There were urban-based agrarian socialists (among the Spenceans in particular), opportunistic adventurers bent on coup d'etat, old Jacobins holding to the notion that London could in 1816 or thereabouts play the role of Paris in 1789, and a parcel of less clearly defined partisans.[91] The London radicals made a number of shows of force which may have been of ideological value (or moral support) to those in the provinces. Their most significant role, however, was performed through oratory and the press. Hunt was master of the former, and Cobbett of the latter. Together they helped to give all of England a common notion of what radicalism was about (especially while they were on friendly terms with each other) and offered advice of various sorts.[92] On a more local scale, the various provincial radical groups communicated with each other, and the Lancashire reformers decided to send missionaries to spread their gospel in Yorkshire and the Midlands. Much was afoot . . .

The absence of self-discipline and organization at a national level, however, left the movement at the mercy of individual leaders. These did not mature at the same rate that a ground swell of support grew after 1816. From the same sources as the vulnerability to demagogues came an intolerance for leadership of any kind from an "equal." Workers would tolerate gentlemen leaders like Henry Hunt, Esq., but resented any of their fellows who appeared to be rising above the common level by fortune or force of personality.[93] This was especially true of the newer, less densely sociated working populations. There was a greater tolerance for difference, and indeed for leadership, in the more stable village communities.[94] This problem was related to a flowering of unrealistic hopes. A reluctance to work in a disciplined organization of many intermediate levels correspondingly makes any movement more dependent on leaders at the highest level and on its own fantasies.

The distance of the leaders from the masses had its consequences for the movement and for the behavior of the leaders themselves. These, in particular, opened themselves to a certain amount of justified blame for encouraging others to commit illegal acts from the consequences of which they themselves escaped.[95] In general, however, the leaders' faults lay in folly more often than in instigation. Their finances and business affairs were a constant source of scandal, second only to their quarrels with each other. Their various schemes for marketing grain substitutes for taxed brews and such like cannot but leave the historian with a raised eyebrow or a chuckle. But this was all part of the price for the personalization of radical politics—perhaps the only form of leadership a nascent movement is likely to develop.[96] Still, these brilliant early personalities, capricious and contradictory almost by definition, served well in many respects. If it is undeniably true that Hunt raised emotions, not principle or strategy, still he drew large numbers of workers together and helped to convince them of their own strength. In some ways the fault lies less with Hunt and his fellows than with the (perhaps structural) incapacity of the movement to move beyond them, to build anything else on the basis of the attention, emotion, and criticism which they generated.[97]

From an early point there were journalists of more sophisticated views and calmer tone. Many of the local leaders of popular radicalism, men like John Knight of Oldham, displayed a more practical and less demagogic orientation and did better work in organizational tasks. These men did not command the devotion of the populace in any manner approaching that of Cobbett and Hunt. The latter were true masters of a rhetoric which drew on widespread popular feelings, fears, sentiments, symbols, and sensibilities. This is not to suggest that their proposals for reform were necessarily unreasonable (though they were not the best thought-out), but that their appeal was not based on the reasonableness of their proposals. To the socially weak and disorganized populace which formed their constituency (and which made charismatic leaders likely) they appealed with two primary stylistic elements. They were first and foremost personalities, whose concrete political proposals were somewhat secondary; and they offered a resolution of present disorders and difficulties in terms of symbols and values which transcended immediate circumstances. As politicians of personality, Cobbett and Hunt were forerunners of one of the most prominent types of mass politician.[98] Their relationships with their constituents were mediated by mass oratory or the mass media. In this they were the opposite of politicians whose strength is based on direct attachment or local leadership, whether these politicians are active in machine politics or trade-union and socialist activism.[99] For every Jaurès or Trotsky, there have been two dozen party functionaries and shop stewards, or even union presidents, whose base was a dense network of relationships within an organization, not an appeal to a weakly organized "mass." The talents demanded for the mobilization of such a popular movement are different from, and partially contradictory to, those required for the building of relatively stable organizations.

Leaders like Cobbett and Hunt did not speak to trade-union issues even when they spoke specifically to workers about the concerns of the laboring classes. Their remedies for the privations of workers never involved the organization of local work forces against their masters, let alone of workers, as a class, against capitalists. The populists spoke of rather broad and general national issues—of the financial system, the standing army, sinecures; and of abstractions—liberty, right, the constitution. They desired to petition Parliament and to threaten it with a grand insurrection, though not a revolution. Such politics appealed to people who had little or no strength to fight concrete battles over their own livelihoods with the sides dictated by the relations of production. As Luddism failed, the expectations of village craftsmen for local solutions within the old order of things faded. These workers turned to a broader but vaguer agitation to secure the reinstatement of that old order, the rescue of constitutional England from corruption. Any extent to which they were revolutionary is due to the absence of local solutions, not just because capital was now national in structure but because a national industry was supplanting their local ones.

As the agitation became increasingly national, the crucial questions concerned ties between communities, and the ideological and organizational denominators which could unite the populace. Ties between communities were difficult to forge, especially when the communities were founded on different crafts or industries. A network of contacts between centers of varying size and outlying villages was in the making.[100] The well-publicized experience of Oliver and other spies and agents provocateurs made people more cautious in accepting delegates from afar on their own recognizance. Rather, bonds were forged primarily on a local scale, and the itinerant preachers of reform, first Cartwright but then most importantly Hunt, provided the primary links. A few of the leaders from each locality began, especially as transportation facilities improved, to become acquainted with each other, but for the most part the infrastructure was the older one of community and kinship bonds.[101] This limited the extent of concerted action which could be brought to bear even had the national leaders been inclined to organize such action (which they were not).[102]

The internal organization of the different industrial districts had a persistent flaw. While the centers varied in the strength of their radical commitment, the villages and small towns around them were consistently stronger. Manchester is the most glaring example, largely because industrial development had gone furthest there in creating a different kind of populace, but also because the rest of southeast Lancashire was so effectively organized. Stockport and Oldham were among the leading radical centers of the country, but Manchester itself was always a problem. There were early difficulties in enlisting the support of Manchester workers. Among the reasons was the fact that Manchester had an active group of middle-class (largely Benthamite) radicals at a time when the outlying towns were more polarized, lacking any middle-class radicalism. Manchester also had a different population of workers, organized in larger, more technologically advanced factories—indeed, more often in factories rather than in homes or small shops.[103] Despite the organization of the spinners, and the fact that they might act with the other radicals on some occasions, no cotton spinner or mill hand was among the Manchester radical leadership. Thompson notes this "curious" fact but makes little of it.[104] It would seem, however, to have been a serious problem for the radicals as they attempted to organize nationally. Certainly it is a problem for the generations of writers, including Marx, who expected that the great economic and demographic centers of the industrial revolution would also be the centers of radical action against industrial capitalism.

If the residents of Manchester had different interests, so was it a different city. By this time it was already significantly larger than the outlying townships.[105] It had spreading slum districts without parallel and was the temporary home of a constant stream of transient immigrants—all factors contributing to a much weaker sense and reality of community cohesion than the various outlying townships might support. Stockport, for example, offered a very different model. It had the radical leadership of the Reverend Joseph Harrison, an erstwhile Methodist, and it had its important community center in its independent Sunday school.[106] But it was the rural villages and smaller townships which were truly dominant in Lancashire radicalism throughout this period.[107] The most significant industrial population represented in these towns and villages was that of handloom weavers. These were, as we have seen, first the beneficiaries and then the victims of laissez-faire industrialization.[108] They shared an ideology of sturdy independence and a traditional and community-based radicalism which kept them in the forefront of action. The kinds of action they pursued, however, were limited by the fact that no obvious political objective—or really any other centralized objective—lay close at hand,

and their organization was too local and insufficiently organized to take national action.[109] These were indeed the dominant participants in this wave of radical agitation, and they were workers for whom the individualistic, personalized and traditional ideology of Hunt and Cobbett held great meaning. But for Thompson to assert that these weavers were the "characteristic" workers of this phase of the industrial revolution stretches the term. Most of all, it obscures the growing divergence between factory workers (whose strength was growing) and outworkers and artisans (who were for the most part losing strength).[110]

It was communities like those of the weavers into which Oliver and other spies and provocateurs traveled in 1817 and 1818. The villages were internally cohesive and often revolutionary to the point of preparing arms (though not to the point of making much use of them, or having any clear idea of how they were going to do so).[111] But their links with each other were minimal; they were frequently geographically isolated, and their bonds to and awareness of urban life were slight.[112] In terms of Thompson's account we must counterpose this discussion of social and geographic isolation and its attendant vulnerability to figures like Oliver to the argument made earlier in The Making that Luddism was in some ways a revolutionary movement. It was this only in thought, never approaching it in deed. Even with the beginnings of the national parliamentary reform campaign there was little if any organization to translate intentions into action. This is the larger, more significant point: culture and ideology, intention and even clear opposition cannot substitute for organization in producing collective action. The organization need not be a formal one, such as a party, but some kind of organization must unite the relevant collectivity. Workers frequently were aware of this and, in addition to joining a variety of clubs, sent missionaries into adjacent areas to attempt to recruit further support.[113] They lacked, however, the social foundations which would have allowed their movement to remain strong when it moved beyond the immediate locality. Moreover, instead of an organizational backbone, to carry the core of the movement along, especially through times of limited popular agitation, the radicals of the early nineteenth century had only ideology. Remembered and republicized ideas were all that maintained the concentration of collective attention from peak to peak of activity.

It was precisely the absence of such an organization that gave Oliver his opportunity.[114] What he did was to step into this near vacuum, offer a connection between communities and a "plan of revolutionary action" to people who desperately wanted one. Oliver was about as close to a national revolutionary party as England developed in this period.

The employment of informers was a routine practice. These were often instigators as well as listeners, repeatedly bringing a premature climax to radical activity. The novelty of Oliver was that he worked on a national scale and he stepped into the crucial organizational void before the radicals had the chance to fill it in any more effective way. This, of course, only begs the question of whether the radicals could have otherwise and effectively filled the organizational gap. There is, no short answer; the present book is in part one possible, and predominantly negative, long one.

The rising at Pentridge shows the problems the radicals faced and the problems in Thompson's interpretation. It was, if not unique, still a wholly isolated event, knit into the larger "plan" of insurrection almost entirely by Oliver's reports in his travels and by rumor. It was led, largely by force of personality, by an alternately heroic and somewhat pathetically imperious Jeremiah Brandreth and involved a couple of hundred knitters and laborers, including a number of colliers. All of its expectations for a general rising were frustrated and its own activity was relatively aimless.[115] The radicals expected a wholly improbable degree of success, and even of mobilization. It is hard to understand what Thompson means when he describes the Pentridge rebels as "not dupes but experienced revolutionaries."[116] For one thing, the two categories are not necessarily mutually exclusive. While it is clear that the rebels did not get their antigovernment ideas from Oliver, it is nonetheless true that he did convince them of grossly inaccurate information which led to death and other punishments for many of them. In short, they were duped, though they were not necessarily fools. Part of Thompson's point is that, even without Oliver's instigations, "some kind of insurrection would probably have been attempted, and perhaps with a greater measure of success."[117] The first clause may well be true, though evidence is scanty, but what sort of success is certainly an open issue. As I have said, there were few if any possible proximate solutions to most of the ills the weavers and their allies suffered. A revolution might indeed have been required, since direct reallocation of resources would seem to be the only "concession" which would have done much good.

As to being "experienced revolutionaries," Brandreth and his associates were perhaps (some of them) experienced in thinking revolutionary thoughts and even in discussing them. They had likely been involved in drilling, in hoarding weapons, and perhaps (for a few) in local insurrections. None of this would seem to add up to experience in waging a revolution. Had any of these people been experienced in national attempts at revolutionary mobilization (let alone organization) he would have known the impracticability of the Pentridge rising.

Their experience, however, was entirely local and primarily cultural, verbal, and symbolic. Thompson is under no illusions about most of this, but nonetheless his terminology and analysis confuse local disruption combined with revolutionary rhetoric with revolution itself. The use of the term "insurrection" further clouds the issue. Thompson describes Pentridge as "one of the first attempts in history to mount a wholly proletarian insurrection, without any middle-class support."[118] The problems in this short passage exemplify my argument with The Making. First, it is never spelled out just what an insurrection amounts to; in what way, for example, Pentridge is to be distinguished from Luddism.[119] Presumably the answer lies in the slightly more sophisticated and substantial political ambitions of the leader(s). They did propose to seize state power. Their followers' appreciation of this is less clear. Secondly, it is dubious whether there is any clear sense in which to understand the "wholly proletarian" nature of the insurrection. It was not based on either a dominant or an ascendant sector of the working class. It did not include a significant proportion or distribution of the members of the working class, however broadly defined.

Luddism was described as only "quasi-insurrectionary," despite the fact that it was vastly better organized and more efficacious than Pentridge (and related events).[120] It would seem to be only "quasi-" because it did not expressly seek state power (though that blurs the distinction between insurrection and revolution). But at Pentridge it was principally one person, and at most only a handful of those involved, who sought state power. Certainly the Luddite delegate meetings had at least as many such, together with occasional hope for French, Irish or Scottish aid.[121] And there were a great many more Luddite meetings, with, it would appear, at least as much reliable communication between them. Thompson reports that Pentridge "is a transitional moment between Luddism and the 'populist' Radicalism of 1818–20 and 1830–32."[122] Earlier he saw "Luddism as a moment of transitional conflict."[123] Neither description is really wrong, since conflict tends to be transitional. Both, however, unjustifiably bolster the implication that each new step in the progress of the working class was a head-and-shoulders advance over its previous state. It seems more plausible to emphasize the similar weaknesses which (together with geographical and communal continuities) unite Luddism and the various rebellions that were touched off by Oliver or were generally brewing at this point. Both movements (if the latter can be so-called) suffered from an extreme of localism and a lack of adequate organization. Luddism balanced this with an extraordinary strength of local solidarity (and a focus on relatively local aims). With Pentridge, it seems to me, we have more the activities of an ex-Luddite rump of extreme radicals and their very distressed fellows. Leadership was, in contrast to Luddism, especially important. The followers of Brandreth may have included a number of colliers, but the leadership certainly fits the artisan model.[124] The words of Henry Hunt are perhaps salutary, regarding the Pentridge "rebellion." After finding cause in the distress of the people, and "the diabolical machinations of the villain Oliver, the spy," he minimizes the rising and compares it with the Spafields meeting:

> This petty riot [at Pentridge], which was put down without any military force, was consequently blazoned forth and proclaimed through the country as an insurrection and open rebellion, and great preparations were making to bring the prisoners to trial for high treason, and a special commission was appointed at Derby to try them. The Ministers had failed in their attempt, in London, to spill the blood of Watson, Thistlewood & Co. whose lives were saved by the honesty of a Middlesex Jury. The despicable riot in London, ridiculous and contemptible as it was, yet it was ten times more like a premeditated insurrection than the Derbyshire riot.[125]

Having failed in their London prosecution, Hunt continues, the ministers were determined to gain a conviction in the country and thus make a show of strength.

The disclosures of the activities of Oliver brought his victims a certain amount of middle-class sympathy. Middle-class reformers were then (as they generally are now) most sensitive to civil libertarian issues, not more radical political or economic goals. This coincided with the major trend of the agitations of the period—the demand for parliamentary reform. Pentridge, Folley Hall, and similar events had been the nationally atypical aftermath of Luddism; numbers dwindled and a rump of extreme radicals was left. More and more moderates were drawn into the reform agitation and away from revolutionary designs (let alone activity). These moderate veterans of earlier agitations were able to expand the numbers of the committed by the extension of their influence into new areas, and by virtue of the growth of the industrial regions in which they were strong, particularly that of southeast Lancashire/Cheshire/the West Riding. The moderate workers also came into contact with the middle-class proponents of parliamentary reform. Hope for collaboration from this quarter further induced them to moderate their tone. The constitutionalism which had long been central to the movement became all but exclusive. As the agitation built up to its (largely involuntary) climax at Peterloo, nearly every town and village in the southeast Lancashire region sent at least one petition to Parliament.[126] Revolutionary conspiracies were rare and clearly not a popular orientation for action. Thompson attributes that to "the lesson of

Oliver" and doesn't consider his own earlier emphasis on the constitutionalist outlook of the people and on the importance of the 1813–15 travels of its foremost advocate, Major Cartwright.[127] Nonetheless, we may agree with him on the result: "From 1817 until Chartist times, the central working-class tradition was that which exploited every means of agitation and protest short of active insurrectionary preparation."[128] We must add, however, that this meant that the workers often acted on the basis of far more mediate groupings than class.

The middle-class reformers made an attempt to co-opt the popular movement as it recoiled from the Oliver episode. The middle-class press suggested that the vulnerability of the workers was evidence that they needed to be led by their "betters." The demand of the popular radicals for manhood (or universal) suffrage, became counterposed to the middle-class insistence that household suffrage would be quite enough.[129] The middle-class leaders were, however, not yet strong enough to offer an alternative line of advance, as they were to do in 1831–32. The movement remained largely the people's own, though the domination of central leaders, like Hunt, was intensified. These saw their opposition to clubs and organizations vindicated and, especially in the case of Hunt, used the suggestion of vulnerability to spies, which the name Oliver symbolized, to fend off attempts to radicalize the movement.[130]

John Wade, a wool-sorter turned journalist, struck a similar theme:

We have raised our voice against violence on the part of the people, because we are persuaded that it would not in the least advance the public cause, and could only serve to strengthen the hand of despotism. Every unsuccessful attempt, and all attempts must, at the present, be unsuccessful, to wrest our rights by *force* from our oppressors, would only afford pretences, still further, to abridge the liberties of the people, to rivet their fetters still stronger, and to deprive them of all means of resistance, when a more favourable moment occurs. . . . The people may guard against all seductions to violence. The tools of corruption will always be at the bottom of every thing of this kind, for it is their interests alone that can be advanced by it.[131]

But Wade, it will be noted, had a fine appreciation of the tactical importance of this imperative. He was not opposed to organization but to taking actions on an insufficient basis of power, including the power which would come from better organization. He quoted Major Cartwright's objections to raising subscriptions for the Pentridge men, and warnings to the reformers not to identify themselves with their action. And Wade warned of the tendency of such violence to offend moderate and middle-class reformers who might otherwise have joined with the laboring population in protesting and resisting government oppression. "But when the zeal of the people broke into outrage, the timid became alarmed and deserted the ranks of the people; and government was quietly suffered to pursue the infernal measures, they had previously planned, against the liberties of the country."[132] On this basis, he counseled moderation, and attempts at a union of the reformers.[133]

There was an accession of strength to the radical movement (in part because it became more moderate) at the same time that there was an increasing isolation of the Liverpool government from middle-class support.[134] In this connection Thompson describes a potentially revolutionary situation; there was a split in the ruling class(es):

> 1819 was a rehearsal for 1832. In both years a revolution was possible (and in the second year it was very close) because the Government was isolated and there were sharp differences within the ruling class. And in 1819 the reformers appeared more powerful than they had ever been before, *because* they came forward in the role of constitutionalists. They laid claim to rights, some of which it was difficult to deny at law, which had never been intended for extension to the "lower orders."[135]

The key long-term significance of the rights demanded was that they could not be granted without undermining the old regime. This can be carried in two directions (Thompson does not follow it up in either): one could hold the gradual gaining of certain reforms to be itself a revolution if, over however long a duration, the changes were significant enough. Or, one could argue that the demand for the rights, while itself only reformist, would nonetheless pose a serious enough threat to produce a revolution. In the former view revolution is measured by the extent, not the suddenness, of change; in the latter it is the product of government intransigence or counterrevolution (which may or may not be the product of a material inability to make the necessary concessions).[136]

Thompson's immediate points in the passage quoted are twofold. First, he suggests that the reformers succeeded in capturing the moderate, constitutionalist ground, while the government came to appear as extreme and intransigent. This situation would become more acute with Peterloo.[137] Second, Thompson suggests that the weakness of the ruling coalition of elite interests was a, if not the, crucial determinant of revolutionary potential. These become especially important considerations because Thompson holds the population to be already polarized into collectivities capable of concerted action. In short, he argues that there was no strong middle position and so politics came to divide primarily on the pro- or antigovernment stands of those involved. Compromise became increasingly unlikely, escalation more and more likely. Because the two sides were capable (minimally, even in Thompson's generous opinion) of collective action, their disjuncture of opinion led to class struggle. Curiously, Thompson's argument, thus boiled down, appears quite similar to that of "bourgeois" political theory: political stability depends on a strong middle class.[138] The primary difference is, of course, that Thompson does not value political stability as highly as most bourgeois political theorists do.

The rights which the workers demanded became less threatening to those in power as the strength of the middle class grew. Reformers in 1818–19 laid claim to rights of political and economic organization, freedom of press and public meeting, and the vote.[139] These were gradually obtained over the next several decades, as social structure (and ideologies) changed.[140] In the meantime the radicals worked to keep a constant pressure on the government, that concessions might be forthcoming. This strategy was pursued in the absence of substantial popular organization. It fits with the intentionally antiorganizational strategy advocated not only by Cobbett and Hunt but by such modern activists as Piven and Cloward, who suggest that disruption is the most effective tool of the poor. The poor ought to interfere however they can in the "normal" political process, and rely on the reverberations of their disruption, which will be considerable in times when the social and political system is dislocated, which are precisely the times when the poor can be moved to disruption. This does not give them much leverage, and their action cannot be effectively planned or its results controlled. The results will be controlled by those who make concessions from above, but concessions will be made.[141] The government's first response in the period of the industrial revolution was to attempt to suppress the rebellion directly—a tactical error. Somewhat more cleverly, it helped to touch off incidents like the Pentridge rising at times and under circumstances of its own choosing, thus deflating the radical movement. Eventually it felt itself strong enough to make concessions, and a middle class developed to which it could make less threatening concessions. In the meantime, there was a great deal of struggle and debate, and there was Peterloo.

On 16 August 1819 a group of local shopkeepers and minor gentry, under orders from the assembled magistrates, charged into an unarmed crowd of workers. The workers had assembled to hear a series of speeches, with Henry Hunt as the headliner. They came from villages and towns all around Manchester, as well as the city itself, and this meeting was the culmination of months of growing activity. Accounts of the event differ; it is known that the local Yeomanry Cavalry killed or injured hundreds of the people in attendance, including women and children. The Cavalry claimed that they were assaulted by the mob; others suggest that they were simply bad horsemen who could not maneuver in close quarters; still others argue that they wantonly attacked. Some members of the Hussars who were also present were reported to have tried to stop the Yeomanry Cavalry from attacking, but with little success. Henry Hunt was arrested and jailed, claiming manhandling and fierce blows to the head. In a sarcastic reference to Britain's great military victory at Waterloo, the event became known as the Peterloo Massacre. It marks one of the fiercest physical confrontations between agents of the government and workers in nineteenth-century England. The labeling of it as a massacre symbolized rejection of such violence among some elites. Workers struggled with no success, however, to get a parliamentary inquiry into the event. A great deal has been written on Peterloo itself; though its significance remains open to debate, it is perhaps more interesting now to ask what happened to radicalism after Peterloo, and why.[142]

As Thompson recognizes, the reform movement had little organized expression or concentrated activity through most of 1818; organization was only minimal in 1819. By the beginning of 1819, though, local societies were rapidly being formed. They were unable, however, to forge strong ties with each other. In the absence of any national organization, these local groups took their lead from the radical press.[143] Cobbett had departed for America, and so the *Political Register*, though still printed, was out of touch with the rapid development of English events.[144] Although no paper could assume the stature of the *Political Register*, a number stepped into the void it left. Most notable were T. J. Wooler's *Black Dwarf*, Wade's *Gorgon*, and Carlile's *Republican* (from March to August, 1819, this was Sherwin's *Political Register*). These and a number of other national organs were joined by significant local radical papers at this point, most notably the *Manchester Observer*.[145]

The last had considerable influence on uniting the reformers of southeast Lancashire and neighboring areas, and providing this region with its peculiarly active and politically oriented movement.[146] In general, however, the papers could help to provide a certain unity of ideas and even coincidence of action; they could not provide the organization necessary to concerted action, especially over the long term. The closest they came, perhaps, was in making radicalism a full-time occupation for their legions of regional agents, booksellers, and itinerant hawkers.[147] This is not to suggest that all the papers shared Cobbett's hostility to formal organization; on the contrary, several advocated it; they just did not provide it. Most conspicuous among these, perhaps, was Wooler's *Black Dwarf*, which supported (and was supported by) Major Cartwright and endorsed societies like that of the Hull "Political

Protestants."[148] These were organized in classes of not more than twenty, and had as their main function the distribution and discussion of radical publications.

In such societies all "secret transactions" were forbidden; spies or even magistrates could appear and examine the books and accounts. Provocation was held to be unlikely, since plans were not being made. The focus was on attitudes and open discussion of the issues of the day. Not just the Political Protestants, but the dominant stream of both concrete organization and radical publicity shared this tactical approach. Through such activities, it was hoped, these organizations would grow and multiply, eventually including all right-thinking people in a single union:

> Those who condemn clubs either do not understand what they can accomplish, or they wish nothing to be done. . . . Let us look at, and emulate the patient resolution of the Quakers. They have conquered *without arms*—without *violence*—without threats. They conquered by union.[149]

Exactly what the Quakers conquered besides opposition to their own existence and a fair amount of wealth is unclear. Obviously, Wooler did not offer an analysis of inevitable conflict based on the political-economic nature of the society. On the contrary, his vision was democratic, and assumed that broadly similar interests were distributed throughout society. People could, in this view, be convinced without force; classes were epiphenomena of attitudes. The organizations were not devoted to concerted action but rather to increasing their memberships and improving their opinions by discussion. Of course, this did not prevent people who knew each other through organizations such as the Political Protestants from attempting concerted action based on their acquaintanceship rather than on the formal organization. They were not encouraged to do so—indeed the opposite—but sometimes they did.

This desire for an all-encompassing unity was widespread. Wade's *Gorgon* sought to achieve a juncture between the more moderate (including utilitarian) reformers and the radical trade unionists and democrats of all stripes:

> What we have most at heart, is to consolidate into one mass the different materials that are hostile to the present system of government. This can only be done by the different *sects* (if we may be allowed a religious term for a prophane purpose) of Reformers, coming to some sort of understanding and compromise on certain unessential points on which they are disunited. We have always thought it rather absurd and premature, to be scrupulously *nice* as

to what ought to be substituted in place of that which yet remains to be abolished.[150]

While the proliferation of journals sometimes encouraged fractious disputes, the constitutionalist reform demonstrations served to reinforce the notion of widespread agreement. This was the tactic preferred by most of the agitators. It was often coupled with presentations of petitions to Parliament or the prince regent; like petitioning, the demonstration was a demand from below for action from above. It displayed the people's opinions, but it did not really render those people capable of translating their opinions into action.[151]

While Thompson rightly stresses the determination of those involved in such demonstrations to show themselves an orderly assemblage rather than a ragged rabble, he exaggerates the capacities of the radical organization of the time. Even in Lancashire, where the movement was most advanced, and the constitutionalist reform demonstration was developed, the participants were more able to show themselves orderly than they were to take any very concerted action. Discipline may indeed have been an important characteristic of popular gatherings culminating in Peterloo, and one quite alarming to the authorities.[152] Nonetheless, despite the authorities' concern, the reaffirmation of collective solidarity at such meetings served as a substitute for more concrete action as much as it stimulated it.

Sentiment had it that "the people," once mobilized, were omnipotent. This was quite likely wrong in any case, and it certainly was when the mobilization was focused primarily on very broad and general ideas rather than on more concrete programs of action. Mass meetings in particular tended to reduce the ideology to a lowest common denominator at the same time that they satisfied a part of their participants' longing for social action, serving as ends in themselves, rather than as means to more distant ends. The local organization of small groups of workers reading the radical literature and discussing courses of action continually came up against an inability to mobilize people much beyond demonstrations. While they could raise their own ideological consciousness to a level of greater sophistication, they lacked the organization to maintain this as a stable characteristic of a larger population. They could discipline workers going to mass meetings, but the ideology remained one common to weakly organized masses. The people sought an affirmation of their commonality, of the injustice done to them, and an easy remedy to the latter which would not conflict with the former. They demanded a consensual validation of their activities. This intolerance for diversity, although really only common beyond the local level, greatly limited the movement.[153]

The radical press filled its pages with fractious and often trivial contention among national leaders and to a lesser extent among local figures in the radical movement. At the same time the sense and sentiments of the participants in the mass meetings was of an overwhelming unity. The two are not really contradictory statements. The dependent attitude of the participants left them vulnerable to the prideful antics of the leaders, and moreover demanded leaders whose strengths were found in forceful and enthralling personalities and transcendent, idealized messages. The very sense of unity, as I have suggested, involved a resistance to differentiation among followers. None wished his fellows to rise above him, even in the collective movement. This emotional sense of commonality furthered the subservience of the group to its leaders at the same time that it weakened its analytic capacities and indeed, made it resistant to real organization. As Slater has summed up from studies of group psychology: "A group . . . cannot effectively revolt so long as it perceives itself as a mob or mass, but only when it can differentiate clearly among its members."[154]

The most crucial demand, of press and "mass" alike, was for radical democracy. A democracy of political representation was central, but an economic democracy and a democracy of expression were also involved. There was nothing wrong or unsophisticated about such an object in itself. The problem was that radical democracy appeared generally as a purely abstract goal once one got beyond the level of face-to-face contact. Whatever its ultimate desirability, it helped in the concrete setting of early nineteenth-century England to make the working class vulnerable to middle-class co-optation and, perhaps more fundamentally, to make it vulnerable to its own notions of "purified community" and of the omnipotence of ideas.[155] Once abstract ideas took over as the focus of attention, obsessive concern with their refinement became at least as likely as their practical application. Much of this appeared in the radical press of 1818–19. Whatever the peculiarities and pettinesses of the national ideological and personal struggles, at the local level groups were cohesive enough to fight on for a time.

The ceremonial of the various mass meetings served to integrate the ideology and the activity into a ritual, to secure the practices of the present to their roots in the past, and to provide a certain discipline and order for the event. A rhetoric of strength (one might sometimes say wildness) united with the pageantry and the numbers to reassure the participants.[156] The meetings grew. Strategies for harassing the radicals were generally met with restraint; pretexts for positive action against them were strained at best. A popular insurgency, albeit without any clear political program or objective of governing, was posing a serious threat to political status quo (if not necessarily either to economic domination or to the continued role of some grouping of the old elite). "Old Corruption," Thompson suggests, had the choice of meeting the reformers with either repression or concession. It had the power, I might add, to succeed in either, but:

> Concession in 1819, would have meant concession to a largely working-class reform movement; the middle-class reformers were not yet strong enough (as they were in 1832) to offer a more moderate line of advance. This is why Peterloo took place.[157]

The workers were insurgent in quite the sense envisaged by Piven and Cloward: while they were not organized for lasting or concerted action, and were not in position to seize control of the government, they were in a position to make life very difficult for members of the elite(s).[158] Repression, it will be noted, was at least a temporarily effective expedient, although in the long run concessions had to be made. The key question which is posed by this is: who among the elite population was threatened and, relatedly, who responded by repression? This is, of course, the old question of the Peterloo Massacre: was Sidmouth responsible or the Manchester Magistrates? I do not propose to offer a new answer here but rather to consider Thompson's answer as it fits into his larger argument.[159]

The question is the mirror image of that I have posed concerning the notion of working-class action: at what point, or in what sense, can local actions be described as class actions? What is the analytical significance of such a description? As in his account of workers, here too Thompson sees class primarily as a motivation and as the framework of opposition in which the participants in struggle saw themselves. He does not see it as an analytic description of the nature of the collectivity taking action. Thompson describes Peterloo as a one-sided "class war."[160] We must interpret this as meaning that the members of the Yeomanry Cavalry acted as they did because they were members of a class and saw their interests in opposition to those of the assembled multitudes, or at least in opposition to their stated goals. It is not feasible to conclude that Thompson means that the Yeomanry were acting *as* a class, unless we reduce class to an essentially local phenomenon.

Thompson is ambiguous. He holds that Peterloo, while not in any direct way ordered by the Home Office, was a consistent part of national policy in dealing with the demands and actions of the disaffected. Its extreme of violence was "less than prudent" in Liverpool's words, but some such confrontation was the inevitable result of government intransigence. Thompson's empirical analysis is entirely of after-the-fact government support for the magistrates, however, combined with analysis of the exacerbated relations particular to Manchester. The significance of Peterloo, to be sure, cannot be understood in terms of an artificially isolated Manchester, but that by itself does not justify a leap to the assertion that it was a class (and thus, by implication, class-wide) activity. Thompson argues that it was the latter because it was a consistent part of a repressive policy on the part of government and magistrates. There is considerable evidence to support this view; most notably, the government did repeatedly issue directives to local authorities to do what they had to do in order to quell popular disturbances.[161] This no doubt helped to create or reinforce intransigent local attitudes, whatever the communications immediately preceding 16 August may have been.[162] While Thompson argues that Sidmouth did know of and assent to the magistrates' plan to arrest Hunt (although he was unprepared for the violence with which this was done), the important part of his argument is not one of direct connection. Rather, he suggests that there was a commonality of attitude and a participation in a common, if not necessarily concerted, sequence of events.[163]

This is largely why Thompson treats the action of the elites as a matter of class; he makes little case for any sociological or economic commonality among them, other than simply being better off than the workers. Their unity is, apparently, to be found in their opposition to the workers or, rather, to the radicals and reformers. Even so, we must question just how much this produced a polarized "ruling class" as opposed to, nationally, a government interest and locally, a coalition of frightened property-holders. Though members of the elite classes were somewhat better organized than the workers, and were in a better position from which to take collective action, they were not very effectively or completely mobilized to defend their real or supposed interests. Against Thompson's suggestion of malicious organization, we must remember his earlier suggestion of fragmentation in the ranks of the ruling class.[164] Magistrates and other privileged members of society had long been accustomed to deference from below—not to concerted activity to maintain order—and they had been accustomed to leave matters of state to the great men and those who sought careers in politics. The industrial revolution, with its attendant concentration of population, and the apparent mobilization of a popular challenge, had changed all that. But, it must be remembered, that things had changed rather more dramatically in Manchester than in the rest of the country. There the yeomanry cavalry, first off, was composed in large part of shopkeepers, lesser manufacturers, and merchants.[165] Not only were they poor horsemen, but they were poorly schooled in the traditions of paternalism—and even in gentlemanly conduct.[166] Secondly, the participants in the 16 August meeting came from a wide geographic range—they were not familiar neighbors to the magistrates and "yeomen," but largely outsiders by reason of geography as well as of class.[167] Thirdly, the agitation of 1818–19 was highly focused on the northwest of England and the industrial regions of Scotland, with secondary activity in other industrializing parts of the country. It was not as much a threat to the government as it was to the manufacturers, whatever its ideology.

The recession of the winter of 1818–19, which helped to spur people into agitation, was focused on (if not entirely contained in) the textile industries.[168] The rest of the country underwent a moderate cyclical downturn, milder than that of 1816. In the textile districts the problem was more severe, and aggravated by the fact that in 1816 the employers had demanded and the workers agreed to a reduction in wages on the understanding that in good times they would be raised again. The employers broke their word in the middle of the heady (and in part artificial and speculative) boom of mid-1818. A strike was broken in September, with humiliation and bitterness apparent after two months of conflict. By late fall the crisis had set in; it peaked in January 1819. The commercial loan obligations undertaken by textile firms soared; many were bankrupted; there was a rise in living costs not offset by a comparable rise in wages; unemployment was severe. Early 1819 industrial agitation, including the demand for a minimum wage, was concentrated in Manchester, Glasgow, and Paisley.[169] In short, pressures, like the responses of workers in industrial and political agitation, were felt mainly in one part of the country.[170] They most threatened one part of the dominant population.

Thompson suggests that there are two key points about Peterloo which have tended to be forgotten: the "actual bloody violence of the day" and the size of the event. To his comments on the first of these we must add the minor caveat that this was an extreme of violence only in England's relatively peaceful domestic history.[171] The second we must further emphasize. On 16 August an entire quite substantial region was mobilized for a common activity—however unfocused that activity was. (The workers of Manchester itself were the only substantial local population apparently not strongly represented.) This was a considerable organizational achievement. But Thompson also means by size, apparently, significance, for that is what he discusses most under the rubric. And he is right. Almost immediately Peterloo acquired near mythic stature in popular culture and, to only a slightly lesser extent, in English historiography. Peterloo was, as radicals at the time sensed and Thompson stresses, a moral victory of sorts.[172] That the epithet "Peterloo" stuck, indeed both demonstrated and further nurtured the ideological strength of antigovernment opinion. To what use that opinion was put, is more dubious. Even stretching himself, Thompson finds few material gains from Peterloo for the workers. But, he maintains, it was an ideological triumph. It drew new adherents to the radical cause, both from among the working population and from other sectors. But, did the radicals or the Whigs emerge the champions of the agitation which followed? And why did radical activity so quickly subside, diverted first into agitation for the redress of grievances attendant on Peterloo and then into the demand for the coronation of Caroline?

Thompson follows the aftermath of Peterloo through the outrage of the "free-born Englishman" into the months of October and November 1819 when, he says, "Radical constitutionalism itself took a revolutionary turn."[173] Certainly there were radicals who armed themselves, but they were few, and fewer still were those who stayed armed for long, or deluded themselves into thinking that they were the spearhead or even a part of the main body of movement. The response of the majority of the workers fell in with that of their "betters." They continued in constitutionalist protest at times, created subscription funds for Peterloo's victims and legal defense funds for their leaders. Many of the radical leaders were, in fact, in the custody of the authorities by the end of 1819. Their place at the center of national attention was taken by a rather more loyal opposition including Benthamite reformers and Whigs. Under their leadership popular protest languished. As Cookson has said of the ensuing campaign, it had an essential weakness:

> Its whole accent was on inquiry, which meant that the chances of success depended in the last resort wholly on the Whigs. In coming forward when they did, Fitzwilliam and others pushed the popular leaders ignominiously into the background. After Peterloo it was not the system but the ministers who were denounced, and they could not be brought to book until parliament met. Immediately the initiative was taken from the people, the drift back to apathy commenced.[174]

This battle between radicals and Whigs for position at the front of the protest movement continued through the Caroline agitation, with constant radical claims of Whig sellouts.

A number of the erstwhile radical leaders struggled to keep their movement meaningfully alive, but they were a minority, and could not overcome, among many other obstacles, the ever-present tendency of the English crowd to prefer leadership from its "betters" to that from its members. Thompson follows one such strain of continued agitation through with Watson and Thistlewood to Cato Street.[175] This last conspiratorial attempt to seize power deserved perhaps as much pathos as fear. In any case, it was manifestly the rump of the previous movement—which Watson and his colleagues had never, even in their heyday, represented or led. There was, to be sure, Cobbett's return to England, bearing the ashes of Tom Paine. His pilgrim's progress from Liverpool was not an unalloyed success, and anyway he joined Hunt in calling for investigations into Peterloo rather than sustaining the agitation of which it had been a part. This preoccupation with a mythologized event stemmed from the inherent weaknesses of the movement, social and psychological, and it effectively defused it and brought about its dissipation. The quarrels in the radical leadership were a problem, but no one really had a forward-looking answer anyway, and these quarrels were part and parcel of the same social and psychological malaise. The Six Acts were unquestionably repressive, and together with the actual imprisonment of many leaders helped to end the agitation. But the internal weaknesses of the movement must be given responsibility for its demise at least equally with the repression of the authorities or the personal failings of leaders.[176]

Four

Populism and Class Consciousness

"I have had too much opportunity of studying men and things to be led astray by any *wild theories about liberty*. I know, that there must be government, and that there must be *law*, without which there can be no such thing as property, nor any safety even for our persons. I want to see no *innovation* in England. All I wish and all I strive for, is *The Constitution of England*, undefiled by corruption."[1]

So wrote Cobbett in 1809, and he remained true to this attitude throughout his life. He was the most widely read popular journalist of the early nineteenth century.[2] Though he did much to shape popular consciousness, he is perhaps the more remarkable for the extent to which he reflected it. But just as such popular consciousness is refractory to any simple categorization, and holds its own logical inconsistencies, so too the work of Cobbett. Further, as I have emphasized, there was no single public to which any or all ideologies appealed. There were many, and Cobbett appealed most to that numerous and vocal populace of small producers, shopkeepers, artisans, small farmers, and consumers who were at the forefront of that first great phase of popular radicalism, that stretching from the Luddites to Peterloo. These people were not all radicals, however, and those who might sometimes wear the label did not do so always, nor did "radical" always mean the same thing. As the above passage indicates, much of Cobbett's stress was on the lost virtues of a purer age, on traditions which held that present society was a deteriorated version of previous society, not the product of positive transformation. He did not see that there was any change in society which necessitated a change in the fundamental bases of social analysis and evaluation. Neither did a large proportion of his readers. His and their battle against corruption was

95

thus as liable to turn to the farcical affair of Caroline of Brunswick as to stick to any continuing criticism of the political or economic systems.

Much is made of Cobbett's switch from Tory supporter of the government against the American colonies to radical opponent in domestic (and still, sometimes, international) affairs. While some writers have been concerned to fit him into the radical tradition, others have suggested that he remained "really a Tory." Thompson points out much of the conservatism in his opinions but finds something radical in "the democratic character of his tone."[3] The Coles emphasize the "continuity between Cobbett the Tory and Cobbett the Radical. . . . He was a Radical, in his own estimation, only because things had gone radically wrong, and no less than radical remedies would avail to put them right."[4] Though Cobbett's stance toward the government of the day did shift, for various reasons, there is indeed more than mere continuity in his work. He was, in his maturity, a Tory, a democrat, a cynic about the politicians of the present, an idealizer of the past, a reactionary and a radical, all at once. This was no simple confusion, though both Cobbett and his followers were sometimes confused. This was, rather, an authentic social criticism and political voice of the sort which came a few generations later, in America, to be called populist.[5]

This English populism was not statist or supportive of reactionary elites, in the manner of some Latin American populisms. Rather, it was a genuine and radical insurgency. It spoke primarily on behalf of "the people." It was against those who would abuse the people, but not necessarily in favor of any specific segment of the population. By the 1830s, this emphasis on the people was competing with a growing analysis of the interests of the working class.[6] English populism had a strongly negative ideology; it was much concerned with a critique of corruption in favor of some postulated prior and better state of society.[7] Its aims were consistently to restore society to this blessed state. Images of this golden age embodied the values of contemporary community life, at least as much as an amalgam of actually remembered virtues of the past. Based on this foundation, the populist movement resisted the industrialization of England. It resisted most of all the particular paths this industrialization was taking, and the injustices which were embodied in the system for reasons of the self-interest of elites rather than the demands of production or the benefit of the nation. But it also resisted the whole transformation of social life which industrialization implied or required. As such, the populist movement was fundamentally conservative. Its strengths and its aims sprang from the communities in which its proponents lived and worked.

At the same time, the populist agitation was very radical, because it demanded things which could not readily be incorporated within the emerging framework of industrial capitalist society. Indeed, it demanded an organization of productive and distributive relations which could fit well into neither capitalist economics nor modern industrial processes. It is in this sense that I have termed the participants in this movement (or movements) the "reactionary radicals." They called for changes which were at once founded on traditional aspirations and almost diametrically opposed to the dominant economic and social trends of their day—that is, the development of capitalist society. The chances of their movement's being socially revolutionary were in direct proportion to its relative social strength, not its ideological clarity. Such social strength was to be found most of all in local communities, least in national organization.[8] This populist pressure from below competed in a zero-sum game, as it were, with the forces pushing for the dominance of capitalist industry. Each side's victories had to take something directly from the other side; there was virtually no ground for compromise.

The class orientations which began to dominate popular collective action as populism receded were not equally radical. However much they might be supported by physical force (or threat of physical force), and even when they united a larger proportion of the population in stronger formal organizations, they did not demand anything which industrial society could not ultimately offer. This is not to suggest either that members of the elites liked making concessions to workers, or that the reforms which the working-class organizations demanded were unrelated to the claims which had been put forward by republicans, Jacobins, and parliamentary reformers for many years. On the contrary, there was considerable continuity in the reformist program, and the struggle to achieve it was a long and often heated one. The critical divergence showed the social foundations of the new working class to differ from those of the older populist agitation. This was reflected in ideology. The populists had not accepted an abstract republicanism but rather grafted democratic principles to strong traditional, especially communal and craft, values. The industrial working class continued some elements of popular ideology as it diverged from this older working population, but it no longer struggled to protect traditional social and economic organization from the disruption of industrialization.

With this perspective one can see the limitations of a statement such as this by Thornton:

> The Chartists' programme for constitutional reforms in the 1830s and '40s was based on the Duke of Richmond's programme of 1780, but they had to fight their battle unpatronized by any "respectable"

leadership from grandee, squire, or merchant. Democracy was not
something that could be trafficked with without loss of reputation:
Burke's *Reflections* had ensured this as the continuing majority
view.[9]

This is all true, but it fails to grasp the importance of the fact that the
new working class could be content with the liberalism of the old
Whigs, while the populists of the intervening period could not. No
simple constitutional reform could express the struggle to maintain a
traditionally valued way of life, however desirable such reform might
also be. The new working class, through Chartism and a variety of other
more narrowly focused mobilizations, could fight for improvements
within the capitalist industrial system without forfeiting its basic identity. However damnably insubordinate and threateningly unstable democracy might seem to the elites, it could be granted in an extended
series of reforms without sacrificing the capitalist industrial society, or
even most of the cultural hegemony and material power of the elite
strata.[10] The most potentially revolutionary claims were those which
demanded that industrial capitalism be resisted in order to protect craft
communities and traditional values. Democracy did not directly speak
to those claims; nor did it directly threaten the emergent social order.
Only when combined with socialism would the claims of the working
class threaten to reorganize fundamentally power in English society
and, especially, to take control over the production and distribution of
wealth.[11]

English populism was guided as often by rich complexes of symbols
as by rationalized theories. It looked backward as much as forward and
varied somewhat with craft and locality. For the most part, it had a
long, traditional pedigree. It was a set of values in everyday life at the
same time that it was a political ideology. This was the source of much
of its strength. What I term populism was not so much a distinct set of
political opinions as a mobilization of people who shared a common
understanding of how life ought to be. Not all of the people were
mobilized at any one time, but the mode of understanding was widespread. As people tried to live in accord with their expectations and
ethics, they found themselves increasingly frustrated by social change.
In the early nineteenth century, it was already impossible, in much of
England, to continue a traditional style of life without drastic
alterations. When times were good economically, these alterations were
easier and more palatable to make than when times were hard.

But such changes in cognitive structures, in the culture which people
share and the personal habits which shape their lives, are not easily
made. As older patterns of thinking fail to account for and order activ-

ity, either new ones must replace them or some manner of defense must be mounted. The latter is at least as common a choice as the former. Defense can range from the discovery of loopholes in traditional pre-scriptions of what ought to happen, to the addition of a separate but congruent explanation for the problem without sacrificing the tradi-tional mode of thought, to an attack on those enemies who appear to be undermining the traditional order. In the last case a passive sense of the order of the world becomes an active political ideology.

The rationalistic, Jacobin radicalism of the 1790s is an example of a new mode of thinking about important public issues. During the period after the French Revolution, this newer radical thought had made some headway in merging with older, more traditional orientations.[12] The popular thought of England as a whole had not been very rationalized, however, had not been very far removed even by the time of Peterloo from its traditional roots.[13] Similarly, it is easy to exaggerate the shift of proportionate population and political activity from London and rural areas to the provincial towns and cities, and the emergence of a new factory-oriented working class in this period.[14] Most of the people in England continued to be moved primarily by traditional values and sentiments. Spokesmen like Cobbett, Wooler, and Hunt represented this traditionalism at least in part—a greater part in the case of Cobbett, perhaps, than of any other. Their papers and speeches mirrored a popular opinion and frame of mind which extended well beyond the radical mobilization of the 1810s. Such popular opinion was as evident in the more widespread Queen Caroline agitation as in the parlia-mentary reform movement.

It is perhaps true that some radicals—e.g., Carlile—rather cynically used older symbols in order to reach their audience, but even that im-plies the power of such symbols. The more their traditional way of life was under challenge, the more adamantly many people stuck by their habits of mind. It was easier to scapegoat King George, or his ministers and Parliament, and thus have a relatively easy explanation for evil, than to undertake a new analysis of the whole system of social organi-zation. After 1822, with acceleration in trade-union activity from 1826 on, and the period of reaction to the weakness of the 1832 reform act, such a reanalysis began to be more elaborately developed and wide-spread. At this point, the new politics of class began, though popular ideology was ambiguous throughout Chartism.[15] Populism did not in-stantaneously vanish in favor of the theoretically more developed analysis of class and political economy.

The most widespread body of political opinion in early nineteenth-century Britain, then, was a defensive criticism of threats to a tradi-tional way of life. Most of the threats can be grouped under the heading "corruption." True Britons were offended by foreigners, notably by Hanoverians, although the reactionary side of this during the Napoleonic wars should not be overlooked. The established church was seen to be growing away from the people. A once-popular king was replaced by a once-popular prince who came to be seen as an increasingly distant and poorly paternal regent and monarch. Worse than the king were the holders of sinecures, placemen, and other leeches on the public revenues. Ostentatious wealth was to be seen everywhere; it was offensive in its newness as well as in its contrast with the poverty of many common people. The rapidity of the acquisition of wealth during the industrial revolution lent credence to the notion that it was comprised of ill-gotten gains. The new elites led the way in neglecting their obligations to the rest of society, but even the older patrician families were seen to be failing to live up to the duties of their stations. Last, but hardly least, the common family was under pressure, it seemed, from all sides: from employers who did not help to keep the family together, from factories which used children, from simple poverty, from a king who wished to abandon his wife.

With political analysis couched in terms of aristocratic theft and corruption, and economic attention turned to the defense of the moral economy, it is clear that this popular ideology hardly matched Marx's idea of class consciousness. In order to fit at all easily with a Marxian understanding of social organization and change, such a consciousness would have to be first and foremost a consciousness of the common exploitation of workers in capitalist production. This it was not.

Neither, for all its admixture with Jacobinism and its continuing admiration of America, was this English populism primarily democratic, at least in the modern sense of fully representative government. Its claims were in some ways more radical, for they called for changes throughout the system of social organization, not merely in electoral politics. Mere representation might have been an advantage for hand-loom weavers, for example, but it would hardly have changed their fundamental circumstances; at most it might have brought a more sympathetic hearing and more ameliorative action. For the most part, workers who sought representation in Parliament did not seek to assume state power as much as to make the existing political structure work properly.[16] Only gradually, from the 1830s, did a substantial segment of the working population begin to plan to use the strength of numbers to gain control of a truly representative government, and it is not clear that this was ever a realistic policy before the formation of the Labour party (and the Labour party of course has not commanded unanimous allegiance from the working class).

The populists were less oriented toward representative politics than toward the sort of direct democracy of mass meetings. The people—or at least all good people—were assumed to be unanimous in their condemnation of corruption. The necessity of continuous representation only gradually became clear to them, for they were opposing the sort of constant revolutionizing of social life which capitalism was bringing; they hoped to restore a more nearly steady state of public affairs. Where populists saw that they were not met with unanimous accord from their fellows, they characteristically assumed that only ignorance stood in the way of understanding and agreement.

A great deal of the time, the radical politics of this period emphasized local rather than national issues or authorities.[17] The democracy of the politics was, correspondingly, far more a matter of internal structure than of external aim. As borrowed from American political history, the term"populism" is used to indicate, not a reified ideology, but an idea of how public affairs ought to be run which starts very locally with the running of communities and the local chapters of larger political organizations.[18] The populists hoped that their movement would directly establish (or reestablish) the good social order by expanding to include all or virtually all of the population. They did not regard the movement as really separate from the end sought; it was a microcosm, not a means.[19] This is one of the central reasons for their seemingly exaggerated emphasis on internal unity, including exaggerated feuds over the purity of leaders and ideology. Like members of many religious groups and communes, the early nineteenth-century populists sought to go "beyond democracy to consensus."[20] This desire for consensus produced problems. It pushed toward an ideological "lowest common denominator" in order to avoid sectarian disputes. Even so, consensus was unlikely outside of close-knit communities where social pressure could be brought on dissident holdouts, and common circumstances and frequent social intercourse helped to promote agreement.

Authoritarian means to radical ends were inconceivable. If anything, the workers' concern for democratic form impeded their accomplishment of any ends at all, as it turned attention inward.[21] Movements of this sort, which see themselves as microcosms of a better society, commonly face a problem when they attempt to move from informal solidarity to formal organization.[22] So it was for these populists; their movement always foundered on the attempt to achieve some level of supralocal, supracraft organization. The direct participation which was the strength of movements from Luddism through parliamentary reform and even Chartism at the local level, gave way to attitudes of naive optimism or uncertainty and dependence at the national level. Where immediate social relations gave people a good idea of what to expect from their fellows, expansion to a national frame of reference meant moving beyond the range of such relations and almost always beyond the range of reliable information.

This lost sense of intimate knowledge is one reason why leaders like Cobbett and Hunt were attractive. They made their followers feel that they knew them personally, could count on them as on their friends. The personalization of popular politics contributed, however, to a pervasive sense that following was enough (though which of the leaders to follow was sometimes in contention). As a song had it:

> With Henry Hunt we'll go, we'll go,
>   with Henry Hunt we'll go;
> We'll raise the cap of liberty,
>   In spite of Nadin Joe.[23]

Cobbett filled the *Political Register* with autobiography and portrayals of himself standing steadfast and often lonely against the beasts of corruption. Hunt's *Memoirs*, published while he was in prison following Peterloo, are a virtuoso example of posturing and self-involvement; they did not lack an audience. This dependent attitude undermined efforts to create effective organizations.[24] Not only did it lead to a certain passivity and lack of initiative, but it fostered (and was fostered by) unrealistically simple analyses of problems and fantasies of solutions. The attack on Old Corruption in the name of the English constitution was such a weak, but extremely popular, analysis. As Wade repeatedly emphasized, in a tone of frustration:

> One thing is certain, that these ancient laws have been a real stumbling block in the way of the Reformers; they have been the subject of endless, unmeaning altercation; they have filled the heads of the people with nonsense, and covered their advocates with contempt and ridicule. That our leaders should continue to stick to these follies, is both provoking and astonishing. Can they bring nothing to bear against the old rotten borough-mongering system but musty parchment, black letter and latin quotations?[25]

It was not an abstract analysis but rather the vision of lost rights which moved English people to protest or rebel. The republicanism of Wade and Carlile never became a mass ideology, a fact which tells of the limits of the influence of Jacobin thought on later popular radicalism.[26] As Hunt wrote, speaking of his political mentor:

> Mr. Clifford never professed to wish for a republican government; he always contended that the English constitution if it were administered in its purity, was quite good enough for Englishmen. In this opinion I then concurred with him, and from this opinion I have never once in my life swerved, up to this hour.[27]

The bulk of the English people in the 1810s had a consciousness of theft and corruption, a very populist consciousness, far more than one of new possibilities opened up either by reason (a Jacobin consciousness) or by technological or social advance (the developing consciousness of both the bourgeoisie and the nascent working class). Wade came far closer to the latter sort of view, when he stressed "the relative degree of comfort and importance enjoyed by the labouring classes of the present day, compared with former periods."[28] He, and others of similar ideological bent, were particularly conscious of the emergent class of factory workers, and of the position of strength from which this newer laboring population could speak, as opposed to the older and more precarious movements of journeymen.[29] Cobbett was convinced, like most of the populist radicals, the members of craft communities, of the virtues of tradition and the real existence of a golden age, the rules to which were preserved in the ancient constitution:

> There is no principle, no precedent, no regulations (except as to mere matter of detail), favourable to freedom, which is not to be found in the Laws of England or in the example of our Ancestors. Therefore, I say we may ask for, and we want *nothing new*. We have great constitutional laws and principles, to which we are immoveably attached. We want *great alteration*, but we want *nothing new*.[30]

Cobbett indeed thought it a pleasant and quite possible prospect that commerce and manufactures could be greatly diminished, the clock turned back, and the factory system averted.[31] This was a vision which held out a good deal to the artisans but very little for the factory workers. Wade's reply was scathing:

> The cause of reform has been injudiciously betrayed by reverting to the supposed rights and privileges enjoyed by our ancestors. We are no sticklers for precedents, nor for dead men's Government; neither do we wish to revert to the institutions of a barbarous age for example to the nineteenth century. Englishmen of the present day can have no more to do with the Government of the Saxons, than of the Romans, the Grecians, or the Carthaginians.[32]

Wade spoke like the good rationalist and realist that he was, and like the utilitarian he was (though not uncritically) becoming. I have discussed his work from the period just before Peterloo here, in order to point out the discontinuity between it (and such similar papers as Carlile's *Republican*) and that of Cobbett and Hunt. This is also a discontinuity between the populist radicalism of the craftsmen and outworkers, reaching its peak in 1816–20, and the increasingly trade-union oriented and pragmatic movements which followed, involving mainly the factory workers. Already in 1818, this was visible as Wade devoted considerable attention to the Manchester spinners' strike, while their organization, perhaps the strongest trade union of the time, held aloof from the radical and reform agitations of Cobbett, Hunt, and others.[33]

Radicalism in this period was still primarily a resistance movement, and the spinners were a part of the factory system against which many of the populist radicals fought. The spinners' interest lay in agitations within, not against, the factory industrial system—though not necessarily in favor of capitalism.[34] Their politics were founded on their trade unionism. They were radicals in the 1820s and 1830s on the basis of their interests and organization as a trade. The political radicalism never superseded the trade unionism; they were never class conscious as opposed to trade-union conscious. In comparison with both handloom weavers and most other factory workers, the spinners enjoyed a relatively privileged position. Their trade-union strength may have helped to defend this; certainly it was built on the foundation provided by relative security of employment and, most of all, a position within the growing factory work force which was not technologically obsolescent.

Attempting to treat of ideologies as though they were somehow free-floating, varying independently of social bonds and economic relations, is a mistake. Imposing the category of class on the activities of working people in the early nineteenth century forces just such a treatment despite the best of intentions to the contrary. Class is too general a category at the level of social foundations, even if it can be stretched in treating of ideology. It obscures the distinction between those for whom a conservative, traditionalist ideology could be the source of radicalism, and those for whom a forward-looking, even anti-capitalist ideology was more often than not the source of reformism. We may apply the notions of class, and class consciousness, with some clarity to the latter group, the industrial workers who grew in collective stature as a part of modern capitalism. Stretching the concept will blind us to the differences between such workers and those artisans, outworkers, and others for whom industrial capitalism posed a threat to their very existence. The confusions of considering the populists in terms of class outweigh the gain of highlighting such continuities as there were in the ideological and social history of English workers.

This is not to exaggerate the chronological sequences of movements, or the clarity of breaks between them. Populist consciousness has continued to exert some strong and direct influences from time to time in the most advanced of capitalist societies. Certainly it was as powerful in Chartism, especially early Chartism, as the nascent analysis of class.

There too, however, the populist ideology had a special relevance for surviving handloom weavers and others for whom modern industry appeared to offer few benefits. I shall look briefly at that survival of populism in the last part of this chapter. Before that, it is important to examine the most widespread of the populist campaigns of the period, one which brings out its traditional roots and shows the symbols with which it spoke in unusual clarity. I refer to the popular agitation on behalf of George IV's spurned consort, Queen Caroline. The agitation has been almost entirely overlooked by historians, despite its extent. It is significant not only for its general insights into what moved English people in the early nineteenth century, and for its insights into popular culture, but also for its demonstration of the limits within which the radicalism of the 1810s had developed.

The Queen Caroline Affair

Cobbett was perhaps more able than any other spokesman to reach the traditional values of Englishmen. The extent to which his use of them was really "radical" varied considerably. His sustained championship of the cause of Queen Caroline was one of the less radical uses. Nonetheless, it was appropriate that Cobbett should emerge as one of the queen's most important defenders, and that he should virtually turn the *Political Register* over to her cause from mid-1820 to early 1822. Along with other popular supporters of the queen, Cobbett gives an indication of the enduring potency of traditional images of the family and of the symbolism of the monarchy.

Caroline was an unlikely heroine. She was an obscure German princess forced upon the Prince of Wales (later to become George IV) by his father. The prince had secretly married an Irish Catholic actress, Mrs. Fitzherbert, several years earlier and was actively engaged in a long and celebrated series of affairs. These did not stop with the arrival of his diplomatically chosen but remarkably indiscreet wife. Caroline was no prize. The fastidious prince was saddled with a wife who did not bathe or change her linen very often, who lacked every vestige of the sophistication he cultivated. Since he had little to do with her (other than bickering) after siring Princess Charlotte, she too began a series of affairs. Her behavior was not much more embarrassing than that of the prince, but nonetheless he twice—in 1806 and 1813—brought charges against her and demanded official investigations in the hope of ending the marriage. First the Tories and then the Whigs came, like good opposition parties, to the princess's aid. As indiscreet as she was, there was insufficient evidence to convict her of adultery. To avoid further embarrassments, she agreed to accept a permanent pension that was granted on the condition that she live abroad. There she associated with Napoleonists and did not improve her personal behavior. The final drama began when George IV acceded to the throne and refused to have Caroline mentioned in the Anglican liturgy. Somehow, despite her past and present character, the would-be queen became a dramatically popular symbol of purity and womanly virtue. This remained at the root of popular support, and radicals could never turn the agitation to more rationalistic ends.

The Queen Caroline agitation was arguably the largest movement of the common people during the early nineteenth century. It spread through the whole of England, involving thousands of workers, along with many others, many of whom had not been direct participants in any of the radical agitations of the preceding years.[35] That it was popular is evidenced by the participation and its distribution. That it had a radical component to its ideology (if not necessarily in practical terms) can be seen in the claims of the radical press to represent the queen's case more justly than did Brougham, her Whiggish "attorney-general." Witness Carlile's suggestion that: "Every step that Mr. Brougham takes in this business adds another proof to his treachery and dishonesty. . . . It is evident that if the cause of the Queen rested in the hands of Mr. Brougham, she would be sold."[36] Wooler hinted that the affair might lead to revolution.[37] Throughout the agitation, though, until almost the end, the Caroline propaganda was overwhelmingly lighthearted.

The radicals (including Carlile in the article quoted above) made much of the king's own violation of the norms of good familial conduct. He was accused (correctly) of bigamy, adultery, and in general of mistreating his wife. Broadsides described him as a wife-beater and threatened him with traditional punishments.[38] Carlile published biblical maxims in support of the queen and a "New Litany or General Supplication" for the queen's opponents to sing to Satan.[39] In fact, during the agitation the radical press showed a greater sense of humor than at any time since the eighteenth century. As much as anything else, the agitation developed the theme of "a woman wronged." Female reform societies sprang up throughout England to espouse the queen's cause.[40] As the queen replied (through numerous addresses and responses the authorship of which must be in doubt) to her supporters, in this case specifically the married females of Bristol: "a deserted Queen be only a deserted woman."[41]

Pressures on the organization of both the family and relations between the sexes provoked responses which had no clear political target. The English people had deeply felt values on both issues, and it seemed to them that what they valued was being undermined. Prostitution and the plight of unwed mothers and their children were prominent in the thoughts and plaints of working people, and the story of the virtuous maid turned by necessity to prostitution could—whether with happy or sad ending—pluck at many heartstrings, if we are to judge by its continuing success in the popular press. The family was an important resource for survival in the midst of the turbulence of the early nineteenth-century growth of cities and factories, and the disruption of local communities. It was not simply an abstractly held value. It was, further, of a piece with the whole complex of traditional ideas about how the world (of social relations in particular) should be structured.

Nonetheless, just as conservatism may underpin radical action, not all the "attacks" on the family need be considered exploitative or socially regressive. The changes which took place in the economic status of women by no means indicated an end to drudgery or poverty, but they did signal a weakening of the grip of a culture and structure of social relations which deprived women of autonomy.[42] Women were paid less than men in factories, but their autonomy in the labor market did give them the chance to delay marriage and exercise greater choice of partners.

It was still marriage, however, which defined a woman's basic status in society. Thus it was that the female reform leagues which developed (most of all in the industrial districts) had an ambivalent attitude toward themselves and social questions in general.[43] Though they were largely independent organizations of women, they did not seek goals particular to women. Women might mobilize around concerns deemed especially feminine (for example, Caroline, food prices, child-care), but they sought not to perpetuate their organizations but to obviate the need for them by restoring propriety of manners and an adequate standard of living. Their aspirations were often defined in terms of the possibility of improving the positions of women as housewives. Thus their relations to factory agitation were generally through their husbands, and were a force for economistic concerns. As Thompson notes: "The Radicalism of northern working women was compounded of nostalgia for lost status and the assertion of new-found rights."[44] This did not, of course, greatly distinguish them from the men of the period.

Thompson goes further than any other writer to point out this ambivalence and to argue that it is not grounds for dismissing the early radical movements as "premature." But even he is trapped by the implicit theoretical assumption that a working class ought to achieve its ends as explicit and forward-looking goals. He battles against the assumption but does not rid himself of it. This leaves him trying to fit the ambivalent workers into conceptual category—class—which, however modified, implies a clarity forged in opposition.

The reactionary-radical ambivalence of English popular protest appears strongly in the Queen Caroline agitation. This has perhaps contributed to the general neglect of it by historians, who are uncertain just what to make of it in terms of conventional categories. Almost all of the major radical leaders of the 1810s were involved in one way or another, yet the content of the agitation seems a jarring shift away from that which led up to Peterloo. Perhaps an excessive preoccupation with London has also misled scholars. It is true that London was the scene of much pro-Caroline activity, and that its press was full of Caroline propaganda throughout. This particular agitation, however, was much more widely diffused throughout the country than any of those immediately preceding it. It was largely the spontaneous product of "the people," not something planned in London and sent out to bucolic audiences.[45] Relative to preceding activities, the Caroline agitation was less prominent in industrial regions like southeast Lancashire and more prominent in rural areas in the South. It is hard to reconcile this massive agitation with the view that the radicalism of the 1810s came to an end not because of any fundamental weaknesses in social foundation or ideology but because of dissension among the leaders and the imposition of the Six Acts.[46] That the Caroline agitation embodied both a ground swell of popular opinion and an active campaign on the part of most of the radical leadership highlights the need for a different understanding.

The post-Peterloo agitation had died down, for the most part, by the early months of 1820. But after the death of George III the public grew increasingly interested in plans for the coronation, including George IV's continuing insistence that his ministers free him from his marriage to Caroline of Brunswick. The princess was a notorious libertine and something of a Napoleonist (though the king was at least as scandalous in his personal morals). The government shuddered and tried to talk the king out of divorce, but he was adamant. A number of the old Whigs, and certain of the city radicals, rallied to the princess's cause, jockeying for positions as her advisors and using the occasion to embarrass the ministers.[47] Caroline dithered a bit about just what stance she was going to take, after initially expressing her indignation at the failure of the government to properly inform her of her father-in-law's death and the intentions of her husband to prevent her ascension to the throne. Eventually, she rejected the various compromises offered by the government, and with more support from Alderman Wood than from the brothers Brougham, decided to return to England.[48] Somewhat to everyone's surprise, she was greeted by an enthusiastic crowd on her arrival at Dover.[49]

No one was quite sure, at first, just what to make of this popular support. "J. S.," a veteran Home Office informer, summed up what was happening in London:

> A Spirit of Loyalty & Affection for his Majesty prevails generally among all classes; and yet, a few of the Leaders of Sedition *are at present* endeavoring to stir up *discontent & disaffection.*
>
> The Editors of the Statesman, Chronicle, Cobbett's Evening post, Wooler's Gazette & Dwarf, the Champion, and others are endeavouring to raise a party in favour of the Princess of Wales. Last night when the Various Congregations were leaving their respective places of Worship, fellows *with Horns* were *proclaiming* the *arrival* of the *Queen* and selling papers to that effect, Printed (as mentioned at the foot of the bill) by Thomas's, Printer, Denmark Court Exeter change.
>
> Colours with emblems, etc., in favour of the Princess of Wales is also in preparation *to raise a Mob* to go to meet *the Princess* and escort her in *triumph* into *Town;* & at the different debating clubs they are advocating her cause.[50]

John Shergoe's calm tone was to prevail in nearly all the communications of the authorities throughout the Caroline agitation, including even such well-known alarmists of the pre-Peterloo period as Colonel Fletcher of Bolton. Only in rural districts where there had been little previous open rebellion did the activities of Caroline's supporters excite much fear. The Home Office thought little, in any case, of the conclusions of immanent revolution reached by clergymen indignant at having their church bells rung without permission or in spite of their active resistance.[51]

The pageantry and rich symbolism at which Shergoe hints were hallmarks of the Caroline agitation. Here, in far brighter colors, appears the traditional English culture which Thompson finds represented in more faded hues in radicalism proper. The theme of the agitation was "a woman wronged." The innocence of the queen was set against the corruption of the ministers (and, indeed, in accounts like Cobbett's, of the Whigs who proclaimed themselves her defenders). Implicit in this was an analogy between the situation of the queen and that of the people. But the arguments by which the radicals found a connection between the queen's cause and theirs were contorted, and go only so far toward explaining the appeal of the queen's case to the supposedly rationalist and advancing "class-conscious" movement of the workers of England. Wrote Cobbett, in one of the less sterling examples of his prose:

> Her Majesty, the Queen, has been accused of *making common cause with the Radicals,* than which nothing can in itself be more ridicu-

lous. For, amongst the imputed sins of the Radicals, that of wishing
to degrade Royalty has always been one. It is ludicrous enough,
therefore, now to accuse them of the crime of thinking, that the
Queen *ought not to be degraded.* But, the fact is, that the Queen's
cause *naturally allies itself* with that of the Radicals. They are *com-
plainants,* and so is the Queen. They have had and have their dun-
geonings; and the Queen has her prosecution. They are threatened
and her Majesty has been threatened. They have had their petitions
rejected, so has the Queen her's. . . .

   Besides all these circumstances of similarity, those who appear as
the prosecutors of the Queen have also been the prosecutors of the
Radicals; and, which is the *great thing of all,* it is as clear as day-
light, *that the Boroughmongers to a man are enemies of the*
Queen.[52]

What was clear as day to Cobbett is a bit harder for us to see, noting that
the Whigs had a number of boroughs in their pockets, the representatives of which voted against the conviction of the queen.

More than anything, the way in which the radicals, and their followers, were able to take up the cause of the queen exemplifies the
essentially populist, restorationist, and non-class-analytic nature of
their radicalism and their rebellion. The affair of Queen Caroline was
no minor episode on the continuous path of historical progress, either.
Rather, it was the largest agitation of the entire pre-Chartist period,
dwarfing that of which Peterloo was a part (though it was comparatively short-lived). It was strongest in the areas in which the earlier
parliamentary reform movement had been weakest; in the Northwest,
although it excited a fair amount of interest, the authorities were not
worried, and the demonstrations were relatively small. Fletcher, Bolton's notorious chaser of radicals and employer of spies (he was one of
the Home Office's most frequent correspondents), reported simply that
there was a partial illumination but "no breach of the peace ensued."[53]
For the most part, people rang bells, staged illuminations, and posted
placards.[54] The content of the last of these was varied. Some called for
illuminations, and were often followed immediately by notice from the
authorities cautioning the inhabitants against "any riotous, unlawful,
or disorderly proceedings."[55] By comparison with the preceding reform agitation, meetings were very infrequently called (the Six Acts no
doubt had something to do with this), and crowd action was particularly important only in the areas where the reform agitation had been
advanced.[56] The illuminations and public gatherings were almost entirely peaceful. The closest to violence most of them came was the
trussing up of recalcitrant clergymen or churchwardens in order that
their bells might be rung without resistance.[57]

In a few instances the houses of those who would not illuminate were attacked.[58] More often there were vague threats, though whether these threatened serious violence or simply a more striking performance of symbolic rebellion is not clear. Typical is a placard posted in Norwich shortly after the queen's acquittal, reporting an "Extraordinary Electrical Effect" which exhilarated the greater number of the inhabitants but rendered the principal church bells unfit for service:

> Each parish is expected to raise a company of FORTY FIVE hand-bell ringers; and as soon as a master of eminence arrives from London, an additional company with marrow bones and cleavers may be expected from Ber-street.—An eminent composer offers his services for the gratification of the public, who by the above arrangements will no longer be dependent on the *little greatness* of any present or future church-wardens for the harmony of sweet sounds.[59]

In general, the radicals positively reveled in the opportunity to turn accusations of disloyalty on their head and to emphasize their legitimacy as supporters of the queen. Far from criticizing the "official" order, they decried an attempt to circumvent the rules of that order. Wrote the inhabitants of Southampton, to the king:

> We cannot conceal from ourselves that there exists a Faction of needy and ambitious Men in this hitherto happy Country, who are active in persecuting your Royal Consort, and thereby inflame the Passions of all Classes of People;—and if they are suffered to continue to do so, they will usurp all lawful Authority, and destroy, through their Means, the Constitution of these Realms, which has been so long the Admiration of the World, and the Cause of our Prosperity as a Nation.[60]

Whether this passage is meant to be satirical or is in sincere ignorance of the king's attitude, it is hardly of a piece with even the ideology of the parliamentary reform movement's more advanced moments, let alone Chartism. It does have, I suggest, rather too much in common with the popular sentiments underlying the earlier movements for it to be discounted as a mere aberration. The authors went on to ask for a change of ministers, and in general the supporters of Caroline interwove other populist demands with their rhetoric about the wronged woman and persecuted queen. But calling for a change of ministers is not the same as calling for a radical reform of Parliament (and even that is not necessarily "class-conscious"). The Whigs still stood most to gain from the Caroline affair.

There were, to be sure, occasional anachronistic reports of French arms and strangers abroad on horseback, reports which sound more like they came from 1792 than 1820, and which perhaps point up the connection of Caroline and many Whigs with Napoleon.[61] This connection was not made in the popular literature, which could even criticize foreign kings while calling for the coronation of a German queen.[62] The popular press took up the cause of the queen with a vengeance. "Her Majesty," wrote Cobbett,

> is under the guardianship of the people in general, and of the press
> in particular. She was sentenced; she was doomed to banishment
> for life from this land, where alone there was a heart to beat for her.
> She was entangled amongst lawyers, creeping deputations, dark
> negociators and intriguers of all descriptions. The Press darted for-
> ward and extricated her from the trammels. The Press called aloud
> to the people, and the people saved her.[63]

It is unclear to what extent the principals of the press campaign thought they simply had a fine opportunity to mock royalty,[64] or seriously identified with the cause of the queen, or were led by their readers. It is hard not to believe that Cobbett was sincere; Wooler's barbs seem more calculated; Carlile is rather in the middle. Some writers, like Carlile, made an effort to keep up other political concerns as well as the affair of the queen. But even Carlile conceded that: "As the subject of the Queen and her treatment is the prevailing topic of discussion, we thought it useless or superfluous to meddle with any other political question this week."[65] And when Henry Hunt replied to the "122,776 Brave Radicals" who signed an address to him on the first anniversary of Peterloo, he referred to the king as "the husband of our excellent and persecuted Queen. . . ."[66]

Carlile was clearly not happy with this state of affairs, although he attempted to make the best possible polemical use of it:

> We have now a practical proof of the observation of Paine, when he
> remarked, how ridiculous it was, that one member of a society
> should be so far elevated above the rest, as by his misconduct to
> disturb and render the whole miserable and unhappy. . . . All minor
> matters, or rather, all major matters, are laid aside, and the Queen
> occupies general attention. The question for reform, the motion for
> inquiry into the cause of the Manchester murders, the provision for
> the representation of Leeds, and the amelioration of our bloody
> criminal code, are all lost sight of.[67]

Adapting himself to popular sentiment, Carlile went along with the affair of the queen, publishing addresses as well as his own comments, and turning for the most part to deistic and anticlerical satires. Still, replying to an address commemorating Peterloo, he thought that "Although the case of the Queen is become more particularly the subject of conversation, yet we shall no sooner see this business ended, than the Manchester murders will blazon from every tongue; particularly if the Queen defeats her enemies."[68] Wooler, though he spent most of his paper on rather old-fashioned, Jacobin-sounding satire, did at least link the cause of the queen directly to "an imperfect representation of the people."[69] And he, like the other republicans and like Place, thought that the affair would diminish the prestige of monarchy:

> The attack upon the Queen has been a fatal oversight. *Monarchy* has received a shock from it already, which its old age, and asthmatic constitution is not well able to sustain. . . . Defenders of the *faith* should not put their *practices* in contrast with the theory of rule— and *publishers* of *proclamations* against vice, immorality, and all profaneness, should beware of being detected in the private sanction of what they publicly condemn.[70]

These hopes proved unfounded. The press was really as much led by the people in the affair of Caroline as it was leading them, and the people made fewer fine distinctions between the queen's Whiggish and popular radical supporters than the latter might have hoped. Far from demystifying the monarch, the affair showed the considerable symbolic strength the crown still carried. Indeed, despite all the propaganda against the king which was a part of the affair of Caroline, and the enormous attendance at her funeral, there was also a large popular gathering, for celebration not condemnation, at the coronation of the king.[71] Blame was generally placed on ministers; the institution of the kingship survived intact.[72]

Prothero has recently argued that the Caroline agitation ought to be seen as part of the continuous development of artisan radicalism and not as a diversion onto a side issue, as many previous accounts have considered it. He suggests that there is a danger of being too intellectual in concentrating on the "dead-end" nature of the issue of the queen's rights or the shift of leadership from ultra-radicals to the parliamentary and Whig radicals who had their eventual victory in 1832: "it may be that the fact of agitation was more important than its ostensible aim. The affair was crucially important in dissipating the constrictions of the six-acts and re-establishing open political campaigning."[73] With his eye almost exclusively on London, Prothero sees the agitation as largely organized by the radical leadership. This leads Thompson to interpret it as a tactic of the radical leadership.[74] In fact, the agitation was widespread and much more spontaneous than such views allow. It was so widespread, I suggest, because it was an outgrowth of the immediate struggle of many people in local contexts to preserve a traditional way of life. Its symbolism expressed their concerns in a language of fairly old heritage, which common people knew well how to speak and understand. The Caroline agitation was continuous with the parliamentary reformism of the 1810s only because that too was both reactionary and radical, based on the struggle against the industrial revolution and attendant social and political changes. Further, the strength of the Caroline agitation in those areas where parliamentary reform was weakest shows how little it was a tactic of the established radicals.

The shift in ideological focus from reform to Caroline allowed the popular movement begun in the late 1810s to achieve its greatest breadth of appeal precisely at the point where it collapsed. The relatively rationalized core of the protest became sufficiently diluted in the Caroline agitation that there was no real radical object on which the mobilization could be focused. The radicals lacked any organizational means of turning the agitation from an airing of grievances to an attack on actual structures of power.[75] Thus at the same time that the defense of the queen shows the strength of traditional sentiments, it shows the weakness of a primarily cultural explanation of collective action. The defenders of Caroline might have done what they did because of their culture or consciousness, but they were unable to do very much because they lacked organizational foundation to give their mobilization concertedness and endurance. Unlike Luddism or early trade-union activity, the Caroline agitation was concerned with national affairs. The radicalism of the 1810s (and some later activity) could base itself effectively on local community bonds because it attacked a local object. This was not the case with Caroline, and I suggest that anything resembling Marx's notion of class action would also have had to have a national focus and would thus have been subject to the same limitations. Only through formal organization could people go beyond destabilizing insurrection to concerted action on the national level.

The argument that the Caroline agitation was a means of preserving or extending the mobilizations of the 1810s at best reduces to the fact that some radicals hoped it would do so. It was not, however, followed by rebirth of the parliamentary reform agitation or of protest over Peterloo, as Carlile and others had hoped. Indeed, with better times there was less protest. Among some workers the development of real trade unions began, and with it rose the possibility of negotiation over reforms and incremental gains in material well-being and working conditions. In many artisan trades, of course, trade societies had a long history, and they played an important part in the Caroline agitation.[76] In London, though not to any considerable degree elsewhere, the demonstrations on behalf of Caroline began a practice of public protests going beyond mere petitions which lasted into Chartism. In London, too, the Caroline agitation was closely related to Jacobinism, its propaganda heavily emphasizing the rights of man (and occasionally woman) and such carry-overs as the liberty tree. This distinguished London from the rest of the country, and from the mobilization of 1817–19, where Jacobinism was much less prominent.

The most important point to be made about the Caroline agitation is that we ought not to overestimate the degree of change, and especially of rationalization, which took place in British popular protest during the 1810s. In a period full of talk and agitation for reform, and even weakly attempted revolution, the most widespread popular agitation was in defense of a queen denied her traditional place. The symbolism of the agitation recalled Jacobitism as well as Jacobinism, pitted the Innocent against Corruption, and defended the "true constitution" against the usurpation of power; Caroline's supporters struggled to reclaim lost rights including the right to address and petition (and be answered), the right to assemble, and even the right to paternalism embodied in the imagery of the Good Princess. The battle was fought in the name of the people as well as the queen. The people were seen as a party, more just than those parliamentary bodies whose members voted for party and self-interest against known right. None of this was trivial, and by no means all of it was retrograde. It is hard, however, to see that the whole represents one of the moments of the continuous development of the working class in the direction of rational, revolutionary collective action. We may better see in the defense of the spurned queen an indication of the complexity and diverse rootedness of the community-based movements which preceded those founded on the category of class and mediated by formal organizations working nationally.

Populism Continues

On a sociological level, the critical shift in the transition to "class" action came with the development of formal organizations which could mobilize workers for national action. On an ideological level, the key to the transition was the development of an argument of exploitation based on the labor theory of value. The 1820s were a major turning point in both of these developments.[77] The growth of trade unions, which was closely tied to the decline of outwork industries and the growth of factories, provided the beginnings of a new organizational infrastructure for collective action. Unlike the bonds of community, this new social basis could readily be extended beyond the local level, could be selective in its aims, and could maintain concertedness over time. Further, trade unions fixed attention on men and women as workers, rather than as consumers, thus laying the groundwork for the development of the theory of exploitation. This theory held that the worker was deprived of his full share of the wealth produced by aid of his labor. More specifically, it held, in the shape given it by the Ricardian socialists, that the worker was deprived directly through the relations of production, through the rate of the worker's exchange of his labor for wages.[78]

This was a critical advance on the earlier theories, which we may lump together rather loosely as populist rather than class theories. Paine and Cobbett, for example, had regarded taxation and, in Cobbett's case, manipulation of the money supply as the central mechanisms of the maldistribution of wealth. The Spenceans, whose following on this was not limited to the small London group, held that cheating the poor of their land had deprived them of their independence and thereby enabled the rich to manipulate the prices of necessary consumer goods and thus rob the poor in unfair exchange. These views continued to be populist inasmuch as they portrayed the people in general as suffering because of aristocratic theft and overgrown government. There can be little doubt that most people did so suffer.

As general theories, whether taken together or separately, these accounts ran into problems. In the first place, they failed to distinguish between the long-standing aristocratic oppression of commoners and the growing capitalist exploitation of workers. This was closely linked to a failure to identify those evils which were due to the activity of the government—e.g., taxation—and those which were more due to its inactivity in the face of new modes of capitalist action. The effect of these failings was to limit the theories to reactive prescriptions for action. The populist theories did not yield an indication of a fundamental transformation in social structure based on an existing pattern in social change. This emerged only with socialist theories founded on the claims of labor and the critique of exploitation. The populists were limited to reactionary radicalism in the idealization of past golden ages—the predominant theme, for example, in Cobbett—or millenarian views of a future which would transcend all existing social arrangements, and which thus could not be extrapolated from any evident pattern in social change.

These limitations did not cause the populist theories to disappear, or the populist ideology to lose its appeal for a wide section of the British populace. Even among members of the new industrial working class, populism remained an important theme in protest. In some ways the struggle between the proponents of moral and physical-force Chartism can be seen as one between those who would win adherents to a cause which in the end would result in harmony and benefit for all, and those who envisaged a struggle between opposing classes in which one must lose as much as the other gained. The issue was complicated by differing degrees of stress on political or economic analysis, and by opposing views on the Malthusian/Owenite controversy over whether productivity must always be severely limited and goods in short supply. However various opinions and allegiance were, it remains the case that at no point during Chartism did the theory of the working class defined by exploitation in production come to dominate. This was, no doubt, partially because ideas have a certain inertia of their own. Perhaps more importantly, however, the endurance of the populist analysis reflects some general advantages it had over the class analysis, and its special relevance for those who continued to sell the products of their labor rather than to exchange their labor for wages directly.

The most important general advantage to the populist analysis was that it encouraged the widest possible collaboration in the reform movement. Writing at or after mid-century, Marx could plausibly assert that workers had the strength of numbers on their side, but it is not entirely clear that he was right even then, depending on how "worker" is understood. Certainly in the 1820s and 1830s there was no readily identifiable population of workers which could hope on its own to win national elections. In the first place, workers needed the monetary support, electoral expertise, and organization of the middle classes. More importantly, however, the working population was internally extremely diverse. The Chartists were quite right to speak of *classes*, not *class*. Marx had lumped together artisans, laborers, and factory workers of various skills, probably greatly overestimating the importance of the last group.[79] Industrial workers were far from a majority throughout the period of Chartism. The "people" were certainly a majority. Equally important, as far as many populist arguments were concerned, the poor and near poor were a majority by many definitions. Too limited a criterion for membership in the politically critical class removed the sanction of democratic right from its actions.

The exploitation-based class analysis was most readily applicable to the circumstances of industrial workers. Since they sold their labor more directly for wages, it was clearer that they received less than their full share of the product of the factory. Those who sold the products of their labor might be conscious of suffering, either in absolute terms or relative to a remembered past, but they were less likely to identify the problem as originating within the relations of production, as opposed to within the relations of exchange which followed production or within changes in the process of production. This point Marx wholly recognized in arguing the importance of the reduction of the work force to a common level of skill which would ensure the consciousness of commonality in the face of capital. The gradual elaboration of more and more complex piece rates, which attempted to take into account such exogenous factors as the state of a given worker's machinery, reflects the tenacity of the older view of the worker as selling a product rather than his labor. The introduction of time-based wage payments marks a qualitative change, not only in accounting but in the workers' self-identification.[80] Workers using the exploitation argument and struggling for higher direct wages were no longer defending a moral economy or notions of a just price.[81]

The populist ideology did not call on workers to abandon their various sectional identities in favor of a single category of "working class." The populist argument placed radical democracy before equalitarianism, politics before economics (which is not to suggest that it disregarded the second term in either phrase). The emphasis on political freedom as opposed to exploitation was critical. It allowed, for example, the most important paper of the period, the *Poor Man's Guardian*, to exhort its readers to "unite and be free":

> it entirely rests with the People themselves whether they will continue to endure the unjust and tyrannical treatment they have hitherto experienced, or whether they will have a government established that shall afford protection to ALL CLASSES of the community. If the people seek for political justice they should unite, and demand their rights. If justice be denied, let them withold the supplies—PAY NO MORE TAXES![82]

Similarly, O'Brien later defended Hetherington from attack: "He has never reviled the master manufacturers as such—he has never attempted to inflame the people against them merely on account of their calling or business; he has only spoken against them as the enemies of the workman's political rights."[83] Generally speaking, the *Guardian* did take an equalitarian line, and it did defend trade societies from attack. Consistently, however, O'Brien and Hetherington sought to persuade workers to put the political struggle first, to see securing universal suffrage as the best means "to establish for the productive classes a complete dominion over the fruits of their own industry."[84] If any demonstration of their distance from the traditional defense of the artisan crafts and the moral economy be needed, it can be found in O'Brien's attack on benefit societies.[85] However much there was an infusion of new ideas and goals into artisan radicalism, most artisans continued to work to protect their traditional positions and the communal institutions which supported them.

The Chartists adopted a variety of descriptions of those they aimed to help: the people, the industrious classes, the working or the useful classes. The language was sometimes militant and sometimes not. As

Prothero has summarized the years to 1840: "the anti-capitalist ideas which evolved in this period were those appropriate to artisans, not opposing all masters but condemning 'merchant capitalism', the monopolist middlemen. It was a theory not of exploitation within production, but of unequal exchange."[86] Papers like the *Poor Man's Guardian* went beyond London's traditional crafts to achieve a considerable audience in the Northwest's emerging textile industry. From the trade-union movements of the 1820s through Chartism, radicalism was in transition, with populism still dominant, and the source of most of the revolutionism in the movements, but the analysis of class was ascendant, particularly among the trade unions. These were generally reformist, and reform was the characteristic stance of collective action on the basis of class.

Changes in the social foundations on which workers were able to take collective action were closely connected to the differentiation of kinds of action they might take. In the first place, these changes in social foundations were part of the more general transformation of the labor force from relatively independent artisans to factory workers, from members of old trades threatened by industrialization to members of skilled (and less-skilled) crafts benefiting from the growth of capitalism. The material conditions and relations of production thus changed, altering the calculus of desirability of various courses of action. Secondly, shifts in the social organization of workers' everyday lives, in community structure, and in workplace patterns of association produced change in the processes by which workers selected among various possible identifications of themselves with groups of others, and corresponding commitments of personal resources to seeking collective goods. Concretely, in southeast Lancashire, as village communities became less important, associations based on place of work became more important. This was a stimulus to trade-union activity but an impediment to the sort of unified populist activities of residential and craft communities which had previously been so important. There was considerable overlap between the two sorts of activity during the Chartist period, but this shift in focus of association is essential to understanding why Chartist political action lost concertedness and faded in the late 1840s while trade-union struggles took firm root.

The Artisan Struggle for Autonomy

Respectable mechanics, skilled artisans, and even practitioners of such degraded crafts as handloom weaving generally did their work with a great deal of autonomy and independence. Some, like shipwrights, worked on projects of sufficient scale that they had to collaborate in "gangs." These were a relatively small proportion of the whole. Even shipwrights' gangs, however, show only the palest hint of the coming factory division of labor and enforcement of work-discipline. The members of a gang knew each other on a face-to-face basis and their informal relations with each other endured over time and extended outside of work. While they had to work with each other, and while each gang had a leader and each yard a foreman, it was still difficult for master-builders to enforce any substantial degree of control from above.[87] The fact that a craftsman had to exercise his own judgment and had to use his own skill and training to execute his productive tasks meant that he could not readily be controlled. The loss of the opportunity to construct a whole product instead of a mere part, and the loss of intellectual involvement in the labor process, have been properly emphasized, most notably by Marx. The implications of this for the aims of individual workers and the orientations of popular collective action have been less fully explored. It has been noted, to be sure, that as the worker's involvement in his work diminished, and productive activity became a neccesary evil performed only for a wage, the worker was apt to turn his attention more and more to his leisure, to see himself more and more critically as consumer rather than producer. The alienating tendencies of this change in the nature of work have been apparent to many observers. It seems to have been less apparent that the same transformation of work producing this alienation altered the organizational conditions for workers who mobilized to do something about their circumstances.

In the 1820s and 1830s, artisans made a number of attempts to retain and perhaps even increase the degree of control they had over their processes of production and in some cases over the distribution of the products. Many of these attempts centered around the loose ideology and set of organizations called "co-operation." They drew on Owen's arguments concerning the sort of new world which could be built if competition, private property, and religion could be prevented from exercising their deleterious influences. They drew on the notion of the fundamental value inherent in labor which Owen had given prominence but which had both a long intellectual heritage and an already existing if less articulate understanding among the artisans. These attempts were all based, fundamentally, on the relative independence of artisans. This was not a mere ideal to be sought; it was a condition for the kinds of actions attempted. Artisans were only occasionally involved in the large-scale cooperative communities for which Owenism is famous. They were much more invested in organizations which provided avenues for the exchange of goods. The artisans sought through cooperation a way to capitalize on the fact that they could do their work either as independent individuals or with the collaboration of a few fellows. Thus the artisans sought to become self-employed; they struggled to socialize not production but exchange.

This was especially true in the advanced urban crafts of London and some other southern towns, though it had its northern analogues as well (for example among the Manchester building crafts).[88] There were extensions of individual self-employment both within and very occasionally among trade societies. These took essentially two simple forms. First, there might be agreements for the exchange of goods. Much more often, a trade society might attempt to provide employment for its own out-of-work members. This could be done either by offering loans to workers and engaging to market their products to the public for them, or by forming something of a joint-stock company which directly employed its members. The latter is the clear ancestor of a number of more recent experiments in industrial cooperation. With such extensions as this, the artisans were able to take some first steps in the direction of moving from a set of solutions based on consumption to one based on the organization of production. These practical efforts were thus directly connected to the emerging analysis of exploitation.[89] Note the limitations of these first steps, however; only a few such attempts to turn trade societies into cooperative producers were made, and most were made as stopgaps during strikes. During the 1830s the great schemes of Owen and others for cooperative exchange overwhelmed the efforts of self-employment. The Labour Exchange drew contributions very largely from trades which were being degraded under pressure from a surplus of labor—tailors and shoemakers, for example. The cooperative movement as a whole rapidly degenerated into the frequently maligned society of "shopkeeper socialists."

If the artisans had difficulties extending their defense of traditional autonomy in the direction of industrial cooperation, the obstacles which faced factory workers were even more formidable. Leaving all other factors aside, the division of labor alone, on which factory work was based and which was a key source of the alienation described by Marx and others, created a tremendous hurdle. For factory workers to engage in industrial cooperation, they needed a scale of organization and capital backing which was all but completely out of the question. Unlike artisans, whose various tasks were essentially similar and who produced whole products, the factory workers were engaged in different tasks and each produced only a part of a product. This meant that any attempt to organize could not proceed simply by accretion of members. That is, if each tailor could produce a whole garment, then a cooperative of tailors could have any number of members. If each factory worker labored on only a part of the process, then a cooperative would have to have a complete set and could not add or subtract members at will. Further, most of the branches of work which were industrialized in factories were dependent not merely on the division of labor but on coupling it with machinery. This further increased the obstacles to cooperative organization.

The upshot of all this was that, while artisans could hold out various hopes of maintaining autonomy, factory workers could not. Factory workers were led of necessity to see themselves always in relation to their employers; they were led to the formation of trade unions and a trade-union consciousness. More specifically, their trade unions were led to a process of continual conflict and negotiation with employers rather than to political objectives or to an attempt to circumvent employers altogether. Beyond ensuring certain "rules of fair play" in labor disputes, these factory-based trade unions had little to gain as such from political activity. While their members might benefit in various ways as individuals, the unions were not in a position to capitalize on political moves to provide workers with autonomy. The hope for a society of independent, autonomous producers belonged to traditional artisans, not modern factory workers, even skilled factory workers.

This difference in the organizational problems facing artisans and factory workers influenced the kinds of goals they sought and helps to explain why leaders like Owen did not develop a notion of class struggle as a central element in the transformation of society. The reason lies not just in Owen's contention that the supply of goods was potentially unlimited but also in his idea that this fundamental transformation could occur gradually, by force of example. This appears more plausible if one realizes that most of the cooperating artisans were envisioning an extension of autonomous organizations of craftspeople to autonomous organizations of factory workers and then to similar organization of all of society. Despite Owen's own experience in factory management, this vision did not have equal appeal to factory workers. They had no autonomy to extend. Rather, they had bargaining positions to protect. Owenism's productive communities drew artisans and unemployed people willing to try anything. Factory workers were interested, for the most part, only in Owenism's cooperative stores.

In this discussion, I have been referring to artisans primarily to designate those who worked out of doors, domestically, or in small workshops. There were, of course, artisans within factories as well. These fit the picture I have drawn of artisans to the extent that they were autonomous in their work and were engaged in some fairly complete process of work. Thus engineers involved in building and maintaining machines were very similar to nonfactory artisans during the 1830s and 1840s. On the other hand, to the extent that artisans in factories worked on some step in the direct process of production, they approximated more to the position of skilled workers. They no longer faced the same circumstances, even where they maintained considerable autonomy due to the degree of their skill. Craftsmen of this latter variety were in immediate and continual danger of having their jobs in the production process subdivided and their specific artisanal position eliminated. We may see the difference between the two groupings clearly in terms of the different sorts of potential strike actions in which they can engage. The artisan can withhold his product from his employer or from the general market. The efficacy of this tactic is directly proportional to the demand for the product. The worker in a more specialized, subdivided organization of production (a factory, in short) gains his leverage from an ability to create a bottleneck at one step in a series of tasks by which a product is produced. He is thus potentially able to cause his employer to suffer costs much greater than his own specific input.[90]

Control over a link in the chain of production is thus critical to the factory worker. Demand itself is critical to the artisan. The one is thus led to see a narrower set of issues arising directly between employer and employee. The other, the artisan, is led to see a broader set of issues between producer and society. The factory worker is able to negotiate wage increases repeatedly over a long period of time; this is a plausible strategy. The artisan must defend an entire process of production: he must prevent his trade from being swollen and degraded, and he must prevent it from being supplanted by mechanized or foreign production. In the pursuit of neither of these goals is he consistently confronted with a singular adversary, an employer. The factory worker can come to see himself simply selling his labor at a more or less desirable or exploitative rate, with more or less of a premium for skill. The artisan cannot, for the essence of being an artisan is the autonomous production of a whole product, thus placing oneself directly at the mercy of the market and thus treating the acquired skill and membership of the craft as capital to be invested rather than labor to be sold. An artisan is a producer who combines the different functions of design, discipline, and fabrication in one person and one craft.

In this light we can see why artisans during the industrial revolution went only a limited distance in developing a class-based, anticapitalist ideology. Since each artisan who emphasized his respectability at the same time emphasized the justness of a system into which he fit, the artisan ideology was for neither leveling nor inverting the social order. It was indeed, in many cases, for warding off the threat of leveling which the growth of factories and degraded industries seemed to present. Artisans might harbor reasonable hopes of rising to be small masters, or of setting up in such businesses as public houses. They were not, thus, against the owners of private property or the masters of the workplace as such. Artisans did, as we have seen, oppose a variety of specific practices on the part of masters, notably the infringement on apprenticeship rules and the production of "cut-ups" and other low-quality goods. Incidentally, in the attempt to preserve the quality of products on the part of artisans like framework knitters we see not just a traditional pride in workmanship but also an awareness of the critical nature for the artisan (as opposed to the factory worker) of the control of supply of goods to the marketplace.[91] The opposition to masters was generally against their behavior, not their existence. The existence of the masters was only challenged when that label was used to denote men who were no longer practitioners of a craft but merely employers. Artisans argued that each man had the right to work for whatever master he wished, and that each man thus had the right to be his own master—either individually or as part of a collectivity. The artisans were struggling to keep the gap between masters and journeymen from growing. As long as masters played by the traditional rules and allowed those who worked for them to maintain their "respectability," the artisans identified more with their employers than with common laborers or with factory workers. This closeness of masters and men is evident in the Luddite disturbances, as small masters were frequently spared the destruction visited on large, and occasionally supported the rebellious weavers in their actions against those with the will and the capital to launch innovations.

The artisans opposed, in short, those masters who wished to abolish artisanal production. They also opposed those capitalists who by engrossing, forestalling, and manipulating parliament and government succeeded in increasing the cost of living while holding increase of wages down. When they considered the justness of their economic situation, they examined their overall standing in the social hierarchy and their absolute means of subsistence. If these were at least holding stable, they were reasonably satisfied. In many trades artisans fared reasonably well and were generally apolitical. In others combinations and some political activity secured them protection for a time. In still others, attempt after unsuccessful attempt was made to maintain a respectable standard of living. In very few cases was there any analysis of exploitation within production. The artisans did not locate their misfortune in any such necessary characteristic of the capitalist system of production but rather in incidental features of the capitalist system of exchange and in political corruption. When, especially during the 1830s, but in some cases earlier, the artisans turned their attention to production, they identified problems not in such general phenomena as exploitation but in specific pressures on the organization of work. Unemployment and underemployment weighed most heavily on the minds of worried artisans, not exploitation. These conditions were generally due either to fluctuations in the economy (or certain sectors of it), or to reorganization of work through division of labor, technological advance, or increase in scale. In some instances degradation of a craft through too easy entry, and in others foreign competition, were identified threats.

In all cases, the artisan solutions emphasized the maintenance or recreation of the traditional autonomy of the artisan. Cobbett and a number of his followers idealized the small farmer and petty commodity producer. Others gave more recognition to the importance of the division of labor and the fact that all workers in modern society live by the exchange of their products and by cooperation in combining individual acts of production into larger wholes. This meant ensuring the maximal level of cooperation and finding the best way of judging the contributions of each worker.[92] Well acquainted with acting as their own supervisors and managers, the artisans were quite prepared to grant these activities a share in the produce of organized labor.[93] They were less convinced about the claims of those who owned property in the means of production and claimed a share in the products on this basis rather than on any contribution of their labor or ingenuity.[94] They were not by any means unanimously opposed to such private property, however; at least as many simply wished recognition for the skill which was the craftsman's capital equal to that accorded by government and law to the fixed capital of proprietors. The result of all this was that artisans generally resisted the notion of a single homogeneous class of workers, even when they presented the claims of those who labored to those who did not. The artisans continued to think of working classes in the plural, indeed England's present-day trade-union organization reflects this traditional legacy; it is perhaps the most predominantly craft-based of any in the world.

During the 1820s factories came for the first time into ascendancy over domestic and small workshop production in the Lancashire textile industry; the rest of England gradually followed. This decade, coming between Peterloo and the "last laborers" revolt (the rural incendiarism of 1830–31) marked the close of the great wave of local-based, communitarian populism which ushered in capitalist industry in England. By the end of the first third of the nineteenth century, the predominantly traditional "old radicalism" was virtually past. It lingered a bit in the opposition to the new Poor Law, in the reform agitation, but in Chartism and the factory agitations of the 1830s and 1840s a new generation of leaders came to the fore and the problems of common people began to be conceptualized in new and different ways. Perhaps most importantly, a greater division among political, industrial, and social problems and mobilizations to solve those problems began to emerge.

This was especially the case at the level of formal organizations extending across the boundaries of local communities; these were themselves assuming an increasing importance.

The age of Chartism and the early factory agitations was dominated, as far as working people's action was concerned, by the split between the older artisan populations and the newer factory and laboring populations. This is not to say that there were simply two opposed camps, but a great many of the partially ideological divisions of the period are easier to understand when seen in the light of the divergent interests and social strengths of these two broad populations. Trade unionism was the great survivor of the period, not political radicalism. Though a number of artisan trades retained their place in production throughout the nineteenth century, from late Chartism onwards the artisans lost their position of preeminence. The political radicalism of the early part of the century had been very strongly tied to these artisans, to their local and craft communities, and to the traditions which they maintained. Much of this was lost or deeply submerged during the Victorian age. The social foundations which had sustained the mobilizations of artisans were transformed. Chartism needs to be seen, in important ways, as an ending as much as a beginning.

It was during Chartism and the factory agitations that Marx and Engels came to examine English society and take the mobilizations of English workers as central to their theory of working-class radicalism. They, like most analysts since, saw the period almost entirely as one of beginnings. These, to be sure, were many. This was the period in which popular politics and the trade-union movement as we now know it both got seriously underway. It was after surviving the crises of 1837 and 1847 that industrial capitalism developed the sense of confidence which characterized it throughout the Victorian age. But Marx's hoped for and predicted working-class movement did not mature as clearly or continuously as capitalism. Marx failed to foresee this development partly because he had treated Chartism as a unified beginning, because he had not realized how much of the radicalism he observed among English workers (and workers of other nationalities) was part of the resistance waged by artisans and small producers of many sorts against modern industrial capitalism. And he had not realized the extent to which the demands of the new factory population could be incorporated within capitalism, unlike the demands of the artisans. By understanding why so much of what Thompson calls "the making of the English working class" is the reactionary radicalism of the artisanate, we are better placed to understand the problems which were incorporated from its beginnings into Marx's theory of revolutionary class struggle.

Five

Beyond Populism: Class and Reform

As late as the mid-nineteenth century there was still considerable theoretical argument in the Chartist periodicals concerning the nature of class and the necessity of class conflict. Marx's follower Ernest Jones stressed that small shopkeepers must come to recognize that their "true interests" lay in an alliance with workingmen, but:

> Capitalists of all kinds will be our foes as long as they exist, and carry on against us a war to the very knife. Therefore, they must BE PUT DOWN. Therefore we MUST have class against class—that is, all the oppressed on one side, and all the oppressors on the other. An amalgamation of classes is impossible where an amalgamation of interests is impossible also.

Jones was uncertain on many particulars—how many "classes" could be incorporated into the larger, more polarized framework of struggle, for example. But he was certain that opposition to capitalism was predicated on a disjuncture of interests. "Class against class—all other mode of proceeding is mere moonshine."[1]

At the same time, Jones's co-worker George Julian Harney was still describing the woes of workers as being due to "that vile system, begot by aristocrats and usurers." In other words, Harney had not fully assimilated the shift in social organization of production which the industrial revolution had brought about. He published proposals for social reform from Louis Blanc, calling for a state extension of credit, social workshops, and the division of "profits" among the workmen in each branch of industry. But he also published Engels's arguments that workers must unite and conquer political power.[2] Harney's editorial policy, in keeping with what passed for theory in his own thought, was eclectic. In time, this cost him the allegiance of Jones and the Marxists (including Marx and Engels). All the same, he could not bring himself wholly into the moderate fold. His analysis was more of political categories than of social structure. He indeed might think of property as theft, but he did not dabble in the complexities of political economy.

The more moderate Chartists were quite remote from any rigorously based class analysis. Lovett not only placed greater faith in the struggle for knowledge than in that for radical social change; he thought in terms of a coexistence and collaboration of classes. His moderation was not only in his desire for peaceful rather than violent change but in the assumption that the object of Chartism should be "to secure to all classes of society their just share of political power."[3] Marx, and those who shared his perspective, thought such an emphasis on political affairs in isolation from social and economic conditions misleading at best. The notion that the various classes could all have political power and continue to exist as distinct classes could not but seem preposterous. The notion that capitalists were entitled to any "just share" of political power for exploiting the workers also seems distant from Marx.

If class struggle was only in its infancy during the Chartist period, and was neither a universally acknowledged nor appreciated infant, then on what basis can one suggest—as do both Thompson and Foster—that there was a class struggle underway still earlier in British history? The first sense in which this might be so is that of a long, gradual development of the struggle. If capitalism is the true source of modern class struggle, then it stands to reason that class struggle should develop alongside the political and economic system, not spring into existence full-grown from the pages of theory. Secondly, there is the point that workers, now almost universally assumed to be the agents, or at least the intended beneficiaries, of class struggle were not the only group with the potential to organize itself to seek collective goods. This is alluded to at the beginning of the quote from Ernest Jones given above; he refers to the capitalists who, as a class, carry on a war against workers "to the very knife." There might, in other words, be a concerted struggle against workers carried out by another class, with workers as the respondents not the initiators. It should be noted that this is not simply a question of who benefits. In the terms established for this discussion, class struggle implies organized and intentional activity; it is not enough to say that industrialists worked within a system which benefited them at the expense of workers. It is necessary that they collectively worked to secure these benefits.[4] Lastly, it may be suggested that workers might participate in class struggle without calling it that.

The last two of these possible arguments open a number of knotty but important questions. They suggest a quantitative difference in the extent to which particular activities may be justifiably termed class struggle, with no qualitative break. Class struggle is at one end of a continuum of concerted collective action. The other activities in which the (potential or actual) members of a class expend their energy, time, and resources are arranged along that continuum to the other end of maximally discrete individual action. These activities need not be the products of "false consciousness."[5] In the first place, workers have multiple and competing interests, not simply one true class interest. Secondly, the relevant variable discriminating among types of action may not be consciousness at all but the social foundations on which such action is based. Here we must notice two problematic dimensions of variance, one suggested by the second and one by the third of the above-listed possibilities for identifying early class struggle. Each of these dimensions is the source of problems in Thompson's and Foster's arguments.

First, to what extent must activities be organized nationally, or include members of all the different trades, in order to be considered class activities? There are no clear and simple answers, though both Thompson and Foster make implicit assumptions. The former assumes that neither dimension is of extreme importance; class activities may be purely local and confined to a single trade—though these he considers somehow a less "made" version. Foster suggests that we can find class struggle within a single town, Oldham, though not necessarily that it can succeed in transforming society when limited to that level. While being nationwide is thus not essential, class struggle must unite all workers. Foster opposes class consciousness to trade-union consciousness. I have attempted to ferret out some of the implications of these implicit assumptions above. It is also noteworthy that if one were to assume that an extreme of national and cross-trades participation is integral to the definition, then there was nothing approaching class struggle until Chartism, if then, and quite likely not even with the formation of the Labour party or with the conflicts of the 1910s through the 1930s.

The other possible formulation, class struggle which appears to its participants on at least one side to be something else,[6] is probably the more contentious and perhaps the more important. Can various intentionally organized activities, none of which by itself constitutes or presupposes class struggle, constitute, collectively, class struggle? At what point, if any, do variables of consciousness or intention take precedence over material actions and their consequences? Consider, for example, the impact of Cobbett's *Political Register* and its sister publications from his radical period. The *Political Register* did not offer a class analysis or a call to class action. Nonetheless, it circulated primarily and widely among the "industrious classes," a demarcated substratum of society. The familiar tone with which Cobbett addressed members of elite society was seldom returned. In addition, the paper did call for political action, though not always of a very focused kind. Cobbett was an individualist, biased against organizations, and a strong believer in the power of the printed word together with "due reflection." The actions he demanded were generally in the "objective interest" of the paper's readership.[7] Further, the paper frequently reported the activities of laborers and workers in widely separated parts of the kingdom; it helped its readership to see the commonalities in their plight and attitudes. This may certainly be considered the beginnings of a class consciousness, even if it lacked the framework for a class analysis. Particular pressures felt at a local level might elicit relatively common responses without further organization, where attitudes had been shaped in part by the same source. Lastly, such political pressures were often only local manifestations of national political and economic crises.[8]

Has one here, with Cobbett's followers in the 1816–20 movement for parliamentary reform, the concerted activities of a class or the common responses of like-thinking individuals to similar pressures? Or, and this is my argument, is there an intermediate level of community organization which was crucial and has tended to be overlooked in a polarized argument? The workers of England had long and strong communal traditions which came to the fore in movements like Ludism and continued to underpin the radicalism of the ensuing years. They were in many ways like members of an acephalous African society. They shared significant elements of common culture, though with important regional variations. They were subject to widespread material and economic pressures but, often, also to local pressures and opportunities which counteracted broader trends. A widely ramifying network of ties knit different parts of the country together laterally, but there was nothing approaching a centralized organization. Such a population one generally does see as socially organized,[9] as having something of a collective identity.[10] But, organized though such a social aggregate may be, its organization is one which is signally unsuited to concerted action. Such concerted action as there was took place primarily in and for the particular interests of local communities. Sometimes (as in the case of Norwich) craft groups were so successful in protecting traditional privileges, prices, and organizational patterns that the industries on which they depended moved to new locales. At other times, radical communities with long histories or strong organizations (like Foster's Oldham) were frustrated in their efforts to restore or change socioeconomic structures by the apparent apathy of neighboring towns and villages (especially in the case of the newly developing industrial districts). Both sorts of experience drove home the lesson of economic interdependence but at the same time made the interdependent workers suspicious of each other.

Localism and craft identification obviously had a tremendous head start over class in the sympathies and social relations of the people. A political movement or trades organization which attempted to base itself exclusively on class loyalties which did not yet exist was doomed to failure or irrelevance. Conversely, the capitalist economic system had wrought widespread and deep interdependencies which were much more sensitive than such earlier market relations as had linked regions. This meant that any movement or organization which based itself exclusively on local bonds could not confront the deepest and most important of its enemies. Not everyone, not even all of the most perceptive leaders, saw the need for a compromise between the two poles of organization. In practice, community took a clear precedence over national class as a motivation for and organization underlying collective action. Communities—often composed of workers—struggled against external threats to their existence or way of life. Class could overlap with this foundation but not escape it.

That there was struggle on the part of laborers, craftsmen, workers, and other groups during the industrial revolution is not in doubt. In what collectivities they struggled, for what reasons, and for what ends are the subjects of debate. It has been my contention that the strength of the first great phase of popular radicalism in England (1810s) derived largely from attempts to protect the communities which workers had built amid poverty, suffering, and uncertainty, and was crucially based on those local and craft communities even when its ideology extended beyond them.

This radicalism was thus in many ways conservative and populist in ideology and localist in orientation. The movement collapsed at the beginning of the 1820s as it extended beyond this basis and attempted to rest itself on links between communities and relationships with national leaders which were not strong enough to sustain it. The sentiments, knowledge, and social relations which bound people together nationally were not sufficient to create an effective, active class. Instead they created a mass—and a mass can take little concerted action. This is one of the reasons that the rather quaint agitation following George IV's treatment of Queen Caroline could come on the heels of the post-Peterloo peak of radical sentiment. The common denominator of the would-be national working class was far less analytically penetrating and self-conscious than that of various localities. Instead, it appealed to dreams of too easy solutions and deep-seated and nostalgic sentiments. The wronged queen was a colossal symbol of injustice, the structural significance of which, unlike that of the Peterloo martyrs, was totally null. When something that was easier to understand as class struggle emerged, it was in the second phase of popular radicalism, that of the 1830s leading into Chartism. At that point it was based on an unstable collaboration of the very different communities of factory workers, artisans, and domestic outworkers.

Thompson's narrative really ends with Peterloo, though his book goes on for over a hundred pages, touching on the 1820s and the beginnings of Chartism. For the most part, however, he considers the story of the making of the English working class to be told, and he turns to examine the consciousness of this class. The dozen or so years after Peterloo were crucial in determining just what legacy of consciousness "Old Radicalism" would leave the new working class.[11] It is this "Old Radicalism" which Thompson chronicled in The Making; it was an extension of Jacobinism and it ended with Cato Street.[12] In the 1820s workers attempted to reconcile the success of the industrial revolution with the defeat of this phase of popular radicalism. The success of the industrial revolution, and its new concentrated organization of production, brought trade unions into increasing prominence. These signaled the increasing importance of collective, and generally formal, organization in the attempt to secure popular goals. This was of course, no more than a match for the increasing scale and complexity of organization in the rest of society, and among the other classes. Formal, self-conscious organization became the characteristic way of getting things done in modern society—a society characterized, as Marx and a thousand others have noted, by its need continually to get things done, to achieve, and in the process to change itself.

The decade of the 1820s was a very prosperous one, especially in its first five years. This was no doubt an important reason for its relative political quiescence. But it should also be borne in mind that concern with political reform was in part giving way to concern with economic organization. Old Radicalism had focused almost exclusively on political issues, the reform of parliament and various libertarian freedoms. This was in part because as radical as it was politically, economically it was a movement of resistance to industrialization. As factory workers came to play a more important role in popular agitation, their concern for changes within the industrial conditions they inherited became increasingly determinant, not only of their own action, but of more general radical ideology. In the agitation up to 1819, radicals formed a highly political picture of their problems and of potential solutions to them.

> They learned to see their own lives as part of a general history of conflict between the loosely defined "industrious classes" on the one hand, and the unreformed House of Commons on the other. From 1830 onwards a more clearly defined class consciousness, in the customary Marxist sense, was maturing, in which working people were aware of continuing both old and new battles on their own.[13]

The continuing importance of older political definitions of the issues facing workers was, nonetheless, one of the reasons that they could be led into their miscalculations concerning the 1832 reform act.

At the same time, however, that this political legacy persisted, with its particular problems and virtues, the much maligned "trade union consciousness" was developing in earnest. In contrasting the two, we must remember that we are also, in part, contrasting two different populations.[14] The trade unions of the 1820s and after were significantly more urban than Old Radicalism. Even where the two prospered in sequence in one community (as in Oldham), it must be remembered that there was a change in the distribution of the various kinds of work over time. The development (or at least change) in consciousness did not take place in abstraction from the concrete circumstances of the workers in question.[15]

By the 1830s, Thompson suggests, the dividing line of class would be not alternative reform strategies but alternative notions of political economy.[16] The importance of this becomes apparent if one considers the extent to which, in histories of the period, the contrast between physical-force and moral-force Chartists seems almost to outweigh that between Chartists and non-Chartists. Political reform remained the most important object of the middle classes until 1832, when they achieved a measure of it, and it was second only to free trade for another thirty-five years. Yet it is equally true that much of the radical legacy was carried on by members of the "labor aristocracy" and the "petit bourgeoisie." Carlile, the greatest editor of the unstamped press, sold his papers primarily to clerks, artisans, shop assistants, booksellers, and the occasional warehouseman, not to weavers or pitmen, the classical figures of the older radical workers. Carlile's readers were freethinkers and utilitarians, not trade unionists.[17] The issue is not one of deciding whom to admit into a purified category of "class." Rather, the diversity must be recognized as all one phenomenon. The extremely individualistic radicalism of Carlile was not in some simple sense a middle-class threat to workers' mobilization or a "false consciousness" nefariously spread among workers. It expressed the aspirations of a portion of the population. And these aspirations were not unrealistic for that portion of the population. The "petit bourgeois" and the skilled worker could expect to advance themselves as individuals. This is not to say that a class consciousness would have been unrealistic for these same people. On the contrary, it is normal to have a multiplicity of practical and possibly beneficial courses of action (and views of the social and political world) open to one. It is more exceptional to have one's hand forced by the conjunction of one's own aspirations with material and political circumstances into a single possible "rational" action.

From the beginning of the Chartist period, debate was to focus on the relationship of such varying segments of the working and petit-bourgeois populations. It would be misleading to think that the alignments developed by the end of the ferment were somehow intrinsic to the social groupings involved. Thus "shopocrat" individualism may have been a "liberalizing" or antipopulist force in 1850; twenty years earlier it was not so narrowly self-interested. The individualism which came to the radicals out of the Enlightenment still carried a libertarian tone and even a certain radicalism in 1830.[18] Though some of this remained, individualism became more and more co-opted as political ideology by the advocates of laissez-faire and self-help. It ceased to refer to the creation of a society which fostered creative and productive individual activity and came to be a rationalization for the stratification which obtained in the society as it stood. Radicals in 1830, and in varying degrees in the preceding forty years as well as in the ensuing hundred and forty, claimed a number of freedoms—of press, speech, public assembly, and personal demeanor. That they did not pose a structural critique of society or uniformly seek fundamental changes to achieve the freedoms they claimed was not due to their being "bourgeois" or to their consciousness being dominated by that of the bourgeoisie. It was, rather, the common characteristic of those schooled in the Enlightenment to assume that such reasonable demands would of their own logic be realized, that means of diffusing light and knowledge were all that was lacking. This ideology indeed grew as part of the same revolution in Western history which spawned the bourgeois domination. None of this, however, negates the fact that many workers pursued this "bourgeois individualism" as their own popular objective in the early years of the industrial revolution.[19]

To be sure, individualism was in part predicated on illusions. Ideas did not have the radical effect, by themselves, which many early radicals had anticipated. From the 1820s on, there was a growing awareness that common interests could not be effectively gained by individuals acting alone. Collective action was identified as necessary, and nowhere was this lesson more deeply learned than in the nascent trade-union movement. This awareness was forced by the decline of traditional communities in which social bonds providing for collective action could be taken more for granted. It was necessary for the new industrial workers deliberately to create such collective organization. This they did on a local scale in a wide variety of organizations. The partially overlapping national trade-union, Owenite socialist, and Chartist movements reflected the same concern. All of these were largely distinct from the strictly knowledge-oriented institutes and programs which grew up during the same period. The same people might belong to both kinds of groups but the two kinds remained distinct. The emphasis on knowledge and the emphasis on organization developed from separate roots in the capitalist industrial transformation of England (and of Western Europe generally). The former had its roots in the Enlightenment and the libertarian push which accompanied capitalism's revolution against the entrenched social, political, cultural, and economic orders of early modern Europe. The latter had its roots in the stabilization of capitalism and industrial society. The two foci were not opposed simply as the concerns of opposing classes; they competed for the attention and effort of the same people at the same time. Knowledge and action are not intrinsically contradictory, but it is hard to study and march at the same time.

There remained in the twenties and thirties large populations of workers both in and out of large-scale industry. This split still determined a considerable amount of the disparity in kinds of popular action. Owenism initially entered factory areas only where it came as part of trade unionism. Even then, it was most likely to appeal to craftsmen like the builders. Its greatest appeal was to those outside of large-scale industry. This differentiation needs to be borne in mind as one considers Thompson's characterization of Owen not so much as the first modern socialist as the last eighteenth-century rationalist.[20] To be sure, Owenism had, by the 1820s, developed an identity largely distinct from Owen himself, but by no means entirely so. The appeal of Owenism followed a division in the kinds of communities in which workers lived, and the kinds of aspirations for which they worked. Owenism continued to build on some of the same premises and attitudes as Old Radicalism, in populations where Old Radicalism had been important. Workers in large-scale industry faced a different set of organizational dilemmas and also sought partially differing ends. This is not to say that Owenism was "backward looking." It could often be practical for many workers. It was unrealistic primarily in the impatience and ambition of its propaganda. Little stores and even communes brought no millennium.[21]

Both trade unionism and Owenism could shift down to the pursuit of local goals with local organization when attempts at national action failed. The same was not true of Chartism. Like the movement for parliamentary reform before it, Chartism aimed at changes which could only effectively be instituted on a national scale. Its attention was largely fixed on the state. A number of Chartist leaders noted the fate of the reform movement and set out explicitly to comprehend class as a general category, and to mobilize all the members of the proletariat for collective action. In this attempt they continued the tradition of emphasis on the printed word but supplemented it with both greater organization and more sustained analysis. In the same vein, they helped to depersonalize the movement, to put it forward as a matter of commitment to an ideology and a program of action, not to a number of leaders. All of this would seem to be tactically sound. It was also ineffective. The new organizations did not succeed in developing an intensity of commitment among the bulk of their members which could rival that of the less sophisticated and less "rational" groupings of the 1818–19 reformers. The movement of English workers became more of a class mobilization, but it also became weaker. This is partly a matter of contrast to the strengthened forces of vested authority but also a matter of "consciousness."

Implicit in notions of class consciousness is the assumption that greater rational clarity of perception of interests is inexorably connected to greater commitment to collective action. It would appear, however, that in England at least, diminished emotional commitment accompanied increased analytic clarity. The concept of class grapples poorly with the complexities of a movement which followed such a contradictory ideology and set of ideologues as popular parliamentary reformism. The assumption has been that radicalization and class consciousness somehow imply a simplification and clarification of perspective. Marx's use of the dialectic suggested that the increasing polarization of classes led to an ultimate negation of the very negation which was class society itself. The clarity of the opposition was thus implicit in his view of class development and revolutionary action.

What if this is wrong? What if it assumes a greater rationality for history than that of which human action admits? Let me suggest that the strength of early radicalism derived in part from the very complexity which makes the notion of class inadequate to describe either workers' consciousness of themselves or the foundations of their collective action.[22] A radical movement is a risky undertaking at any time; it certainly was so for the workers in the age of the combination acts, Peterloo, and the Six Acts. Any successful radical mobilization must depend on more than the rational calculations of the potential participants. These people must have strong emotional ties with each other, a faith in their strength, and an identification with the collectivity in which they are to act. None of this makes it necessary, or even very likely, that their perceptions of what is going on would always satisfy the outside analyst. We must recognize that the analyst's view is as limited as that of the participants. If the one can never view his situation with the cool detachment of the other, still the latter cannot truly understand the feelings of the former. He can only approach them by indirection, as Thompson does so well, and with sympathy. And as Thompson implicitly argues, if we leave the nonrational out of our accounts, we make much of human action inexplicable and apparently unmotivated.

That people were open to a religion of frenzy and enthusiasm is not a sign that they could not have been radicals or revolutionaries. On the contrary, it is a sign that they could have been. Both radicalism and Methodism attempted to tame the emotional expression of their adherents and tie it to ideologically sound and organizationally sanctioned occasions.[23] This resulted on the one hand in the earnestness and sobriety which Thompson records in both movements.[24] That is, it created in part a self-conscious and controlled devotion. But this was not all; there was also, with fluctuating success, a real emotional depth in both Methodism and radicalism. Symbols took root in personal consciousness and images of social life were deeply etched on the minds of participants. This is a key part of the significance of ritual in any movement—or in a relatively stable society.[25] It is not a diversion from rational thought and thus a complete loss to the progress of history. It is another kind of cognitive action, weak in its ability to focus, abstract, and analyze, strong in its ability to motivate and give preconscious order to perceptions. The involvement of the early radicals—and their contemporary nonradical fellows—in a variety of symbolically rich ritual actions, and enthusiasms both religious and political is an indication that these people were deeply enough involved in their own emotional lives, and those of the groups in which they lived and worked, to respond with strength and feeling. One can scarcely imagine them taking concerted radical action without such strength and feeling.

Chartism marked no night-and-day change, of course. It had its own distinctive ritual elements, and it continued a number of earlier elements of symbol and culture. Nonetheless, it can readily be asserted that the proportionate influence of these "nonrational" but ordered aspects of social life declined, and with the decline some of the strength of the mobilization was sapped. At no point during the first half of the nineteenth century was a synthesis forged between the local social strengths of radicalism and the national organization needed to win fundamental victories. This was partly so because the local mobilization was based on a hostility to industrialization while it was the common position of workers in industrial society which called for (and provided the potential for) national class action. There was only a gradual growth of the proportion of workers in large-scale "modern" industry. It seems unreasonable to ascribe total determination to such general factors, however; no doubt a myriad of particular influences worked against the juncture of local struggles and national class organization. In any event, this would seem to be a far more telling contrast, at least in the English case, than the vaunted Leninist distinction between "trade-union" and "class" consciousness.

In the last pages of his book Thompson makes the curiously juxtaposed comments that 1832–33 is the threshold past which the working-class presence can be felt throughout England; and in 1832 the middle classes succeeded in co-opting the lead the workers had established in the politics of reform.[26] The two comments are not necessarily contradictory; in fact, they are both true. Their juxtaposition without comment, however, belies the conflict in Thompson's account over recognition of their connection. The conflict is present because Thompson accepts, somewhat preanalytically, the notion that class development can be equated with the progress of radicalism. His argument on a number of particular empirical points, as I have shown, strains to demonstrate just the opposite. In part this problem results from the polemic Thompson is carrying on with those modern Marxists (among others) who would dismiss pre- and early industrial workers out of hand as potential class actors. Whatever the reason, Thompson finds it surprising that he must conclude that workers were stronger in some ways before the maturity of their class consciousness: "It had been the peculiar feature of English development that where we would expect to find a growing middle-class reform movement, with a working-class tail, only later succeeded by an independent agitation of the working class, in fact this process was reversed."[27]

In this passage, Thompson leaves himself open to some of the criticism he later levels at others for failing to give full credit to the importance of the English Revolution of the seventeenth century.[28] More to the point, it is not entirely clear that England is peculiar in this feature. Members of the (loosely defined) middle classes were significant in the seventeenth century, not least of all on the Leveller "left"; they were all but dominant in the Jacobin agitations; and they (together with the official Whig opposition) lost their hold over the reformist banner during the Napoleonic wars when, in large part, they joined in the twin anti-Gallican and antiproletarian panics. In all of their periods of importance, their hand was being forced by a more popular "left-wing" to their movement. The same can be said for the French revolutionaries of 1789 and 1830. The bourgeoisie clearly retained the leadership in both cases but was often forced into the position of reacting to the initiatives of its supposed "working-class tail."[29]

The argument to which Thompson is pointing out a perhaps not very exceptional exception is essentially that of Marx in his analysis of the class struggles in France, 1848–50.[30] Thompson's point is justified in that, at the time he wrote, Marx's position held a certain force of orthodoxy. It has since been often challenged and greatly revised—just as Marx himself revised his early unilinear view of the development of class struggle. It is important, as Thompson emphasizes, to see history in terms not of continuous progress but also of fits and starts, slips backward as well as steps forward. Perhaps even more to the point, steps forward in any one direction are just as surely steps not taken toward another possible future.

Thompson's story is that of many men seeking the future in differing ways. He shows them struggling at times to work in concert, succeeding only briefly beyond the most local scale. The dreams for which these workers struggled were often vague, ambiguous, even contradictory, but this was not the primary reason for their failure (and it was not an entire failure at that). If we think of the revolution for which some of these workers fought as a rational undertaking to bring about a clearly foreseen future, then it was hopeless from its inception—but then so was every revolution to which the label has ever been applied. It is not likely that English workers could have seized control of the government at all, still less held it for long or effected the transformation of society in consonance with their dreams. When Thompson suggests that revolution was possible in 1832,[31] we ought to think rather of a breech in the walls of order and predictability. Nonetheless, the cultural and social groundwork of England was such that, had there been a revolution, of however modest an aim, there could conceivably have been a profound radicalization after the revolution began.[32]

The working-class radical movement did not contribute to a revolutionary destabilization of the old regime. Rather, fear of the working class provided the various middle- and upper-class elites with an incentive to reach some compromise on their own differences so that the scope of political debate could be kept within safe bounds. The dominant groups in English society awoke to class politics at about the same time the workers did. In the early 1830s the workers were meeting to debate the nature of class; from this point forward the radical and Chartist press worried constantly about the definition and implications of class.[33] Only a handful of defenders of the old regime were of any illusion about the emerging class to which they did not belong—however else they might see their position in society. The middle and upper classes were in a far better position to engage in class politics, and they assessed and handled their situation very expediently. The workers, it must be said, did not. They had dozens of different dreams, rather than a single existing system to defend, and their activity and attention were scattered. The fact of their exclusion from political and economic control was the most unifying ideological concern of the would-be working class; it hardly provided for equal social unity. In the years after 1795, as Thompson notes, counterrevolution had helped to keep the radical movement limited to workers of various descriptions.[34] After 1820, and especially from 1832 on, there was a great deal more ideological competition for the hearts and minds of working people.

So what was "the making of the English working class"? Thompson perhaps describes the subject of his book as clearly in the last line of his 1968 postscript as anywhere, where he terms it a "process of self-discovery and of self-definition."[35] In describing such a process, Thompson is indeed describing "cultural formations," but he draws conclusions which presuppose a great deal more than culture. He leaves implicit in his analysis the mechanism for translating culture into social action; that is what I have been trying to make explicit.

Class and Reform

A good deal of effort has been expended in constructing explanations of the historical "defeat" of the working class. Such accounts, whether phrased in terms of "liberalization" from above or "fragmentation" and the development of a "labor aristocracy" within the working class, tend to assume either the prior existence of a revolutionary class, or a "natural," evolutionary course of development toward such consciousness and mobilization.[36] I have argued in this work against both assumptions. In particular, I have distinguished between the mobilizations of "old" and "new" workers, especially as the former sought more radical, but at the same time more populist, goals, and the latter more reformist aims. The former, I suggested, fought on the basis of strong community foundations but against the preponderant forces of economic change. The latter fought on a weaker social basis but within the emergent industrial order. This distinction militates strongly against a notion of the continuous development and increasing radicalization of the working class. Instead, it suggests that revolutionism may most likely be found at the onset of capitalist industrialization while reformism is the characteristic stance of the working class. Such reformism may be either more or less extreme in its aims; the important point is that those aims can be sought in a gradualist or incrementalist fashion. While the communities of traditional workers had to transform the basis of the British economy or cease to exist, the new working class could gain an indefinite range of ameliorative reforms without fundamentally altering its collective existence.

Suggesting that reformism is the "natural" or characteristic form of working-class action implies that much of the argument concerning fragmentation and liberalization is redundant, or at least must be seen in a new light. This is especially the case where such argument holds that specific intentional action on the part of the "bourgeoisie" was integral to the limitation of working-class revolt. Thus Foster holds that "Liberalization was in fact a collective ruling-class response to a social system in crisis and integrally related to a preceding period of working-class consciousness."[37] Most of this part of Foster's argument carries beyond the temporal boundaries of the present research. In the first chapter, however, I directly challenged his argument concerning the existence of class consciousness and its social foundations in the 1830s. I have also challenged the arguments of Thompson and other historians who find extensive working-class mobilization still earlier. Instead, I have suggested that the radicalism of the 1810s and to a lesser extent the 1830s drew heavily on the communities of domestic crafts-men and others who were either in the process of displacement by economic change or else under immediate threat of the disruption of collective life. I have argued that these workers should not be in-corporated into a single conceptualization of the working class but rather that their differences from factory and other "new" workers should be emphasized. These new workers were never dominant in a potentially revolutionary or even very radical movement (at least not until after the turn of the century). At most, they demanded reformist concessions with threats of physical force during some periods of Chartist agitation. No special explanation is needed, thus, to account for the relative quiescence of the Victorian working class or its accep-tance of economic concessions in lieu of political gains. This is not to suggest that no concessions were made to workers, or that these were not important, merely that they were not necessary to the containment of any "natural" revolutionism.

Lenin's famous considerations on the role of the party and the radical intelligentsia suggest that he regarded the activity of the working class as naturally limited to trade-union economism (and perhaps liberal democracy) and requiring external intervention to go beyond this. Foster follows this lead in part, as he bases much of his argument on the local leaders and the ideological positions which they espouse. Thus he holds that the growth, for various reasons, of a significant group of liberal leaders worked to undermine the more class-conscious influ-ences of earlier years. The material basis for this process was provided by the super-profits of imperialism and the use of those super-profits to buy off a stratum of skilled workers. The implication is that had this not happened, had this not been possible for the "ruling-class" or had another strategy been chosen, then the working class might have proceeded in a class-conscious and potentially revolutionary manner.[38] I have attempted to show that this is not the case, that the workers would have been unlikely anyway to pursue such a course of action because of the existence of mediate, less extreme, interests and because of the relative weakness of the social foundations for collective action available to workers.

Foster suggests that "Oldham's bougeoisie consciously used its industrial power (and the economic and psychological reality of empire) to split the labour force and bribe its upper layers into political acquiescence."[39] He terms this process "restabilization." It is important to ask, however, when there had been extensive previous stability. One would have to go back well into the eighteenth century to find a period of more than a decade without major popular mobilizations. In other words, one observes in the 1840s and 1850s the stabilization of capitalist industrial society.[40] The movements of workers in the first decades of the century were most importantly movements of resistance against the introduction of capitalist industry. Imperialist super-profits could not have bought off the communities of traditional craft workers. Unlike the emerging working class, this older communal order did not divide neatly into layers. It was not possible to offer special privileges to a single stratum in order to divide it from the rest. There is no reason to believe that money would not have been welcomed by any and all traditional groups, but as long as the community structure remained intact, the older population of domestic workers and other craftspeople could not fit economically or socially into the new order of society. They could fit only as individuals leaving their communal and craft roots behind, and then not always easily.

The wealth of capitalist industry and trade could be redistributed in part to the members of the new working class without requiring the dissolution of that class as a social formation. The working class could find a niche in capitalist society and fight for a more gradual accession of benefits. Neither the reality of exploitation nor simple relative poverty provide necessary—or even probable—causes for radical, potentially revolutionary collective action. One may thus agree with Reid:

> The process of containment of the working class does not then require "special" explanations whether in the form of a labour aristocracy, social control or the cultural subordination of crucial strata, all of which tend to assume that, left to itself, the working class would be spontaneously united and revolutionary due to its economic position. On the contrary, defeat is the normal not the abnormal condition of the working class under capitalism, for in the absence of consciously formulated politics and carefully con-

structed alliances, it is only able spontaneously to sustain temporary sectional revolts.[41]

Reform is the most likely focus for concerted working class action. This
obviously, is close to Lenin's formulation in *What Is to Be Done?* My
explanation for this situation, however, is not that which Lenin went
on to argue in his studies of imperialism.

Marxists have adduced three major kinds of reasons for the political
behavior (real or anticipated) of the working class. The first is
consciousness—an emphasis on the opinions, aims, and analyses of the
class. Within this line of reasoning some follow Lenin in stressing the
incapacity of the workers themselves to develop a revolutionary class
consciousness and in stressing, therefore, the need for the radical intelligentsia to lead the masses.[42] In extreme forms of this position the
consciousness of the "vanguard party" comes to substitute for that of
the workers themselves in determining what is to be done. Others stress
not the consciousness of the elites but that of the workers themselves;
they hold that it is not the clarity of an ideological position or the acuity
of the analysis on which it is based which is most important. Rather, it
is the context of consciousness in concrete engagements of class struggle which matters most. In this treatment Gramscian arguments concerning cultural and ideological hegemony come to the fore with the
key question becoming whether or how much the consciousness of the
working class can escape the determination of elite control over cultural institutions and, perhaps, become dominant itself. Thus in
Thompson's usage, class becomes a principle for understanding the
organization of consciousness in many circumstances, and in some the
principle which in fact does organize consciousness.[43]

The second major kind of explanatory basis for working-class politics
is "structure." By structure is meant, generally, objective position in
society; in other words, the structure into which the class fits, not the
structure of the class itself, especially not the internal social relationships of its members. The implication is that workers will engage in
this or that political action because they stand in definite relations to
the means of production and possibly to the institutional framework
and political organization of a society. Rational interests are important
in this sort of analysis and are treated as subject to objective analysis
rather more than subjective choice. This view is not incompatible with
the Leninist position concerning consciousness. It becomes important
in such a view to assess who is specifically a member of the working
class and thus subject to definite determinations leading ultimately
toward revolution; who is in an ambivalent position and thus subject to

indefinite determinations; and who is definitely opposed to the interests of the workers and determined to support the capitalist order.[44]

The third line of reasoning could be seen as a subcategory of the second. It involves extending the frame of analysis to include the international division of labor. This may be done either to explain the relative quiescence of workers in "core" industrial countries or to argue that the "true proletariat" is now to be found in the third world. In both cases the position of workers in relation to the directly economic results of exploitation—specifically wealth—is taken as crucial. The workers in advanced industrial societies become part of the exploitative class because they share in their societies' wealth; those in the third world are exploited.[45]

All three of these lines of reasoning leave out of consideration the fundamental question of on what social foundations the working class is to organize for collective action. The distinctive area of social relations among workers is relegated to the status of epiphenomenon. Either collective action is the direct result of consciousness or it is the determinate result of the structure in which the collectivity is embedded. In either case the constitution of the collectivity itself is left relatively unexamined. One of the distinctions of Foster's work is that he asks what the "social being" of the collectivity "working class" might have been. Although there are serious problems with his analysis, he raises an important question, the answer to which might have great significance, and he gives some help in answering it. Unfortunately, almost as soon as the question is raised, it is lost. The analytic significance of Foster's partial answer is sacrificed to an overall analytic framework which has room only for a Leninist conception of consciousness and a structural concern with the intermediate strata occupied by the petty bourgeoisie and labor aristocracy.

By concentrating on the immediate contexts in which workers lived, and especially on community, I am trying to show early nineteenth-century popular agitations in a new light. Traditional local and craft communities supported and collectively participated in populist agitations motivated largely by the attempt to resist the disruption of communal life by capitalist industrialization. The working class emerged as an essentially reformist grouping. Once one has separated the populist agitations which peaked in the 1810s (but included some of early Chartism) from the nascent class agitations of the 1830s and 1840s, this becomes much clearer.[46] The greater radical potential of the populist mobilizations becomes apparent. Likewise, the failure of the working class to wage revolution becomes explicable. It is not simply the ideology of workers or the co-optation of intermediate strata which is problematic, but the social organization of various groupings of workers.

If a class mobilization were to have the social strength which has characterized populist movments it would have to be founded on a basis in social relations making of the class a complex of interlinked communities. It is not enough that workers combine on the basis of their specific interests as workers in capitalist society, even in times when the pressures on them are severe or the "ruling class" is fragmented. It is necessary that workers form sentient groups, communities, which are congruent with the class mobilization. The existence of such communities cannot be based on purely instrumental relations, on conscious decisions or collective interest in the objective sense. As Max Weber argued:

> Every social relationship which goes beyond the pursuit of immediate common ends, which hence lasts for long periods, involves relatively permanent social relationships between the same persons, and these cannot be exclusively confined to the technically necessary activities.[47]

It is necessary that community work to define interests, that communal relationships be invested with moral authority. In other words, the bonds among members of a community must constrain, order, and indeed partially constitute the material action of those members and its significance to the rest of the community and to the actor himself. For this kind of social strength to obtain, the individual must be inextricably a part of the community, not simply a follower of an optional cause, however much he would objectively benefit from the success of that cause.

In the second half of this book, I shall delineate in more detail just what I mean by communal foundations for collective action, and why I see no opposition between traditional culture and radicalism. Though the remaining chapters will include much more substantial theoretical discussion, they do not abandon empirical consideration of early nineteenth-century England. They do, however, abandon the broadly chronological organization of the analysis up to this point. Their concern will be to make greater sense of the transition which I have seen most focused in the decade of the 1820s, but resistance to which, I have argued, dominated popular radicalism from the eighteenth century into early Chartism. The disruption of traditional community life against which populists—"reactionary radicals"—fought did indeed take place. It not only changed society in general, it transformed the social foundations of collective action for English workers. Both the ease of individualistic accommodations[48] and the struggles (usually reformist,

I claim) organized in terms of the working class, date from after this transition. I shall not only discuss conceptualizations of "before" and "after" but also try to state my theoretical position in terms of variables which can be—at least in principle—measured comparatively. One such comparison of communities in southeast Lancashire in the 1830s—alas, with inadequate data—is included.

Part Two

Six

The Radicalism of Traditional Communities

In Lancashire, wrote William Cobbett in 1817, "every hamlet is a village, every village a town, and every town a city."[1] Sheer size and a shocking rate of growth were perhaps foremost in the minds of contemporaries who thought about changes in community during the industrial revolution. Among cities, the capital was the only model by which they could judge the new industrial centers, and even London itself continued to grow rapidly, swallowing outlying towns and villages. The new industrial cities and towns presented a different aspect from the old, even the largest of the old. The new towns seemed to observers crowded, polluted with the smoke of factory chimneys, athrob with such rapidity of motion that calm was all but impossible. Observers contrasted these new urban centers, for the most part, not with each other or with the old cities, but with rural life. The old village was seen by many to be vanishing, was held up by many as the repository of all that was good and moral in social life.

It was in reflection on the dramatic changes wrought in the late eighteenth and nineteenth centuries that the concept of community took the shape in which we receive it today. It bears, as a result, a number of connotations specific to the historical context of its formation, which have led at least one social historian to suggest recently that it ought to be abandoned.[2] The concept does, however, refer to some real and important phenomena. It is thus important that we refine it rather than abandon it.[3]

In two important ways, the concept of community is central to an adequate understanding of the popular protest movements of the early nineteenth century. First, these movements were largely based on the social foundations of local communities. The people they mobilized were knit together through personal bonds within these communities much more than they were unified as a class. As such movements attempted to go beyond local communities in their mobilization or objects, they foundered. Second, the early nineteenth-century protests were largely aimed at the preservation of the communities in which workers lived. These populist movements defended various traditional values, notably those of family and craft loyalty. Families and crafts were not distinct from communities; the social bonds with which they knit people to each other were part and parcel of community. Only with the aid of such bonds had workers been able to organize over the years to fight for notions of a just price, occasional improvements in their standard of living, and security against the vicissitudes of capitalist markets and human life. Workers did not abandon their communities or their crafts willingly during the industrial revolution. Those who held themselves above most of their fellows as "respectable mechanics" were among the most important radicals of the period, yet they sought not to maximize their gains from industrialization but to preserve the position they already occupied. To dismiss them as backward would be to dismiss one of the most vital of popular forces and the eventual source of much of the modern radical tradition. Yet to treat them through a rationalized concept of class is to neglect or obscure their traditionalism and communitarianism. During the industrial revolution many of the most respectable mechanics and such degraded artisans as handloom weavers shared in a sequence of social movements based on local community and craft bonds and designed to preserve those very communities and crafts.

The Recognition of Community

Those who lived in early nineteenth-century England were well aware that dramatic changes, social as well as economic, were going on around them. It is sometimes hard for us to grasp that they were only erratically aware of what those changes were. Cobbett continued to think that the population of England was in a decline even after the first three censuses had been taken. Enclosures had been used not so much to improve agriculture as to misappropriate land and livelihood properly belonging to the people:

> The farmhouses have long been growing fewer and fewer; and it is manifest to every man who has eyes to see with, that the villages are regularly wasting away. . . . In all the really agricultural villages and parts of the kingdom, there is a *shocking decay*; a great dilapidation and constant pulling down or falling down of houses. . . . And all the *useful* people become less numerous. . . . There are all manner of

schemes have been resorted to get rid of the necessity of *hands;* and, I am quite convinced, that the population, upon the whole, has not increased, in England, one single soul since I was born.[4]

Cobbett was wrong about the population of England, of course, but the depopulation of some rural areas was quite real. Cobbett found it difficult to visualize the scale of what was new in England; he was far more able to see the destruction of older patterns of life. In this he was representative of his contemporaries. Even those who had themselves made great fortunes in manufacturing found it difficult, at first, to believe that the growth of production could continue at any comparable pace. Through the Napoleonic wars, at least, there was a widespread tendency to view manufacturing as simply an offshoot of trade, to see home productive activities as a way of fostering mercantile strength abroad. A crucial lesson of the new political economy was its stress on the independent importance of production. In short, the dramatic changes which were taking place in England could not escape notice, as a general phenomenon. What specifically they amounted to, however, was not any more clear to contemporaries than what political and moral stands they ought to take on those changes—indeed often much less so! There were different things to see as well as different evaluations to make.

In the early nineteenth century, Englishmen were just beginning distinctively to conceptualize *social* life, and to consolidate their somewhat earlier recognition of the distinctiveness of *economic* life. Political economy from Smith to Marx involved elements of both conceptions.[5] Parliamentary debates and journal articles increasingly treated questions of the reform of politics in order to take account of social and economic changes. The dimensions of change ranged from shifting distributions of population to the growth of new "interests," to the increasing organization and concentration of demands imposed on the politicians and the forces of "social order" by the disenfranchised and the dispossessed. A great deal has been made of the language of class which came gradually to all but dominate political debate. At least as widespread, and perhaps even more important in the first half of the nineteenth century in England, was a language of community. To be sure, the language had an old heritage, and had reached a prior centrality in Puritan social thought, with the doctrine of the commonweal and the theology of the new covenant.[6] Although the Levellers and others of the seventeenth century had extended the discussion of community from political to social criticism, this usage did not take root until the period of the industrial revolution. The dramatic demographic changes and the changes in the social organization of population aggregates both drew attention to communities. This meant examination of men's relations with each other, personally, through their social positions and attendant expectations for behavior, and in aggregates. The physical and economic changes brought by industrialization served to reinforce this shift of attention, and occasionally to confuse its results. Urbanization and industrialization became quite early and quite firmly linked both in popular consciousness and in the minds of more specialized intellectual observers.

When thought about community became common, it was rooted, for the most part, in the contraposition of ideas of country and city.[7] This simple opposition, however, did little justice to the complexity and variety of communal life before, during, or after the industrial revolution. The differences between the capital and the old country towns, and between both of these and the new manufacturing cities were great, and yet none was much like the agricultural village idealized by the partisans of "Old England." The retrospective vision which placed all its attention on agricultural villages or the yeoman farmer forgot both the varieties of agricultural community in preindustrial England and the increasing importance of manufacturing, in both craft and outwork forms of organization. The hamlets and villages surrounding Norwich, feeding its textile-producing population and gradually moving more into manufacture (especially weaving), presented a very different picture in the eighteenth century, for example, than did southeast Lancashire, even with the similarity of products in the two regions. Manchester did not overwhelm its surrounding area as did the walled city of Norwich. A number of the other substantial towns in the region of Manchester—Oldham and Stockport, for example—were centers in their own right. One of Lancashire's most distinctive characteristics was the great preponderance of small holdings whose proprietors were part-time outworkers; another was the weakness of the greater gentry (which was strong in Norfolk).[8]

Southeast Lancashire and Norfolk were in some ways relatively similar, and so the contrasts between them become particularly interesting. But the whole notion of comparing aspects of community, of treating it as a cluster of variables rather than simply a place or a population is ill-developed in social history.[9] Such a process, however, is of vital importance if we are to move beyond mere characterizations of specific instances or comparisons of isolated dimensions without consideration of how they fit into the overall life of the populations in question. The language of community was elaborated in the nineteenth century to deal with just such comparisons—though in a highly value-loaded way. As country and city were contrasted, an analysis developed of the decline of community as implicit in the transition from country to city. "Community" characterized a valued moral dimension in social relations. The idea of community was used to discuss the ways in which social relations contributed to proper personal behavior and, only half distinctly, to public order and an acceptance of authority as being exercised in the public good.

Some of the early observers went beyond the simple contrast of country and city to hint at more complex comparisons. Howitt, for example, held that the sophistication of urban dwellers could somewhat ameliorate the corruption of their moral life, but:

> It is in those rural districts into which manufactories have spread—that are partly manufacturing and partly agricultural—that the population assumes its worst shape. The state of morals and manners amongst the working population of our great towns is terrible—far more so than casual observers are aware of. After all that has been done to reform and educate the working class, the torrent of corruption rolls on. . . . Where the rural population, in its simplicity, comes in contact with this spirit, it receives the contagion in its most exaggerated form—a desolating moral pestilence; and suffers in person and in mind. There spread all the vice and baseness of the lowest grade of the town, made hideous by still greater vulgarity and ignorance, and unawed by the higher authorities, unchecked by the better influences which there prevail, in the example and exertions of a higher caste of society. . . . The evil lies deeper than the surface; it lies in the distorted nature of our social relations.[10]

An implicit connection was made between industrialization and urbanization. Howitt was aware that much industry of his time was located outside the great new cities, but he assumed that there was a common "demoralizing" social influence; he did not quite ask himself whether it was city life or manufacturing work which was the corrupting agent.[11] Further, Howitt rather ambivalently attributed certain virtues of knowledge and "better influences" to cities, against the general grain of his argument. It may be that he was remembering the quite different eighteenth-century (especially capital) city, at some points, and at others thinking (no doubt with a shudder) of Manchester or Newcastle.

Clearly physical factors loomed large in the view of the manufacturing city held by its early nineteenth-century critics (and indeed its supporters). Size and rate of growth stood out among the novelties, but there were many specific aspects which observers found at least as provoking, if not always as remarkable. There were aesthetic objections to the nuisances created by factories directly—air pollution, for example, and to some eyes, the marring of the horizon by chimneys. But more to the point were objections to the living conditions the city imposed. Poverty had never, perhaps, been pleasant to look at, but in the early nineteenth century those of the privileged classes who noticed the living conditions of the poor found a new concentration of what Ruskin was to call "illth." Slums matured into a newly substantial social phenomenon, but also one newly hidden from sensitive eyes. Part of the outrage of complaint was directly about the physical privations under which the poor and the workers suffered. At least as much, however, was about the social and moral implications of this new organization and concentration of poverty.

Dr. Kay's investigations into "the moral and physical condition of the working classes" drew little distinction between the two varieties of condition, suggesting, if there was a statement of order at all, that one could not expect much in the way of civilized manners and morals from a population made to live like animals. Neither could a manufacturer expect a full complement of energy from a work force which was demoralized or ill—and so it was in the interest of bourgeois Manchester to reform the conditions in which the workers lived.[12] Writing from a similar perspective, Cooke Taylor pointed out the extent to which even the physical debilities of the population stemmed from the social characteristics of the community, where the factory operatives and the wretched poor below even them must live, "hidden from the view of the higher ranks by piles of stores, mills, warehouses, and manufacturing establishments, less known to their wealthy neighbours,— who reside chiefly in the open spaces of Cheetham, Broughton, and Chorlton,—than the inhabitants of New Zealand or Kamtschatka."[13] Taylor's graphic illustration has been often quoted and is representative of an outpouring of comment in the late 1830s and early 1840s, having perhaps its locus classicus in Engels's *The Condition of the Working Class in England*.[14] Taylor, and especially Engels, went on to consider what impact this fragmentation of the population must have on its ability to form a cohesive, or even stable, society. The two reached very different conclusions about the viability of capitalist industrial society, but nonetheless they had both reached the point of phrasing the question in social terms. What, they asked, given its social organization and resources, is a population of people able or likely to do? In some ways, observers of the development of industry and of urbanization had been working toward the ability to ask that question clearly through the entire industrial revolution. They had been inventing the sociological categories in which to think about the impact of these social changes. They could thus ask about the significance of the reduction of social relations to a cash nexus, or wonder what the impact of fluctuations of trade would be on different sorts of community.[15]

Writers from Cobbett to Coleridge recognized and bemoaned the loss of older self-regulating mechanisms of community, although they tended to attribute rather more, and more recent, vitality to the traditional English community than seems justified. Those who would use "before and after" contrasts of community and dissociation need to have their perspectives broadened, in general by an "elsewhere" criterion. But even traditional or tribal societies do not form an ideal type exemplifying total self-regulation. Beyond the most fleeting of communal experiences,[16] some regulatory mechanisms must be developed. In many tribal societies kinship systems perform this function and may knit together millions of people in some degree. The more innovative the action which a group attempts, however, the more elaborate must be its external or specialized regulatory mechanisms. Its communal nature will be proportionately jeopardized. A corollary of the present definition of community, thus, is that new, ordered, and directed actions will be difficult to sustain for any substantial period of time on the basis of communal bonds alone. Conversely, the ability to alter the order or direction of action is limited by the necessary conservatism of the communal bonds, if any, on which it is founded.

A community, in this usage, is able to pursue only implicit or traditional ends, or to respond to external threats to its ability to follow its traditional way of life. This is important, for from communal bonds comes a great deal of the potential strength of motivation for social action. Different types of social organization yield different capabilities for social action. On the one hand, there is the development of analytic capabilities, and mechanisms for social decision-making and intentional organization. On the other hand, there are the stronger, but less consciously directed, bonds of community, which may provide for much longer-term coordination of social activity. There is a partial contradiction between the focus with which a social aggregate can attack a problem, and the strength and endurance of motivation which underpin its attention.

In a community, the manifold immediate connections among people—social actors—may be quite conscious, but "this does not mean, of course, that each member of a society is conscious of such an abstract notion of unity. It means that he is absorbed in innumerable, specific relations and in the feeling and the knowledge of determining others and of being determined by them."[17] It is largely in these specific relations and determinations that community exists. Clearly, such community cannot everywhere equally obtain, and other mechanisms for social integration must exist, if indeed there is to be any social integration. In a large or dispersed set of people, or one divided into relatively noninteracting subgroups:

mechanisms of association must make up for the loss of community character; techniques of communication will make the wide-range coordination of behavior possible; and administrative machinery will enforce it; and idea systems will sustain the awareness of belonging together which can no longer spring from proximity and familiarity.[18]

The more distant and the less frequently actualized that ties among actors are, the more important external regulations and political power become. Where people are only loosely connected to each other, they may choose, for example, to prolong a conflict or abandon the community which proposes a solution they do not like—unless prevented by material power. The self-regulation of community is dependent on dense, multiplex bonds which force people to accept resolutions to conflicts and give weight to "public opinion."[19] The organization of community is based on particular ties among social actors, even in kin-dominated societies. There is always an imperfect fit between the narrower social field of community and both the formal and informal overall organization of society.

Community, as a pattern of social organization and as a culturally defined way of life, depends on a fairly high degree of stability. The bonds of community are indeed bonds: they tie social actors to each other and to their own pasts. Communal bonds are loaded with the expectations which both actors and the interested public bring to their evaluations of social interaction. These expectations derive from broad cultural rules and both localized and widespread traditions. Thus each social actor develops a reputation and also plays a role. "Tradition," as anthropologists have often noted, is malleable and is not infrequently developed for or adapted to the demands of a new situation by enterprising persons.[20] In seeking consensual validation for their interpretations, they draw upon both broader cultural patterns for the construction of traditions, and upon their own social resources (including, for example, obligations which their fellows may have toward them). The malleability of tradition is, to be sure, wholly relative. It can nowhere be totally absent, or the practices and ideas of communities and societies would become brittle and fail to adapt to changing conditions. On the other hand, where tradition's real links with the past become almost totally lost, it is unlikely to be the source of any enduring consensus. Actual social practice and tradition are constantly interrelated and mutually determining, though the weight of determination may vary.[21]

Community is made up of relationships among social actors, and relations among these relationships. That is, the concept draws our attention to the ways in which specific social actors are linked to each other, and to the aggregate characteristics of these links within a bounded population. This relational level of analysis is basic. It is the foundation upon which discussions of other characteristics of communities must be based; it is the objective aspect of community, which can be analyzed more or less in and of itself, but without which the subjective aspect cannot be understood. I shall now spell out this conceptualization in greater detail.

The Concept Systematically Summarized

There are three orders of communal bonds: those based on familiarity, specific obligations, and diffuse obligations. A relationship may, but need not, be limited to one of the three orders of bonds. All three are generally involved, but in varying proportions, in making any particular community as communal as it may be. Familiarity offers the least indication of community, diffuse obligation the most. The influence of familiarity is great, however, helping even to distinguish the strength of various diffuse obligations. We have a certain investment in the familiar, even when it is not what we might choose. Thus simple frequency of interaction and the built-up familiarity and predictability which it entails can be a major factor in strengthening a social relationship. A more significant, more binding, sort of relationship is that which carries specific obligations. At the first level, both economic interdependence and comembership of formal organizations form this order of bond. Such relationships imply relatively clear and usually clearly stated or contractual obligations between or among their parties. Such relationships may, however, be either more or less a part of a broader system of moral or, in Parsonian language, "diffuse" obligations. Contractual obligations are attendant on the social relationships themselves. Where community pressures enforce the "sanctity of contract," it should be emphasized, this is not a characteristic of the contract but of the membership of its parties in the community. Thus kinship, and in most societies, friendship, are relations identified and sanctioned by public opinion as well as the immediate investment and agreement of the parties. Bonds of kinship and friendship not only link particular parties to each other but involve each specific relationship in a wider network of social relations, in which the whole is governed by more or less commonly accepted principles. They thus provide for long-term social bonds which are not dependent on continuing reactivation for all of their binding force.[22] These are bonds of a quite different order from familiarity or immediate interest.

Here I begin to touch on the matter of relations among relationships, the other dimension of my analysis of community. The general phenomena here are the implication of a wide range of potential actors in the activities of a smaller number and the replication of bonds forged in one context in another. This is crucial to community, and it appears under three aspects. First, there is the relatively simple matter of density.[23] A small-scale local community is likely to have all or most actors directly related to each other in one way or another. The West Riding village of Cleckheaton is shown to have a dense familiarity among its inhabitants in the early nineteenth century by the fact that its children relieved the monotony of repetitive tasks by reciting the names of every inhabitant of the village as they worked.[24] In some very small towns, three or four surnames account for a majority of the inhabitants.

The second important relationship among bonds may be called systematicness or corporateness. This involves the linkage of individuals to social groups, and the ordering of groups in some unifying system of incorporation. Thus, in a segmentary society, kinship will make a person a member of an entire hierarchy of corporate groups, the smaller of which are components of the larger. The actions of an individual member may implicate the whole; accordingly, the corporation has strong powers of coercion over the individual.[25] One effect of such systematicness is to provide social actors with determinate identities. Such identities are constraints on the range of possible actions open to either party in any interaction.

> In the small corporate groups of pre-industrial societies, and in their relationships with one another, disputes between individuals are far more likely to be disruptive to the social fabric than in impersonal, large-scale societies. In part, this is inherently so because of the small numbers, but it is the more so because of the way in which structurally determined partisan commitments spread the effects of what start as individual disputes.[26]

Corporateness thus increases the motivation of a population to settle its internal disputes. Systematicness also involves the existence of common principles which establish and order social relationships. It is thus guaranteed that, as far as such a system is in operation, any set of social actors may readily establish their relationships to each other.

The last of the relations among bonds is that of multiplexity. This refers to the extent to which individuals who are linked in one type of relationship—say kinship—are also linked in other types—co-residence, co-religion, and economic interdependence, for example. Each kind of bond implies another social context in which the same parties are co-actors. The responsibility for meeting the claims of one relationship is enforced by the other strands which also tie its parties together. As Gluckman has noted: "Because men and women in tribal society play so many of their varied purposive roles with the same set of fellows, each action in addition is charged with high moral import."[27] Such "moral import" forces people to look beyond the immediate instrumental considerations which might otherwise determine their actions. The same is true of "those many situations in modern life where we find 'pockets' of social relations which resemble those of tribal society in that there are 'groups' whose members live together in such a way that their relations in one set of roles directly influence their performance of other roles."[28] We might alternatively say that the roles played by people in such multiplex social networks are not fragmented into so many separate social dramas as are those of most of us.[29]

Through bonds of this kind, social actors are knit together into communities. They are not discrete and wholly independent individuals—*homo economicus*—but social persons subject to innumerable constraints on their individual autonomy and in return receiving collective supports. As social persons, their behavior can involve other social persons, involuntarily, in a stream of actions either through interpersonal bonds or as members of corporate groups. For these reasons:

> Communities . . . do not leave their members free to go their own way and explore every possible avenue of behavior. They operate with a set of rules or standards which define appropriate action under a variety of circumstances. The rules, by and large, operate to eliminate conflict of interest by defining what it is people can expect from certain of their fellows. This has the healthy effect of limiting demands and allowing the public to judge performance.[30]

It is in this sense, as well as in that of accumulated esoterica and personal familiarity, that the community is a culturally defined way of life. It holds its members to a set of rules and standards which allow them the intensity of their interaction. These norms may also govern patterns of consumption and production in favor of longer-term continuity, like a far more effective "invisible hand" than any which has ruled since "laissez-faire" became self-conscious theory or policy.

Community and Authority

A central question regarding community life is that of how obedience to rules and standards is enforced when social pressure proves inadequate. A corollary to this question asks how changes in communal life and public opinion are collectively legitimated. I have stressed in my preceding discussion the relative absence of specialized agencies of coercion or regulation in communities. That is, there are no independent chiefs or bureaucracies capable of enforcing laws or announcing changes in them. When these are absent, however, there must be some method for expressing communal opinion. In tribal societies, such mechanisms, particularly divination, are often bound up with ancestor worship. Reverence for ancestors expresses reverence for the community, as ancestors symbolically represent lines of collective affiliation in lineage-structured societies. The ancestors are made the repositories of authority over the affairs of the living, but evidence of the supernatural power of ancestors can only be had after the fact, generally through divination. In divination, though the diviner himself may command a certain amount of respect, he must generally produce a divination which is in accord with the general body of public opinion and the normal pattern of divination, if his report is to be accepted. Failing this, he or other diviners may be asked to repeat the entreaty to the spiritual world until the signs offered are in accord with present social constraints and standards. In other words, the ancestors have all formal authority but no intentional power. They "act" to express the will of the community, and thus act with a great deal of moral and social strength.[31] But the range of possible actions which the ancestors may sanction is limited; ancestral authority cannot readily be used to support a new concerted collective action, but may order the activity of the members of a community over extended periods of time and sanction the defense of this social order.

We may understand the notion of "moral economy" in a similar sense.[32] E. P. Thompson, as we saw, brought this notion into currency to refer to the slowly evolved but carefully maintained community consensus on many fundamental issues which ordered and legitimated responses to the disruption of the community's way of life. Thus, food riots in preindustrial England were not blind or instinctive responses of base and hungry creatures. They were indeed responses to crises, but:

> The men and women in the crowd were informed by the belief that they were defending traditional rights or customs: and, in general, that they were supported by the wider consensus of the community. On occasion this popular consensus was endorsed by some measure of license afforded by the authorities. More commonly, the consensus was so strong that it overrode motives of fear or deference.[33]

Two particularly interesting questions are raised by this passage. One involves the relationship of authority to power in community life; the other concerns the relationship among community, consensus, and the taking of collective action.

Authority is not the same as power; those who speak with authority may speak also with a varying proportion of private or sectional motives and a varying amount of power.[34] It is communal consensus as to what is right which confirms the voice of authority. In a society as complex as pre- and early industrial England, no population was wholly self-contained and thus a perfect example of my model of community. In varying degrees on different dimensions, population aggregates were communally organized. But the nature of those aggregates was changing. Further, England was not organized on a single monistic principle, in which a single hierarchy ordered social relations at all levels, with aggregates at each level discretely added together to form those at the next higher level. On the contrary, even in eighteenth-century England, members of the gentry can be seen to have been at once members of local communities and members of the broader but no less influential and binding communities of county society and landed society in general. During the industrial revolution, these people were increasingly removed from the dense, multiplex, and systematic bonds of local communities. It was part of the emergence of class structure that communities of workers and communities of various elites were formed in separation from and often in opposition to each other.

It was in the countryside that traditional patterns of authority continued to function longest. In industrial villages and in small town and urban communities of artisans and outworkers, there were no substantial resident, especially not gentry, authorities. These artisans and outworkers were much more significantly autonomous as communities of workers than any other nonelite grouping, and they were thus much more capable of concerted collective action. In the new industrial towns, workers of relatively low skill tended often to be so disorganized that they had relatively little community. In some cases there, and quite often in the villages dominated by a single factory, they were under the direct and active control of manufacturers, especially in the workplace but also out of it. The remainder of this chapter will take up the traditional system of community-level authority, its decline, and the beginnings of its transformation in some detail. I shall treat of the relationships between community and collective action more briefly, as they are taken up in considerable detail throughout the rest of this work.

Traditional Authority in Local Communities

The basic criterion for authority in rural England was the ownership of land. Landowners could be divided into the somewhat indistinct gradations of small holders, lesser and greater gentry, and aristocracy.[35] For all levels in this hierarchy the family was more important than the individual. The family, which was involved as a unit of property holding and a frame of social reference, grew broader in genealogical scope as one moved up the social scale. Though the amount of land owned was preeminently important in distinguishing the ranks of the farmers, gentry, and aristocracy, it was not exclusively so. Various qualities of character, the length of attachment to a given estate or community, and even personal choice were all significant.[36] In the last instance, acceptance by the community determined a claim. There was a scale of deference and prestige which governed not only relations between landowners and everyone else but also structured relations among members of the almost infinitely graded groupings on each side of that great divide. Just as an aristocrat might look down on a somewhat wealthier man because of his bearing, breeding, or the source of his wealth, so a "mechanic" in one of the most respectable trades might look down on an upstart master who was getting rich by employing nonapprenticed labor and by adopting quality-cutting methods. A remarkable characteristic of the years before the 1790s is the extent to which everyone of a given level in the hierarchy knew on whom they should look down and to whom they should defer.

This knowledge was dependent on a localism of attitude and a relatively low rate of geographical mobility and social change. Although it was weakened throughout the eighteenth century, it was only in the nineteenth that it was disrupted in ways from which it could not recover. The stability on which familiarity with the social positions of oneself and others was founded is difficult to quantify. Even the rate of emigration from rural communities in the second half of the eighteenth century is uncertain, though it was not inconsiderable.[37] This was primarily a loss of laborers drawn into manufacturing occupations, and in particular drawn from villages undergoing enclosure or other forms of improvement which alienated small farmers from their land and made laborers more susceptible to cyclical, including seasonal, unemployment. The differentiation of status among landless laborers was about as low as that among any aggregate of the population before the great increase in the ranks of the rural poor. It was certainly much less than that among factory workers, whom Marx expected to see reduced to a complete objective commonality of position. The gentry would appear to have been less mobile, even into the later nineteenth century. Almost all Justices of the Peace in southeast Lancashire appear to have served for most of their lives and southeast Lancashire's overall rate of mobility was high. If they, or other gentry, left, it was usually to go to another family estate—somewhere where their place in society would be fairly clear. The overall stability of the deference system in rural communities would seem to have been very gradually weakening since the end of the seventeenth century.[38] Laslett describes the enduring mesh of agrarian relations in that period as follows: "a labourer, or a craftsman, a cottager or even a lowly husbandman could very well have been a servant in one of the larger houses in the locality, and his sons and daughters might in fact be in that position at the same time. Each of them might well have to look to those same substantial householders for a day's work all his life."[39] People knew as a matter of course which families were which, what property they owned, and who was the eldest son—not to mention a variety of more esoteric lore. As Foster notes, one of the effects of this knowledge was to minimize the formation of an autonomous labor community: "Instead of allowing labour to develop its own 'solution'—its own subcultures—the Puritan household attempted to eliminate the tension at source: to bind the worker so tightly into the cultural group of the employer that any consciousness of a loss of control was minimized."[40]

Localism also narrowed the range of phenomena with which people felt it necessary or found it possible to concern themselves. Whether by choice or not, most members of the gentry and almost all of those below them were unable to influence national affairs directly. Their influence was likely to be small even in the restricted field of the county (though in this regard it grew during the nineteenth century). Although they owned a larger total share of the land than the aristocrats, they owned it in much smaller lots. The very expense of contesting an election—which routinely ran into the thousands of pounds—put Parliament beyond their reach unless they were patronized by one of the great political families.[41] This was the general mode of their integration into national affairs: patronage. While the higher ranks might contest the right to govern the country, the lesser gentry were more concerned with their own communities—if indeed they had any political ambitions at all. They were most likely to become justices of the peace, an office which grew in both number of occupants and importance during the course of the late eighteenth and early nineteenth centuries.[42] They were also voters, of course, but as such they primarily possessed the right to choose among the candidates put forward by the great landowners at infrequent elections. They seem very much to have followed the lead of their patrons, those to whom they owed deference and from whom they might feel they could claim favors.[43] Personal ties to members of the elite were the way in which the gentry secured favors both for themselves and for those who, yet lower in the scale, owed them deference. It was therefore not merely a matter of habit or affection but also one of interest to vote for those with whom they had some personal bond. These bonds grew primarily out of proximity and kinship among the landed, and were reinforced by generations of reciprocity, deference in return for paternalism.

At an increasing rate, this reciprocity was forfeited during the industrial and agricultural revolutions; with it went the bonds of authority and community between the landed elite and those who worked on their estates. A variety of factors contributed to this deterioration of bonds of community across the levels of the social hierarchy: the accelerated building of great houses, the increasing proportion of absentee landlords, the growing importance of clerical (and thus nonnative) magistrates, and the centralization of landholdings. Perhaps nothing was more important than the simple increase in scale of local populations, especially those which turned to outwork or factories. Industrial discipline itself became increasingly impersonal in part for the same reason. The traditional authorities felt themselves under increasing pressure. They and other people of similar rank were threatened from three directions. First, the great landowners above them were transforming agriculture into a capitalist industry much more dependent than before on changes in technique and capital improvements. Second, outsiders to the traditional hierarchy and local community were gaining in importance; first middlemen and engrossers and then tenant farmers and factory owners upset the local social balance and, in the case of the latter, produced "great blots on the beauteous landscape." Last, but emphatically not least, were the occasionally insurgent poor. As local authorities proved less and less able to help the poor find meliorations or solutions to their complaints, would-be paternally benevolent landlords came increasingly to fear for the security of their own property. They were not sure that outbreaks of popular violence would remain limited to middlemen and innovators. Although the landed gentry liked to think of themselves, not entirely unreasonably, as in harmony with the lower ranks of their vicinity, they were in fact becoming more and more estranged from them. As the lowest level of the rural hierarchy was swollen with an increasing number of landless laborers and small farmers—the former "sturdy yeomen of England"—what continuity there had been across ranks was broken. Workers might be knit into local communities, but local landowners were increasingly excluded.

This is the inverse of the observation of the Hammonds, that the poor were becoming isolated.[44] The Hammonds are indeed correct, if one is considering isolation from the center of political life, and from the traditional welfare system which gave the English economy some of its semblance of humanity. But the reverse is equally true, for as the pageantry of the Queen Caroline agitation and the incendiarism of the "last laborers' revolt" were to show, the local representatives of traditional authority were estranged and isolated from the poor. A solitary magistrate on his estate might feel very vulnerable indeed, without the protective bonds of community and the soothing lubricant of deference. In a community in which such authority is respected, for anyone to fail to follow it will bring repercussions throughout the network of multiplex personal relations. To fail to follow authority is to fail to maintain one's place in the web of social relations of which it is a part. But clearly, even in the years before English industrialization, it was necessary on occasion to back up the word of authority with economic sanctions and public bloodshed—in other words, with power. The local "authorities" were not always voicing the consensus of the community, and the implicit sanctions were not always working.

There are, of course, always exceptions to the rule of authority; man is not completely socialized. No society is so completely free of contradictions, either, that the breaking of customary rules is not normal and does not require the active exercise of power if it is to be kept in check. Authority is, however, weakest at the joints of corporate or communal organization. It is, crudely, when those who are most socially important to an individual support his violation of authority that power is most likely to be necessary. Feuds thus occur in ancestor-worshipping societies, despite the existence of overarching common authority. Similarly, crises of authority occur where counterbalancing and cross-cutting ties are absent or weak and a social split develops in what had hitherto been a more unified community. Such a crisis of authority is what made for the extension of the death penalty and then the campaign for reform of the criminal justice system in late eighteenth- and early nineteenth-century England.[45] Resistance to the rule of law was not new, but it was intensified, and the traditional bridges across the "ranks" of society became increasingly hard to maintain. As Hay has described the eighteenth century:

> The fabric of authority was torn and reknit constantly. The important fact remains, however, that it was reknit readily. The closer mesh of economic and social ties in rural society, the public nature of those relationships compared to the complexity and obscurity of much metropolitan life, allowed the creation of an ideology that was much more pervasive than in London.[46]

In the nineteenth century, many of the landowners on whom the traditional system of authority depended, worked to maintain their political positions at the expense of close ties to their communities.[47] Perhaps more importantly, the proportion of the total population which lived in the more traditional communities shrank rapidly, if unevenly. In the new industrial districts new ties had to be formed; traditional communal bonds did not support an established system of authority, and before a new paternalism was forged (to the extent it ever was) power was especially important.

The gentry were perhaps more interested in the security of the traditional system of authority than any other group, and worked longer and harder to preserve it. It was this security which had allowed them to develop their farms and their local communities over the course of innumerable generations.

> The long continuity of many gentry, and of some yeomen too, gave to their districts a degree of permanence and a stable base to society and so helped to create the sense of a real county community.
> ...This sense of community had no small influence on the independence of provincial opinion and local freedom of action, and played a major part in the varying reaction of the counties to the series of crises stemming from the Great Rebellion.[48]

The gentry were, thus, able to maintain a degree of independence from the great families through their local communities—for a time. They were also more able than lesser farmers to resist the inroads of industrialization and, indeed, less likely than the Whig families to become a part of it through investment, marriage, friendship, or direct participation.[49] They maintained their independence, some of them, and fought for a long time the battle of "the true conservatives" and on occasion of "the Tory Radicals" against the merely wealthy: "much of the long rearguard action fought against the modernising, centralising and standardising tendencies of national legislation was inspired by the old tradition of local independence among the country gentry and their sympathisers in the provincial towns. It was an action doomed to eventual failure."[50]

In the long run, despite their initial closeness to yeomen and to local communities, the gentry were assimilated for the most part into the aristocracy. Like the great families, they began to interpose professional managers between themselves and their estates (and thus between themselves and those who worked for or near them). They had become a smaller proportion of the English population but remained a privileged group. The main period of their transformation came in the middle third of the nineteenth century. With the innovation of paid managers, "deference to the gentry might remain," but "the roots of deference in a personally administered paternalism were being snapped."[51]

Deference and paternalism were the forms of social interaction which expressed the relationship of people at different levels in the traditional hierarchy of authority. Concern for the poor was considered important as one of the qualities of a gentleman and as an element of his political good sense: "In general, concern for the well-being of the propertyless poor, who were directly or indirectly his dependents, was as much a part of the character of the landed gentleman as it was an essential element in the structure of the deference society."[52] Nonetheless, this concern became less prevalent and less practicable. The increasing scale of agriculture made this so as it increased the proportion of laborers. Paternalism might be a planned characteristic of the well-run estate—as it was of the well-run factory under an Owen or Wedgwood—but that was not the same as the paternalism-deference relationship held "from time immemorial" and carried on in generation after generation. And it was not the same when transmitted through an intermediary servant of the landowner, such as his steward, instead of through the personal interactions of the principals.

Throughout the eighteenth and nineteenth centuries, those who expected and commended deference bemoaned the fact that they were not getting it—at least not in the quantity and quality they expected. It was only after the Reform Act, however, that it became common to link this absence of deference to a failure of paternalism. In Disraeli's famous words: "if that principle of duty had not been lost sight of for the last fifty years, you would never have heard of the classes into which England is divided." As Thornton has observed, there is in such lines an echo of Cobbett.[53] It is worth remembering how much Cobbett spoke for, as well as from, the position of the small farmer. This makes his turnabout from Tory to radical more comprehensible—it was not as much of a turnabout as it seemed. In 1844, Howitt, writing rather rhapsodically of the country life, quotes Cobbett freely, with none of the sense of danger which impelled the magistrates in Manchester to keep the publisher of the *Political Register* out of the town on his return from America twenty years earlier. Ironically, perhaps, Howitt—by no means a radical but living in a different age—is able to reprove Cobbett for his conservatism in suggesting that "the farmer has been spoiled by the growth of luxurious habits and effeminacy in the nation." Cobbett's disdain for pianos in rural parlors, daughters at boarding school, and sons who become clerks instead of sturdy husbandmen is given a brief rebuke: "it should be recollected that Cobbett was opposed to popular education altogether. He would have the rural population physically well off, but it should be physically only." Howitt reminds his readers of the nobility and humanity of "partaking, as far as their circumstances will allow them, of the pleasures of the mind."[54]

Local Authority in Transition

In the mid-eighteenth century, the local gentry had had a considerable degree of independence in managing the public affairs of their own vicinities.

The social leadership of the squires was matched by their administrative and political predominance. It was the strength of the landowner's control of local government in the counties which gave him
his self-confident independence. It is an error to think of local government in 1760 as a subordinate authority operating within defined
limits. On the contrary, the effective government of England was, as
far as concerned everyday things, conducted on a county or
borough basis with little interference from London.[55]

Things began to change in the 1790s, but by the 1830s local authorities
were still very jealous of their traditional rights.[56] The members of the
gentry were, as I have suggested, bound with ties of deference to greater
landowners, but they were not functionaries. Increasingly, in the early
nineteenth century, the local authorities became bound to the government and the crown, particularly where matters of public order were
concerned.[57] This was one of the most significant manifestations of the
tendency toward centralization which was strong during the period of
the industrial revolution.

Throughout the late eighteenth and early nineteenth centuries, the
primary local authorities were the justices of the peace. The lord-
lieutenant of each county was in theory the representative of the central
government, but a predominant family's claim on the office was difficult to resist. The lord-lieutenant was either nominally or in practice
the head of the justices. The other local offices were high sheriff (a royal
appointee whose importance had waned), coroner (elected by free-
holders—a post of little prestige but a good deal of profit), and high
constable (in effect an agent of the justices).[58] As long as there was local
rural and village authority, it was the justices who represented it. From
the late eighteenth century, solitary magistrates had administered
summary judgment on such matters as infractions of the game laws.
Sitting together, the justices constituted the Courts of Quarter Sessions,
which were

> genuine legislatures engaged in building up from quarter to quarter
> a new code of law under the pretext of interpreting the old. In this
> capacity they put together during the last years of the eighteenth
> century a complete poor law, first in one county, then in another,
> acting on their own initiative, without any interference by the cen-
> tral government.[59]

Centralization of the economy and anomalies magnified by growth
made this system of local authority increasingly untenable. It was, by
the early nineteenth century, a considerable problem to have different
rulings on such matters as relations between masters and men, since
industry did not have to remain within the bounds of local authority

but could pick up and move to more hospitable locales. The un-incorporated towns and industrial villages had no local authorities of their own under the traditional system and so were dependent on the county magistracy.[60] The squirearchy was neither interested in and familiar with the problems of industry nor prepared to act with the initiative required by constantly and rapidly changing circumstances.

> The reaction against the extra-legal autocratic oligarchy which had been established in the county government was dramatic in its sud-denness. The uncontrolled power of the Rulers of the County stood, in 1815, unchallenged either by Parliament or by public opinion. By 1835 the Justices had forfeited a great part of their administrative functions.[61]

The Webbs reveal their own biases in the passage just quoted. Their policy proposals, like most which have come from the British left, called for great centralization. The question they ask (with mixed won-der and annoyance) at the end of their first volume is that of why the justices survived.[62] Yet, one of the features which distinguished Brit-ain's early reactionary radicals from the later predominant tendency of the left was a steadfast opposition to centralization of govern-ment. In this they were very close indeed to the local Tories, if not always to the parliamentary party of that name. In any case, the Webbs were more or less preoccupied with legislation, and therefore tended to equate the legal status of the magistracy with actual practice. In fact, as we shall see, a number of factors worked informally to weaken the autonomy of the justices, most especially their own helplessness. This feeling of helplessness—whether due to real danger or paranoia—caused them to call on the central authorities for aid or even advice, which the authorities were frequently unwilling to provide. The numerous exchanges of letters between the local magistrates in "dis-turbed areas" and the Home Office regarding disturbances in these years is ample evidence of the growing involvement of the state in local affairs.[63]

Since 1732 the property qualification for the Commission of the Peace had been £100. This was enough to bar the mass of the popula-tion, but in fact the real criteria of respect and family position tended to place justices somewhat higher in the social hierarchy than property qualification alone would suggest.[64] Still, the majority were squires and members of the lesser gentry. In particular, these were the classes likely (along with, and occasionally overlapping with, the increasing numbers of the clergy) to make up the minority of active justices.[65] Those of much higher rank and civic ambitions (or sense of re-sponsibility) might be admitted to the Commission, but they did their main work more often in Westminster than on the local scene. The justices were responsible for appointing all the administrative officers of their parishes—the most important of which were commissioners for poor-law administration and various local improvements. The parish vestry was the only surviving unit of government with popular meetings. Although it had no direct control over the administration of the parish, it could raise complaints or reinforce decisions of the justices. Its accessibility made it a likely target for struggles between workers and manufacturers in the developing industrial towns.[66] The vestry system worked at its best in country villages where the more or less consensually recognized leaders were the ones to consider the activities of the justices. In doing so, they were evaluating the performance of men who were their personal acquaintances and approximate social equals. In a town like Manchester, on the other hand, with its confused administration and overgrown population, the vestry did not even check the accounts of officials.[67]

> Devoid of instructions or guidance from London, local authorities were left to handle their individual problems as best they could. It is not surprising that the tendency of the more articulate reformers to gravitate toward London, together with the absences of adequate channels through which the new urban population could make their aspirations known, permitted the traditional oligarchies that controlled local government to fulfill their limited objectives before attempting to satisfy the basic needs of the community at large. Endowed with the economic and administrative means to undertake effective planning, the urban middle class did not hesitate to sacrifice the community interest to its own.[68]

Until civic reform began quite late in the first third of the nineteenth century, Manchester was appealing annually (and successfully) for a renewal of an act of Parliament for the lighting, watching, and cleaning of the town and the ability to administer a police tax. All of these and various other similar efforts were administered by commissioners from among the boroughreeve, constables, warden, and fellows of the Collegiate Church, together with owners and occupiers paying rents of £30 a year.[69] When instructions of any sort came from the central government, they were usually concerned with public order, not with matters of ordinary local administration. As Vigier observes, however, when the means for efficient action were available, there was no guarantee that this action would be in the public interest. Although the middle class early identified its own interest as being the national interest, where there were conflicts it was quite likely to choose the former over the latter. This did not radically distinguish it from the country gentry.

The difference was that the changes which were disrupting England were in the interests of the middle class far more than in those of the gentry.

It should be borne in mind that these formally vested officers had no monopoly on authority but were rather representatives of a system of authority. This system designated some people as more authoritative than others in a relative, not a static, fashion. To say that the system did not define a class is not to minimize the extent of hierarchical privilege or to deny oppression and exploitation. It is to indicate that no single collectivity was at issue. Public opinion was the sanction of authority, and the relevant public was a variable matter—a matter of community. Public opinion by no means always referred to majority opinion; influence was very differentially distributed. But at no level of the hierarchy could those in official positions act in contradiction to the will of the public (be it a majority or a considerable minority of the affected population) for very long.[70] In country villages, those who held positions of authority held them more or less on the sufferance of their friends and neighbors—and held them largely to gain the respect of their friends and neighbors as well as for the common good.

With such a community feeling among those eligible for participation in political affairs, most men of the higher ranks saw little reason to seek public office. This was true on occasion of gentlemen and more often of the middle classes; as public offices were onerous and often costly duties, they were not only not sought but actively avoided.[71] So much did the Manchester bourgeoisie crave exemption from some of these civic duties that bogus records of felonious criminal activity—Tyburn tickets—were sold on the open market in order that their purchasers might be declared ineligible. The going price in Manchester in 1816 is reported to have been £350−400 while in London Tyburn tickets cost only £23.[72] In the country, justices were also likely to be out of pocket more than the 4d daily expenses allotted them, but the respect the position entailed kept applicants prepared to meet the cost.[73] The country gentry considered amateurism in politics and public affairs desirable, at both local and national levels. It was an indication that officials would remain bound to the interests of their communities rather than become independent seekers after private gain.[74] For the middle classes to opt out of public affairs was to leave the field open to professional politicians—and simultaneously indicated the unworthiness of the middle classes for involvement in political affairs.

Despite the widespread agreement among those high in the scale of deference as to essentials of local government, and despite the considerable social pressures which could be used to produce consensus and persuade officials, there were conflicts. There were disputes among officials over jurisdiction and among local authorities over policies. There were on occasion localized versions of the national rivalries among Whigs, Tories, and other more ephemeral ideological groupings and political factions. Not least of all, "Property-owners might present a united front against the pretensions of the propertyless, but this did not prevent them from fighting over property among themselves."[75] A stable society need not be free of conflicts. What it requires is that conflicts not follow the lines of structural cleavages without counterbalancing commonality. This they did not do under the system of traditional authority before the 1790s.

The division of a hierarchy into ranks and degrees, as opposed to classes, was not an arbitrary linguistic convention, to be altered as an autonomous shift of consciousness.[76] Rather, it reflected the existence of bonds which bound people across the levels of the hierarchy, in daily interaction and both specific and diffuse obligations. This system of interhierarchical bonds was eroding through the eighteenth century and was disrupted with accelerating pace in the nineteenth. Small landowners declined as an identifiable part of the population.[77] The gentry were drawn together with the aristocracy to form a landed interest which largely excluded mere farmers and what were once called yeomen and squires.[78] Both William Cobbett and Henry Hunt identified themselves with this disappearing station in life.

A good many of the country magistrates fought to preserve the passing way of life with which they had grown up. In the struggle they shared a common interest with the skilled workers and agricultural laborers of the villages in their vicinity. They had very little ability to act directly against disrupting influences; their authority was responsive, not intiative. On occasion, though, they did intervene to fix wage rates and more often allowed "the common people" to protest food prices or bargain for wages by rioting. With this consideration, we may return to E. P. Thompson's evocation of the notion of the "moral economy," seeing in it not only an ideological value but a part of a traditional way of life based on community and authority rather than discrete and instrumental relations and power:

> the final years of the eighteenth century saw a last desperate effort by the people to reimpose the older moral economy as against the economy of the free-market. In this they received some support from old-fashioned J.P.s, who threatened to prosecute forestallers, tightened controls over markets, or issued proclamations against engrossers who bought up growing corn in the fields.[79]

Some magistrates, of a more "modern" sort, attempted to impose order on communities by external agency. They were not a part of the

same communities as the common people, and so could not be a part of
the self-regulation of integrated communities. The traditional magistrates who opposed the encroachments of market relations frequently
tolerated or encouraged the actions of crowds against grain dealers and
other middlemen. This sort of authority, however, allowed magistrates
to give license rather more than to take action. As defenders of a way of
life and a set of values, they might implicitly or explicitly approve of
actions against middlemen, but they had little or no power to move
against these engrossers and forestallers themselves. To the extent that
the role of the middlemen and other shifts in the relations of production were new, the magistrates were made ineffective by the very conservatism of their own authority. They were slow to realize the threat to
their way of life, and slower still to adopt "popular" solutions, but this
can only partly be attributed to personal failings. The intrinsic limitations of authority were also involved:

> As a regulatory capacity, authority is legitimated and identified by
> the rules, traditions, and precedents which embody it and which
> govern its exercise and objects. Power is also regulatory, but is
> neither fully prescribed nor governed by norms and rules. Whereas
> authority presumes and expresses normative consensus, power is
> most evident in conflict and contraposition where dissensus
> obtains.[80]

Such power as the magistrates had came from the central government,
and this put them in an ambivalent position. On the one hand, their
authority depended on their status in the local community and the
congruence of their activities with public opinion. On the other hand,
their power obliged them to represent interests sometimes contrary to
those of their local communities.[81]

On the local level, the authority of magistrates enabled them to carry
out proceedings which were backed by the apparent opinion of the
community. In general, this meant proceedings against particular individuals who transgressed against the laws. The community might
either support the specific laws or at least the general right of king and
Parliament to establish such laws and magistrates to enforce them. This
did not necessarily mean that the community members individually
felt compelled to follow these laws.[82] Unpopular laws (or interpretations of the law), moreover, might engender opposition as well as
disobedience. Herein entered the difficulty. To put down popular opposition always meant to act against the community, not simply against
members of the community. It made it obvious that, far from being
representatives of the community, and of public opinion, the magistrates were acting on behalf of external interests and were using exter-

nal powers. Magistrates were increasingly called upon to enforce certain abstract rights (such as that of selling commodities at the price one chooses) against the weight of custom. Not infrequently a large domestic army was needed to back up the magistrates as they attempted to enforce laws which lacked authority in local communities.[83]

The crucial issue here is the breakdown of the structure of hierarchical incorporation which knit local communities into the society as a whole. The authority of the law in the eighteenth century was maintained in part by the collaboration of the interlinked levels. Thus suspects might be apprehended locally, tried by visiting justices (representing national authority), and convicted. After conviction, local authorities might petition regional or national ones in order to obtain a commutation of the sentence by royal mercy.[84] In this way, local notables both upheld the law and alleviated the sufferings of the members of the community (upon the satisfaction of certain criteria of worthiness, not the least of which was being well-integrated into the web of social relations). In the course of thus managing the ambiguity of their position, they were able to demonstrate to the locals that they had the ear of people at court (either directly or indirectly). Such a process still obtains at a local level and within many institutions. Nationally, it is attenuated beyond all recognition. If one writes to one's MP to get a wrong redressed, one generally writes as just a "constituent," not as someone "personally very well known to . . ."—a standard eighteenth- and nineteenth-century locution. Other "rationalized" mechanisms have taken the place of personal connections in accomplishing most transactions between local and national levels (though of course one's standing in the social hierarchy may influence the performance of bureaucrats). During the period of the industrial revolution, however, the older hierarchical organization of authority underwent its crisis without an effective substitute being provided. This is one of the factors which caused community to be reorganized along class lines in Britain.[85]

Community and Collective Action

As the fissure of class distinction began more and more to be recognized, and as demographic and other factors made self-regulating working-class communities possible, the identification of the bonds of community shifted. The corporate system into which people were most strongly linked was confined within the major lines of class. Friendly societies, trade unions, and political unions linked workers primarily to each other. At the same time, the growth of working-class collective action depended on the social integration of working-class communities.[86] Protest movements before the 1820s and 1830s did not depend to any significant extent on formal organizations. Such formal bodies as there were generally added a dimension of increased organization to social bonds which went on both before and after them. The radicals were linked to each other by kinship and personal friendship, as neighbors and co-workers. Their political mobilizations followed these lines; they were not distinct from them.

The result of this was that strong communities were in the best position to launch political or economic protests. These communities were of two sorts. First, there were relatively small, homogeneous towns and villages where simple propinquity helped to ensure frequent interaction, and small size led to greater density and multiplexity of bonds. These were the communities, for example, which preponderated in Luddite disturbances, especially in Nottinghamshire and the West Riding of Yorkshire. Second, there were communities of urban artisans, in which common craft and workplace were at least as important as propinquity and often more so.[87] Eventually, some of these artisans formed a community based largely on political opinion, one that crossed craft line. Leaders like Gast of the Thames shipwrights worked together with printers, journalists, and full-time activists in a community of largely self-educated London radicals.[88] Those for whom political allegiances became a primary source of community bonds remained, however, a minority and in most cases an elite. For most of the artisans, their first loyalty was to their craft and to the associations which occasionally formalized its cohesion: benefit societies, trade societies, reading clubs, and local pubs.

The significance and strength of the relationship between community and collective action suggested in the preceding paragraph may not be entirely clear. I shall therefore set it out more fully. The central issue is, under what circumstances is a given population aggregate likely to mobilize for collective action? Secondarily, what sort of action is it likely to sustain? For purposes of the present discussion, we may conveniently assume that all collectivities under consideration have equal "objective" reasons for taking action. Thus, confining ourselves to revolutionary or radical action, all the collectivities have equal complaints of poverty, disenfranchisement, and so on.[89] What happens?

Marx, it will be recalled, argued that the concentration of workers in large factories and urban areas increased the chances of successful revolution, by increasing the interconnectedness of the workers and their consciousness of themselves as a class.[90] I have already defined community in such a way that it may be taken as a continuously variable measure of interconnectedness. In my contention that Marx was wrong, one critical issue is why such community bonds were unlikely to preponderate among members of the urban working class. Had they preponderated, then it would have been more plausible to hold, with Marx, that the working class would achieve solidarity through its social being and become subjectively capable of concerted collective action. The reasons for the absence of bonds, however, are very largely formal, not merely contingent on particularities of historical circumstance. The most important of those reasons may be termed the argument from size.

This argument is simple, but within the limits of its formalism quite strong.[91] Its basic question is, How does group size affect the structuration of interaction within a group and between the members of different groups? If one works with the assumption of a random propensity for people to relate to each other, for example, it is obvious that the density of relationships is a declining function of size. The more people within a population aggregate, the less likely that any one of them will be related to any other, or set of others, and the smaller will be the proportion of total possible relationships actualized. Not only does net density decline, but its evenness declines. It follows from the assumption of random interaction or relationship that, the larger a group, the more likely it is to be subdivided into clusters. These clusters of relationships are likely to occur, given random interaction; where people's relations with each other are shaped by various structural patterns which encourage in-group association—e.g., sharing a place of work—the tendency is intensified.

This has three important implications. First, the larger a population aggregate, the more likely it is to depend on intermediate levels of association in order to act collectively; if it lacks such intermediate levels, or if they seek purposes conflicting with those desirable for the largest aggregate, that largest aggregate loses its capacity to act.[92] More specifically, for workers to be organized for class action requires a hierarchy of intermediate foci of association, each incorporating those below it. Without such intermediate associations, the possibility of class action is replaced by, at most, the simultaneous action of a number of mobs sharing common external characteristics. If the intermediate associations collectively act toward other goals than those of the class, these goals, whether or not they actually conflict, will divert attention and resources from the class as a whole, and its capacity for collective action is correspondingly reduced. A large potential collective actor, therefore, such as a class, must be internally differentiated into groups of such a size that their members may be fairly closely knit with each other; for the class rather than the groups to be the relevant locus of collective action, the different subgroups must be linked together in such a way that they are cohesive at the highest level. For class action to take place, the component units of the class, such as communities and crafts, must be strong, but their in-group association must not so completely predominate over their affiliation with other groups that they are not densely knit into a web of class relations. During the early nineteenth century, English workers attempting class action ran into problems on this score, not only with craft exclusiveness, which has often enough been noted, but with the inability to effectively transcend local community bonds. Thus the Luddites were strong in their communities but were unable to mount concerted action even regionally, let alone as a national working class, however political their "motives" might have been.[93] Similarly, the Pentridge rebels were duped by Oliver the spy into believing they had the backing of a national rising, information they would have doubted if they had had strong social relationships beyond their immediate vicinity; the Blanketeers in Lancashire marched with increasingly despairing expectations of being met by fellow rebels at each turn of the road; and so forth. The limits of an account which stresses motives or attitudes at the expense of social structure are obvious.

The second major implication of the clustering of relationships within large populations concerns variations in the extent of relationship across group boundaries as these affect individual groups. Briefly, if a population is divided into two groups of unequal size, any given rate of relationship across their boundaries will be proportionately greater for the smaller group. If a West Riding village, for example, were to contain two hundred weavers and ten shopkeepers, and there were fifty relationships (of some specific sort, e.g., personal friendship) across group lines, then there would be a mean of five relationships per shopkeeper and 0.25 per weaver. In a village dominated by weavers, thus, but having also several coalminers, shopkeepers, and others, the latter groups would be much more densely tied to the weavers than the weavers would be to them. This factor was of considerable importance in securing community-wide concertedness of action in villages and small towns during the industrial revolution.

Thirdly, clustering has an impact on power and control within groups. Just as it is formally demonstrable that, given random interrelatedness, the density of bonds, and hence presumably the likeliness to participate in collective action, is a decreasing function of group size, so, conversely, is the narrowness of oligarchic control an increasing function of size. This has important implications for both the argument concerning the role of labor aristocracy in defusing a potential English popular revolution and the nature of organization for collective action among such large groups as classes. Contrary to Marx's expectations, the larger a collectivity, the more concentration of power is likely within it.[94] Moreover, if the proportionate size of the lowest strata in a collectivity increases at the expense of the highest, net inequality within the total collectivity increases.[95] While this is in accord with Marx's expectation of a growing concentration of wealth within capitalist society as a whole, it raises the initially unexamined problem that a privileged stratum is formally likely to emerge within the working class. This came to be seen as the problem of the labor aristocracy, the interests of which diverge from those of the rest of the working class.

Is working-class action likely to be organized by a relatively narrow elite, or is it likely to be the direct action of the mass of workers? The argument from size indicates that the former is much more likely. To the extent that the working population in question is a class only, is defined externally by common position in the relations of production, and is thus viewed as made up of individuals,[96] it shows an overwhelming vulnerability to oligarchical control. This control may take several forms. Michels's notion of the "iron law of oligarchy" is the most famous.[97] Leninist substitutionism is formally similar. The vulnerability of large, minimally differentiated crowds to demagogic leadership is another version. During the early nineteenth century, whenever popular activity extended beyond the local community and craft level, demagogues tended to intervene as the only means of leadership. The alternative—formal organization—did not begin in a significant way until the 1820s and especially the 1830s. Formal organization does not in itself solve the problem of oligarchic control. What it generally does, and for the most part began to do in England in the middle third of the nineteenth century, is to replace independent demagogues with those who can run the organizations. During the Chartist period these people were still often charismatic figures, for the organizations were not yet strong enough to stand wholly on their own. The Chartist leaders had to combine the fiery oratory of Henry Hunt with the more bureaucratic skills which would predominate in trade unionism. The tendency toward oligarchy is mitigated primarily by strong intermediate associations. A union, for example, with strong regional and local organization may be seen on the national level as composed of subgroups, not individuals. The number of actors is the formal underpinning of the push toward oligarchy; such corporate actors as local branches are necessarily fewer than are individuals.

In short, for an entire class, or even any very large proportion of one, to be mobilized for collective action, a hierarchy of intermediate-level associations is necessary to steer the mobilization between the extremes of autocracy and complete disorganization. Such intermediate associations may be local communities, specific craft groupings, or component segments of national formal organizations. In the last case, however, it is important that such groups be able to command considerable amounts of commitment from their members, and be able to act with a fair amount of autonomy and self-regulation. If they do not meet these conditions, which preexisting communities generally do, then they will be unable to effectively mediate between individuals' private interests and the specific interests or aims of the oligarchy. Generally, in a very large group such as a class, no individual will have sufficient control of what goes on or enough confidence in the outcome to risk much of his material resouces, time, or effort. In order to take such a risk, individuals generally require some assurance that others will contribute their share and some reason to believe that action will be successful.

Revolutionary class action is particularly problematic. Its success depends on the participation of a great many people, and the taking of a great many risks. Messianic fervor might well convince potential participants that success is guaranteed, thus making them willing to risk their lives and resources. Messianic fervor might also convince each one that all others will soon share his willingness to participate. In the absence of such fervor, however, there are weighty reasons why an individual would not participate. In order for it to be rational for a person to do so, he must either be so desperate that any outcome is preferable to the continuation of his present circumstances, or he must believe that there is some reasonable probability of success. If we assume, as in the case of early nineteenth-century England I think it is quite safe to assume, that the repressive power of elites and government is not sufficient to unconditionally prevent revolution, then the critical issue becomes whether or not the revolutionaries can command sufficient participation. Let me rephrase the question: did the two hundred or so Derbyshire men involved in the abortive Pentridge "Levellution" of 1817 have reason to believe that they could succeed in toppling the government of England, were they so desperate that anything was worth a try, or were they acting irrationally? My own answer is that a considerable measure of desperation made these men willing to believe bad predictions of their eventual success. They were not so much irrational as remarkably misinformed. Let us look for a moment at the case not from the point of view of the Pentridge rising's failure to find a corresponding national rising but from the point of view of an individual participant. This man has reason to believe that almost everyone he knows will participate in the rising. Further, he is knit together with these people by a complex network of social bonds. This provides him with some assurance that they will not betray him and with considerable coercion to act in concert with them and not against them.

It is a central tenet of the theory of collective goods that unless an actor's anticipated benefits from the collective good outweigh his costs, making it worthwhile for him to provide the good alone, there must be coercion or selective inducements to ensure the contributions of the entire collectivity.[98] Community bonds may act as inducements to participation. Coercion need not be an application of external force. If a community acts to defend itself or secure some long-term collective good, the very relationships which constitute the community provide coercion over any individual who might seek to be a free rider on the community's gains or spare himself the risk of participation in collective action. The amount of external force which would have to be applied to recalcitrant individuals to equal the strength of a community's inducements over its members would be vast. Communities may, indeed, even mobilize people for collective action over long periods of time, in pursuit of highly uncertain goals and at high personal costs. This is the essential strength of guerrilla warfare, as many a Western military commander has learned with difficulty and regret.

I am arguing that the populations which were able to mobilize for radical collective action in early nineteenth-century England were those socially knit together in local communities or craft groupings.[99] Associations at this level provided the major social foundation for protest. Whatever their ideologies, at no point before Chartism, and only haltingly then, were popular and working-class political movements able to work effectively at a national level or, indeed, at any level very much above the local. They were limited by problems of their own internal organization, principally the absence of any effective system of intercommunity links uniting local and craft groupings into a national organization which they might have strengthened as intermediate associations. It was also at the national level, not within local communities, that the government was able to mount effective repressive measures. In addition, as I have summarized above, the most traditional populations of English workers, which were the ones with the most internal social potential for radical action, were also quite strongly connected to members of local elites by interhierarchical bonds. Those populations which were most completely abandoned by the old paternalist pattern of authority and aid were precisely those in the weakest position initially to organize themselves for collective action; the low-skilled laborers of burgeoning Manchester are an obvious example.[100] Societies which have had revolutions have shown much more complete and autonomous community among the "masses," and much weaker interhierarchical linkages to those they wished to overthrow, than existed in England. "Wars of national liberation," in considerable part for this reason, have been much more common than revolutionary wars against wholly indigenous rulers—let alone exploiters who had

not themselves gained full control of the political apparatus and therefore did not have a corresponding clarity of identity to those below
them.

It has commonly been observed that those societies with the greatest
and most manifest disparities of wealth are the most prone to revolutionary movements. The existence of strong and numerous middle
classes is conventionally and plausibly held to be a great safeguard
against revolution. There is a good deal to this view, but it may prof-
itably be expanded by attention to some of the issues I have raised in
the preceding pages. Clearly, alien rule, or the rule of a very distinct,
readily identifiable domestic class (e.g., the statist nobilities of a
number of Eastern European countries in the nineteenth century), af-
fords an easy identification of "them" and "us." Where such rule is at
the expense of opportunities for social mobility, it no doubt leads to
considerable frustration. People are led to pinpoint the highest stratum
as their enemies and not to divert their efforts into attacks on small-
time exploiters immediately above them in a social hierarchy. But there
is another important factor in the vulnerability of such discontinuous
hierarchies. Wars of national liberation and most successful revolutions have pitted a hierarchically inclusive, corporate society, a highly
systemic society with strong traditional foundations and intermediate-
level associations such as communities, against an external or clearly
differentiated power.

War within a class society is a much different matter. A class very
seldom has the social strength and community basis of a traditional
society. Nor, usually, does it have the economic and intellectual self-
sufficiency a more "complete" society may have. This is particularly
true in the highly mobile societies of advanced industrial capitalism.
Where the members of a colonial society may inherit the social foundations for a revolution from precolonial society, it is the very nature of
the creation of an industrial, class society to destroy such continuities.
Only up to the point of transition, as during the industrial revolution in
England, are there still large numbers of workers organized in the sort
of traditional community and craft associations which provide for concerted collective action.

The working populations emerging from such an industrial transition have to build such social foundations largely anew. For them the
creation of extensive formal organizations is the only real hope of successful action on either political or economic fronts. Where a traditional peasant society may have a ready network of communication
through widely ramifying bonds of kinship (and, in some cases, trade),
a modern industrial working class must intentionally create such
channels of communication. During the transition to capitalist industry

in England (as in most such transitions elsewhere) social and geographical mobility, long hours of work, and the active repression of corporate groups such as trade societies worked against both the maintenance and the development of a strong social foundation for working-class action. During the early nineteenth century, those workers who were able to draw on preexisting community and craft bonds were the workers most able to take collective action. This they did, but their objectives were reactionary as well as radical, and they were demonstrably not the working class of Marx's vision.

Seven

Community in the Southeast Lancashire Textile Region

Looking at mobilizations of the working people of Lancashire, one sees a shift beginning in the 1820s and apparent in the fragmentation of the Chartist period. Preeminently, communitarian "reactionary" radicalism gave way to formal organizations and the fundamentally reformist activities of the new working class. Some of the important changes were not in the social organization of the Lancashire population as such. The improvement in means of communication and transport which, for example, took place nationally, increased the possibilities for coordination of action among the members of a much wider "class" of workers than had been possible in the 1810s. The most crucial improvements in this area, however, did not take place until the railways had been widely constructed, that is, until about mid-century. The changes on which I shall dwell were primarily in local social organization. My concern is more to differentiate the organization of workers in the earlier period from that of the later, than to examine in detail the social foundations of Chartism. This involves looking not only at direct measures of change, however, but also at differences among a set of fairly similar towns at the same points in time. This is partly because it is very difficult to construct any useful series of data over time. It is also because many of the differences with which I am concerned appear more clearly when one looks across populations. While there was a long-term trend throughout the nineteenth century toward increasing centralization of work in ever-larger factories, this tendency did not affect all towns at an identical rate. It moved faster, for example, in Bolton than in Oldham or Stockport, partly, it would appear, because of the greater strength of traditional craft organization in the latter communities and relatedly because of their greater concentration of work in such new skilled occupations as engineering.

Demographic Background

When it is suggested that "England" was somehow half urban, half rural in 1851, it must be obvious that not every parish or every county was so. The traditional local social organization, already a variable phenomenon, survived the period of the industrial revolution much more intact in some areas than others. Even in the areas which were most affected, the changes came more gradually and unevenly than is often suggested. Such a "classic" cotton town as Oldham was by no means wholly devoted to cotton manufacture or to industry generally. In 1826 Baines's directory listed eight farmers (proprietors) among the inhabitants; Middleton and Newton each had nineteen, Bury and Warrington seventeen. There were none in Manchester.[1] How is one to compare the growth of Chorlton-Row with that of Blackley, Burnage, Moss-side, or Moston? The first grew from 675 in 1801 to 20,569 in 1831 as Manchester's urban concentration spread, yet none of the others grew by more than the 32 percent of Burnage in the same period.[2] All are located in Manchester Parish. That the growth of Chorlton-Row was extraordinary and could not be incorporated into extant patterns of organization is clear. The other districts present more ambiguous cases. If one is going to speak, as many authors have, of the significance of the new urban masses of workers, one must be careful not to generalize too much as to where the masses were.

One must not allow oneself to be misled by examples of growth on the scale of Chorlton-Row. More important, perhaps, are towns which grew at approximately the average rate for all of Lancashire—about 25 percent per decade. Haslingden is such a town. The population of the Chapelry in 1801 was 4,040. It grew in successive decades to 5,127, 6,595, and, in 1831, 7,776. Today Haslingden is about double its 1831 size. Although the extension of the motorway from Manchester is likely to transform it into something of a dormitory suburb, it still retains a decidedly village flavor. The librarians recognize the foreigner with an interest in local history on each successive return. Shopkeepers sometimes suggest that one stop back with cash later rather than bother to write a check—but take the goods along now. Telling someone the street number of one's house may lead to a puzzled expression; telling them the name of one's neighbor will bring instant recognition. In other words, what strikes me as a sense of community has not yet been destroyed over the course of two centuries by growth, changing economic fortunes, or even the introduction of television. There is, in short, a danger in depending too much on inexplicit connotations of the term "community," and perhaps even a danger in taking at face value the apocalyptic assertions of contemporaries about change in their "communities." There have been changes, of course. The question is what we, shaped by different standards and experiences, but also possessed of a more explicit and better-researched understanding, are to make of them.

The changes are important and deserving of more careful analysis than is contained in simple assertions of the rapid growth and industrial change of the textile district, the inadequacy of old patterns of organization or government, the slow pace at which new ones were developed. Class has not lost its significance for Haslingden today. Its meaning is visible in the contrasts between old rows of houses marked for demolition, their bland replacements, the tiny but well-kept terraces which, in their narrow streets, overlook the mills in the valley, the maintained or renovated eighteenth-century farmhouses, and the occasional brick bungalow. "Occasional" is a word to remember when describing the homes of the middle and upper classes in towns like Haslingden. If they are thin on the ground now, they were more so a hundred and fifty years ago. We are considering a community composed primarily of workers. Class is a tangible factor, but not necessarily one which competes with the bonds of community. It is, rather, a part of those bonds, though again, what is made of it is a different matter. On 15 November 1819, not long after Peterloo, a procession of some two hundred Haslingden men marched to Burnley for a radical meeting which was attended by several thousand people. A flag carried by the marchers bore the words: "thou was covered with anger and persecuted us. Thou has slain us and hast not pitied us. Cursed be their anger, for it was fierce, and their wrath, for it was cruel."[3] The turning of religious language to political ends should be familiar to readers of The Making of the English Working Class. It is also interesting to note the clear identification with those who were killed and injured at St. Peter's Fields. Few workers in the country, let alone in the region, failed to know instantly with whom to identify. But this was the last such demonstration in Haslingden for twenty years, until well into the Chartist period. The cotton famine provoked another crisis, and there have indeed been some since. But the Conservative Club, built in 1901, is one of the most substantial buildings in town, and Haslingden, if no longer the solid Conservative constituency it once was, still hardly votes with revolutionary class consciousness.

Haslingden is representative of the relatively small outlying towns which provided considerable support for the parliamentary reform movement of the 1810s. These towns, which were then still largely peopled by domestic workers, dwindled in importance during the Chartist era as the larger towns dominated political activity. Haslingden was slow to develop a "modern" class consciousness in part because of the same strength of traditionalism and community which supported its participation in the pre-1820 movements. Haslingden was the sort of town which gave its allegiance to the Tory radicals rather than to the more systematic Chartists during the 1830s and 1840s.

A rationalistic perspective holds collective action to be explicable in terms of individual interests and strategies, an economistic calculus of self-interest.[4] I suggest that selection among the wide range of objective individual interests is largely socially determined, both through socialization and especially through the constraints on and resources for collective and individual action provided by social structures. A rationalist perspective offers insufficient explanation for the variety of collective actions people take, and in particular for the changing patterns of collective action in early nineteenth-century England. It was not simply the interests of individual workers, but also of communities of workers, which underpinned the movements of the 1810s. The communal element explains why the seemingly class-based movement could turn so rapidly to the obviously traditionalist agitation in favor of Queen Caroline. The national ideology was rudimentary and essentially populist. With some shift in the state of the economy and in the localities most involved, the tone of the protest could be transformed. To whatever extent local communities were truly radical—or even revolutionary—during the 1810s, the economistic calculus of rational individualism fails to account for it. The mobilizations of the 1830s and after are a different matter. To a much greater degree they reveal the sort of limited, reformist collective action which we would expect from formal organizations acting on behalf of relatively free individuals (not communities) with a range of options.

A normative perspective, on the other hand, sees in collective action mere behavior, disturbance.[5] Such disturbances are held to result from the failure of mechanisms of social control, the shaping and channeling constraints of integration into a social order. This view is problematic, macroscopically, in its assumption of a smoothly functioning social order, its neglect of internal conflict or contradictions. In the somewhat narrower context of the present argument, the notion of collective *behavior* as "disturbance" fails to appreciate the social strengths necessary to engage in collective *action*, especially with any degree of concertedness. It is difficult, drawing on a normative perspective, to explain the discontinuity of the movements of the 1810s and 1830s. This discontinuity was the result of changes in social strengths of certain key populations, on the one hand, and the divergent possibilities each had for ameliorative reform, on the other. The functionalist perspective adopted by many writers (Smelser is one) in this mode of analysis highlights so much the "needs" and operation of the postulated "whole society" that it neglects the possibly—and in the present case frequently—divergent needs and values of subgroups such as local communities. Social organization is not as monolithic as the functionalists have assumed. Where communities as I have defined them exist, by that very definition they are at least partially autonomous organizations and thus capable of autonomous activity and requiring specific analysis. In this macroscopic orientation functionalism is similar to the Marxian position which has held that the proletariat would somehow grow to meet the historical needs of the overall system—a view formulated with inadequate attention to the foundations on which the collective action of the proletariat was to be based.

Different sorts of communities were apt to be involved in different agitations, and involved in agitation to different degrees. This was partly because of the different strengths of social and material resources which they could bring to the support of their action, partly because of the different trades which gave their members economic interests, and partly because of the different social values which gave the members of those trades moral interests in one or another kind of agitation. The "resource mobilization" perspective of sociological analysis has focused on propensity to engage in collective action, and rather heavily on material resources. I shall examine these and other factors below, as I challenge the normative view of collective action during the industrial revolution, especially as put forward by Smelser. This view holds, essentially, that the activity of the 1830s was the result of a disruption in the established constraining organization of the family during the 1820s. I shall argue that two different populations of workers were involved, one—the domestic workers—losing its position of strength during the 1820s, the other—factory workers—gaining community strength on which to base collective action.

Industrial development and concomitant urbanization brought a variety of pressures to bear on the traditional communities of Lancashire. These were concentrated for the most part in a semicircle from northwest of Manchester up through the lower Pennines and down to the southeast where the Manchester region extended into Cheshire. This was essentially the area in which water power was readily available during the early years of the industrial revolution. In this region growth was fairly evenly divided between the larger towns and outlying areas. Ashton, Bolton, Manchester, and Oldham grew more rapidly; Rochdale grew at approximately the same decennial rate of a little above or below 25 percent as the whole of Lancashire, and Stockport more slowly, during the first three decades of the nineteenth cen-

TABLE 7.1
Population Summary (Figures in Parentheses Indicate % Increase over Previous Decade).

	1801	1811	1821	1831
Ashton	15,632	19,053 (22%)	25,967 (36%)	33,597 (29%)
Bolton	17,416	24,149 (39%)	31,295 (30%)	41,195 (32%)
Manchester	70,409	79,459 (12%)	108,016 (36%)	142,026 (31%)
Oldham	12,024	16,690 (39%)	21,662 (30%)	32,381 (49%)
Rochdale	17,789	22,036 (24%)	27,798 (26%)	35,764 (29%)
Stockport	14,830	17,545 (18%)	21,726 (24%)	25,469 (17%)

tury (see table 7.1 for a summary of the urban population growth).[6] Unlike the overwhelming urban-led growth of the rest of Lancashire and other parts of England, the Manchester region did not see the major towns grow much faster than the surrounding areas in this period. As table 7.2 reveals, the proportion of parish population in the urban center did not change dramatically, taking the region as a whole. Relatively close relations were maintained between the various towns and the outlying communities around them. Manchester, much larger and more sprawling, was the only exception to this rule, though of course the rule applied variably, perhaps most of all to Oldham, which had close relations with Chadderton, Crompton, and Royton.

Despite the relatively consistent pattern of growth in southeast Lancashire, it must be remembered that this was a very rapid growth and was subject to some fluctuations in specific content. For example, the proportion of female occupants in the industrial towns rose rapidly between the census years of 1801 and 1811, and fell off even more rapidly thereafter (see figure 7.1). The ratio of women to men working in factories appears to have risen continuously through the early nineteenth century.[7] The fluctuation in the proportion of male residents seems, then, likely to be due to other factors. In particular, the availability of nonfactory work was important, and the relatively low proportion of men in the early years is indicative of the fact that factories only began to dominate the labor force after the post-Napoleonic

TABLE 7.2
Town Population as Percentage of Parish Total

	1801	1831
Ashton	n.a.	n.a.
Bolton	58%	65%
Manchester	63	52
Oldham	39	48
Rochdale	59	61
Stockport	55	38

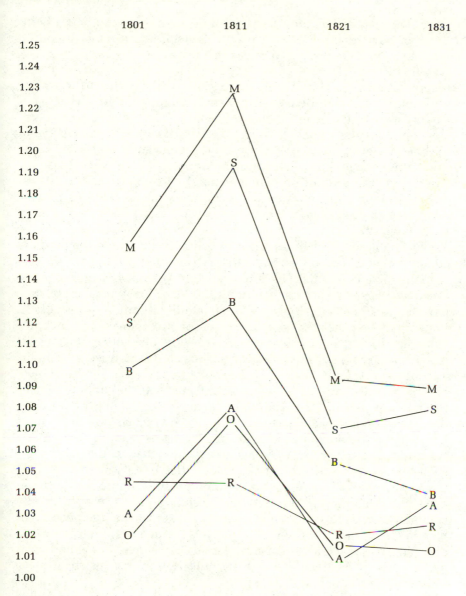

FIGURE 7.1: Ratio of female to male occupants. A = Ashton, B = Bolton, M = Manchester, O = Oldham, R = Rochdale, S =Stockport.

recession ended. 1811 came during a low period of textile production; this was one of the causes of Luddism. Men were more likely than women to be employed in casual labor and they were much more likely than women to leave town and seek work in the countryside, for example, in harvesting.[8] Lancashire's growth owed a great deal more to

migration than did that of other counties, including such partially industrialized ones as the West Riding of Yorkshire.[9] Since this migration
was of recent date, people were apt still to have some ties to the areas
they had left.[10] A further possibility is that young single women were
disproportionately sent, during the distress of the early 1810s, to live
with relatives in the towns, or in boarding houses, with the hope of
finding work in the factories.[11] Manufacturers also advertised on occasion for "healthy strong girls" and "families chiefly consisting of
girls."[12] It seems unlikely, however, that factors such as the last could
account for the specific fluctuation as opposed to the overall trend.[13]
After 1821, the proportion of members of each sex in the towns remained quite consistent despite the continued increase in the proportion of female factory workers; indeed, the disparity decreased slightly
in the long run.

The demographic changes noted may have been due to the partially
counterposed operation of two distinct pressures, acting on at least
partially distinct populations. The availability of jobs in factories, combined with a surplus of male agricultural labor in rural districts, may
have led to a relatively high rate of female in-migration, especially in
Bolton and Manchester. Conversely, the pressures on domestic craft-
work may have led many weavers to seek work elsewhere, thus resulting in some male out-migration. If this account is correct, it explains
why Stockport, with a low rate of population increase, should show a
high imbalance between the sexes. Stockport had the highest proportion of weavers in its population of the towns for which I have clear
data.[14] Bolton and Manchester each had a low proportion of weavers
but many more women than men. In such cases one may tentatively
conclude that the lure of the factories more than compensated for
such loss of domestic workers as those cities underwent. In Oldham
there was a rapidly growing population but little imbalance between
the sexes. This may be an early manifestation of the strength of the
community of workers there, which was able to protect the position of
men in the work force. Either alternatively, or in addition, this may be
due to the fact that Oldham specialized in the relatively finer and more
skilled end of the textile industry while Bolton, for instance, did a
greater proportion of cruder work.[15]

These considerations indicate some instabilities in the underlying
structure of much urban community life, at least one of which—sexual
imbalance—abated during and after the 1810s. If factory-oriented
communities had the chance to grow stronger after the 1810s, the opposite was true of communities of outworkers, especially weavers. As
we shall see below, the late 1820s and early 1830s were precisely the
periods when these communities were torn apart.

Family Structure and Factory Agitation

Smelser, in holding the collective action of workers to be an implicitly irrational response to "disturbances" in family patterns, argues that it was not until the decade of the 1820s that family life was greatly altered, an alteration that resulted in the agitations of the 1830s. Drawing on scattered evidence that adult male spinners retained their "moral authority" in the factory, often hired their own assistants, and were part of a web of kinship controls on abuse of child workers and common employment of families, he suggests that we must

> question some accepted views of urban-factory life. Almost as a matter of definition we associate the factory system with a decline of the family and the onset of social anonymity. Certainly the steam-powered mule created a new type of factory system. By virtue of an intricate set of controls based on kinship and community ties, and by virtue of the continuing authority of the spinner, however, the potential anonymity of factory life was far from being complete in 1820, even though the factory system had been prospering for four decades.[16]

The extent to which the factory system had been prospering for four decades before 1820 is certainly questionable; it had been extending its influence but in few areas dominated employment. This is all the more significant since Smelser tends to conduct his argument in terms of a "typical" factory family. His suggestion that "depersonalization and differentiation did not reach a critical point until the 1820s"[17] is intended to explain why the Chartist "disturbance" and trade unionism "took off" then and not earlier, and were of greater scale than earlier "disturbances." Smelser's evidence, however, is almost entirely drawn from testimony before parliamentary inquiries on child labor, combinations, and factories (and generally from owners, managers, and witnesses sympathetic to them). In almost all cases it is indistinct what type and size of mill is being referred to and where it might be located. The only mill for which Smelser presents detailed data is the Catrine Works in the county of Ayr, Scotland. Whatever might be said for or against the use of this data to illustrate an argument concerning Lancashire, Smelser is forced to admit that the Catrine Works constitutes an exception to the rule he lays down. It did not employ adult male spinners and did employ many children of nonfactory operatives.[18]

The period from the 1790s to 1820s is, for Smelser, something called a "transitional equilibrium." The apparent meaning of this odd term is that there were changes, but they didn't upset things too much. In other words, the basic structure of the family survived intact, but there were a number of shifts in the specific content of family members' roles. In the period from the mid-1820s to the 1840s, the families of workers moved to a new level of differentiation. By this is meant that the families became more complex structures, with each member's role less closely and immediately connected to those of the others, even though the whole is still assumed to constitute a social system and thus to be interdependent. The traditional functions of the family are treated largely in terms of authority and training. Curiously, both are assumed without discussion to be almost entirely male preserves. But, as has been observed: "In terms of a textile family entering a factory, the loss of the female training function, and the gain of a new adult male training function, altered dramatically the industrial training roles of adult males and females."[19] Further, adult women, as well as men, faced competition from child labor increasingly into the nineteenth century.[20] We clearly are in need of a better way of assessing just what changes were taking place—and whether any were as dramatic as Smelser suggests.

Smelser's assertion that considerable disruption in the division of labor within factory families took place in the twenty-year period *after* 1825 seems hard to credit. There simply is very little evidence that there was substantial employment of whole families (or even substantial parts of families) as cohesive work-units in the early mills. Only fairly young children were employed as piecers (assistants to the spinners). Certainly very few adult spinners would have been able consistently to employ their own children as piecers, since very few would have had children at the right age at any one time. Anderson has shown that, from what limited evidence exists, the age distribution of spinners does not appear to have altered significantly between the early 1830s and 1851. As he summarizes: "If there was a trend away from family employment on the shop floor over the first third of the nineteenth century it cannot have been very great, because such employment was at no time particularly widespread."[21]

Smelser's analysis is crucially one of stages: increasing pressures on the family division of labor initially being held in check by "corrective mechanisms," then eventually forcing a new structural adjustment. The pressures come from certain technological advances in textile production resulting in larger factories and more individualistic employment (and presumably, though less explicitly, production) practices. The corrective mechanism is family employment. In the 1820s it is weakened by new technology; the result is that factory workers enter Chartism, factory agitation, trade unions, and manifest a variety of other "disturbances."[22] The structure of the argument is implicitly one of temporal conjuncture; Smelser gives no direct evidence of a connection between family structure and the protest and agitation undertaken by factory workers.[23] He rather suggests that factory workers were passive and quiescent prior to the 1820s, but beginning in that decade they "were drawn into massive protest against the progress of the Industrial Revolution for the first time."[24]

The factory agitation was, however, about many things, from wages to the possibility of technological unemployment to the material conditions and hours of work. Child labor was only one aspect, and only partially connected to traditional notions of family division of labor (some general values concerning abuse of children were also important). Nonetheless, it is possible that a threat to traditional family structure by industrial change was involved. There are two links which need to be empirically verified in such a proposition. First, it needs to be established that there was in fact a strong precondition of family employment which the new technology disrupted. Anderson and Edwards and Lloyd-Jones argue convincingly against this. The second part of the proposition calls for a specification of the characteristics of industrial change held to be disruptive and an attempt to establish whether they are systematically tied to mobilization for protest (disturbance). I shall argue that comparing the changes Smelser emphasizes (e.g., increasing factory size) among towns in the Manchester region, one finds wide diversity, and, if there is any systematic variation, the greatest mobilization of workers occurred where Smelser's conditions obtained least.[25]

Smelser does not at any point engage in comparative analysis. He does offer a rather abstracted contrast between "the new factory proletariat" and the "surviving domestic workers." Before the 1820s, he argues:

> The quiescence of the factory operatives is traceable to the persistence of certain fundamental family relations in the factory setting. In many ways their lot was hard and their adjustments many; but these family traditions were being preserved. The pressures on the surviving domestic workers, by contrast, were to abandon a total traditional way of life.[26]

Smelser is quite right to note the distinction between the domestic workers—notably handloom weavers—and the factory workers. But his location of the source of protest in the disruption of families is problematic. The relevant contrast may be between the social strength of insurgent weavers and the lack of such solidarity among factory workers. Five points are important: (1) The prosperity of handloom weavers was of recent date, a transitional product of industrialization. As Bythell has indicated,

The history of the cotton handloom weavers coincides almost exactly with the traditional time limits of the classic English industrial revolution. Before the 1770s, the cotton hand weavers as a body had not existed; by the late 1840s, they had effectively vanished. In three generations, the process of economic change had first created and then destroyed a new type of labour.[27]

Weaving could be a "traditional way of life" only because weavers could incorporate the over 30 percent growth in their number (from 184,000 to 240,000) into strong, ongoing communities.[28] (2) If anything, it was the weavers who were best able to maintain the domestic family division of labor, although at the expense of rather extreme physical demands on the family members.[29] (3) Recruits to factory work were seldom ex-weavers. Rather they were frequently ex-agricultural laborers and farm servants—populations which had already experienced a good deal of "differentiation" of the family unit—perhaps, indeed more than was the case in cotton towns.[30] (4) The clearest distinction between factory workers and handloom weavers does not lie in their respective family relations but in their relative prosperity. It seems plausible that this might be considered a source of differential rates of mobilization for protest. (5) Further, factory workers generally experienced economic crises as individuals or families during the early years of industrialization. Particular factories failed with astonishing frequency, but there were only a few major industry-wide crises. Handloom weavers, on the other hand, experienced privations as communities. The miseries which affected any of them affected all of them. They were also apt to live in smaller and, we may safely assume, more densely knit units of population.

Smelser is right to suggest that domestic workers were under threat of losing their entire way of life, while factory workers were not. Whatever the fluctuations of real wages, working conditions, and rate of employment for factory workers, these were relatively continuous. They made the workers' situation better or worse but did not threaten them with collective eradication. This only serves further to point out the relative irrelevance of the family structure which Smelser makes his primary variable. Instead, it is first the extreme of suffering the weavers experienced, and second the absence of any plausible mediate or local solution to their problems, which predisposed them to radicalism. Factory workers, on the other hand, could reasonably be reformist. One might ask why they were not more widely involved in reform agitation earlier. Essentially, the answer is that they had not developed the strength of communal and/or formal organization which would enable them to do so.[31] The migrants into factory towns, far from being quiescent because they preserved a traditional family structure, were quiet because they had very little communal organization on which to base extensive collective action. These migrants did not often or readily fit into a preexisting structure, and so had to build community anew. Those towns which were most active in the early phases of protest (pre-1820) were those with the greatest strength of communal bonds, the most differentiated industry, and the smallest factories.

Edwards and Lloyd-Jones have noted, from an analysis of data for Preston in 1816, that although children working as assistants were unlikely to be employed by their relatives anywhere, they were more often so employed in the district around Preston than in the town itself.[32] It would appear that Smelser's "corrective mechanism" was tied to other characteristics of the community.[33] If the same disproportion had obtained in the Manchester district (we have no evidence, but there is little reason to assume that Preston was atypical in this regard), it would interestingly supplement the evidence presented in figure 7.1 on fluctuations and variations in proportions of female residents and in table 7.3 below on factory work-force characteristics. The census sources indicate that smaller towns and villages had more even proportions of men and women and did not comparably experience the leap in proportion of women in the 1811 enumeration. The disproportionate representation of women in the population is greatest in Manchester and least in the smaller outlying districts, towns, and villages. This suggests that "traditional family structure" obtained least in the areas Smelser considers most advanced in the development of the factory system.

It is true that two of the great leaps in the rate of factory construction—1823–25 and 1832–34—coincide approximately with the dramatic acceleration Smelser finds in the pressures of industrialization on family structure. He places considerable stress on the concentration of mills in towns, their increasing size, and "the general lack of intimacy associated with increasing scale."[34] These factors are no doubt important, but the conclusions Smelser bases on them are surprising. He treats these changes (and the technological developments with which they were associated) entirely in terms of "a 'dissatisfaction' for the operatives' family economy in the sense that family members were no longer able to offer labour to the industry on the new terms and at the same time maintain the traditional organization of family life."[35] His universal interpolation of "family structure and values" as a key variable in every explanatory chain seems to be empirically quite arbitrary, following only from his general theory. It would make more sense to point out that the rapid growth of factories and the generally good commercial situation for the textile industry gave the factory operatives a stronger bargaining position than they had had for years. Although the powerloom threatened changes in the organization of work, it was primarily a threat to the livelihood of handloom weavers.[36] Its improvements in fact rendered the position of the factory worker more secure by limiting the extent to which his bargaining position could be undercut by his employer's recourse to handloom work. It was in these years that the number of handloom weavers began to decline for the first time.

By treating all of the workers' responses to changes in the conditions under which they lived and worked as disturbances in the smooth evolutionary development of industrial society, Smelser renders them uninterpretable.[37] He is unable, for example, to see the shift in orientation of workers' movements from the essentially resistance campaigns of the 1810s to the agitation for industrial reform in the 1830s. This shift is easily understood when one notes the changing population which was involved in the two efforts. Chartism's diverse collection of political claims and relations to industrial issues falls into clearer focus when one looks at it from the very different perspectives of artisans and outworkers on the one hand and factory workers on the other. The latter fought for gains internal to the growing factory system. The defense of a way of life was critical to artisans and outworkers; it was never so in equal degree to factory workers.[38]

Work-place Organization and Protest Mobilization

The increasing scale and "impersonality" of factories may well have given workers more just complaints during the latter years of the industrial revolution. But the workers were never short of just complaints. A more important consideration is that of how it may have affected which claims they put forward against the prevailing systems of political and economic power. The factory workers were in a stronger position than outworkers to make internal claims—to demand wage increases or shorter hours, for example. They attempted collective action from a relatively weak communal base, however. This was part of the impact of the increasing scale and impersonality of factories and the mobility of the work force. Collective action could seldom be for these urban factory workers what it had been for artisans and outworkers—a direct extension of community.[39]

I have presented only a very limited amount of comparative evidence on industrial organization during the industrial revolution. Although it is insufficient foundation for the erection of any very grand analytic edifice, its tendencies are nonetheless clear (see tables 7.3 and 7.4). Evidence on factories is available for four of the six towns discussed

TABLE 7.3
Factory Labor Force in 1833

	Bolton*	Manchester	Oldham	Stockport*
Factories in sample	12 (9)	38	22	19 (17)
Spinners	5,010	12,103	2,409	2,659
Weavers	351	3,057	1,261	3,507
Mechanics, etc.	108	518	97	126
Total	5,469	15,678	3,775	6,292
Mean number of employees	455.75 (607.6)	412.58	171.59	331.16 (370.12)
Average weekly earnings (pence)	111.50	122.64	127.09	132.02
Adult males	1,443	4,421	1,318	2,314
Adult females	1,279	5,731	824	2,176
Ratio f:m	0.89:1	1.30:1	0.63:1	0.94:1
Male children	1,425	3,801	813	1,556
Female children	1,322	3,437	820	1,446
Ratio f:m	0.93:1	0.90:1	1.01:1	0.93:1
Ratio child:adult	1.01:1	0.71:1	0.76:1	0.67:1
Combined ratio female:male	1.10:1	1.12:1	0.77:1	0.94:1
Ratio all others to adult males	2.79:1	2.93:1	1.86:1	2.24:1

SOURCE: Stanway's survey of 151 mills, May and June, 1833, reported in Ure, *The Cotton Manufacture of Great Britain*, pp. 390–407.

*Figures in parentheses indicate result if factories owned by one firm are counted as one.

earlier. It divides them into two pairs. Stockport and Oldham had greater balance between weaving and spinning in factories.[40] Spinners overwhelmingly dominated in both Manchester and Bolton. Oldham and Stockport appear to have offered higher wages (in 1833), followed by Manchester with Bolton significantly lower. The proportion of men in the work-force was greatest in Oldham, least in Manchester. In short, on a number of important dimensions, Oldham and Stockport come out consistently at one end of the spectrum.[41]

Oldham and Stockport were also the towns in which pre-Chartist radicalism seems to have been the strongest. Although quantitative evidence for membership in these early radical movements and qualitative evidence concerning their organization is extremely scarce, the trend seems clear. The more "proletarian" towns such as Bolton and Ashton produced none of the major pre-1821 radical leaders. All of the towns were of course active by the standards of the country as a whole. Comparison is made especially difficult by the fact that Stockport and Bolton each had an unusually zealous local magistrate taking an interest in supplying the Home Office with evidence concerning radical activities. But Stockport and Oldham did produce important radical leaders as well as followers. They were also the scenes of important popular meetings—notably the Sandy Brow meeting which preceded Peterloo and the demonstrations surrounding the inquest on the body of John Lees afterward. Such activity as appears during the first quarter of the century in Bolton and Ashton is heavily concentrated in trade unionism. But in fact the most unionized workers—machine spinners—were also conspicuously absent from the radical leadership. When Bolton figures as the scene of significant protest, this protest is almost always found among the town's and the surrounding area's weaving population, not among its factory workers.[42]

Small factories can be seen as important "resources" for collective action, since small size is, as we have seen, conducive to the formation of community and hence to collective action.[43] Wages are certainly to be valued in themselves, but they are also a resource making a variety of both collective and private actions possible. The proportion of adult men in factories again seems most likely to be a condition predisposing the population to organization for collective action. It can also be seen as a result, for men fought sustained struggles to keep women from threatening their employment.[44] As Table 7.3 reveals, Bolton and Manchester tend overall to differ from Oldham and Stockport on these mentioned dimensions. While it would be a mistake to treat these figures as especially reliable, the trend which they reveal would seem to be clear.[45] The factory work force of the towns known to have been disproportionately the home of collectively active workers was generally speaking more adult, more male, better paid, more evenly divided between weaving and spinning, and worked in smaller factories than that of the less active towns. Table 7.4 reinforces the general findings on factory size and indicates that they still obtained in 1841, more or less independently of the branch of the cotton industry in which any factory worked.[46] All of these chatracteristics seem potentially contributing factors to the collective mobilization of the towns. In particular, I contend that relatively large populations were likely only to be mobilized on the basis of smaller component groupings, if at all. While Marx had held, and was implicitly followed by most other writers, that the large urban workplaces ought to be central to the collective mobilization of workers, it would appear that the opposite was the case. Had

TABLE 7.4
Size of Factory Workforce in 1841

	No. of Mills	Capacity Work Force	Work Force at Time of Visit	Mean Size of Factory (capacity)
		Working Full Time *Fine Spinning*		
Ashton	14	1,555	1,555	111.07
Bolton	13	2,007	1,921	154.38
Manchester	20	7,126	6,877	356.30
Oldham	10	635	635	63.50
Rochdale	0	—	—	—
Stockport	na	na	na	na
		Coarse Spinning		
Ashton	36	4,662	4,526	129.50
Bolton	16	2,564	1,906	160.25
Manchester	29	6,767	6,290	233.34
Oldham	65	4,887	4,492	75.18
Rochdale	52	5,137	4,890	98.79
Stockport	na	na	na	na
		Spinning and Power *Weaving Combined*		
Ashton	13	6,783	6,522	521.77
Bolton	12	3,660	3,581	305.00
Manchester	35	14,833	13,843	423.80
Oldham	32	7,137	7,061	223.03
Rochdale	17	3,073	2,644	180.76
Stockport	na	na	na	na
		Power Weaving		
Ashton	5	390	310	78.00
Bolton	0	—	—	—
Manchester	15	1,461	1,393	97.40
Oldham	6	406	406	67.60
Rochdale	0	—	—	—
Stockport			na	
		Doubling Yarn		
Manchester	6	302	297	50.33
Oldham	21	230	220	10.95
		Working Short Time (All)		
Ashton	25	10,505	9,533	420.20
Bolton	14	4,657	4,557	332.64
Manchester	10	1,900	1,614	190.00
Oldham	20	2,273	2,271	113.65
Rochdale	8	682	550	85.25
Stockport			na	

table continued next page

TABLE 7.4, continued

	No. of Mills	Capacity Work Force	Not at Work (All) Work Force at Time of Visit	Mean Size of Factory (capacity)
Ashton	9	899		99.80
Bolton	6	1,710	.	285.00
Manchester	43	5,713		132.86
Oldham	23	1,936		84.17
Rochdale (includes Middleton)	13	1,157		89.00

SOURCE: *Reports of the Inspectors of Factories*, PP (1842), App. I, pp. 33–78, Report of L. Horner.

the large factories been subdivided into smaller work-groups, this might have reversed the effect, but adults were generally isolated, working together with only child assistants and youths on relatively large and noisy machines.[47] British industry did not begin to match the division of labor *among* workplaces with division of labor *within* workplaces until after 1830, and even then this process proceeded rather slowly.[48]

In research on work organizations it has been found that structural differentiation generally increases with size, but such internal differentiation most promotes relations among members of different subunits in small organizations.[49] Size and differentiation have opposite implications for the social relations among a population of workers, and hence for their capability and thus propensity to engage in collective action. With differentiation held constant, increasing size tends to inhibit succesful organization (as for example it is likely to lower the density and multiplicity of social relations among the population). With size held constant, increasing differentiation makes it more likely that the members of any one group will have social relations with the members of other groups. Further, the subgroups of the larger population are potential foci for the formation of dense and multiplex social networks.[50]

The same line of reasoning may be applied to towns and other population aggregates as well as to work organizations. It is thus significant that in Bolton and Manchester (one can say nothing stronger on the basis of the limited evidence of tables 7.3 and 7.4) the working populations appear to have been divided into fewer subunits of employment. That is, the same places which had the largest factories had the fewest factories.[51] On simple numerical logic, the propensity toward interrelationships among separate work forces goes down as the number of such work forces goes down and their size goes up (total population held constant). It becomes all the more clear, following such considerations, why the activity of the emergent population of factory workers (the template for many conceptions of the working class) could only mobilize for collective action through the agency and mediation of formal organizations.[52]

In general, the capacity of workers to mobilize for collective action is positively associated with the structuration of tasks, so that work is performed by groups rather than individuals, with relatively numerous and small places of work, with subdivision within larger places of work, and with smaller total population units (assuming in each case the other factors are held constant). This suggests that artisans, out-workers, skilled factory workers, workers in small factories, and work-ers in towns with a large number of relatively small factories were all more likely to engage in collective action than were those low-skilled workers in large, metropolitan factories who figure so prominently in the vision of the proletariat willed us by Karl Marx.[53]

For the most part, my concern in the immediately preceding discus-sion has been with factory workers. These only began to assume a significant role in workers' struggles during the 1810s, and did not fully come into their own until the 1830s. A key question is just how that transition was made. That is, if the initial (pre-1820) thrust of the movements of British workers came disproportionately from artisans, craftsmen, and outworkers, what happened to the movement as the balance of the working population shifted; where was it most able to continue; and why?

The early strength of protest was built on the foundation of small preindustrial communities.[54] The impetus shifted to those industrial towns which were able to build relatively strong new communal foun-dations. Lacking much in the way of direct evidence for the social bonds making up relative strengths of community, I have considered a number of predisposing conditions. That is, smaller factory work forces did not make community, but they did make it much easier to construct community, much more likely that people did so. Similarly, the pro-portion of the work force which was female did not somehow act as a direct impediment to the formation of community on which to base collective action. Rather, in addition to any cultural reasons which may have made women less likely to organize, four special characteris-tics of the female labor-force indicate problems for stable community organization, in and out of the workplace. First, women factory workers were much more likely than men to be single.[55] Second, women tended frequently to work on an intermittent basis (especially those who were married).[56] Third, women tended to work at relatively low-skilled jobs, and thus were in an inferior bargaining position as they could more readily be replaced.[57] Fourth, women were paid less, and therefore had lesser resources.[58] In addition, the employment of women tended to drive men from work; men, in this situation, were more likely to leave the community in search of work (even if married) than were women.[59]

This comparison of towns in the textile district of southeast Lancashire is hardly complete in itself, let alone representative of the range of community structures throughout England. In the Manchester region there were, in addition to towns of the sort I have considered, country mills with their largely self-contained but highly transient (and frequently very young) work forces;[60] villages, either devoted to handloom weaving primarily, or to a mix in which weaving gave way to factory employment; the outlying townships around the larger towns already considered, often growing in step and sometimes merging with the center; and the new extensions of almost exclusively factory work forces which tended generally to sooner or later be absorbed into the towns of longer standing. Of the last, some, like Chorlton-Row, became largely residential areas for workers employed in nearby mills; others, like Duckinfield, were manufacturing locations in their own right.[61] Both these sorts of populations grew quite rapidly, indeed, suddenly. Duckinfield was less than one-eighth the size of Stockport in 1801, and well over half in 1831, itself increasing by eight and a half times.[62] Village workers in general, and handloom weavers in particular, were disproportionately important to workers' movements well into the Chartist period. Although workers from each of the types of population aggregate were at some times active, those from the middle-sized towns, and especially those with the head start I have described in community development, were most likely to carry on the struggles, adapting them to their own particular situations. This adaptation meant, among other things, that the struggles became increasingly internal to the emerging industrial system and less and less matters of resistance to it. Many of the smaller communities were economically disabled by the decline of domestic industries and the weak competitive position of small factories. The working population of Manchester itself was relatively weak socially, and had a high concentration of low-skilled workers. The most active were not low-skilled workers, however, but urban artisans, members of the building trades, and, in specifically trade-union activity, the privileged spinners. This again points to the importance of community, which gives social foundations on which to organize collective action.[63]

I cannot even summarize the picture of community variation throughout Britain but rather only suggest that it is an important subject for study, together with more conventional variables such as local prosperity, technical changes putting pressures on populations of workers, and political traditions giving direction to thoughts and actions. The special importance of the Manchester region is that, during the 1820s and 1830s, this was one of the places where new communities of workers were most particularly being formed.[64] The older communities which had been the mainstay of the earlier period of revolt and protest were losing their strength, both economically and socially, and, indeed, their preponderance of numbers. A consciousness of class did develop along with the new urban populations. The uneven development of community, however, impeded the workers' ability to act on the broader basis of class. While Oldham was relatively advanced, Manchester was more backward. Class activity necessarily turned to those forms of action which could be pursued in common by at least a large proportion of the class. And the definition of class, in this sense, could not be local, for class structure was not fundamentally a local phenomenon, though class consciousness might be. If the immediate overturning of capitalist society was too distant a goal to be based on the available social foundations, political democratization and improved working conditions and standards of living were not. Trade unionism, unlike revolutionary class struggle, could successfully be pursued up to a point, on a local level.

Eight

The Foundations of Collective Action

In the southeast Lancashire textile district, the 1820s were the pivotal decade in a substantial shift in the social foundations on which workers could organize for collective action. This shift involved the proportions of workers in the three major occupational categories—artisans, outworkers, and factory laborers; the internal organization of various occupations, as for example among artisans, some of whom went to work in factories; the rewards offered for different kinds of labor; and the organization of communities and workplaces, as both became larger. Related transitions took place in other regions of Great Britain at varying rates through the rest of the century.

The shift in social foundations for collective action was discontinuous. The movements which emerged from the 1830s in Lancashire had very different structural roots than did those of the 1810s. Lancashire was particularly important for the rest of Britain; along with Clydeside and the Black Country it led in the transformation of work brought by the industrial revolution. This was particularly true because of the large number of workers employed in the labor-intensive manufacturing of textiles.

Much previous analysis has treated the 1820s as a lull in an essentially continuous process of development of the working class. This is the position of Thompson's *The Making of the English Working Class*: Jacobinism leads directly into the resistance movements of the early years of the Napoleonic wars; the foundations laid by Jacobinism and mated with traditional notions of the moral economy provide the basis for the rebirth of radicalism in Luddism and the parliamentary reform agitation of the 1810s; by the conclusion of this decade the working class is "essentially made"; organization proceeds apace on the local level through the 1820s and England nearly has a revolution in the early Chartist period with the reaction against the limited reforms of 1832 and the resistance to the poor law of 1834. The most common alternative position, widespread before the appearance of Thompson's book, was to regard the earlier movements as rather backward and primitive and to trace the rise of the working class and of British popular radicalism from the Chartist period.[1]

Both positions are wrong. While the latter accurately appreciates the difference between the movements of the 1810s and the 1830s, it inaccurately dismisses the former as backward-looking *and therefore less radical*, as less formally organized *and therefore weaker*. Such a view is not based on the evidence, or on a sound use of social theory. Rather, it comes from the pervasive assumption of a continuous relationship among the variables in social change. In fact, the backward-looking, less formally organized movements of the 1810s were in many ways more radical than the later mobilizations of the working class at a more "advanced stage of development." The movements of the 1810s also provide a closer analogue to those popular mobilizations which have historically resulted in revolutions. Thompson's work performs the very substantial service of pointing out the richness and strength of the earlier popular activity but, by assimilating it, however erratically, to the model of working-class development, obscures both its historical nature and its theoretical significance. There was not a continuous development of rationalism, radicalism, and strength among the members of a single working class.

Rather, there was a discontinuous shift from traditionally oriented, communally based mobilizations toward more rationalistic mobilizations founded on formal organizations. The former were, however, more radical than the latter. Each type had its strengths, but strengths of different kinds. In the present study, I have focused on the reactionary radicals of the earlier period. In the textile district of southeast Lancashire, they predominated before the 1820s and were fading from leadership by the early 1830s. I have suggested that one can see something of the relationship between communal foundations and radical mobilization in looking at differences among populations in the factory towns of the district at the same time. Of course, changes which Lancashire, the Midlands and part of Scotland experienced in the early part of the century struck other parts of Britain later, and similar changes are affecting populations in many parts of the world today.

Surprisingly, the theories which are advanced to account for revolutionary and other mobilizations do not deal very well with "reactionary radicals." The predominant strands of Western social thought have persisted since the Enlightenment in seeing rationality linked to progress and strength and opposed to tradition in its weakness, informality, and conservatism. Marxists and liberals alike have struggled to explain popular mobilizations in terms of the rational appreciation of objective interests. Attention to the subjective and sometimes nonrational factors which may unite people for collective action has been left largely to those on the right who see in such behavior symptoms of mental deficiency resulting only in social "disturbance." Even the notion of community has become almost entirely the intellectual property of conservatives.[2] Western Marxists, indeed, come very close on occasion to implying that alienation is a good thing, if it "frees" people from the bonds of traditional communities and thus readies them for participation in the formal organizations of the rational, class-based revolution.

In this concluding chapter, I propose to turn my attention to our theoretical incapacity to explain—or in some cases even accept—the connection between reaction and radicalism in mobilizations based on traditional communities. I shall look first, but only briefly, at the "disturbance" and "rational individualist" strands of non-Marxist sociological thought suggesting as central criticisms that both neglect the social foundations of collective action and fail to explain concerted, enduring, radical mobilizations. Then, at more length, I shall consider the theory of the working class as a revolutionary collective actor, focusing on Marx. Lastly, I shall suggest that an understanding of the reactionary radicals of early nineteenth-century England, and, I think, of most radical mobilizations and much of all social action, requires some modification of our pervasive rationalism, so that we give greater attention to tradition, and some limitation of our stress on objective structures, so that we see people acting within webs of personal social relations and in communities.

Collective Behavior as a Symptom of Disturbance

At least since the work of LeBon, the dominant treatment of popular mobilizations and crowds in social theory has been to regard them as examples of social or psychological maladjustment, regression, or failures of mechanisms of control. This position was characteristic of much nonacademic social thought long before (and remains so today).[3] The mob was an object of fear; the crowd seemed a mindless multitude which could only be destructive. Such was the opinion of those who would defend a social order against attack, or in many cases against any change at all.[4] It became the position of those academics who took the social order as in some sense a "given." LeBon, for example, was concerned with the French Revolution of 1789, which seemed to him to reveal the primitive thought of the crowd in stark contrast to "civilization."[5]

Much the same perspective shaped the work of the early anthropologists who sought to understand traditional societies through the concept of "group mind."[6] For them, the apparent simplicity of social and cultural organizations (often measured by technological sophistication) was the result of an inferior individual development. This was also held to be revealed in the greater similarity of individuals. The member of the crowd (who, not coincidentally, was generally a member of the lower classes) and the member of the tribal society were seen as similar in the "primitive" nature of their appreciations of causality, contradiction, and other logical notions. This has remained a crucial problem both for anthropologists who would contrast systems of thought[7] and for students of collective action. A perennial question for the latter is: how much do the members of crowds understand why they do what they do and, following on this, how much can they make the results of their collective action fit their reasons for taking part?

Freud took up similar questions, and argued that individuals were likely to behave more "crudely" or emotionally in groups than out of them. This is because, in order to become a part of a group, the individual must surrender some of his most sophisticated (and thus individually distinctive) adaptations to social life and accommodations to internal drives. In other words, group membership is incompatible with mature functioning and involves for Freud a regression toward something of a "lowest common denominator" of personality. As a member of a group, the individual's

> liability to affect becomes extraordinarily intensified, while his intellectual ability is markedly reduced, both processes being evidently in the direction of an approximation to the other individuals in the group; and this result can only be reached by the removal of those inhibitions upon his instincts which are peculiar to each individual, and by his resigning those expressions of his inclinations which are especially his own.[8]

The individual is only able to maintain this more sophisticated identity in a social situation which tolerates it and provides cultural and interpersonal contexts for it.[9] As the situation in which he lives becomes indeterminate and unpredictable, it is hard for the individual to maintain a determinate identity.[10] Thus, failures of identity are not purely personal matters; Freud's argument is quite similar to that embodied in Durkheim's concept of *anomie*.[11] The environment contributes to the individual's development of the potential to survive or succumb to crises,[12] produces the context for the particular crises he will encounter,[13] and influences the statistical frequency of such crises in society.[14] Freud and Durkheim together offer a perspective in which we can see reasons for the emotional impact of such factors on individuals.

Taking such contextual explanation still further, Smelser analyzes collective "behavior" (he specifically does not use the term "action") as the response to situational pressures grown too great for "conventional handling": "This is one reason for defining collective behaviour as uninstitutionalized; it occurs when structured social action is under strain and when institutionalized means of overcoming the strain are inadequate."[15] Smelser's theory is the most sophisticated of the many functionalist theories which, in the Durkheimian tradition, see collective behavior as a response of individuals to disturbances in social order, to social disorganization.[16] We are not told by Smelser where the groups which take part in collective behavior originate. The issue is almost defined out of question, for those who engage in collective behavior are supposed to be deprived of any strong communal organization.[17]

Smelser agrees with Freud as to the lack of mental sophistication characteristic of crowds, but he sees a different (or at least additional) reason for it. The key lies in his conception of "value-added" series in the enactments of components of the social order.[18] He supposes there to be four basic components of action: values, norms, mobilization (which refers to motivation, not commitment of resources), and situational facilities. These are hierarchically ordered, and each is further broken down into levels. Changes at any level necessarily produce changes at those below it, but not necessarily above it. Social action assumes the operation of all components in all four series up to the level at which the action is to have effect. Collective behavior, according to Smelser, is an attempt to "short-circuit" this necessary path of steps and go straight to the high-level problem which is identified as the source of the strain.[19] It is thus by definition an error in rational judgment. It is not the characteristics of group membership which lower its sophistication; it is the intensity of the need to attack a felt social problem and the uncertainty of the means. The occurrence of collective action is seen as a symptom of disturbance in a system which should run smoothly.

In Smelser's view, when social life fails to work in the ways to which people are accustomed, to satisfy their values, people often develop "generalized beliefs"; these beliefs Smelser sees as *the critical feature of collective behaviour.*[20] The process is very much like that described by Freud; distinctive individual purposiveness is lost, and people collaborate in fantasizing unrealistic solutions to their perceived problems. Somewhat surprisingly, Smelser offers the following statement, which stresses the purposive nature of generalized beliefs:

> My basic theory of generalized beliefs is that they are purposive
> collective efforts to redefine and restructure the social environment,
> that crystallize when individuals and groups are subjected to cer-
> tain stresses (strain) and certain types of constraints on their op-
> portunities to resolve these stresses (conduciveness).[21]

The terms in parentheses are the structural complements of the statements in terms of individuals and groups. What is meant by "purposive" here is quite unclear (unless it is a phenomenological statement of
the ultimate intentionality of perception, which seems unlikely). Presumably Smelser does not define "purposive"as necessarily conscious,
but this does not help us much to know what it does mean. It seems a
somewhat gratuitous response to critics who have taken Smelser to task
for emphasizing the "irrational" too much.[22] The problem may be more
that he had no adequate rationale for stressing—or treating—the irrational when he did so. Another problem with the passage just quoted is
that it treats generalized beliefs as collective efforts that crystallize
when individuals (as well as groups) are in situations of strain. There is
an unexplored psychological postulate here that individuals under
"certain" stresses gather in collectivities to produce generalized beliefs. But where do the groups come from? Seeking support from a
group is only one possible response of an individual under intractable
stress—he may, for example, suffer a psychotic episode quite individually. In general, it would seem more tenable to hold that participating
in collective action fosters generalized beliefs than the other way
around.[23]

"Collective behaviour," says Smelser, "is the action of the impa-
tient."[24] If it "succeeds" in producing social change, this will generally
not be because of its practical nature but because it allows for the
components of social action to be "first destructured, then re-
structured."[25] As I have observed, in Smelser's framework collective
behavior occurs, by definition, when the system is not "adequate" to
withstand the strain imposed on it (as manifested in the form of individually and collectively experienced stress). There is an implicit assumption of continuous increase in strain, to the point at which "one
more straw will break the camel's back." To find this point in particular
cases, Smelser makes an elaborate reference to circumstances, which
are only classified, not explained, by the general theory. This problem
is compounded by the fact that his consideration of "mobilization"
gives attention only to the external sources of motivation and not to the
internal organization of a movement which changes its own circumstances.[26] "Structural conduciveness" is given disproportionately more
attention than concerted action. In this Smelser is typical—indeed, he
is the most sophisticated representative—of the view of collective

action as an inappropriate response to a disturbance in social organization. In the following discussion I will place a great deal more emphasis on the social foundations which enable people to engage in collective action.

Collective Action as Rational Individual Choice

Many writers have sought to remove the label "deviant" from collective action. They have tried, by way of tactics, to demonstrate the "rational" nature of participation in collective events. For this task they have taken both the utilitarian tradition generally and modern microeconomics in particular as guides. The individual, out to maximize his interests (however identified), and equipped with a transitive preference-ordering, has been incarnated as a sort of *homo sociologus* as well as *homo economicus*. Like the neoclassical economists, the sociological rationalists share both a claim to avoid grand theory (they construct limited "pragmatic" theories) and a remarkable doctrinal consistency. Most of their efforts in the area of collective action have been either empirical works, giving voice to the presence of intellect and intention in particular collective actions, or critiques of theories and studies which did not do so.[27] Until recently, there had not been much attempt to build a comprehensive conceptual alternative. Rather, in demonstrating the conscious reasons and tactics of rioters, rebellious peasants, and student protestors, writers from this position have offered a healthy corrective to what Gary Marx has called "the Gustave LeBon—Ronald Reagan 'mad dog' image" of those engaged in collective action.[28] Like Marx, I would suggest that the pendulum may have swung too far the other way.

This side of the argument has two main points: to show that collective actions have their "rational utility" and are not simply misguided affective outbursts; and to show that actors maintain their distinctive aims and make rational choices during collective actions. The disagreement seems to be less over the occurrence and structural determinants of collective action than over the psychological-intellectual status of the participants and the mechanisms by which collective action produces its results. Berk and Weller and Quarantelli suggest that collective behavior can be characterized by concerted group activity when previous norms or social relationships fail to meet immediate needs.[29] This is very close to Smelser's position as described above. The chief faults for which Berk criticizes the "normative theorists" are that they assume "crippled cognition" and that they never systematically examine the origins of norms.[30] The critics have yet to produce a comparative argument showing *equal* rationality among groups, however, as opposed to simply showing some rationality.[31] As to the second criticism, it is not very much different in substance from some which can readily be leveled at assumptions of both rational and maximizing man, and at revealed preference theory: to say that activity "reveals" individual preference is neither more nor less an unproven postulate than to say that it reveals collective norms.

The most important question for the rationalistic theories, as for the "disturbance" theories, is, from where do the collectivities come? Smelser's theory holds that, by and large, individual action is normal, collective action is deviant; the rationalists start from the premise that all action is essentially individual. Rationality is introduced at the level of individual decisions.[32] In the case of collective action, one must assess the independence-interdependence of the actors. As Coleman treats it: "An outcome of an event, partially controlled by each of a set of individual actors, will be described as an action or inaction of a collectivity of which these individual actors are members."[33] Such a definition only begs the question, however, of what membership in a collectivity means. Workable enough in formal terms, it fails to take account of two empirical problems: the unconscious part of each actor's control, especially in relatively informal face-to-face interactions; and the change in extent of "individuality" characteristic of the member of a meaningful group (when he is acting as a member of the group).[34] Coleman brings interdependence into his model but only as an external relationship between subjects who are assumed to have as discrete personal boundaries and as individualistic aims and identities within the group as without it. His model of collective action works much better when it is applied to aggregates of discrete individuals than when it is applied to communities. In this it manifests an ironic characteristic of most social-choice theory. It is concerned with establishing the integrated product—decision or action—of nonintegrated individuals. Problems of social choice arise as people make choices which are not sociated but isolated, discrete, or idiosyncratic. The more social are choices, the less useful is a social-choice theory based on individuals and their preferences.

The Requirements for Concerted Action

The "disturbance" theories are at their best in accounting for unorganized mobs, millennial movements, and ecstatic religious gatherings. Applied to early nineteenth-century England, they say rather more about Johanna Southcott and even Methodism than they do about either early or late radical political action. The rationalistic theories are at their best in accounting for fairly stably organized, relatively low-intensity groupings pursuing clearly defined objectives. They provide better explanations of trade-union activity and indeed of many mobilizations on a wider front during the Chartist era, than they do for the earlier, more community-based agitations of Luddites and followers of Cobbett and Hunt. Both sides of the main theoretical debate thus work poorly to account for the movements with which this book is concerned. This is largely because they neglect the social-structural foundations of collective action.

There is increasing evidence from comparative research to suggest that the movements of the 1810s rest, as I have argued, on communal foundations that indicate neither an aberrant nor, in any simple and dismissive sense, a backward movement. Wolf, for example, has emphasized the dependence of peasant movements on high prior communal organization.[35] Studies of the French Revolution since Lefebvre have shown the coherence of crowd action and its dependence on preexisting communal bonds.[36] It would appear that the early generalizations which linked the dissociating tendencies of capitalist industrialization to popular radicalism and revolutionary potential were faulty. Consider the conclusions of the Tillys in their comparative study of late nineteenth- and early twentieth-century France, Italy, and Germany:

> So far as we can detect . . . there is no tendency for recent migrants to Italian, German, and French cities to become exceptionally involved in movements of protest or in collective violence; on the contrary, we have some small indications of their under-involvement. . . . Communication, organization, and leadership take a long time to build up; once they are built up, new recruits respond to them rapidly. Since the early nineteenth century, communications, organization and leadership have tended to build up within firms, industries, and social classes, but not within territorial communities. In this sense, industrialization has affected collective action more profoundly than urbanization has.
>
> The major qualification to that conclusion is a negative case. At the beginning of our period, communities as such appeared in collective violence with fair frequency; the movements against taxation, conscription, and removal of food ordinarily recruited from individual communities; they activated communal claims over the money, labor, or commodities in question. As cities became more dominant in Germany, Italy, and France, both the bases of those claims and the capacity of members of communities to act together on them declined.[37]

In the period of English history on which I have reported, threats to and pressures on communal organization were certainly important motivations for collective action. At the same time, it was the enduring strength of traditional communities which lent concertedness to the social movements which did occur. Further, the fact that a cluster of nondiscrete values—family, craft, neighborhood—was generally being defended by the "reactionary radicals" made it especially likely that their movements would be radical, since economically ameliorative reform would not speak directly to many of their grievances. I am able, thus, to arrive at something of a specification of why it should be that revolutions have occurred not in the advanced industrial societies but in societies still largely traditional in organization but beginning to confront the pressures posed by industrialization or by the intervention of industrial powers. Communities had both the social strength and the need for revolution; the modern working class usually had at most the rational interest.

Oberschall, in emphasizing that social movements organized for conflict seldom are composed of people weakly linked to each other (as the "mass society" theorists would have it), distinguishes communal from associational links. Strength of either kind of internal sociation, as well as strength of connections between the conflict group and the larger society, predisposes a population to mobilize. Oberschall thus adds a very important, specifically social, dimension to the resource mobilization model of collective action.[38] The present analysis extends this distinction in pointing out the priority of community over class foundations for collective action in early nineteenth-century England. As I have suggested, the earlier, more communally based movements provide in most ways the closer analogue to revolutionary mobilizations. The later, more associationally based movements better deserve the label "class actions," but were essentially reformist in orientation and in structural predisposition. A variety of considerable gains were available to them from gradual reform that were not available, for example, to the Luddites.

The Working Class as a Collective Actor

The notion of working-class collective action was in large part a product of the very early nineteenth-century movements which this book has examined. Yet, it developed *out of* them as a goal, not *within* them as a self-description. As we have seen, it was only during the Chartist period that the definition of a singular working class based on exploitation within capitalist industry became widespread.[39] Even then, it did not predominate over popular mobilization. It remained commonplace to speak of the working classes, in the plural. Moreover, if the definition was uncertain, the imputation of a necessary radicalism to the collective action of the working class was confined to a still narrower segment of the population. I think that Marx's and Engels's own polemics reveal that they did not feel that they could take such a position to be firmly established even among the activists in the movements with which they were themselves associated.

In England, popular mobilizations were becoming less widespread and less radical by the time that Marx, Engels, and others were giving the theory of working-class radicalism its decisive formulation, but neither Marx nor Engels fixed his attention exclusively on England. Indeed, such preeminence as it had in their thought was largely due to the notion that the rest of Europe could learn of its future by studying what had already happened in the most advanced of capitalist countries. Their writings on revolutionary mobilization, far more than those on economics, have to be understood as programmatic in intent. Marx and Engels wrote in the hope that the strength of popular radicalism could be melded with the accuracy of scientific analysis in order to produce a supremely rational and supremely radical social transformation through the collective action of the working class. The continued strength of popular mobilizations—especially, beginning in 1848, on the Continent—fueled their hope. But the inadequacy of their sociological analysis of the basis of mobilization left them placing too much emphasis on workers' consciousness. And in the analysis of consciousness, they were too unremittingly rationalistic.

The idea of a commonality of circumstance and interest is central to the Marxian notion of class. Circumstance and interest are, in this view, objective, determinable by external observers and thus essentially amenable to rational analysis. The Marxian concern with consciousness, therefore, need not be a focus on subjective variability but rather an evaluation of how close the individual members of an externally defined category came to recognizing their true interests. In this way, the notion of class, in its most important derivation, rests on an individualistic basis. It arose historically out of the dissolution of local community and trade bonds and the lessening of sectional dissimilarities. It argued that new, more global and abstract, forces determined the relevant categories of social action. Scientific analysis could reveal the interests of these categories of individuals, and as rational human beings they would come to recognize the fundamental commonality which their circumstances gave them. Their unity was to be consciously understood, learned anew, not acquired from tradition, erected upon the largely unconscious foundation of life in communities.

Of course, this is not the whole of Marx's position. Nor do I pretend that it is the only way in which his work can be understood. I do suggest, though, that it is a central tendency in Marx's work. Marx's writings are ambiguous on the matter. As we shall see, some of the early writings give very specific attention to the limitations of "objective, rational" analysis. But Marx's successors have more often followed up his "objectivist" side. Leninism presents the emphasis on rational consciousness in still more extreme form, nearly completely negating Marx's own emphasis on the sufficiency of workers' experience in ordinary life and struggle—rather than direction from above—to produce class consciousness.

Only the proletariat could serve as a true template for Marx's conception of class, as only it would develop as a self-conscious and unified actor. The bourgeoisie became unified only in response to the demands made by the nascent proletariat.[40] It thus never fit the model of classes held in the relation of oppressor and oppressed, as suggested in the *Communist Manifesto*. The aristocracy of land and the bourgeoisie, Marx indicated, developed in competition with each other but not in a relationship of exploitation of the latter by the former. The proletariat, on the other hand, was defined in large part by exploitation; indeed, the particular circumstances of that exploitation were what called the proletariat into being and conditioned its reproduction. Even in relatively early work where the notion of exploitation is not developed, Marx sets the terminology and the model out in a fashion which has had enduring influence:

> Economic conditions had first transformed the mass of the people of the country into workers. The domination of capital has created for this mass a common situation, common interests. This mass is thus already a class as against capital, but not yet for itself. In the struggle, of which we have pointed out only a few phases, this mass becomes united, and constitutes itself as a class for itself. The interests it defends become class interests. But the struggle of class against class is a political struggle.[41]

The terms recur: class in itself, class for itself; class as an object of historical forces external to it, class as the subject of history. The Hegelian and more generally idealist legacy is clear; a distinction is made between external and essential existence. Moreover, the class thus being defined goes from being the negative object of capital to a positive subjective actor for itself, but with its own interests also being the interests of society (humanity), so that it becomes "the negative representative of society."[42] It is able to do this because it is the majority class, part of a polarized society, the negation of the negative state of that society.[43]

The fundamental relationship between the class *in* itself and the class *for* itself is left unclear. Dialectical and positive reasoning are intertwined. Is Marx suggesting that class in itself (class externally defined) precedes class for itself (class internally defined), temporally as well as theoretically? Is he suggesting that the initial definition of class is economic, but that in political struggle it develops subjectivity? Is this subjectivity superstructural as opposed to basic? What is the role of class-consciousness in turning the class in itself into a class for itself? Is the contraposition of one class to another structurally prior to the political struggle between them? Is the bourgeoisie in any sense a class for itself? Are there gradations of individual vs. class consciousness as the intersts defended by the members of a class gradually become class interests? Or, is the class consciousness somehow homogeneous in nature—a category, not a continuum?[44]

These questions are not simply matters of textual interest to scholars of Marx's thought. They stem from the way in which the concept of class was developed and the historical circumstances which conditioned that development. Other thinkers as well as Marx contributed to the ambiguity in the foundations of the theory of working-class radicalism. This is in no small part because most of these thinkers began their deliberations from the naturalistic assumption of discrete individuals. This assumption was not arbitrary but tied to the reality of atomization, individualization under the absolutist and then, especially, the capitalist state.[45] Nonetheless, it was carried in an ambiguous, ambivalent fashion into the conceptualization of the class opposed to that state. Even Marx, dedicated as he was to showing how much individualism was a part of "bourgeois ideology" never succeeded in transcending it at the most fundamental level. Though his theory was one of social actors (e.g., classes) and social relations (e.g., exploitation),[46] it was also one of individual freedom and agency. This was the most important ground on which he differed from Hegel in the latter's analysis of the constitutional state—Hegel had found no place for freedom, emancipation.[47] This ambivalence has contributed to repeated quarrels within the Marxist camp; more to the point of the present argument, it mirrors an ambivalence in the popular social thought and actual social reality of England in the age of the industrial revolution. By opting for one side or the other of Marx's ambivalent whole, analysts have failed to grasp the complexities of collective action in that critical age.

Marx foresaw a struggle between two classes, each defined in relationship to the other and compelled by historical necessity to come into conflict. Such notions had developed in embryo before Marx arrived on the scene. What was most lacking, and what Marx, for all his brilliance in developing other issues, failed to provide, was a clear answer to the question of what would turn the proletariat into a subjective actor. Marx deduced the role of the proletariat less from its internal characteristics (though he hardly ignored these) than from what history demanded of it, if the (bureaucratic) state was not to be the sole and permanent repository of rationality in history. Rationality is the driving force. The state will "wither away" after the revolution because it will be replaced, transcended by organized social relations, most especially, it would appear, among individuals (rather than groups). It is in social determination that Marx finds the possibility for the elimination of political domination. The proletariat must unite and successfully wage class struggle, because that is the only way in which the rationality of human history can progress beyond the bounds of capitalist society. Thus, "It is not a question of what this or that proletarian, or even the whole proletariat at the moment regards as its aim. It is a question of *what the proletariat is*, and what, in accordance with this being, it will historically be compelled to do."[48] Fair enough, but what is the proletariat? Marx gives us a satisfactory answer only in external terms: the proletariat is the class of wage laborers who must sell their labor-power to capital(ists) if they are to survive. Yet the weight of the whole of Marx's work is to suggest that such an external definition is insufficient. He hints occasionally at ways in which the proletariat's social organization and experience makes it a potential subjective actor: its concentration in cities and factories, its subjection to the authority and discipline of the workplace, the collective participation of its members in more particular, narrow economic, and even political struggles.[49] Most of all, Marx held that recognition of common interests would unite the working class. The leveling effect of industrial capitalism would give all workers the same poor standard of living and the same desperate wants.[50]

Marx's successors have had less faith in the direct efficacy of the social being of workers and have introduced the radical mediation of the Leninist party. Interestingly, Marx did not see the party in the same relationship to the working class as, in his view, the state held to the whole society. This would have been a reasonable view. Marx argued that the state was made necessary by the fact that people pursued "private" interests which they identified as separate from "general" interests. The state coerced them to accept their own best interests in the name of a general interest separate from any of them.[51] Now the same alienation which necessitated the state would, one might think, appear among the membership of the proletariat and be the reason why the workers must be united in a strong party. This notion is compatible with Lenin's position, but Marx refused to take it, perhaps because it failed to imply the transcendance of alienation and power politics in the very nature of the proletariat. In any case, Marx held that common interests would unite the working class to the point where it might act for itself and not require the intervention of such an analogue to the state as a Leninist party.

The problem, put simply, is that Marx did not have a sociological account of what turned an aggregate of individuals into a grouping capable of concerted collective action. Such a sociology must consider the internal relationships of the members, not simply their individual existences or the role of the whole in the progress of rationality. Marx put the weight of his theoretical and empirical attack on the issue of what the proletariat would be historically compelled to do, on external circumstances conditioning this action, and not on internal relations making it possible.

Both the Hegelian idealism and the Feuerbachian materialism from which Marx took his initial bearings aspired to universalistic statements. That is, they both wished to make truth claims which transcended mere contingencies of perspective or situatedness, and to speak to fundamental characteristics, either of the human condition, in Feuerbach's case, or of spirit, as Hegel saw it dialectically developing. In both materialism and idealism, Marx saw a passivity which he wished to transcend.[52] He was, thus, fundamentally attempting to create a theory of action. At the same time, however, Marx did not find it easy to abandon the universalistic claims of his predecessors. He sought, through his largely Hegelian theory of historical development, to give a singularly "true" and final statement of the proper sources of the directionality of thought. Marx admitted, in the words of his second thesis on Feuerbach, that human activity in the world is "this-sided." He did not, however, give up on discovering the necessary condition of a universally true theory of action, one which would transcend mere contingency and self-interest in the narrow sense. He argued that the establishment of certain social conditions provided the source of premises of thought which were neither arbitrary nor limited. This is the significance of the proletariat as a transcendent actor, one whose action is shaped by universal chains.[53] The cognitive activity of individual proletarians, shaped by the same premises in social circumstances, would thus constitute a singular consciousness. Because of the place of those circumstances in universal historical development, that consciousness would not be arbitrary but rather the embodiment of historical progress. Revolutionary class consciousness thus became necessary for Marx and not subject to competition from more mediate options or to ethical considerations based on mere particularities.

It is precisely this argument of necessity which Weber challenged:

Thus every class may be the carrier of any one of the innumerable possible forms of class action, but this is not necessarily so. In any case, a class does not in itself constitute a group *(Gemeinschaft)*. To treat "class" conceptually as being equivalent to "group" leads to distortion. That men in the same class situation regularly react in mass actions to such tangible situations as economic ones in the direction of those interests that are most adequate to their average number is an important and after all simple fact for the understanding of historical events. However, this fact must not lead to that kind of pseudo-scientific operation with the concepts of class and class interests which is so frequent these days and which has found its most classic expression in the statement of a talented author, that the individual may be in error concerning his interests but that the class is infallible about its interests.[54]

While many modern Marxists may fall immediately and justifiably victim to Weber's criticism, inasmuch as they merely assume an identity between class interests, class consciousness, and class action, Marx had at least the vestiges of a counterargument. Its weakness is in its lack of a substantial sociology and social psychology which would account for the postulated sharing of interests as a class rather than merely aggregating individual interests, and for collective action on that basis.

In his neglect of such a sociological and psychological argument, Marx fell back on his basic rationalism. This left him open to Weber's critique, for it placed explanatory weight primarily on thinking individuals. Both Marx's Enlightenment rationalism and his nineteenth-century scientism led him to treat immediate sociality and tradition as essentially arbitrary and thus divorced from fundamental truth.[55] Only such immediate sociality and traditional premises in thought make it possible to conceive of social action, however, rather than some form of social-structural or culturalogical determinism. It is the weakness of this part of Marx's argument which has led to the analytic separation of "objective" and "subjective" dimensions of class. This has led on the one hand to asking what objective circumstances are required to make (in some simple causal sense) a class into a subjective actor (e.g., concentration, immiseration, etc.). On the other hand, those emphasizing the subjective dimension have tended to reduce it to a matter simply of what people think rather than a consideration of all the conditions which may produce collective action.

If a class exists separately from its consciousness of itself and its collective action, then it must be seen to exist in some external characteristics common to its members: wealth, income, control or noncontrol of political events, and so forth. But, crucially, in such an account one postulates no collective entity, only individuals. Take, for example, the notion of a class defined by access to goods in a marketplace.[56] The members of such a class might develop a particular style of life based on the goods which they consume; they might even be recognizable to each other. The similarities in the behavior and appearance of individual members do not, however, imply any interconnections among them. The consumption of identical goods does not imply the consumption of collective goods.[57] It may, of course, provide for a predisposition to secure collective goods. Housing is often concentrated in part by cost, and residential proximity may lead to the formation of social ties and the decision to pursue such collective goods as clean or safe streets. Members of a "class" based on level of consumption might band together in a consumers' union or purchasing cooperative. They might then secure collective benefits and exert concerted pressures on producers and markets. As an organized collectivity, however, they cease to be defined by their common level of consumption (though that may still define the population which will share in the collective goods) and become defined by their social relationships. Not an aggregate of individuals but a social organization is at issue. With a social organization, collective action, not merely similar actions, becomes possible.[58]

The leap from the existence of an aggregate of individuals with common external characteristics, or subject to common constraints, to a class potentially able to take collective action is problematic and has not been adequately dealt with either in theoretical sociology or in historical analysis.[59] Crude interpretation of the Marxian base/superstructure dichotomy (and its partial analogue, class-in-itself/class-for-itself) implies such a leap, *within* the general framework of class. Poulantzas, among others, has firmly repudiated such a usage:

> For Marxism, social classes involve in one and the same process both class contradictions and class struggle; social classes do not firstly exist as such, and only then enter into a class struggle. Social classes coincide with class practices, i.e., the class struggle, and are only defined in their mutual opposition.[60]

The difference between seeing class arising out of different levels of material consumption and seeing it arising as a part of the relations of production is manifest in this connection. Among other things, it provided Marx with the foundation for his doctrine of the revolutionary significance of class struggle. The relations of production under capitalism implied, he suggested, a concentration of the working population and its organization and discipline in the workplace. However initially oppressive this might appear, it also had the hidden virtue of uniting and training the future revolutionary class. In other words the (relevant) objective conditions implied the organization necessary (though perhaps not sufficient) to subjective action.[61] Marx was preceded in such a view by English activists such as Thelwall of the London Corresponding Society, who argued that we ought to see every "manufactory" as a potential center of rebellion.[62]

Starting from "consciousness" and attempting to work toward an explanation of collective action can be just as problematic as starting from objective conditions. The leap from thought to action is no less an issue than that from material circumstances to action.[63] Attention is needed to all that goes into making a social aggregate a collective actor. People may share opinions without sharing either the will or the capability to translate those opinions into concerted action. Class is only one of the many kinds of collectivities in which people may choose to act; they may also pursue more individual courses of action. What will happen depends on the extent to which (a) individuals identify with a class,[64] (b) the class is organized to secure participation and take concerted action, (c) other social collectivities are congruent with class organization, (d) other goods than those requiring class action are available, and last, and most likely least, (e) individuals estimate the probable success of class action.[65]

Marx gave his attention most of all to "d," suggesting that capitalism must accelerate the rate and scope of exploitation, the relative material difference between bourgeoisie and proletariat. His suggestion was not just that other goods were not available to workers but that workers were necessarily in competition with the bourgeoisie for these goods, and the bourgeoisie could not relinquish them and maintain its own existence. There was, thus, no nonconflictual way for the working class to improve its position in society. It has often been pointed out that capitalism proved more able than Marx anticipated to offer concessions to workers.[66] These may be variously seen as the fruits of long and bitter struggle or as clever devices by elite groups to secure their positions in advance of open conflict.[67] In either case, the point does not demand any fundamental shift in Marxist theory (though it has sometimes stimulated such shifts). It is perfectly possible to incorporate the resilience of capitalism in the suggestion of a longer horizon before the revolutionary dawn. Some writers suggest that the capitalist transformation of the world is a precondition of the socialist transformation and that in the meantime, the toils of third-world laborers pay for the luxury of relative complacency among the workers of advanced capitalist countries. However practically significant, the length of the capitalist epoch is not crucial to Marx's theory of class struggle.

What is crucial is Marx's argument for the necessity of universalization of class struggle.[68] According to Marx, the inherent tendency of capitalism was to polarize class conflict into a single opposition between the owners and nonowners of the means of production. Even when he considered the growing numbers of relatively privileged and powerful nonowners, he did not give up this notion of the all-encompassing opposition.[69] The import of this is that the workers would *have* to struggle with the owners of the means of production, if not immediately then later; if not for the absolute conditions of existence, then for the relative conditions of existence. This was not simply a conflict of interests but a necessary struggle for existence, a competition over resources which were limited and forms of organization which were contradictory.

Marx's theory is radically challenged on this point only by the suggestion that (a) capitalism can generate sufficient productivity and wide enough distribution to meet the demands upon it without radical class conflict,[70] or (b) that there are ends which workers can and will seek which do not bring them so directly and radically into conflict with the owners of the means of production. Most of the attention of left and right alike has been drawn to the redistribution of the products of capitalism as its means of maintaining itself. This is the "a" challenge above. The "b" challenge turns the question around: one may ask what capitalism can give, or what workers will seek.[71]

Premises of Collective Action

If one assumes that the selection of what ends to seek is open and not obvious or simply rationally ascertainable, a whole new set of problems arises. It becomes an empirical question just what it was that workers in any one place or time were seeking or might seek. Further, the external circumstances of workers cannot be regarded as a sufficient explanation for their aims or activity. The understanding of workers' action must then turn on a more complex concept of consciousness than any simple "reflection" theory or notion of purely "scientific" understanding.[72] Thompson's conceptualization of class was developed, I think, precisely to incorporate a notion of consciousness which includes human agency.[73] Yet, as I have suggested, some of Thompson's innovations in conceptualization, like many of his subtle empirical analyses, are in (not fully admitted) conflict with the main strain of Marxist thought and much of the work of Marx himself.

Marx treated class consciousness as an essentially rational phenomenon. For most of his followers, including especially the Leninists, this usage has continued. Class consciousness is treated as the correct, scientific understanding of external, objective circumstances. For a minority, of some prominence among twentieth-century

Marxists, this has too much devalued the notion of consciousness and too far removed it from Marx's nondeterminist notion of the self-creation of the working class. Thus, in different ways, the early Lukács, Gramsci, and members of the Frankfurt school each struggled to come to grips with the variable and not wholly determined features of human thought and emotion. Marxism, in short, split on the wedge of two different interpretations of class consciousness. The Leninist interpretation made correct class consciousness the prerequisite to class struggle. The other made class consciousness largely the outcome of that struggle.

As different as these two views are, however, they share a crucial common ground. Both see class consciousness as more radical than previous or other nonclass consciousness. The progress of rational analysis is assumed to be tied to the increase of radicalism. It is, of course, my argument that this is not the case. It is my suggestion that both the social organizational basis and the consciousness which preceded the emergence of the modern working class were more likely foundations for radical collective action. I shall attempt, briefly, to sustain this point by arguing that rootedness in tradition and immediate social relations is the essential basis of a radical response to social change; and that neither motives nor interests, however rationally understood, provide a sufficient reason for collective action and, furthermore, that their sufficiency diminishes with the radicalism of the contemplated action.[74]

Leninism developed its insistence on the correct, scientific party line largely in the course of struggles against revisionists and anarchists and in rejection of conventional social democratic tactics. The theme of class consciousness took on new meaning when counterposed to "mere" trade-union consciousness.[75] Marx had always held that any and all collective activity among workers contributed to the transformation of the class in itself into the class for itself. He had suggested no limits to this self-creation but merely emphasized the determinant importance of activity in opposition to the bourgeoisie. This is one of the ways, perhaps, in which Marx remained most Hegelian.[76] Lenin, of course, thought differently—no doubt in part because he observed a very different set of historical circumstances. Lenin substituted a more positivist notion of science for Marx's critical stance[77] and, in the same vein, substituted the Communist party for the working class as the knowing subject of revolutionary action.[78]

Lenin's stance was not altogether foreign to that of Marx. Lenin furthered Marx's own emphasis on conscious self-awareness, placing even more weight on explicit and rational choices based on "correct" understandings of empirical situations. Class interests, in this view, are the objective products of material circumstances and thus matters wholly of scientific analysis, not personal preference. The goal of Marxist-Leninist social analysis is to overcome ideological interference with the "natural" process of identifying objective interests. The assumption is that the rational result of accurate empirical knowledge is revolution. In Eric Olin Wright's recent formulation:

> Class interests in capitalist society are those potential objectives which become actual objectives of struggle in the absence of the mystifications and distortions of capitalist relations. Class interests, therefore, are in a sense hypotheses: they are hypotheses about the objectives of struggle which would occur if the actors in the struggle had a scientifically correct understanding of their situations.[79]

Such a rationalist, positivist emphasis on "correct" analysis follows up one side of an ambivalence in Marx's work. The other side of Marx's account gave a somewhat greater weight to immediately lived social reality, to the directionality implicit in ordinary practical activity. Marx could merge the two sides of his ambivalence into an apparent whole, because he shared the general post-Enlightenment assumptions of rationalism and progress. That is, like Hegel, from whom he drew more than he declared on this, Marx believed that the progress of social life was directly matched in the progress of consciousness, that what truly mattered in human history appeared as rational in human consciousness even if consciousness was not, as Hegel had thought, its source.[80] Thus the materialism which Marx espoused was one which stressed not the externality of material phenomena but their incorporation into human life through practical activity, of which conscious awareness and, indeed, control were always a critical part.[81]

It was through the concept of practice that Marx gave attention to immediately lived social reality, but the potential importance of the concept was to some extent undercut by its assimilation to the idealist emphasis on the primacy of consciousness. I do not want to enter into the debate on how much Marx himself intended the notion of consciousness to imply rational, self-aware thought. I want, rather, to suggest that Marx was sufficiently ambiguous (because, I think, he was ambivalent) that it has been easy for later commentators to attribute extreme views on this point to him. There was unquestionably a part of Marx, increasingly important as his life went on, which believed strongly in the power of scientific knowledge. But there was also a part of Marx which never stopped appreciating the realm of lived reality, of what has more recently been called tacit knowledge.[82] Marx had little intellectual apparatus for considering that which was neither rational consciousness nor simple passion.[83] It was his rationalism which most limited Marx's ability to develop such a line of analysis and which has so deeply permeated latter-day Marxism.

Marx made not inconsiderable strides in coming to terms with the practical significance of knowledge, its directionality as interested or useful action—what Marx called the "this-sidedness" of thinking which is forced upon it by the fact that the thinker is always a human being engaging in practice.[84] He also was careful to give the importance of the material, objective world its due, to emphasize that people think usually as creatures in relation to their needs and to a world of things which could potentially satisfy them.[85] Marx was also firm in his grasp of the historicity of all social action. This is the meaning of his famous statement that "men make their own history but they do not make it just as they please."[86] All action occurs only within the crucial sequence of historical events and is shaped in its essentials by its historical location.[87] Marx's rationalism, however, along with the notion of progress which he shared with most modern thinkers under the influence of the Enlightenment, and the particular political struggles in which he was engaged, severely constrained his ability to appreciate the importance of tradition. Marx's faith in the creation of understanding de novo was too great.

In the second thesis on Feuerbach, Marx had implied, with his notion of the "this-sidedness," a limit to such rationalism. Marx himself and, especially, many of his followers ignored that limit. Like other heirs of the Enlightenment, they struggled for freedom from prejudices. Accepting some of Hume's and Kant's critiques, they did not learn from those masters that pure reason, however well-executed, could go only so far in approaching the practical world. So firmly pejorative have modern ideas of prejudice been, that it has become difficult to recognize the necessity of prerational premises to all thought and experience. It is in this vein that Gadamer has sought to restore something of a positive aspect to the concept of prejudice: "Prejudices are not necessarily unjustified and erroneous, so that they inevitably distort the truth. In fact, the historicity of our existence entails that prejudices, in the literal sense of the word, constitute the initial directedness of our whole openness to the world. They are simply conditions whereby we experience something."[88] It is in this sense that culture is crucial to experience, and in particular that tradition was crucial to the way in which the reactionary radicals experienced the industrial revolution. Thompson is quite right, in opposition to Althusser's rationalism, to argue a case for the importance of experience, everyday life, and common culture.[89]

Culture, however, is not the only source of the premises underlying thought and experience. It is not even the only source of the premises which make that experience shared and thus a potential basis for collective action. Immediate social relations are also important. Indeed, it is in practical relationships with one another that people are able to reshape tradition, keeping culture in touch with new circumstances and experiences.[90] Further, it is social relationships formed in practical activity which make experience something mutual rather than merely common. The mutuality of experience in a closely knit community is a much more likely and solid foundation for collective action than is the similarity of experiences among the members of a class defined in external terms.

Tradition must mean different things to different people, and its meaning must change as society changes. To deny its significance as a basis for thought and action because of this would be a mistake. Tradition need not be the hard cake of culture, absolutely determinant of all thought, for us to recognize its efficacy.[91] In fact, its efficacy is partially independent of its continuity.[92] Immediate social relations provide for new experiences even within a largely traditional framework. Further, each individual is always embedded in a particular constellation of relationships, which gives him a particular perspective on social reality. Such cultural inheritances and immediate social relations must constantly be interpreted in, just as they give shape to, practical activity. Together, culture—which I understand as a collective product, and thus always in some part traditional—and social relations form the primary premises of our thought about social action.

Culture and social relations thus provide a necessary part of the basis for any social action, insofar as action must be directed. They are not, however, sufficient explanations of action. In the first place, still on the subjective side of the matter, to speak of action is to speak of human will. It is the role of will which Thompson is often concerned to discover in his historical (and political) writings. He sometimes conflates will, which I think is best understood as a fundamentally individual phenomenon, with culture. This is confusing, and his relative neglect of immediate social relations further clouds the issue by making tradition too much the hard cake of culture. These problems, however, are internal to Thompson's account; he himself has in a pioneering, if unclear, fashion pointed the way to their resolution. The problems are internal because they are a part of Thompson's fundamental effort to give a subjective explanation of history. It is objective social structure which produces the greater problem, because Thompson neglects it more completely.

An account of social structure is not, however, antithetical to explanation in terms of action; it is essential to it. The idea of action implies choice. It is only meaningful to conceive of any course of action as voluntary where other courses of action are possible. Possibility is frequently determined by objective structural conditions. In particular, collective action is doubly so determined. Like all social action, it is conditioned by the behavior of other actors—as for example the possibility of a coup d'etat depends in part on the strength of police protection of the government or the loyalty of the military—their willingness to shoot their fellow countrymen. But, collective action is also partially determined by internal structural characteristics, the organization of the collectivity itself. Whether or not a particular collectivity, such as the working class, will become a collective actor is a question which can only be answered with attention to objective as well as subjective issues.[93]

Class action is subject to the general difficulties of collective action; there are formal obstacles to the rational provision of collective or public goods. Political economists before Marx had barely noticed the existence of this problem, even in connection with its most obvious manifestation, the provision of services by the state.[94] Saint-Simon, Fourier, Owen, and Marx all brought to the foreground of discussion those goods which individuals could not readily provide for themselves. Marx, in particular, conceptualized the state in terms of its ability to provide collective goods for certain classes of the population. Just as he left the connection between class-in-itself and class-for-itself inexplicit, however, Marx left it unclear just how and why the state should perform for the bourgeoisie. He suggests that it is a direct extension of the rational self-interest of the bourgeois; yet, is it not an agency which coerces the bourgeois to forego his individual self-interest in favor of the interests of his class? Does it not ask him (or, rather, compel him) to give up such immediate benefits as freedom from taxation for such longer-term ones as freedom from foreign invasion? This separate and coercive existence of the state reveals the alienated condition of society.[95]

Collective action is a problem, because the self-interest of rational actors does not cause them always to provide collective goods even when these are in the interest of all members of a collectivity. In other words, groups of individuals with common interests do not necessarily act on behalf of their common interests. This failure is particularly likely to occur with groupings beyond the range where face-to-face contact, dense and multiplex relations, and relative certainty of the participation of others can be had without extensive formal organization.[96] Small, stable groupings, in other words, may act in concert fairly readily. Large groupings tend to be only latent collective actors, for it is difficult to mobilize them without selective inducements for individual participation, distinct from the collective good itself. In a nation-state, for example, it would not be in the interest of rational actors to pay taxes, even for public services which they desire, since those services would be provided whether or not they individually pay part of the cost. States do not rely solely on the goodwill of their citizens in this matter but punish those who do not pay and thus coerce the rest. Without a selective inducement, it would always be rational to attempt to be a free rider, but, since each would make the same attempt, the good would never be provided. There are also, it should be noted, intermediate-size groupings in which each individual's contribution or lack of contribution could be noticed and would affect the outcome, but in a degree less than the cost of his contribution. It is thus logically indeterminate whether such a grouping would provide a collective good.

Collective goods are, quite simply, those which, once provided, may be enjoyed by all members of a collectivity. Selective inducements discriminate between those who participate or fail to participate in providing the collective goods. One reason small groups are at such an advantage in providing collective goods is that it is far easier for them to identify free riders and exercise some form of internal discipline. The costs and difficulty of organization grow rapidly with increasing size and decreasing density, multiplexity, and flow of information. Without an organization able to operate a scheme of selective inducements, it will generally not be (individually) rational for members of a large collectivity to provide themselves with the benefits of any sort of collective goods. There may of course be various nonrational reasons why they would do so. The latter case would not fit, however, with an assumption such as Marx's that there is a direct connection between the rationality of individuals and the rationality of classes.

A collective good may sometimes be provided because it is worth enough to one or several members of the collectivity for them to pay all of the costs of providing it. This is only likely to be the case where costs are trivial (an empirically rare phenomenon) or where one member of the collectivity is disproportionately interested in whatever their common interests are. An instance of the latter sort would be found in an industry so dominated by a few giant firms that it would be worthwhile for these giants to increase the demand for their common product even if this would also be to the benefit of some of their pygmy fellows who might be unwilling to share the cost. Such disproportion is only likely in small groups. It is further only likely where actors vary greatly either in the extent of their interest (certain common interests are peripheral to some group members, central to others) or in the resources they can devote to acquiring the collective good. Concentration of resources differentiates situations of potential oligopoly—relatively frequent in markets—from those in which actors are more or less equal—typically the case in attempts to mobilize a population for a mass movement. No matter what his personal interest in living in a democracy, for example, no single individual could overthrow an autocratic system and institute a democracy. He would lack the resources for the overthrowing, and a one-person democracy is nonsensical. Certain kinds of goods which workers in the period of the industrial revolution sought, and especially the resources with which they had to wage their battles, made collective action a necessity.

The common interests of the workers made them collectively a potential revolutionary class actor. In this Marx was right: it was rational for the class to seek those goods, and there was no other way to do so than as a class. Where Marx appears to have been wrong was in arguing that the class must supersede all other collectivities for the workers, that those interests which they had in common as members of the working class must become their exclusive interests, and that, therefore, it was individually rational for each worker to participate in the collectively rational overthrow of capitalist domination by the working class. There is no logical error in this part of Marx's analysis, as some critics have suggested.[97] Rather, the empirical conditions do not seem to have been met. Class relations have not, in any advanced capitalist society, been universalized to the point where workers identify primarily with their class, and seek the rational goals of that class. Workers have sought other, less radical, ends than the revolutionary transcendence of capitalism; they have aligned themselves on the basis of other, less universal, more mediate collectivities. Furthermore, as long as there were other options, workers were individually rational to persist in this collective irrationality.[98] Class action was costly, its success uncertain, and being a "free rider" easy.

This was manifestly the case during the industrial revolution. The key to organizational effectiveness, to security from the authorities, and to strength of participation was the extent of the linkage between any organization and the local community. Political organizations tended always to suffer on this account. They drew members from a wider area than did trade organizations, for example, at least in the early part of the century, and they included members drawn from widely varying social groups. The trade organizations grew out of more distinctively local conditions and often directly out of workshops. While Thompson brings this up in connection with vulnerability to spies, it is of wider importance.[99] It points out an early pressure in the direction of mobilization for collective action on local community as opposed to national class issues. It also suggests the importance of the attachment of any political campaign to such local community organization and interests.

Lenin based his argument for a strong, centralized, and independent revolutionary party partially on similar considerations. "The history of all countries," he wrote,

> shows that the working class, exclusively by its own effort, is able to develop only trade union consciousness, i.e., the conviction that it is necessary to combine in unions, fight the employers, and strive to compel the government to pass necessary labour legislation, etc. . . . The spontaneous working-class movement is trade-unionism . . . and trade-unionism means the ideological enslavement of the workers by the bourgeoisie. Hence, our task, the task of Social-Democracy, is to combat spontaneity, to divert the working-class movement from this spontaneous, trade-unionist striving to come under the wing of the bourgeoisie, and to bring it under the wing of revolutionary Social-Democracy.[100]

Although Lenin maintained that he was directly representing Marx, in contrast to the misinterpretations or revisionism of others, he was in fact responding to a problem in Marxian theory.[101] Marx and Engels had initially held that workers' participation in trade-union and related political struggles would directly radicalize them and give them the experience and organization necessary to become successful revolutionaries.[102] By the end of the nineteenth century, the notion of a continuous "maturation" of working-class politics toward a socialist revolution was under a challenge based on recent European history. Trade-union strength and workers' collective action had indeed grown, but not strictly in the direction envisaged. In response, Marxists split into three groups. The left-communists were for the intensification of mass action, insurrection, and revolution at the expense of strong party control. The revisionists were for reformist participation in democratic politics, sacrificing notions of discontinuous revolutionary change. Lenin and his colleagues were for the development of a revolutionary vanguard party, strong, centralized, and able to seize power in a systematic fashion when a crisis immobilized or weakened the forces of an old regime or the bourgeoisie.[103]

All of these responses to the unexpected strength of European (and international) capitalism are crucially founded on notions of class consciousness. The first holds that class consciousness is immediately revolutionary (but that revolution is a matter of insurrection first and organization second).[104] The second holds that class consciousness is essentially reformist and that both the interests and the inclinations of the workers are met in trade-union and parliamentary activity.[105] Lenin's position, and the new orthodoxy which grew (or was fashioned selectively) out of it, was a slightly more complex two-stage one. Lenin held that the immediate consciousness of the working class would be a false consciousness, tending toward trade unionism and dominated by bourgeois ideology. This, however, was to be supplanted by a class consciousness which was founded on advanced intellectual analysis of the state of society under the paradigm of historical materialism. This was "class consciousness" not because of who held it but because of its content. It was necessarily revolutionary because the great transformation to socialism could only come by means of revolution. It was also likely to be the consciousness only of a minority, though one which was able to gain access to and assume leadership of "the masses."

One of the things which is lost from Marx in the Leninist treatment is the argument that the social being of workers will lead them toward and provide the foundation for the transformation to socialism. Marx did not discount the importance of organizations or of intellectuals, of course, but neither did he abstract the development of class consciousness from the concrete social life of the members of the working class. Marx was right to place great stress on the analysis of social foundations; he was wrong in holding that the social foundations of mature European capitalism would underpin revolution. This is one of the reasons that the present work insists on the importance of the shift from community-based populist radicalism to a great dependence on formal organizations representing larger, less communal populations. This shift marked the emergence of the typically, and logically, "reformist" modern working class.

This new working class was typically reformist because it could seek a variety of ends within capitalist society. In contrast, the very existence of the older, more traditional communities of artisans and other workers was threatened by capitalism. On a social-psychological level, the most fundamental premises organizing the thought and lives of the older craftsmen were challenged. Their communities, families, and sense of who, exactly, they were all came under attack. The newer working class derived this sort of fundamental sense of identity from capitalist society, and struggled over more transient, malleable, and optional goals.[106]

Let us think back to Marx's description of the proletariat as a class with radical chains, a class compelled to produce a single direction of collective action:

> It is not a question of what this or that proletarian, or even the whole proletariat, at the moment regards as its aim. It is a question of what the proletariat is, and what, in accordance with this being, it will historically be compelled to do. Its aim and historical action is visibly and irrevocably foreshadowed in its own life situation as well as in the whole organization of bourgeois society today.[107]

What is the nature of this compulsion? What so radically alters the relationship of individual subject to collectivity that the latter becomes both the "real" subject and a radically historically determined one? The best answer, I think, is that at the most fundamental level of social and psychological identity, the individual proletarian cannot continue to exist except by defending certain shared, collective premises which are integral to his consciousness but which are also the products of culture and social relations.

Implicit in this answer is the notion that people act to preserve stability in both their psyches and their social environments. In terms of the former, new information is fit in the most consistent way possible into existing patterns of interpretation. Action is taken, further, in ways which keep the individual's environment maximally in line with his expectations. New information is likely to make the individual change only his more superficial or transient patterns of interpretation. He will usually maintain his fundamental self-consciousness and orientation in the world, attempting to change the world, when necessary, to do so.[108] Obviously, the world is usually changed only in the smallest of ways. Individuals act to rescue their marriages, keep their jobs, or protect their property when these are bound up in a fundamental way with their identities. Only in the cumulation of such individual acts do most macrosociological changes come about.

As Bourdieu has pointed out, in order for social life to take place at all in the infinitude of slightly varying contexts which are naturally and socially given to action, there must be continual improvisation on the part of individual actors. Such improvisation is, however, regulated by what Bourdieu terms the "habitus."[109] This structured orientation to the world works to provide for the generation of improvisations in such a way as to reproduce the objective conditions of social action, as well as to reproduce the regularities in responses to such conditions. The habitus is the result of the learning of traditional culture and the experience of actual social relations. It precedes and directs the exercise of personal will.

Even disregarding the effects of purely novel, initiative individual activity, the dialectic between habitus and objective structures provides for only a variable, never a perfect, degree of reproduction. There can be more individual variability in response, and individual-level accommodations, the less near the roots of social existence (the habitus) the practical demands of any situation strike. This is precisely the grounding of the passage just quoted from Marx concerning what the proletariat is compelled to do. Individual wills are the source of all sorts of varying activity so long as the fundamental basis of personal existence is not seriously threatened. These individual acts cumulate in one sort of history—history without a single subject, in which the history itself is not intended.[110] Further, these individuals may cooperate to seek various collective ends, subject to the constraints already outlined on the rationality governing calculations about collective action.

Despite their analytic acumen, and no matter how scientific their understanding of the world, those individual wills will not ordinarily produce radical collective action. To do so would be to subject voluntarily the very ground of their own existence to disruption—a most irrational act. The will of the whole proletariat (in the first sentence of the passage above from Marx) is apt to be a reformist will. Where does radicalism come from? It comes from those the premises of whose existence (whose habitus) are already threatened. In capitalist society as we have so far seen it develop, this means the workers tied to other modes of production and social existence whom capitalism displaces.[111] The "historical action" which "is visibly and irrevocably foreshadowed in its own life situation as well as in the whole organization of bourgeois society today," results from an existential compulsion. The individual must respond, and he must respond as part of a social whole, not in isolation. I believe that this is what Marx had in mind, though he failed to see that it was not the new working class but instead the members of traditional crafts and communities who must react to the conditions of their lives in a radical way.

Summary

It is important to pay close attention to the fields of social relations within which individuals act. These immediate relationships extend across different personal purposes, exerting an influence on individual understanding, calculation, feeling, and activity which transcends instrumentality. Such relationships are partially beyond conscious manipulation, not just because of "values" which they may express or which may order them, but because the capacity of a single consciousness to give attention to many foci is quite limited.[112] Further, in our struggle for cognitive consistency, we continually try to fit our experience and our affective relations into a manageable pattern.

As social relationships are established, in the course of an individual's life, they become part of the set of fundamental premises which gives direction to further action. Relationships may be considered more established as the cognitive, affective, and material costs of violating their premises or disengaging from them increase, along with the rewards of maintaining them. This happens, in terms of particular content, as relationships become more familiar and come to carry specific or (with still more involvement) diffuse obligations. Structurally, an individual becomes more deeply woven into a web of relationships and they become a part of his established premises of action. This happens as relationships become dense within a social field (so that activity in each involves a considerable range of others as an implicitly relevant public), as relationships become multiplex (so that each involves many purposes and qualities of bond), and as relationships become systematic (so that each has its existence not independently, or voluntarily, but rather as part of a differentiated set of relationships each of which presumes the others, as in kinship). This is community.[113]

Clearly, collective action is much more likely where the collectivity in question is already presumed in the activity of individual members. It is not necessary in such circumstances to bring people together, to create organization. Rather, people can be mobilized on the basis of existing bonds. Such communal patterns of organization may, in many cases, provide for much stronger, if less analytically focused, mobilizations than those provided by formal organizations. They solve several of the often noted problems of organizing—such as those of "free riders" and multiple low-level commitments. In communal organizations, free riders can be directly sanctioned by the refusal of others to maintain normal relations. And, in societies where communities are all-inclusive, their bonds multiplex, it is unlikely that individuals will have significant commitments outside of them.

Collective action is likely to be radical where it defends established premises of thought and action against fundamental attacks. Social relations and traditional culture are both important parts of such premises. When people are closely and stably knit together in communities, when traditional culture is vital in giving direction and meaning to personal and social life, people are apt to engage in considerable adjustment of other aspects of their situations, emotions, or ideas in order to maintain this basic structure. People will, in short, resist the disruption of the communities and ideas within which they are oriented to the world.[114] In Marxian terms, they will resist alienation. Reactionary radicals, like the early nineteenth-century English workers discussed in this book, derive their strength of mobilization and their radicalism alike from the very social and cultural bonds which alienation attacks. They are not the embodiment of the most extreme moment of the dialectic—complete alienation preceding radical unification. Far from being freed of all biases and made perfectly rational (an empty, nonsensical idea), these sometimes revolutionary workers were radical (as the word implies) because of their roots.

No degree of simple material suffering could produce either this radicalism or this social strength. Where workers in capitalist industrial production could be offered a wide variety of material rewards,

incentives for cooperation in politics and production, no moderate reform could provide much amelioration to the plight of the reactionary
radicals. The handloom weavers, for example, in their attempt to
maintain a way of life which brought them together in communities
and fulfilled traditional aspirations, stood in direct contradiction to the
development of capitalist industry. The factory workers, on the other
hand, could struggle for improvements within capitalism. For factory
workers to devote themselves to revolution would have involved (as
sometimes it has done) a rejection or sacrifice of other less radical ends.
Marx thought that workers in advanced capitalism would be compelled
to seek social revolution because, in part, of a lack of alternatives. In
fact, they have alternatives. It is workers facing the transition from one
mode of production, and one traditional orientation in the world, who
lack alternatives. They are often not even involved in a transition taking them in any identifiable direction; their way of life is simply being
obliterated. They protest, and sometimes they revolt.

Epilogue

The contrast between relatively traditional communities of craftsmen and less traditional, less communal aggregations of workers within industrial capitalism has formed a central theme of this book. It should be noted that to draw this contrast among workers in early nineteenth-century England is hardly to present an extreme picture of either pattern. The traditional communities in which I have found the basis for an important English radicalism were not committed to an unchanging way of life and livelihood. Their members worked in a capitalist economy and lived in a largely modern if not yet corporate and centralized society. Many, like the northern handloom weavers, were indeed products of an economic transition; only for a short period did they maintain communal organizations and traditions linking them to pre-industrial England. In the same vein, the factory workers who began to form the modern English working class in the 1820s and 1830s did not come to predominate in English popular activism for several decades after that. Craftsmen and others with direct ties to traditional occupations and communities were disproportionately important. To this day, English workers are often densely knit into local communities and fiercely loyal to particularist traditions—much more so, for example, than their American counterparts. In short, in describing the transition of work forces in early nineteenth-century England, I have considered variance only within the middle range of a much broader variable of the social and cultural foundations for popular mobilization. It may be well to suggest something of what I take to be the rest of the variance.

England's struggles at the onset of industrialization were distinctive in the first place because England had already had a political revolution which had not only strengthened nascent capitalism but minimized the role of repressive central power in maintaining internal peace and labor control. English workers confronted a mixed, not an absolutist, government. It did not represent them, but neither did it form the strong arm of repressive labor control on behalf of a landowning class. The converse of this nonabsolutist government was the heterogeneous working population. England was far from a nation of peasants; her internal division of labor was quite advanced. This meant, first, that no single class of elites could be the beneficiary of a singular policy of state repression. At the same time, hardships and provocations to insurgency often hit different parts of the population at different points, thus making unified action difficult. One dimension of this split can be seen in the contrast of the emergent articulation of political and economic claims in the parliamentary reform agitation leading up to Peterloo, with the charivari-like, culturally focused, expressive protest of the Caroline agitation. The demands of the former movement drove a socially radical wedge between the solidary communities of those protesting and the elites who attempted to repress their insurgency. In the Caroline agitation, the focus of the widespread mobilization did not separate any solidary population from those who played the game of high politics; rather, it linked common people to certain elites. The unlikelihood of a national revolutionary mobilization can be seen in the difficult position of the members of the radical press as they attempted to confront the popularity of the Caroline movement without sacrificing their earlier positions and constituencies. The Caroline agitation could not readily be used for radical purposes; the cause of reform could be confounded with that of the Queen but not effectively combined with it to mobilize a truly massive insurgency.

Where revolutions have taken place, the picture is different. As works of comparative history have repeatedly shown, these societies have been predominantly agrarian. Even the broadest listing of where social revolutions have occurred gives a good sense of this: France, Russia, Mexico, China, Yugoslavia, Vietnam, Algeria, Turkey, Cuba, Indonesia, Iran, Angola, Nicaragua, and Peru. (I consider England and the United States to have had political but not social revolutions.) The list hardly describes the advanced capitalist countries of the world. The French revolution was led largely by urban craftsmen and was radicalized significantly by the claims of peasants. Though debate remains over the role of the working class in the communist revolutions of the twentieth century, in none of the countries involved did the working class comprise even a near majority of the insurgents, let alone of the population. In the Third World, nationalist, anticolonial sentiment has been central in revolutionary insurgency, and peasants and members of other agrarian classes have been crucial, if not exclusive, agents.

Two further points can be derived from even a superficial consideration of the commonalities among societies undergoing revolutions. First, revolutions tend to have involved the collaboration of disparate classes (if classes are understood to be defined by external, structural characteristics). Second, revolutions appear to have been waged against readily identifiable, often alien, oppressors. It should furthermore be borne in mind that the protagonists of revolutions need not be the beneficiaries of their own actions; many struggles have been waged by groups who suffered oppression under the new regimes. Those who have secured power in postrevolutionary societies have frequently been representatives of special-interest groups, and of urban as opposed to rural bases. The facts that revolutions have depended largely on peasants, that they have occurred more often at the onset of capitalist industrialization, that those who waged revolutionary struggle could not in very many cases become the primary beneficiaries of the new regime are all challenges to a stereotypical Marxist understanding of such movements. At the same time, the polarization which amalgamates different class interests in times of revolutionary ferment, the external and often economic difficulties which plague prerevolutionary regimes, the importance of a clear division between oppressors and oppressed, and the very existence of revolutions instead of gradual capitalist "progress" all suggest the strength of Marxist theory.

A variety of works have attempted to develop a Marxist understanding of social revolutions, modifying Marxism where necessary. Most have chosen to concentrate on external and "objective structural" factors; characteristics of states, in particular, have occupied the center of the analytic stage. For the most part, such theories have been rigidly determinist. The present work has taken up a different strand of the argument. Where others have maintained that exigencies of state power have accounted for the necessity of revolutionary resolutions to domestic and international crises, I have held that contradictions between traditional communities and crafts on the one hand, and capitalist industrialization on the other, have given some groups of people the motivation and strength for revolutionary action. I think that my argument has something to say about why peasants have predominated in revolutionary mobilizations. Peasants are often knit together in strong local communities, bound by traditional identifications to each other and to a certain manner of living. The break is clear between their relatively autonomous communities and the social organizations of their exploiters and oppressors—even those who, like the United States in Vietnam, would help them by destroying their land and way of life.

From Marx's day to the present, the conditions of revolutionary mobilization have been continuously eroded in the advanced capitalist countries. This does not in itself mean that workers have increased their share of capitalist wealth or lost the "objective interests" they may once have had in a different form of society. It need not even mean that techniques of ideological cooptation or police repression have improved or their use intensified. What it does mean is that the social strength of workers' communities, their links to each other, and their dependence on a traditional way of life incompatible with modern capitalism have been greatly reduced. At the same time, the distinction between the beneficiaries and victims of capitalism has become less clear.

Workers have almost never had nothing to lose but their chains, and in any case the degree of their immiseration hardly predicts their radicalism. On the contrary, the question is what workers have had to defend. Some defenses need to be radical, even revolutionary, because workers (or peasants, or "the people") cannot both save what they value and adjust to capitalist, colonial, or imperialist conditions. Other defenses can be reformist, because there is no fundamental and immediate contradiction between what workers want and what elites need, only a quantitative competition. The economic, social, and cultural goods which people have are more important motivations and bases for collective action than what they stand possibly to gain.

In early nineteenth-century England, because of the strength of their traditions and their communities, many radical artisans, craftsmen, and their fellows were in some ways more like the peasants and others who have made revolutions than like the working class of today's advanced capitalist societies, which struggles for a variety of greater and lesser reforms. These early English radicals had a sense of what traditional, preindustrial life was like; they had local and craft communities in which they found both the social foundations for collective action and practical experience in popular, democratic decision-making. Their successors have lost more of the immediate control over their lives to large-scale formal organizations and "experts"; they have come to think of themselves as members of capitalist industrial society and to frame their goals from within that social context.

It will not do to obscure these distinctions by extending Marx's theory of working-class radicalism (or its close relatives) to craftsmen, peasants, small proprietors, and others. These groups are most often radical in reaction to efforts to make them a part of that industrial working class. The maintenance or rediscovery of some of their traditions has been crucial to those movements of radical action which have occurred on behalf of the modern proletariat. Nonetheless, the social foundations for this radical, democratic vision and action have not often been made a part of the life of modern workers. Whether well-paid or poor, the "new" workers have different personal experiences and social capabilities. They are a "class" in a way their predecessors were not, but that is more an indicator of isolation as individuals than of unity. New social foundations for radicalism may yet be made, but they are no longer inherited as they were before and during industrialization.

Notes

Chapter One

1. On the Pentridge rising and Oliver, see J. L. and B. Hammond, *The Skilled Labourer*, chap. 12; White, *From Waterloo to Peterloo*, chap. 13; and Thompson, *The Making of the English Working Class* (hereafter cited as *The Making*), pp. 711–34.

2. Thompson terms the rising "a transitional moment between Luddism and the 'populist' Radicalism of 1818–20 and 1830–32," (*The Making*, p. 733). Just what he means by "populist" remains unclear, though apparently the qualification is ideological.

3. *The Making*, pp. 212–13.

4. Nairn, *The Break-Up of Britain*, pp. 303–4, and Anderson, "Socialism and Pseudo-Empiricism," began this particular part of the long argument between Thompson and the post-1963 editors of the *New Left Review*.

5. Thompson, *Poverty of Theory* (revised version of "The Peculiarities"), p. iii. For Anderson's suggestion that Thompson has overreacted, see *Arguments within English Marxism*, pp. 140–41.

6. Consider especially Marx's historical essays "The Eighteenth Brumaire of Louis Napoleon" and "Class Struggles in France, 1848–50."

7. *Poverty of Theory*, p. ii.

8. Jones, *Notes to the People* (1851), pp. 1016–17.

9. Similarly, the concept of community took its modern shape in an emphasis on certain, but not all, aspects of a remembered past, and the observed and experienced remnants of more traditional society.

10. See chap. 6, above.

11. The best source on Owen and his followers is Harrison, *Robert Owen and the Owenites*. See also Pollard and Salt, eds., *Robert Owen: Prophet of the Poor*.

12. In his later work, Thompson has decided to push the continuity back even earlier. This leads to a certain amount of confusion if one is not careful to attend to the sources of differing statements. Thus, in *The Making*, p. 463, we are told that the eighteenth-century mob had become conscious and organized by the nineteenth century. In "The Moral Economy of the English Crowd," we are told that the eighteenth century "mob" was already conscious and organized. Thompson attempts both to show progress and to idealize the past.

13. Donnelly's defense of Thompson's "theoretical clarity and historical objectivity" does not withstand scrutiny ("Ideology and Early English Working-Class History: Edward Thompson and His Critics," p. 219). One may agree with Donnelly's suggestion that Thompson's critics have been ideologically motivated, theoretically unclear, and, not infrequently, wrong, without holding that Thompson himself is wholly clear. Indeed, clarity and value ought not to be confused; there is perhaps more of the latter than of the former in *The Making*. The most extended discussion of Thompson's theoretical work—indeed the only one—is Anderson, *Arguments within English Marxism*, which, however, gives very little attention to *The Making*.

14. *The Making*, p. 781.

15. Outworkers did grow in number through most of the industrial revolution, and, as Thompson notes, were disproportionately important in Chartism. See *The Making*, pp. 295, 307, 325, and pp. 53–58, above. One of Chartism's greatest weaknesses, correspondingly, was the split between factory workers on the one hand and artisan and outwork populations on the other. The pulling apart of the movement in the late 1830s and 1840s followed largely these lines.

16. *The Making*, p. 914. Curiously, Thompson criticizes just such a tendency elsewhere: "'It'—the bourgeoisie or working class—is supposed to remain the same individual personality, albeit at different steps of maturity, throughout whole epochs; and the fact that we are discussing different people, with changing traditions, in changing relationships both as between each other and as between themselves and other social groups, becomes forgotten" ("The Peculiarities of the English," p. 342). Once again, it is important to distinguish between Thompson's empirical treatments—which are fine-grained discussions of just such changes—and his summary statements.

17. *The Making*, pp. 913–15.

18. Ibid., p. 9.

19. Ibid., p. 12.

20. In this, Thompson was part of a prominent current in 1960s social science which argued for the use of ordinary language or "native" accounts rather than objectivism or analytic distancing. This subjectivism may, however, have been as limited as objectivism, and just as prone to the reification of mere statements and of conscious awareness.

21. *The Making*, p. 13. This statement is made in a more general context in "The Peculiarities," in which Thompson brings his political theory and historiographic policies into the foreground, and into conjuncture: "So let us look at history *as* history—men placed in actual contexts which they have not chosen, and confronted by indivertible forces, with an overwhelming immediacy of relations and duties and with only a scanty opportunity for inserting their own agency—and not as a text for hectoring might-have-beens" (p. 342). In this passage, Thompson is criticizing colleagues on the left for denying the complexity of history and ignoring the real actors—acting, sometimes, in their "blind alleys." In *The Making*, the right was more often, but no more or less justly, the target of similar criticism.

22. Ibid., p. 13.

23. In this discussion I am primarily concerned with Thompson's argument in *The Making* regarding the late eighteenth and early nineteenth centuries. His argument on the early eighteenth century is related but not identical; see "Eighteenth-Century English Society: Class Struggle without Class" (hereafter cited by its subtitle alone).

24. See Anderson's brief but important discussion of this; *Arguments*, chap. 2, esp. pp. 40–42. Anderson suggests that Thompson's "class struggle" might just as well be termed "social conflict."

25. This is a point which, Thompson says in his Postscript to the 1968 edition of *The Making*, p. 923, he would now stress even more, especially the link of Jacobinism with the events of 1816–20.

26. Currie and Hartwell surprisingly get this backward and suggest that Thompson does "not like the artisans" ("The Making of the English Working Class?" pp. 638–39).

27. *The Making*, p. 278.

28. Social mobility was (and is) central to what liberal ideology offered, and yet, whatever the prospects, statistically indicated, there was still a problem in that such advancement was always individual. It thus violated the value on collective advancement, family, and communal welfare. Social mobility also meant the opportunity to be an outsider in a world other than that in which one was raised, a world in which those born to the higher classes were insiders.

29. It may be observed in passing that this distinction corresponds to splits in the socialist movement over the last century and a half between radical democrats (providing most of the ground strength in labor and socialist parties in Western Europe) and more orthodox Marxists (starting with Marx) who have treated class as an ideal construct and the proletariat as the agent of a radical historical transformation, rather than as a social movement within a relatively continuous historical process.

30. In 1819, white hats were banned (along with some other symbols of radicalism) by Sunday school authorities in the Manchester area. *Manchester Observer*, 24 September 1819.

31. A term coined by Victor Turner, *The Forest of Symbols*, p. 7, to describe the way in which the different symbols speak simultaneously to many issues and resonate differently in different minds.

32. Thus modern democratic political activity depends largely on the symbolically motivated activities (e.g., voting, donating money) of individuals. It includes relatively few occasions for concerted group activity outside of the campaign or administrative staff organizations at the center. This may, of course, be one reason why political participation has declined with "voter apathy."

33. See, for examples, *The Making*, pp. 456–69, 557–58; Postgate, *The Builder's History*, pp. 61–67; Cole, *Attempts at General Union*, pp. 70–75. It is important to remember that this significance of ritual did not immediately disappear with the rationality of industrial society and the development of "instrumental" trade-union activity.

34. See chap. 6, above.

35. This should be recognized as essentially Durkheim's notion of collective representations, generalized somewhat from his specific analysis of representative rites. *The Elementary Forms of the Religious Life*, pp. 414–34.

36. Thompson, "Eighteenth-Century English Society: Structure, Field-of-Force, Dialectic," esp. pp. 25–26; see also "Patrician Society, Plebeian Culture." In "Class Struggle without Class," Thompson clarifies this conceptualization of the priority of class struggle to class as entity.

37. At this point, in other words, Thompson uses "dialectic" in its classical Greek rather than its Hegelian sense.

38. The relationship of this process of self-creation of consciousness to mate-

rial factors is unclear in Thompson's account. The specific nature of the "existence" being recognized was continually changing as political and productive relations were altered. Thus, Thompson's "working class" is not defined primarily in terms of exploitative capitalist production, as Marx's is.

39. This point—the identification of the class interests of opponents—is also central to Thompson's argument in The Making. Thus, he emphasizes the fact that "A Journeyman Cotton Spinner" in an 1818 Manchester address (almost completely reprinted in The Making, pp. 218–21) "spoke of the 'masters', not as an aggregate of individuals, but as a class" (p. 226).

40. Thompson, "Eighteenth-Century English Society," p. 28. Thompson is attempting to work his way around the limitations of the distinction between objective and subjective definitions of class, without abandoning it altogether.

41. Thompson, "The Peculiarities," p. 320.

42. Indeed, as we shall see, Thompson's dialectical view of class suggests that a "class" may not be identified outside of particular historical contexts. It is always a complex of concrete relations, qualitatively distinct, and interpretable only in terms which change with context. Thompson is generally against ideal-type constructs. See "Peculiarities," p. 321.

43. Thompson is aware of this; he points out the special connection of "class" to nineteenth-century theory, but considers this outweighed by the absence of a better term for application to earlier societies "Eighteenth-Century English Society," p. 25.

44. The Making, p. 9. The plural usage was, however, the most common among people of the early nineteenth century.

45. The usages have not all been crude. The most sophisticated variant in current prominence is the Althusserian distinction between determinant and dominant structures. See Althusser and Balibar, Reading Capital; Althusser, For Marx; Poulantzas, Political Power and Social Classes; and Godelier, Rationality and Irrationality in Economics. In this formation, considerable stress is laid on the relative autonomy of the superstructure or "structure in dominance." Other, cruder formulations focus more directly on the causal links between the levels, and tend to fall from economics to economism. Marx's own classic statement is to be found in the Preface to "A Contribution to the Critique of Political Economy." Engels's statement of the base/superstructure position in "Socialism: Utopian and Scientific" (the Anti-Dühring) has been influential, though it is a polemical and popularizing oversimplification of Marx (see esp. pp. 88–89). See also Thompson's partial rejection of the base/superstructure model in his recent work "Class Struggle without Class," p. 152; and his critique of Althusser in The Poverty of Theory. See also Anderson's analysis of the last in Arguments. Thompson's rejection of the metaphor falters because he does not have an alternative.

46. The extent to which the economic is held directly to "cause" the specific characteristics of other domains varies. No serious treatment argues for a complete reduction of the latter to the former, as that would vitiate the need for any analytic distinction. Most structuralists hold that there is fairly extensive autonomy within the general notion that the economic is determinant "in the last instance." The separation of the economic, political, and ideological domains is held to be a historical product, with the economic dominant as well as determinant only in the capitalist mode of production. Poulantzas also points out that the characteristics of the realm of the economic are not identical in all structures. Political Power and Social Classes, esp. pp. 20–21, 27–28. As Anderson has shown, Thompson misreads Althusser on this; see Arguments,

chap. 3. It is curious that Thompson nearly completely ignores Poulantzas. I view the constructivist metaphor as a trap, and would extend similar criticism to the claim that logical priority can usefully be distinguished from temporal precedence. Compare Poulantzas, *State, Power and Socialism*, chap. 1.

47. Thompson at no point argues that those interests are all economic, either in the conceptions of actors or in retrospect. "Freedom," for example, was a collective and individual goal for workers which was not limited to their economic state, and which was occasionally sought at the expense of material well-being. It is also one which Thompson would by no means denigrate. The structure of his argument remains the same, however, when he considers political liberty as when he considers economic autonomy or material well-being.

48. *The Making*, p. 207. This is the position Marx and Engels took up in England when they decided that the resocialization of previously disunited workers in factories would create the class for itself and that the factory system would be the blueprint of the revolution. See chap. 8, above.

49. *The Making*, p. 259.

50. Ibid., p. 9. Not a casual statement, this appears again in "The Peculiarities," p. 357: "class is not a thing, it is a happening," and is quoted from that source in the Postscript to the 1968 edition of *The Making*, p. 939.

51. Colonized populations may well, for this and other reasons, be more likely to wage revolutions than alienated industrial populations. This does not, however, mean that the term "class" ought to be stretched to include both.

52. For present purposes, exploitation can be quite simply defined: it is the appropriation of value at the expense of the producer of that value, not compensated by other equal value. It should not be forgotten, though, that the term carried more complex implications in Marx's work.

53. See chap. 8 for further discussion of this aspect of Marx's theory.

54. The suggestion that politics was only secondary in Marx's analyses of class may seem strange to followers of some recent Marxisms, but is reasonable. Marx never devoted much attention to the strictly political activities of the working class, except to argue against premature seizures of power. This is so even in "The Civil War in France," one of his more opportunistic essays, and the last time the Commune of 1871 would get such praise from him. Economic activities would lead the workers on to the world-historical stage in Marx's view, though their struggles would inevitably include politics. See Cohen's vigorous defense of the traditional Marxist economic definition of class, *Karl Marx's Theory of History—A Defense*, esp. p. 73.

55. Thompson, *Poverty of Theory*, p. 295. Original emphases.

56. Ibid., p. 8. Original emphases.

57. See the discussion of premises of collective action in chap. 8, above.

58. Thompson, "Class Struggle without Class," p. 149. The argument which I have just developed is largely (though not quite exactly) consonant with that which Anderson has recently advanced in *Arguments*, pp. 29–43.

59. Foster, *Class Struggle*, p. 5. Foster's theoretical discussion is remarkably dense and unclear, though his conclusions are categorical. Somewhat surprisingly, he has received considerable praise for his theorizing; see, for example, Tilly, *From Mobilization to Revolution*, pp. 47–48. Note the similarity of Foster's definition to Weber's anti-Marxist one. See further discussion, above, pp. 219–20.

60. On this, see Lenin, *What Is to Be Done?*, and, in general, see above, chap. 8.

61. *Class Struggle*, p. 1. Foster's discussion of "liberalization," a major part of his book, concerns a later period and is not considered in detail in the present work, though see above, chap. 5.

62. Empirically, Foster looks at three very different towns—Northampton, South Shields, and Oldham—and finds revolutionary class consciousness and active struggle only in the last. One problem with this procedure is that the towns are so different that it is difficult to isolate the extent of variance caused by any one independent variable.

63. This consideration of how people attempted to live their social lives, and what they in fact valued and attempted to maintain in their social lives, is a large part of *The Making*.

64. Foster, *Class Struggle*, p. 4.

65. Ibid., pp. 5–6.

66. Ibid., pp. 6, 74, 123–24.

67. Ibid., p. 43.

68. None of this, it should be noted, seriously threatened the property of the bourgeoisie.

69. See, on these and other problems, Jones's critique, "Class Struggle and the Industrial Revolution." Although critical on many other points, Jones is unjustifiably impressed with Foster's statistics, which are, as I shall argue, somewhat problematic in themselves and used in support of very dubious reasoning.

70. Foster, *Class Struggle*, p. 69.

71. See ibid., chap. 2, esp. pp. 41–43.

72. Ibid., pp. 139–49, esp. p. 146.

73. Ibid., pp. 107, 114, 124; Jones, "Class Struggle and the Industrial Revolution," pp. 38–41.

74. Ibid., p. 148.

75. Ibid., pp. 116–18.

76. The context of the strike is almost entirely absent from Foster's account (one of several such instances). It did not pass by Engels unnoticed; see *The Condition of the Working Class in England*, pp. 520–22, though note that Engels characteristically managed to turn his analysis to the optimistic conclusion that this effectively ended class collaboration.

77. See Gammage's account, *History of the Chartist Movement*, pp. 216–25.

78. See Gayer, Rostow, and Schwartz, *The Growth and Fluctuation of the British Economy*, vol. 1, pp. 301–3; vol. 2, chap. 11.

79. For an analysis published about the same time as Foster's, with somewhat more detail, and taking the opposite view, see Mather, "The General Strike of 1842." Mather does agree that authority was challenged.

80. Based on reports in the *Manchester Observer* and *Guardian*.

81. See Rose, "The Plug Plot Riots of 1842 in Lancashire and Cheshire."

82. Foster, *Class Struggle*, p. 125.

83. Data on neighboring come from the 1851 (and in one instance 1841) census. On intermarriage, they come from parish records. Neighboring, by the way, is done on a basis of next-door neighboring rather than the probably preferable technique of cluster-sampling and density measures.

84. Poverty is treated, not actual income distributions. A measure of concentration of population within a distance (in pence) from the poverty line is used. It is never fully explained.

85. All figures are from p. 126 of Foster, *Class Struggle*.

86. Ibid., p. 127.

87. Foster appears to have classified weavers, however, as "semi-skilled," p. 292; just what the categories "craft" and "laborer" mean in his computation is unclear.

88. We can get an idea from Wood's estimates of the numbers of handloom weavers and factory workers in the industry more generally. In 1831, factory workers were 44 percent of the total and weavers 56 percent; in 1841 the figures were 71 percent and 29 percent respectively and in 1851, 89 percent and 11 percent. The differences are dramatic enough to potentially wash out all of Foster's results (or, rather, the possibility of extending them backwards in time). Mitchell and Deane, *Abstract of British Historical Statistics*, p. 187 (my computations). Of course, new crafts emerged, but their members were not sufficiently populous in this period to compensate for the decline of handloom weaving. Foster does not say how "overlap" was computed. By simple numerical logic, if two groups are of very different size, any given rate of "overlap" of interconnection must involve a much larger proportion of the smaller group. See Blau, *Inequality and Heterogeneity*.

89. Foster, *Class Struggle*, p. 4.

90. Ibid., p. 128. There is no other acknowledgment of this problem.

91. Wadsworth and Mann, *The Cotton Trade and Industrial Lancashire, 1600–1780*, pp. 315, 346–47.

92. Foster, *Class Struggle*, pp. 99–100.

93. Jones, "Class Struggle and the Industrial Revolution," pp. 56–57.

Chapter Two

1. Not, of course, in the philosophical but in the practical sense of the term "radical;" populist movements may be deeper-rooted, their effects more extreme.

2. *The Making*, p. 23.

3. Ibid., p. 9.

4. See above, pp. 11–23, for a more abstract discussion of Thompson's conceptualization of class.

5. See Parkin, "Strategies of Social Closure in Class Formation," for a modern Weberian approach taking this as its central feature. See also, however, Prothero's suggestion that this was an old, common, and not terribly significant line borrowed from the rules of benefit societies. *Artisans and Politics*, p. 85.

6. This point is developed by Richard Sennett in *The Fall of Public Man*, especially chap. 4.

7. Though such transactions began to decline at this point in London, their influence did not disappear, and the public realm remained in other ways as well a more available milieu for communication. There was, in fact, some growth in the numbers of coffeehouses, generally of the smaller kind and, around 1808 and 1809, perhaps those more oriented to the press. See M. D. George, *London Life in the Eighteenth Century*, pp. 296–97.

8. On the moral economy, see the next section of this chapter.

9. Indeed, these attitudes may have preceded the initial working out of the newer justifications, although these of course had roots at least as far back as the seventeenth century. To show that the early eighteenth century was not a uniform calm of deference and paternalism has been the object of much of Thompson's work since the publication of *The Making*. See, for example, *Whigs and Hunters*, "Patrician Society, Plebeian Culture," and, especially,

"The Crime of Anonymity," sec. 7. At the same time that Thompson unearths evidence of disrespect, however, he endorses Hay's argument as to the efficacy of law in maintaining public order and patrician hierarchy, not least of all through an imposing social drama. See Hay, "Property, Authority and the Criminal Law."

10. *The Making*, pp. 57–58.

11. Ibid., pp. 88–91; certainly with enclosures and game laws, press gangs, engrossing, and forestalling middlemen he had experience enough of not being left alone. See p. 148 of *The Making* on Hardy as a popular image of independence and political rebellion and p. 191 on the libertarian bias of the London crowd. Also, Rudé, *Wilkes and Liberty*.

12. It is partially in this sense that Thompson refers to "the continuing traditions and the context that has changed" (*The Making*, p. 27). It was often not the phrases of Jacobinism but their use in a political ideology which attempted to speak for common people that alarmed authorities and excited crowds. After all, Locke was no great radical, though Lockean liberties without his qualifications were a good deal more than the populace had gained in 1792.

13. Jacobinism did not petition mildly for privileges but demanded rights. With some exaggeration Thompson refers to this as breaking down the flood gates of constitutionalism (*The Making*, p. 111). Those flood gates may have been opened a crack, but the dam was certainly still standing and significant for the duration of the period dealt with in Thompson's book. Thompson is on target, though, when he likens the English Jacobins to the Parisian sans-culottes (p. 171). They were urban craftsmen and shopkeepers and, in their different contexts, each quickened the pace of political action, forced the hands of their "betters" but was unable to directly assume power (in no small part because their individualism inhibited organization). See G. Williams, *Artisans and Sans-Culottes* on the comparison. Soboul, *Les Sans-Culottes Parisiens de l'An II*, and Rudé, *The Crowd in the French Revolution* are detailed sources; see also the salutory comments of Cobban in *The Social Interpretation of the French Revolution*, especially chap. 11.

14. *The Making*, p. 181.

15. Ibid., p. 194.

16. Ibid., p. 125.

17. Ibid., p. 123, 151, 158–59. The French Revolution in some ways helped the consolidation of "Old Corruption," Thompson suggests, by uniting the propertied classes in a common fear (p. 195). Moreover, the Jacobin leaders were caught on the horns of a dilemma equally problematic to that of the Chartists forty years later: they called for unlimited agitation but rejected underground revolutionary organization. That left them precious narrow ground on which to stand (p. 176).

18. Ibid., p. 924. A classic example is John Knight of Oldham (erroneously considered a Manchester resident by Bamford, *Passages in the Life of a Radical*, p. 9). His career, spanning nearly fifty years of agitation, is summarized by Foster, *Class Struggle and the Industrial Revolution*, pp. 139–40. See also Prothero, *Artisans and Politics*, especially pp. 70, 85, 89–93, 122–31, on the continuities of Jacobinism among certain London radicals.

19. The ideology was preserved in the writings of Paine, especially; in those of Godwin, Wollstonecraft, Spence, Tooke, Cartwright; and in the odd newspaper.

20. See Prothero's very gentle disagreement with Thompson near the end of a book which avoids the language of class and implicitly contests much of

Thompson's argument throughout. *Artisans and Politics,* p. 337.

21. See pp. 42–48, 159–61.

22. The ideas were not linked simply because of any internal similarities, but because they were united in a common opposition to the degrading and oppressive order (intellectual and social) of the day. In this they fit well with Thompson's notion of class defined solely through opposition.

23. See chap. 4, above.

24. *The Making,* pp. 491–92.

25. Ibid., p. 531.

26. See Thompson's closing comment on England's loss in the failure of radical artisans and romantics ever to achieve full juncture (ibid., p. 915).

27. Ibid., p. 495.

28. *Political Register,* June 1807, p. 215 of *Cobbett's Political Works,* vol. 2.

29. See *The Making,* pp. 495–96; Thompson quotes Sheridan pointedly.

30. See the *Political Register* for the fall of 1804; also, *The Making,* pp. 497–504; there is further discussion of Cobbett in chap. 4, above.

31. *The Making,* p. 499.

32. Ibid., p. 509.

33. Ibid., p. 508.

34. Ibid., p. 510.

35. See chap. 4, above.

36. See Stevenson, "Food Riots in England, 1792–1818."

37. *The Making,* pp. 516–22. The Despard affair also took place in this period and revealed some links between the provinces and the capital. Thompson suggests that it is not totally anomalous, that Despard was a well- and long-connected radical, and thus that the affair can be seen as something of a tip to the iceberg. *The Making,* pp. 521–28.

38. See H.O. 42, fols. 56–74.

39. *The Making,* pp. 517–20.

40. Ibid., p. 527.

41. Ibid., p. 531; they found it more and more necessary to resort to spycraft to have any idea at all what was going on.

42. Ibid., p. 536.

43. Ibid., p. 73.

44. See above, chap. 6.

45. Not only in England is this so but throughout the world, as peasant, petty-commodity, and pre-industrial craft producers are confronted with the economic changes attendant on entrance into the capitalist-dominated world-system.

46. See Hobsbawm and Rudé, *Captain Swing,* and the Hammonds, *The Village Labourer* (not really as completely superseded an account as Hobsbawm and Rudé suggest); Luddism is discussed in more detail in the next chapter.

47. The most detailed and explicit statement of his position is in "The Moral Economy of the English Crowd"; the term is often applied in quite similar ways in *The Making;* see, for example, pp. 66 and 70, but there are a number of differences, notably with regard to his dating of changes in the crowd and its attitudes.

48. *The Making,* p. 68.

49. See the series of articles in Cobbett's *Collected Works,* vol. 2. On food riots, see also Rose, "Eighteenth Century Riots in England, 1792–1818," and Tilly, "Food Supply and Public Order in Modern Europe."

50. There were no major changes in the organization of mine production

during this period; extractive work retained its traditional character. Similarly, after the transition from small farmer to landless laborer, agricultural workers saw little major alteration of their situation in the relations of production.

51. I do not mean to suggest that we can find the ideology neatly differentiated in every instance; certainly any such event as a food riot could become an occasion expressing a variety of grievances. Further, such grievances could probably be understood by many members of the relevant elite "audience" at this social drama. What I do suggest is that we can fairly well delimit the potential collective actors for whom both themes were simultaneously issues.

52. Prothero, *Artisans and Politics*, p. 40, original emphasis.

53. Thus the Benthamite radical paper the *Gorgon* was not a typical representative of London artisan opinion. It was more appropriate to the skilled workers within the new industrial organizations, for example the Manchester cotton spinners. It stood alone in supporting their strike in 1818.

54. It is important to see that the shift in the orientations of collective action was the result of the failure of conservatism to defend traditional values rather than a "modernization" of values. Smelser, *Social Change in the Industrial Revolution*, following Parsons, is inclined to see values leading the way.

55. Prothero, *Artisans and Politics*, p. 67.

56. Ibid., p. 167.

57. "Artisans sought remedies through preserving traditional stints, rates, privileges and hours, insisting that masters and men should have served a regular apprenticeship, banning female labour and enforcing a closed shop. They saw high food prices and taxation as not only reducing artisans' earnings but also, by increasing the cost of living, as making foreign competition more dangerous. They sought remedies in co-operative trading, repeal of the Corn Laws and tax reform" (ibid., p. 330). See also the more complete listing on pp. 337–38 of the same work.

58. Handloom weavers were reduced far more to this level than were the factory workers whom Marx expected, partially on this account, to be in the forefront of the revolution. See the discussion in chap. 7, above.

59. It is difficult to demonstrate such communal organization except with instances and indirect evidence—some of which is gathered in the next chapter and in chap. 6. Numerous authors have made the same assertion; for example, Prothero, perhaps the most authoritative historian of the London artisans, agrees that "domestic outworkers like handloom weavers...[exhibited] a much greater communal solidarity and social egalitarianism" (*Artisans and Politics*, p. 336; also pp. 74 and 93). In chap. 6 I shall also argue that there are formal reasons to think community greater in these small population aggregates.

60. Of the various groups involved in London agitation during the 1790s and the Napoleonic wars, "the artisans had not only a clearer perception of their specific identity and interests, but they also had the greatest organization and communication network. By the end of the wars it was to the artisans that the Jacobins looked as the potentially revolutionary class" (Prothero, *Artisans and Politics*, p. 70).

61. Thompson sometimes emphasizes social relations in general terms. In "The Peculiarities," p. 354, he refers to them in terms of a unification of "economic values" and "social and moral obligations." He still treats this mainly as "culture," however. See also "The Moral Economy of the English Crowd," p. 79.

62. Williams, *Culture and Society, 1780–1950*, p. 263.

63. See above, pp. 18–19.

64. George Orwell, *1984*, pp. 181–82.

65. Contrast Foster's assertion that such characteristics of social existence as high rates of intermarriage among families of different occupational groupings are the result, rather than the cause, of class consciousness.

66. *Poverty of Theory*, p. 9; see also pp. 32–33.

67. In "The Peculiarities," Thompson at once affirms the importance of social being and reveals his own bias: "The dialectical intercourse between social being and social consciousness—or 'culture' and '*not* culture'—is at the heart of any comprehension of the historical process within the Marxist tradition" (p. 351). Notice that it is "culture" and a residual category of "not culture" of which Thompson speaks.

68. This important combination of an articulate institutional level and a localistic and ill-formulated foundation in consensual assumptions—two varieties of intellectual or cultural influence—is emphasized by Thompson in "The Peculiarities," p. 335.

69. *The Making*, p. 12.

70. Little distinction is made between the concepts of "objective conditions or influences" and "objective evidence." A good deal of Thompson's attack is, in fact, on the positivist stress on and treatment of the latter.

71. See chap. 6 on the concept of community and chap. 7 on specific aspects of community structure in early nineteenth-century Lancashire.

72. In part, perhaps, because it is conceived of as discussing the residual category of "not culture"; see n. 67 above. By no means all of the diverse topics covered in Part Two of *The Making* are reconsidered here. In particular, I have nothing new to add to the disproportionately extensive discussion of Thompson's treatment of Methodism which has already taken place.

73. *The Making*, p. 486.

74. To take a moderate example, the first organizations of industrial workers in the American South suffered defeats more totally devastating, and leaving deeper psychic scars and prejudices against class consciousness and trade unions (for example, at Gastonia and Henderson, North Carolina) than anything which happened to workers during the industrial revolution in England. In the latter case, something, pride at least, was often salvaged.

75. "By 1840 most people were better off' than their forerunners had been fifty years before, but they had suffered and continued to suffer this slight improvement as a catastrophic experience" (*The Making*, p. 231).

76. Not least of all among these were wage disputes, but there were also conflicts over working conditions and apprenticeship, quality of production, etc. See *The Making*, pp. 284–86; none of Thompson's examples is drawn from specifically factory work; he discusses, rather, the "honorable" trades and artisans in general.

77. *The Making*, pp. 207–13.

78. It is perhaps implicitly rejected, for Thompson notes that "It is questionable whether factory hands—except in the cotton districts—formed the nucleus of the Labour Movement at any time before the late 1840s (and, in some northern and Midland towns, the years 1832–34, leading up to the great lockouts)" (ibid., p. 211). Thompson of course suggests that the working class had been made by 1830.

79. Marx and Engels, "Manifesto of the Communist Party," p. 496.

80. Engels, "Socialism: Utopian and Scientific," pp. 97–98; original emphases.

81. But see secs. 13–15 of *Poverty of Theory*, where Marx's "silences" are pointed out.

82. Foster, *Class Struggle*, pp. 177–86, offers some interesting data on the cohesion of Oldham area capitalists. See also Ashton, *An Economic History of England: the 18th Century*, pp. 122–24; Chapman, *The Early Factory Masters*, especially chaps. 5 and 6; Pollard, *The Genesis of Modern Management*, pp. 156–59. This is also implied by Smelser's analysis of structural differentiation in spinning and weaving, although activity takes second place to functional necessity in his theory; *Social Change in the Industrial Revolution*, chaps. 4–7.

83. *The Making*, p. 217; Clapham, *An Economic History of Modern Britain: The Early Railway Age*, pp. 172–84; Bythell, *The Handloom Weavers*, pp. 29–36.

84. *The Making*, p. 265; Thompson occasionally makes use of both sides of the degradation-of-labor argument without explicitly showing how situations differ. When we are considering a skilled craftsman and when a low-skilled outworker under the category of "domestic worker" is sometimes uncertain. The distinction which he recognizes, following Clapham, is that the true outworker industry is one which has entirely lost its artisan status; Clapham, *An Economic History*, p. 179; *The Making*, p. 287. This leaves intermediate, or less "true," types uncertain.

85. See above, chaps. 6 and 7.

86. See Hobsbawm, "The Tramping Artisan"; Leeson, *Travelling Brothers*; and, especially, Prothero, *Artisans and Politics*, chap. 2, pp. 35–36.

87. Prothero, *Artisans and Politics*, p. 24.

88. These communal rituals and organizations are discussed in *The Making*, chap. 8 and chap. 12, part 2, and in Prothero, *Artisans and Politics*, chap. 2; Smelser, *Social Change*, chap. 13, contains some useful information on friendly societies; the rituals were also a favorite topic of artisans' memoirs, for example Lovett's *Life and Struggles*, pp. 24–27; these "upwardly mobile" artisans often used the occasion of their memoirs to condemn such "irrational" practices.

89. Marx did distinguish new from old varieties of domestic industries, stressing the decline of independence of the worker (*Capital*, vol. 1, chap. 15, sec. 86).

90. *The Making*, p. 288; Smelser, *Social Change in the Industrial Revolution*, pp. 65–67, 129–31; regarding handloom weavers, Wood's estimates show steady increase parallel with that of factory workers (including spinners) from 1806 through 1831, after which the numbers of handloom weavers began to decline. Mitchell and Deane, *Abstract of British Historical Statistics*, p. 187.

91. He does not argue that the rural laborers were political in anything approaching the manner and extent of artisans and outworkers, but he does argue that they were in the process of becoming part of the working class. That this was a class dispossessed of land was a factor about to become potent in radical ideology. See *The Making*, chap. 7, especially p. 255.

92. Donnelly defends Thompson's concentration on the craftsmen, artisans, and domestic workers as "entirely justified: they are the groups crucial to the emergence of the class movement of the 1830s" ("Ideology and Early English Working-Class History," p. 222). But the point is not the justice of the emphasis but its theoretical implications, and that is precisely what Thompson's presentation obscures.

93. On the labor aristocracy argument, see Hobsbawm, "The Labour Aristocracy in Nineteenth-Century Britain"; Foster, *Class Struggle*, chap. 7, Stedman Jones, "Class Struggle and the Industrial Revolution," pp. 61–69; Moorhouse, "The Marxist Theory of the Labour Aristocracy"; and, briefly, chap. 5, above.

94. *The Making*, p. 340.

95. Estimates of G. H. Wood, in Mitchell and Deane, *Abstract of British Historical Statistics*, p. 187; the figures are:

Year	Factory workers	Weavers
1820	126,000	240,000
1833	208,000	213,000
1840	262,000	123,000

96. "Since at least 1816 the common objective of all Lancashire cotton workers had been to get Parliament to pass a short-time Act. Far more than immediate wage bargaining, it was this which provided the spinners with their one continuing base for organizational unity" (Foster, *Class Struggle*, p. 108). Note that Foster leaves the outworkers (who would be unaffected by short-time legislation) out of the picture—as did the spinners, to a large degree.

97. "The old skill and the new were almost always the perquisite of different people" (*The Making*, p. 274). See also Smelser, *Social Change in the Industrial Revolution*, p. 181, and, for further discussion, chap. 7, above.

98. *The Making*, p. 322.

99. Marx, *Capital*, 1: 434. See also p. 407 on "the unequal contest of the old handicrafts and manufactures with machinery," and on handloom weavers in particular.

100. The same was true of artisans. We may agree with Prothero that "the artisans were the most numerous and most important of all the organized groups of workers in the first half of the nineteenth century, though this fact is only beginning to be recognized" (*Artisans and Politics*, p. 336). The incorporation of such recognition within the Marxian conceptualization of the working class, however, raises considerable problems.

101. Thompson suggests that, even in Mayhew's mid-century London, artisans remained distinct from and more political than laborers. *The Making*, p. 266.

102. Ibid., pp. 262–65, 270, 277.

103. As Thompson observes, unfavorable contrasts between factory and domestic workers were often resented as much by the former as by their employers (*The Making*, p. 452). They had no desire to be seen as debased workers, though they did wish to see improvements in their lot; they had little wish to hear their homes described in terms of urban squalor, though that did not mean they were opposed to sewer development.

104. Prothero, *Artisans and Politics*, pp. 5–6, 26–27, 66, 229; *The Making*, p. 328. And the ranks of weavers continued to increase well after wages began their long decline (Bythell, *The Handloom Weavers*, pp. 114–19; *The Making*, p. 307; Smelser, *Social Change*, pp. 219–20).

105. After which time they began to be joined by, or merge with, some of the newer "aristocrats of labor" such as engineers.

106. "The first-half of the nineteenth century must be seen as a period of chronic under-employment, in which the skilled trades are like islands threatened on every side by technological innovation and by the inrush of

unskilled or juvenile labour" (*The Making,* p. 269; see also p. 342, and Prothero, *Artisans and Politics,* especially p. 330).

107. See Rushton, "Housing Conditions and the Family Economy in the Victorian Slum: A Study of a Manchester District, 1790–1871," chap. 7.

108. *The Making,* p. 289. Prothero's evidence supports Thompson overall, though he makes more of the qualification that some artisans were secure, and hence not very radical (*Artisans and Politics,* especially p. 229); see also p. 5: "Level of proletarianization is in itself no explanation of their action. . . ." Artisans such as Gast thought those who were well enough off to engage in collective action had an obligation to lead the country (p. 184).

109. *The Making,* p. 279; Tucker, "The Real Wages of Artisans in London, 1729–1935," p. 29; Gayer, Rostow, and Schwartz, *Growth and Fluctuation of the British Economy,* 1:135–36; 827–33.

110. *The Making,* p. 292; Prothero, *Artisans and Politics,* pp. 27, 64–65, and chap. 11. Factory work was also likely to be casual labor for many, especially in the early years; Collier, *The Family Economy of the Working Classes,* pp. 16–17 and 31–33. See also chap. 7, above.

111. *The Making,* pp. 315–16.

112. Gayer, Rostow, and Schwartz, *Growth and Fluctuation,* 2:950–53.

113. *The Making,* p. 294; the debate on the standard of living is recorded in some detail and with reference to a variety of sources in Taylor, ed., *The Standard of Living in the Industrial Revolution,* and in Seldon, ed., *The Long Debate on Poverty,* the latter of which records that side of the debate which holds, essentially, that there was very little poverty and that what there was had little to do with either capitalism or industrialism. See also Inglis, *Poverty and the Industrial Revolution,* for a good summary.

114. *Mechanics Magazine,* 6 September 1823; cited in *The Making,* p. 277; the theme of low wages yielding an unequal distribution of work among craftsmen was widespread; see also *The Making,* p. 289; Prothero, *Artisans and Politics,* chap. 11.

115. *The Making,* p. 329.

116. Ibid., p. 217.

117. Ibid., p. 222; after 1830 a new form of paternalism began to develop, but for the first three decades of the century exploitation was peculiarly bald.

118. See Pollard, *The Genesis of Modern Management;* on housing, see *The Making,* pp. 355–56; Gauldie, *Cruel Habitation,* p. 123; numerous observers commented on this, and of course Engels made a major point of it in *The Condition of the Working Class in England in 1844;* see also Rushton, *Housing Conditions,* and the forthcoming work of E. V. Walters on the evolution of the slum.

119. Thompson pointedly notes that it is this minority opinion which Smelser terms the "dominant value structure" of the day (*The Making,* p. 331). Smelser takes it for granted in his analysis rather like the natural resources of the countryside. He does not consider that a "value structure" might dominate because of the power of those who hold it or in whose interest it works. Smelser, *Social Change,* especially p. 247.

120. When, for example, they checked in 1833 on the activities of the assistant commissioners and in general attempted to influence the Factory Commission. *The Making,* p. 372.

121. Ibid., pp. 374, 377, 380 and 384.

122. Ibid., p. 375.

123. See discussion in chap. 5, above. Leisure was also an issue of importance, only partly connected to the (socially respectable) desire to spend time with one's family or in "self-improvement." See on this, and in general on resistance to routinization of work (and of the rest of life) Thompson's superb essay "Time, Work-Discipline, and Industrial Capitalism."

Chapter Three

1. See *The Making*, pp. 546, 548. Consider also Peel, *The Risings of the Luddites*, pp. 52–60, in which a meeting between "Painite" democrats and Luddite croppers is described (a description which, one must admit, tends to mix oral history with a great deal of imaginative reconstruction). The Painites argue in terms of national issues and Jacobin principles; the Luddites (particularly Mellor) suggest the prior significance of local issues and industrial oppression: "We'll reckon with the aristocrats in London in due time, but, friends, is there not some work nearer home to be done first? I know of no aristocrats who are bigger tyrants than our own master, and I'm for squaring with them the first." Note also that such discussion as there was of national issues was in terms of aristocrats, taxation, and the usurpation of the Englishman's natural inheritance.

2. Thompson titles his opening section on the Luddites "The Opaque Society" (*The Making*, pp. 529–43). As Peel put it: "The systematic combination, however, with which the outrages were conducted, the terror which they inspired, and the disposition of many of the working classes to favour rather than oppose them, made it very difficult to discover the offenders, to apprehend them if discovered, or to obtain evidence to convict those who were apprehended of the crimes with which they were charged" (*The Risings of the Luddites*, p. 32). This was so because "The whole population in fact seemed at that time to consist of one large family" (Peel, "Old Cleckheaton," cited in Thompson, New Introduction to *The Risings of the Luddites*, p. x).

3. See *The Making*, p. 543, on this aspect of Spence's notions, and more generally pp. 151–52 and 176–79. Spence's agrarian radicalism, at its most popular among urban artisans (including such successful ones as Alexander Galloway, later Hume's friendly witness before the select committee on artisans and machinery, P.P. (1824), vol. V, and one of London's largest engineering employers) well represents the populism of the early nineteenth century. It was indeed a relatively sophisticated variant, with unusually thorough attention to both tactical questions and issues of how society could be reorganized in favor of its still relatively traditional values. Through such measures as abolishing private property in land, Spence wished to be, in the words of an 1801 publication, "The Restorer of Society to its Natural State." The Spencean Philanthropists were an enduring, if always fairly small, group, cropping up again in the *First Report of the Committee of Secrecy*, P.P. (1817), vol. VI. See Rudkin, *Thomas Spence and His Connections*, excerpts in Cole and Filson, *British Working Class Movements*, pp. 124–31, and the works cited in *The Making*, p. 179, n. 1.

4. *The Making*, pp. 544–45.

5. Even in the West Riding, cropping and finishing shops employing traditional methods were much smaller than mills such as Cartwright's at Rawfolds; Peel suggests most of the former employed only three or four men (*The Risings of the Luddites*, p. 10). This dimension of relative size of workplace takes on

more significance as one looks at town Luddism—at Stockport for example— rather than at the already closely-knit villages of the West Riding. See chap. 7, above.

6. This of course strengthens Thompson's argument that the Acts were a piece of class legislation, motivated by hostility as much as practicality. See *The Making*, pp. 550–52. It is worth remembering also that the Acts symbolized repression more than they enabled it. Older laws continued to be used more frequently, in part because they could be more easily used.

7. On the masters' greater ease of combination, see various of the replies to Hume's questions in the *First Report from the Select Committee on Artisans and Machinery*, *P.P.* (1824), vol. V, for example, pp. 12 and 40. The committee was embarked on its curious argument (under guidance from Francis Place) that the anticombination legislation encouraged combination which would not take place if it were legal.

8. *The Making*, p. 552; Prothero, *Artisans and Radicals*, pp. 165–66. This was especially true where there was a strong tradition in the trade and the little masters had not already clearly lost their battle, for example, in London and Birmingham.

9. An example is Moore's and Henson's bill against the Combination Acts.

10. This bill marked also the first and perhaps the greatest of Place's exercises in Parliamentary string-pulling and organization; see Wallas, *The Life of Francis Place*, chap. 8. As Thompson notes, it is not clear whether Hume's bill was tolerated as a palliative to prevent Moore's or out of boredom, or what (*The Making*, pp. 568–69). Wallas treats it as a single-handed victory for Place. Thompson also suggests, I think accurately, that the workmen's organizations were less involved in class collaboration and more autonomous than Place's retrospective account indicates. There is little evidence, however, that the workmen's organizations of the 1820s were inclined to extend their trade-unionist activity very far in the direction of Marxist class consciousness. They were more likely to follow Owenite cooperation if they did move to extend their field of battle at all.

11. Byron's speech is quoted in Peel, *The Risings of the Luddites*, p. 76. The speech was specifically in response to Percival's bill to make frame-breaking a capital offense. Halévy, rather inaccurately but not unlike a number of other historians, suggests that Byron "sang the praises of the Luddites" (*England in 1815*, p. 303). In fact, Byron was not so much praising the Luddites as attacking those who would persecute them. He was in some ways less a radical than Shelley, for example; his concern was in the older tradition of exposure of and opposition to ministerial malfeasance and failure in paternalistic duty. Watson gives an accurate, if brief, reading of this in *The Reign of George III, 1760–1815*, pp. 538–39.

12. The outworkers, such as handloom weavers, occupied an anomalous intermediate position (which may be partly why they were worst-off of all). They were for the most part similar to the older artisan craftsmen, but without equal ability to appeal to traditional relationships and economic order.

13. The question of just how effective Luddite action was in securing material concessions has been debated. Thomis suggests that "it is difficult to see the apparent triumphs of the Luddites as anything more than the superficial appearance of victory" (*The Luddites*, p. 161). This has been the traditional view of economic history. Hobsbawm, on the other hand, argues that "collec-

tive bargaining by riot was at least as effective as any other means of bringing trade union pressure, and probably *more* effective than any other means available before the era of national trade unions to such groups as weavers, seamen and coal-miners" ("The Machine Breakers," p. 16). He concludes, however: "That is not to claim much." His view is closer to Thompson's as both combat the view of Luddites as backward-looking, almost foolish, and fighting a hopeless battle with an ineffective weapon. The crucial distinction may be between local and national effectiveness, as Hobsbawm implies. Luddites could not hope to win their battle against the overall forces for industrialization and the control of industrial society because their strengths were entirely internal to local communities and crafts. Such earlier local victories as that of the Norwich weavers had eventually caused industry to move elsewhere; see Clapham, "The Transference of the Worsted Industry from Norfolk to the West Riding." In 1811–12, large employers were more often intransigent, and relied on greater military aid; see Darvall, *Popular Disturbances*, pp. 214 and 234–49.

14. This is a point Thompson emphasizes in *The Making*, pp. 552–53.

15. Thus, Hobsbawm's "collective bargaining by riot" ("The Machine Breakers") and the English versions of *taxation populaire* described by Thompson, in "The Moral Economy of the English Crowd in the Eighteenth Century," among numerous others.

16. See, for example, Peel, *The Risings of the Luddites*, p. 127.

17. See pp. 161–67, above.

18. *The Making*, pp. 552–53.

19. See discussion of size of workplace and related issues in chap. 7, above.

20. Equally importantly, it was easier to split and to make concessions to. See chap. 7, above.

21. While this was immediately true of outworkers, skilled artisans often maintained a privileged place in factory work for a very long time. The degradation of artisan work is still an active process.

22. On the oaths, see *The Making*, pp. 557–58; Thomis, *The Luddites*, pp. 126–28; Darvall, *Popular Disturbances*, pp. 182–83, with reference to Bolton; and the Hammonds, *The Skilled Labourer*, pp. 275–78 (on Lancashire oath-taking) and 325–29 (a discussion of the oaths in general). Oaths and ritual are not simply important as indications of traditionalism, in some abstract sense of being "time-honored" or "old-fashioned," but because their symbolism and their strength are bound up with enduring communities.

23. See, for example, Postgate, *The Builders' History*, pp. 63–64, and note the inclination to standardize traditional ceremonials under Owenite influence in the 1830s.

24. *The Making*, p. 561.

25. Ibid., p. 575. Workers made unsuccessful proposals for a tax on new machinery to provide a relief fund for workers the machinery threw out of employment, and for the gradual introduction of such machinery.

26. It should be borne in mind, however, that if it was not the first appearance of the new machinery which motivated the outburst of 1811–12, neither was that the first outbreak of machine-breaking. Rather, it was the latest in a long sequence, even, perhaps, in a unified campaign. See Hobsbawm, "The Machine Breakers"; "The Luddites in the Period 1779–1830"; and Thomis, *The Luddites*, pp. 12–17. Henson speaks of the destruction of machinery and cutting of warps in 1770, as the weavers "kept up their rate of wages by dint of terror"

(*History of the Framework Knitters*, p. 377). The Hammonds's *The Skilled Labourer* remains an important source, indicating some of the history of disagreement, if yet treating the Luddites as largely backward-looking.

27. Peel, *The Risings of the Luddites*, p. 25.

28. *The Making*, p. 575; the Hammonds, *The Skilled Labourer*, pp. 170–71.

29. *The Making*, pp. 576–77; the Hammonds, *The Skilled Labourer*. The little masters' empathy was reciprocated; see H.O. 40/1/20, a letter threatening a fire which was postponed to enable small masters who rented space to avoid injury (16/4/1812). The *Times* found it remarkable that the Nottingham Luddites were so selective in their destruction: "One poor man begged of the rioters to spare two frames that had been the fruit of his industry for many years: his request was granted" (2 December 1811). In general, the focus of Luddite action, as opposed to expectations of indiscriminate destruction, surprised the elites.

30. Thus it was that croppers' organizations could claim 100 percent membership and, in addition, some local weavers and small masters (*The Making*, p. 576).

31. Ibid., p. 594.

32. Ibid., p. 604.

33. Darvall, *Popular Disturbances*, p. 314.

34. Contrast, for example, the calmness of the military officers with the hysteria of local authorities in H.O. 40/1, e.g., item 17 in which Garside of Stockport sees "the most desperate, the best organized conspiracy, that the world has ever witnessed."

35. Hobsbawn, "Should the Poor Organize?" p. 48.

36. See Gluckman, "Rituals of Rebellion in South-East Africa," Introduction to *Order and Rebellion in Africa*, and *Custom and Conflict in Africa*, chap. 5. Gluckman's main point is that there are tendencies to rebellion inherent generally in political systems, and that these find expression (and containment) in rituals, in those societies socially stable and strong enough to tolerate such public expression of their basic structural conflicts.

37. This is not to say that there were no resources which could have been used to make the Luddites' plight easier, but rather that there was little or no way for capitalists, acting as such (and especially within the ideology of the time), to negotiate a mutually tolerable settlement with the traditionalists. Unlike a zero-sum proposal regarding the allocation of money (e.g., wage rates vs. profits), the conflict between Luddites and their employers (of the newer sort) was between two different sets of values and ways of organizing the productive process.

38. *The Making*, p. 608. But again, this was partly because the Lancashire and Yorkshire Luddites were less dependent on specific leaders. See also Thomis, *The Luddites*, p. 160, and diary of events, pp. 177–86. Such Luddism as continued in the Midlands seems often to have featured a sort of quasi-professional body, available on hire to break frames (Darvall, *Popular Disturbances*, pp. 187–88). See the Hammonds, *The Skilled Labourer*, pp. 236–43, on the 1816 recrudescence of Midlands Luddism.

39. *The Making*, p. 618.

40. The first volume of the Home Office disturbance books is full of such informations, from magistrates' and other reports (H.O. 40/1). Thompson suggests that "there is only one reason for believing that the various depositions in the Home Office papers as to its revolutionary features are false, and this is the assumption that any such evidence is bound to be false" (*The*

Making, p. 648). There is a halfway position, though, which involves being selective. The revolutionary ideas and plans may have been a great deal more real than the organization (also asserted) to carry them into practice. There is little evidence to show that the many local sergeants and captains were part of a universal system of military rank.

41. *The Making,* pp. 656–57; this characterization is close to the argument of the present work. Thompson at no point suggests that there *was* national organization, but by using the term "organization" in a number of different and unspecified senses, he makes himself unclear. Papers like the *Times* (cf. 31 January 1812) were alarmed at *any* organization, but even when they thought they saw the coordinating hand of one leader, they did not think his "army" was truly national.

42. *The Making,* p. 593. This quandary develops in part because Thompson continues, almost despite himself one thinks, to work with a developmental view of working-class history, in which those who come earlier are of necessity less a part of the final product (see the discussion in chapter 1, above). Curiously, this continuous evolutionary view is undialectical as well as non-positivist. Its effect in the present instance is to make Thompson want to show early development (assumed to be on lines later more developed) in order to rationalize Luddite action. This quest runs counter to the general grain of his work.

43. These features, however, were not necessarily the most general. See the discussion of Lenin on trade-union attitudes, including political as well as economic content, below, pp. 230–31.

44. As Thompson seems to suggest they do, for example on p. 643 of *The Making.*

45. Thompson gives a relatively concise statement of these on pp. 643–54 of *The Making* as he sums up the course of Luddism, focusing on Lancashire.

46. See *The Making,* p. 647, on reasons for Luddites to be insurrectionary. Just what Thompson means by "insurrectionary" is unclear. While he seems to use the term to emphasize something more than merely an unfocused rising, the *Oxford English Dictionary* defines the term as referring to "open resistance against established authority or governmental restraint, . . . an armed rising, a revolt; an incipient or limited rebellion." It would appear that an insurrection is an uprising of the people, negatively defined, not an organized movement attempting to make a specific substitution for constituted authority. If one reads Thompson's usage strictly in this sense (and not through his connotations) he is right; the Luddites were insurrectionary, and specifically not revolutionary. See Buckle's distinction of the two sorts of collective action, *History of Civilization,* 2:593.

47. See above, n. 2. Thompson suggests that "not one of the leaders of the movement of 1811–12 was ever, with any certainty, convicted" (*The Making,* p. 626). This is unquestionably an exaggeration; Mellor and Baines, prominent in Peel's narrative of West Riding Luddism (endorsed by Thompson), were both convicted and sentenced. But they were local leaders; what Thompson seems to be assuming is that there were "higher-ups," the "real leaders," who got away. There is as little certainty regarding their existence as their conviction.

48. *The Making,* pp. 633–34.

49. Ibid., p. 638. The Home Office files are full of panicky letters from magistrates, though this panic was not shared by the Home Office itself. A great deal of the activity of the military officers, such as Maitland, and much of the

correspondence between them and the Home Office concerned attempts to quiet the unreasonable fears of the local authorities, and appease (without granting) their demands upon the central government. As Darvall remarks: "The agents of Government, magistrates, members of the local force, constables, though they became in effect, since to put down the disturbances would play into the hands of the employers, the agents of the latter, were almost always perfectly safe. The authorities might be eluded and their commands ignored but they were not resisted or directly attacked. The Luddites' quarrel was not with the Government but with particular employers" (*Popular Disturbances*, pp. 314–15).

50. See Peel, *The Risings of the Luddites*, chaps. 10 and 11; Darvall, *Popular Disturbances*, pp. 115–17; and *The Making*, pp. 613–14.

51. Peel, *The Risings of the Luddites*, p. 145; *The Making*, pp. 624–25. Whatever might be thought of his behavior, Horsfall belonged in the community.

52. *The Making*, p. 624. It is, presumably, no mere accident that the Home Office began keeping entry books on disturbances, i.e., H.O. 40, with this mobilization.

53. H.O. 40/1/42; statement of Humphrey Yarwood at Stockport gaol, 22 June 1812. This, along with other informations from Lloyd, the Stockport magistrate, in the same file, is the source of several of Thompson's uncited quotations. See also *The Making*, p. 652, on the exclusion of Manchester delegates (who refused to contribute financially) from a regional meeting.

54. *The Making*, p. 637.

55. Ibid., p. 640.

56. This is not to deny that Luddite ranks sometimes included people such as colliers and weavers who were not a part of the trade primarily involved in a locality. Coal miners, by virtue of the social and technological organization of their work, have always been particularly prone to take direct action. For the most part, Luddite villages were dominated by a single trade; to have ties with any large body of workers in another meant transcending the local bounds of organization and attention.

57. *The Times*, 31 January 1812.

58. The *Times* was occasionally pleased to use the Luddite disturbances as an occasion to goad the ministry on the subject of the corn laws, never failing to point out that the high price of provisions was as important as the low wages or new machinery in a trade. It also found pleasure in commenting on the inefficiency of government action to put down disorder.

59. See discussion in Darvall, *Popular Disturbances*, pp. 220–21.

60. Even Cobbett did not devote much attention to the Luddites until July 1812 when the government began to contemplate taking extraordinary measures for their suppression; see *Political Register* for that year.

61. *The Making*, p. 654.

62. It is hard to imagine what contributions there were on the level of grand ideology. Thompson suggests none. Rather, Luddism's cultural contribution was in the spreading of the word and the strengthening of the sense of opposition between craftsmen and masters.

63. *The Making*, p. 654.

64. Ibid., p. 657.

65. Ibid.

66. Ibid., p. 658. Compare *Whigs and Hunters* or "The Moral Economy of the English Crowd in the Eighteenth Century."

67. Prothero, in his study of London artisans, also finds the shift of leadership away from the capital (*Artisans and Politics*, pp. 107, 293, 323).

68. *The Making*, p. 657.

69. If the government could find no agitators, no plots, Cobbett wrote, then Luddism was "a movement of the people's own, as far as it goes." Either it was caused by distress, or the government must look to itself for the reasons (*Political Register*, July 1812; *Cobbett's Political Works*, 4:167).

70. Particularly in chap. 2 of *The Making*.

71. *The Making*, p. 640.

72. If this was true of religion, it was all the more true of the older popular symbolic culture. This may have given Luddism its charivari-like character, with men dressed in women's clothes or their own inside out (cf. Peel, *The Risings of the Luddites*, p. 78), but it limited it to traditional ritualized opposition—to a mode of rebellion grown ineffective with the increasing insulation of "the powerful" from "the people." Such rituals of reversal reveal a cultural order, but that cognitive system, whatever its merits, was not capable of analyzing the new and complex turns which society was taking, though it might well be capable of rejecting them. See for a similar, and perhaps even more telling instance, the discussion of the Queen Caroline affair above, in chap. 4.

73. Hobsbawm, "Should the Poor Organize?" p. 44.

74. *The Making*, p. 660.

75. Its active participants were of course still a minority nationally, if generally dominant in their own communities.

76. *The Making*, p. 663. Thompson does not refer to "aid" or "show of force" but simply says that the government was maintained by force in 1816. But no government was ever maintained wholly by force, and the English home army would have been a weak weapon against a really concerted insurrection. Similarly, "deference and consent" were always backed up with the threat of execution as well as the majesty of judicial pomp and ceremony. In 1816 the military was deployed to bolster weak points in the defense of deference.

77. Ibid., p. 662.

78. As Thompson points out, the difficulties of communication before the railway can be—and have been—exaggerated (ibid., p. 667).

79. F. D. Cartwright, ed., *The Life and Correspondence of Major Cartwright*, 2:31. Osborne, *John Cartwright*, offers background and narrative, see especially chaps. 6 and 7.

80. Cartwright, *Life and Correspondence*, 2:21, letter of 19 July 1811.

81. Ibid., pp. 31–32.

82. Ibid., p. 46.

83. Places visited are listed in ibid., p. 47.

84. As Thompson points out, Cobbett exaggerated the power of his particular medium, the printed word; he belittled organizations. See *The Making*, p. 699, and above, chap. 4.

85. Osborne, *John Cartwright*, chaps. 6 and 7; *The Making*, p. 668; Kinsey, "Some Aspects of Lancashire Radicalism, 1816–21," p. 36. As Osborne points out (p. 110), Cartwright had little understanding of the economic situation or needs of the working people; his concerns were entirely political.

86. *The Making*, p. 670.

87. One of the virtues of Foster's study is showing this to have been true of Oldham; see his Ph.D. thesis, "Oldham," as well as *Class Struggle*; much the

same was true of Stockport in the early years with figures such as Harrison. See discussion in chap. 5, above.

88. *The Making*, p. 691.

89. See Bion, *Experiences in Groups*, and Slater, *Microcosm*, for sociopsychological considerations of the reasons for this tendency. One could regard the Leninist theory of the revolutionary vanguard as an adaptation to this stage of development, rather than a means of leading a mature working class. Thompson emphasizes the extent to which dependency on leaders was due to the illegality of party organization rather than immaturity of the movement.

90. *The Making*, pp. 688–89; Prothero, *Artisans and Politics*, pp. 283–84.

91. These are discussed at length in Prothero, *Artisans and Politics*; see also *The Making*, pp. 672–75.

92. As for example when Bolton radicals wrote to Cobbett and to Knight, the experienced Oldham radical, for legal advice in 1816 (*The Making*, p. 677).

93. Ibid., sec. 2 of chap. 15 and especially pp. 682–83.

94. This is what sociopsychological studies would lead one to expect— dependence on a glorified leader is linked with an exaggerated desire for equality beneath that leader. See Bion, *Experiences in Groups*; Slater, *Microcosm*; and Gibbard, Hartman, and Mann, eds., *Analysis of Groups*.

95. *The Making*, p. 685; see Bamford's comments on Benbow's pre-Peterloo suggestion that the people "present their petitions at the point of sword and pike" and his subsequent departure for America (*Passages in the Life of a Radical*, pp. 167–68).

96. On such personalization of radicalism, see *The Making*, pp. 686–90.

97. While Wade, Carlile, and Gast offered pointed analysis, they never commanded the respect of the movement the way Cobbett and, to a lesser extent, Hunt did. Even in the 1830s, Cobbett, though long since analytically surpassed, was the key in maintaining the identity of the popular movement. He was a master of its symbols, and he was one of those symbols. See *The Making*, pp. 836–37, and chap. 4, above.

98. On this aspect of modern political culture, discussed under the rubric of charisma, see Sennett, *The Fall of Public Man*, chap. 12.

99. Something of this is suggested in Weber's scattered comments on machine politics; see discussion by Gerth and Mills, *From Max Weber*, pp. 17–18.

100. *The Making*, p. 702; the tendency of political historians to focus on the capital and social historians on local community studies has left us short of information on such links. The autobiographies of central figures such as Bamford's *Passages in the Life of a Radical*, Hunt's *Memoirs* and *Autobiography*, and, to a lesser extent, *The Life and Struggles of William Lovett, in His Pursuit of Bread, Knowledge, and Freedom*, give a general idea of how such ties were made.

101. A spy's report listing the founders of the Hollinwood Club indicates that six of the twenty-two founders had a brother in the group and two others were brothers of prominent local radicals who had been arrested (Kinsey, "Some Aspects of Lancashire Radicalism, 1816–21," pp. 37–38).

102. As in the reform movement of twelve years later, those national leaders who wished for dramatic changes in the government thought most often in terms of "a continual increase in activity until there was a mass movement confronting the authorities" (Prothero, *Artisans and Politics*, p. 289).

103. See chap. 7, tables 3 and 4.

104. *The Making*, pp. 705–6.

105. Manchester township alone had reached nearly 80,000 in 1811, and would approach 110,000 in 1821; Oldham at the same dates was going on 17,000 and 22,000 and Stockport was about the same size. *P.P., Census Summary*, (1831), vol. XVIII.

106. *The Making*, p. 709; see also Laqueur, *Religion and Respectability*, pp. 196–200; Wearmouth, *Some Working-Class Movements of the Nineteenth Century*, p. 35; and Read, *Peterloo: The "Massacre" and Its Background*, chap. 4.

107. *The Making*, pp. 708–9. Read's *Peterloo* somewhat obscures this by concentrating almost exclusively on the immediate Manchester area, and indeed on Manchester itself.

108. See above, pp. 54–58.

109. They did have national ambitions, or at least hopes. In March 1817, the central committee of delegates for southeast Lancashire sent a representative to London "to ascertain what number of men in the Metropolis could be relied on to come forward in case the insurrection broke out in the country" (Kinsey, "Aspects," pp. 87–88).

110. *The Making*, pp. 710–11.

111. Few radical leaders, and none of the national leaders of the parliamentary reform agitation, were engaged in preparation for an armed insurrection. Few would deny, however, the right of wronged Englishmen to do so (*The Making*, p. 683). Cobbett was uncertain about the right to armed insurrection; in 1812 he blamed the prevalence of such a notion on loyalist praise of French insurrections against Napoleon (quite improbably, be it said) (*Political Register*, July 1812, quoted from *Cobbett's Political Works* 4:159).

112. *The Making*, pp. 712, 715.

113. There is a lengthy discussion from local sources of these efforts in Kinsey, "Aspects," pp. 50–58, 94–98.

114. Oliver is discussed on pp. 713–36 of *The Making*. See also the Hammonds's classic account in *The Skilled Labourer*, pp. 341–76, and the opening pages of the present work.

115. For the most part Brandreth and his followers attempted to gather arms, and marched about from village to village and to isolated farmhouses firing their guns, shouting, and blowing horns. The only bloodshed was a largely accidental shooting of a farm servant by Brandreth. See *The Making*, pp. 723–26. Thompson builds his argument largely as a polemic against two quite minor historical accounts which played down the role of Oliver and the radicalism of the Pentridge men: Fremantle's "The Truth about Oliver the Spy," and White's *From Waterloo to Peterloo*. Not only are both accounts inferior to that of the Hammonds in *The Skilled Labourer*, pp. 341–76, but they are much less widely read. This polemical intention leads Thompson to much overstate his case.

116. *The Making*, p. 733.

117. Ibid., pp. 733–34.

118. Ibid., p. 733.

119. See above, pp. 64–69, and especially n. 46.

120. *The Making*, p. 604.

121. As Thompson affirms in ibid., p. 657.

122. Ibid., p. 733.

123. Ibid., p. 603.

124. It should be noted that the colliers were hardly workers in modern mass

industrial organizations. Most mines employed only a couple of score, many fewer, and only the greatest approached a hundred (Clapham, *An Economic History*, 1:185–86).

125. Hunt, *Memoirs*, 3:492–93.

126. Kinsey, "Aspects," p. 111.

127. *The Making*, pp. 665–66; see also above, pp. 72–74.

128. *The Making*, p. 735.

129. This distinction did not provide quite as clear a dividing line as Thompson suggests in ibid. p. 698. Cobbett initially held that household suffrage, the limitation of the vote to those directly taxed, was an appropriate object for reform agitation. Hunt continued to chide him for this for years. See Cobbett's detailed discussion in the *Political Register*, 19 October 1816; *Cobbett's Political Works*, especially 2:519; Hunt, *Memoirs*, 3:355; also the *Gorgon*, 25 July 1818, pp. 75–76, on the range of opinions from "Delicate Reformers" through household franchise supporters to advocates of universal suffrage. Wade was in the last camp, and perhaps extreme even there, rejecting quibbles over exclusions and holding that "The only simple and consistent scheme [is] that which includes the whole *biped* race, without distinction of age, sex, rank, or condition."

130. *The Making*, pp. 735–36, 749.

131. *The Gorgon*, 11 July 1818, pp. 62–63.

132. Ibid., pp. 63.

133. Ibid., 25 July 1818, pp. 73–74. If the laboring classes attempt to act on their own the middle classes will naturally desert them "and would wink at measures on the part of the Government, which, under other circumstances, they would resolutely oppose."

134. *The Making*, p. 736. For a description of the government's troubles with public opinion and with the Commons, see Cookson, *Lord Liverpool's Administration*, chap. 3.

135. *The Making*, p. 737.

136. See the admirable presentation of these issues in Wertheim, *Evolution and Revolution*, 127–36.

137. The collapse of the movement after Peterloo indicates the limits of any benefit derived from this situation. Capturing the middle ground tends to force one to fight on the middle ground—which is not a very revolutionary locale.

138. Just how weakly formed the middle class was is beyond the scope of my argument, and indeed Thompson more asserts than demonstrates it. Papers like the *Times* were already more than simply a Whig opposition, though middle-class reformers had not yet coalesced into a body demanding power in government. See Perkin, *The Origins of Modern English Society*, chaps. 6–9. He dates the emergence of the middle class from this same period of 1815–20. See also Briggs, "Middle Class Consciousness in English Politics, 1780–1846."

139. *The Making*, p. 738.

140. This argument coincides with that of D. C. Moore in "Concession or Cure: the Sociological Premises of the First Reform Act." This is also discussed by Foster, from a rather different point of view, as the phenomenon of "liberalization," in *Class Struggle*, chap. 7; see also above, chap. 5.

141. Piven and Cloward, *Poor People's Movements*, chap. 1; see also Hobsbawm's critique, "Should the Poor Organize?" The emphasis on the weakness of the poor as opposed to the strength of the working class clearly distinguishes this genre of radicalism from Marxism.

142. Even Thompson's (and nearly everyone else's) arch-critic, Walmsley, does not offer a strikingly different narrative of the events of 16 August, but rather differs concerning the intentions and characters of the participants (*Peterloo: The Case Re-Opened*).

143. *The Making*, pp. 736, 739.

144. Cobbett's sudden departure was yet another source of dissension in the radical ranks; see Hunt's recriminations in the *Memoirs*, 3:461–79.

145. *The Making*, p. 740; Prothero, *Artisans and Radicals*, p. 94; Wickwar, *The Struggle for the Freedom of the Press, 1819–1832*; Aspinall, *Politics and the Press, 1780–1850*; Hollis, *The Pauper Press*.

146. Kinsey, "Aspects," is largely based on the *Observer*, and includes an argument as to its importance.

147. *The Making*, p. 740.

148. An indication of the *Black Dwarf*'s visibility can perhaps be seen in the establishment of a Tory opposition paper, the *White Dwarf*.

149. The quotation is from the *Black Dwarf*, 9 September 1818, but it could just as easily have come from Wade or Carlile (in the latter case probably without any religious allusion) as from Wooler. See also *The Making*, pp. 740–41, and Halévy, *The Liberal Awakening*, pp. 59–61.

150. *The Gorgon*, 25 July 1818, pp. 74–75.

151. Thistlewood, the younger Watson, and some other extreme radicals continued to hope that a mass meeting would provide the occasion for a seizure of power. They were mistaken. For a good discussion see Prothero, *Artisans and Politics*, chap. 6.

152. Thompson documents this, emphasizing General Byng's revealing comment that "the peaceable demeanour of so many thousand unemployed Men is not natural" (*The Making*, p. 747).

153. The mobilization did not, in any case, include the entire English people but rather was concentrated in certain parts of the country, and among village craftsmen first and foremost, urban artisans and workers secondly, and rural laborers least of all.

154. Slater, *Microcosm*, p. 176.

155. The phrase "purified community" is borrowed from Sennett's *The Uses of Disorder*; although his empirical context is different, I believe the underlying phenomenon to be quite similar.

156. *The Making*, pp. 745–49; see also Bamford's description of, and emphasis on, the orderliness of the processions in his *Passages in the Life of a Radical*, chaps. 33 and 34.

157. *The Making*, p. 749. I, of course, suggest that it was the new working class as much as the middle class which was moderate in 1832.

158. Piven and Cloward, *Poor People's Movements*.

159. Thompson's comments on Peterloo are in *The Making*, pp. 748–59. Read's *Peterloo* gives more detailed local information; since Thompson's book was published, Walmsley has gone over the record laboriously in *Peterloo: The Case Re-Opened*, and constructed a defense of William Hulton, the magistrate who gave the order for the hussars to disperse the meeting.

160. *The Making*, p. 753.

161. Several such instances are listed by Halévy in *The Liberal Awakening*, p. 64. See also Stevenson, "Social Control and the Prevention of Riots in England, 1789–1829."

162. There is some indication that these communications were cautionary.

See Read's discussion of communications between Sidmouth and the magistrates, especially the letter of the former on 4 August, advising against "an attempt to disperse the Assembly by force" (*Peterloo*, pp. 118–22).

163. *The Making*, pp. 750–51, especially the footnote on p. 750.

164. Ibid., p. 737.

165. A letter to the *Manchester Observer* called them "the feather-bed cavalry" (17 July 1819). The yeomanry cavalry was the object of abuse from the radicals well before Peterloo, not least of all for its ineffectuality.

166. This is part of what is behind the widely cited incident reported in the *Inquest of John Lees* (p. 180) involving an officer of the hussars who shamed the yeomanry for cutting at people who could not escape. After the officer turned his back, the yeomanry returned to their swords.

167. This was exacerbated by the size of Manchester (and surrounds), the distinction of its residential districts by class, and its function as a center to a district.

168. Gayer, Rostow, and Schwartz, *The Growth and Fluctuation of the British Economy, 1790–1850*, vol. I, pt. 1, chap. 3; pt. 2, secs. 4, 5, and 6.

169. Radical papers with a heavy bent towards industrial issues, such as the *Gorgon*, derived almost all of their provincial sales from the textile region.

170. Thompson does not recognize this at this point in his account, but only earlier (and implicitly) when he notices that London no longer dominated the countryside in radical agitation (*The Making*, pp. 699–70); the activists, conversely, often waited for the London lead which never came. An idea of the districts most affected can be gotten from the list of disturbed counties in Art. 8 of 60 Geo. cap. 2: Lancashire, Cheshire, West Riding of Yorkshire, Warwickshire, Staffordshire, Derbyshire, Leicestershire, Nottinghamshire, Cumberland, Westmorland, Northumberland, Durham, Renfrew, Lanark, the Counties of the Towns of Newcastle-upon-Tyne and Nottingham and of the City of Coventry. See also Halévy, *The Liberal Awakening*, p. 67.

171. Cf. Read's comment that "The successful designation of Peterloo as a 'massacre' represents another piece of successful propaganda. Perhaps only in peace-loving England could a death-roll of only eleven persons have been so described" (*Peterloo*, p. vii). Be this as it may, the point remains that the violence at St. Peter's Fields was relatively extreme, and experience and perception are quite relative things.

172. See *The Making*, pp. 754–55, and Read, *Peterloo*, pt. 4.

173. *The Making*, pp. 757, 759.

174. Cookson, *Lord Liverpool's Administration, 1815–1822*, p. 179.

175. *The Making*, pp. 761–81; see also the account in Prothero, *Artisans and Politics*, chap. 6.

176. Thompson attempts to limit the reasons for the collapse to the dissension among the leaders and to the Six Acts (*The Making*, p. 761).

Chapter Four

1. Cobbett, *Political Register*, May 1809, p. 214 of Cobbett's *Political Works*, vol. 2.

2. At its height, Cobbett's two-penny *Political Register* had a circulation of between 40,000 and 60,000 copies a week, many times the number of its nearest competitors—including those of the "legitimate" press. See Thompson, *The*

Making, pp. 789–90, and R. K. Webb, *The British Working-Class Reader, 1790–1848*, pp. 79–154.

3. *The Making*, p. 833; on Cobbett in general, see pp. 820–37.

4. Introduction, *The Opinions of William Cobbett*, p. 13.

5. To read too much of intellectual, rationalistic radicalism into populism is an error. Cobbett and Hunt may have been "plebeian and populist in tone," but they were not "vehemently hostile to established forms of authority.... [appropriating] the traditions of the Left, rooted in the Enlightenment and the French Revolution" (Tholfson, *Working Class Radicalism in Mid-Victorian England*, p. 49).

6. Hollis, for example, observes that "Place spoke the language of aristocracy and People, and within the People there could be no division of class. Hetherington spoke the language of class" (*The Pauper Press*, p. 8).

7. "For it was always the abuse of authority, not the authority itself, that was the immediate target of attack, even although other targets might present themselves as a campaign progressed" (Thornton, *The Habit of Authority*, p. 14).

8. This continued into the early Chartist years. As Dorothy Thompson has commented, "The real threat to authority in these years was in the community-rooted organizations of the provincial Chartists, less articulate though its leadership may have been than the French-inspired rhetoric of Harney or Taylor" (*The Early Chartists*, pp. 19–20).

9. *The Habit of Authority*, p. 86.

10. See the argument of D. C. Moore in *The Politics of Deference*.

11. Note that the stated issue is *control over* production and distribution, not production processes or distribution in themselves.

12. See above, pp. 35–42.

13. Thus Thompson overestimates the pace of rationalization in much of the general argument of *The Making*.

14. As for example Stevenson does in "The Queen Caroline Affair."

15. This prompted Engels to speculate that perhaps "the English proletarian movement in its old traditional Chartist form must perish completely before it can develop in a new, viable form" (Letter to Marx, October 7, 1858, in *Marx and Engels on Britain*, p. 491). Engels was upset over Jones's attempt to form an alliance with members of the middle classes in the struggle over the franchise.

16. This was the constant program of the National Union of the Working Classes and of the *Poor Man's Guardian*. Both felt compelled to preach it constantly to doubters. Even in these quarters, there was uncertainty as to whether outright control of government would be necessary.

17. See Prothero, *Artisans and Politics*, p. 293, for a suggestion of the continuing truth of this.

18. I thus refer in American history less to such elite figures as William Jennings Bryan than to grass roots movements such as the Farmers' Alliance. These movements were organized in large part from the bottom up, and remained responsive to the rank and file throughout. For a perceptive account which returns the term to these roots rather than its political and historical popularizations and assimilations, see Goodwyn's *Democratic Promise*.

19. This characteristic was shared with millenarian movements throughout history, as well as with various religious revitalizations and such recent similar movements as that of the "Woodstock generation."

20. The phrase is from Macrae, "Populism as an Ideology," p. 162. On the

problem of obtaining and maintaining community consensus in a variety of settings, see Colson, *Tradition and Contract: The Problem of Order*; Gluckman. *Politics, Law and Ritual in Tribal Society*; Peters, "Aspects of the Control of Moral Ambiguities: A Comparative Analysis of Two Culturally Disparate Modes of Social Control"; and Abarbanel, "The Dilemma of Economic Competition in an Israeli Moshav." Historians have recently taken up some of this anthropological analysis; see Thompson, "'Rough Music': Le Charivari Anglais," and Davis, *Society and Culture in Early Modern France*, especially the discussion of the "reasons of misrule."

21. "It seems at times that half a dozen working men could scarcely sit in a room together without appointing a Chairman, raising a point-of-order, or moving the Previous Question" (*The Making*, p. 738).

22. Sociologists and psychologists have traced these problems in considerable detail in studies of small groups and organizations. See Bion, *Experiences in Groups*; Slater, *Microcosm*; and Miller and Rice, *Systems of Organization*, for three classics. Recent research is well anthologized in Gibbard, Hartman and Mann, eds., *Analysis of Groups*.

23. The song comes from Harland, *Ballads and Songs of Lancashire*, p. 262, cited in *The Making*, p. 689. Joseph Nadin was the hated stipendiary constable of Manchester.

24. In no small part because the demagogues preferred "spontaneous" mass protest to organized action. Even such would-be revolutionaries as Watson and other Spenceans in London long hoped that mass meetings would turn into revolution. See Prothero, *Artisans and Politics*, p. 127.

25. *The Gorgon*, 20 June 1818, p. 35. It is perhaps telling to note that Wade published his paper anonymously; he did not personalize politics like the demagogues.

26. Republicanism was always more important at the center than at the local roots.

27. *Memoirs of Henry Hunt*, 1:505.

28. *Gorgon*, 23 May 1818, p. 8.

29. Ibid., 20 June 1818, pp. 33–34; 1 August 1818, p. 85, and in general the last several issues, devoted primarily to problems of workers' organization.

30. "Address to the Journeymen and Labourers of England, Wales, Scotland, and Ireland," *Political Register* 2 November 1816, quoted from the Coles, *The Opinions of William Cobbett*, p. 216.

31. See, for example, *Political Register*, November 1807, pp. 346–66 of vol. 2 of *Cobbett's Political Works*.

32. *Gorgon*, 23 May 1818, p. 5. Major Cartwright was, of course, also an object of Wade's attack.

33. *Gorgon*, especially 15 August 1818; Kirby and Musson, *The Voice of the People*, pp. 18–22; *The Making*, pp. 706–8.

34. On the spinners, see Kirby and Musson, *The Voice of the People*.

35. There is virtually no account of the Caroline agitation's popular components in the literature. It has been regarded by most historians as a distasteful aberration in royal decorum or popular good sense. Francis Place thought it at least demystifying of royalty; other reformers have found it more embarrassing (witness Martineau's nose-pinching disdain, *History of England during the Peace*, p. 125). Where it has attracted attention at all, this has been focused on the divorce case and trial, the shenanigans of Whigs and city radicals such as Brougham and Wood (see Bowman, *The Divorce Case of Queen Caroline*; Ful-

ford, *The Trial of Queen Caroline*). The Coles's collection of *The Opinions of William Cobbett* includes none of the Caroline material, from either 1813 or 1820–21. Halévy offers some discussion, *The Liberal Awakening*, pp. 80–106, as does Maccoby, *English Radicalism, 1786–1832*, pp. 369–75. Stevenson in "The Queen Caroline Affair," and Prothero, in *Artisans and Politics*, chap. 7, have each recently given an account of the London radicals' involvement. Thompson devotes one paragraph to the events, *The Making*, p. 778, and two ensuing mentions (pp. 794 and 810) which imply that its greatest significance lay in occasioning a number of satirical prints and cartoons. My own research on the Caroline agitation has been aided by collaboration with Thomas Laqueur, who will publish his own study of the literary and symbolic aspects of this social drama.

36. *The Republican*, 30 June 1820, p. 325.

37. *The Black Dwarf*, 28 June 1820, p. 881.

38. Three volumes of the Home Office papers contain numerous examples of such, along with dozens of worried letters to Sidmouth: H.O. 40/14, 15, and 16.

39. *The Republican*, 16 June 1820, p. 277, and 30 June 1820, p. 327.

40. Numerous examples of addresses from these societies to the queen, together with several responses, may be found in the *Political Register*.

41. *Political Register*, 7 October 1820, p. 830.

42. See Pinchbeck, *Women Workers and the Industrial Revolution, 1750–1850*, chap. 9.

43. These female reform societies date primarily from about 1818, with a leap in numbers during the Caroline agitation. In addition to sources already mentioned, they appear frequently in the pages of the *Manchester Observer*. Thompson discusses these issues briefly on pp. 453–56 of *The Making*.

44. *The Making*, p. 455.

45. Thus Prothero is quite wrong to assert without qualification that "The 'Queenite' agitation was much stronger in London than anywhere else" (*Artisans and Politics*, p. 143).

46. The latter argument is offered by Thompson in *The Making*, p. 761.

47. See Lean, *The Napoleonists: A Study in Political Disaffection, 1760–1960*, pp. 90–103; Cookson, *Lord Liverpool's Administration, 1815–1822*, chaps. 5 and 6. The king's dislike for his wife had twice previously—in 1806 and 1813—brought the marriage into public and parliamentary debate.

48. See Lean, *The Napoleonists*, pp. 116–17; Halévy, *The Liberal Awakening*, pp. 86–92; and the several letters from various parties in Aspinall, ed., *The Letters of George IV*, vol. 2, letters 801, 819–22; Brougham, *Life and Times of Henry, Lord Brougham*, 2:357–66; Yonge, *The Life and Administration of Robert Banks, Second Earl of Liverpool*, 3:65–68. Woodward, *The Age of Reform*, p. 67, agrees as to the priority of Wood's support over that of Brougham in the queen's decision. See also Cobbett, *Political Register*, 10 June 1820, "A Defense of the Queen Against the Defence made by her 'Constitutional Defender'," the first of Cobbett's series of attacks on Brougham's handling of the queen's case. Cobbett remarks: "Happy I am to say that that man was not a Radical" (p. 596).

49. Aspinall, *Lord Brougham and the Whig Party*, p. 145. Cobbett addressed his letter on the occasion of the queen's triumph to the people of Dover, because "If people less zealous, less active, less prompt and less resolute than you had been placed on the frontier; had been placed as an advance guard to the nation, the result might have been very different" (*Political Register*, 18 November

1820, p. 1202). See also *An Impartial and Authentic Memoir of the Life of Her Late Most Gracious Majesty Queen Caroline*, p. 25. Note the problem this poses for arguments such as Prothero's *(Artisans and Politics*, p. 133) that the London radicals cooked up the popular support.

50. H.O 40/15/6, letter of 14 February; Hone has identified "J. S." as John Shergoe. On 12 June, Shergoe reported that radical papers were being read with more than usual zeal (40/15/24), and by 7 July that medallions were being struck (40/15/31) (traditional for coronations; see Report of a Committee of the Privy Council, May 1820, in Aspinall, *The Letters of George IV*, p. 329). In general, Shergoe played down the danger from the agitation concerning the queen, and playing danger down was hardly habitual to those who earned their living as informers. He did subscribe to a conspiracy theory which was inappropriate to Caroline's defense but not to all acts of the London radicals. Remember that these events transpired just before the exposure of the Cato Street conspiracy.

51. A scene which seems to have occurred in literally hundreds of villages throughout the countryside, usually on the occasion of the passing of a noted Whig defender of the queen.

52. *Political Register*, 29 July 1820, pp. 77–78.

53. H.O. 40/15/108; letter of 15 November 1820. Norris thought the Manchester illumination a "great failure" (letter of 20 November 1820, H.O. 40/15/170). The same was true of Stockport (item 220, 40/17/20).

54. There were two occasions when the "large representation of a human eye" over the entrance to the *Manchester Observer* office was illuminated: Hunt's birthday and the end of the queen's trial. Illuminations took place with varying degrees of success throughout the country; they were most successful in the smaller villages. See H.O. 40/15.

55. Cf. placards from the Borough of Devizes, H.O. 40/15/114 and 115.

56. And, sometimes, in towns of older radical fame, as for example Norwich (H.O. 40/15/147). The mayor there was petitioned to call a Common-Hall for the purpose of congratulating Her Majesty on 16 November 1820. The Court of the Mayoralty was not favorable (item 149).

57. Churchwardens and such were intimidated by keelmen in Bishop Wearmouth and by laborers in St. Ives, Huntingdonshire (H.O. 40/15/118, 126). A Belfry was broken into in Swansea (item 181).

58. In Llanurst and Sevenoaks, for example (H.O. 40/15/213, 244); in Wincanton, a captain of the local yeomanry had his cow stall and hay rick burnt as a consequence of "having taken an active part in preventing illumination and other disgraceful Proceedings" (item 232). The locations listed in this and the preceding note are typical, and indicative of the widespread following Caroline had, and of the relatively pacific state of the previously most disturbed districts.

59. H.O. 40/15/177. The significance of the number of hand-bell ringers called for is obvious. Jacobitism still had popular symbolic value. Another placard from the same printer emphasized the peaceful intentions and moderation of the celebrants: "All they claim for themselves is the right to express their own exultation at the triumph of her Majesty; a right which they presume all *truly* loyal men will be proud to exercize. And they hereby caution their Fellow Citizens on *no account whatever* to suffer themselves to be *ensnared* or *incited* to the commission of any outrage, but if any should be committed, from

whatsoever quarter, to assist in delivering the offenders into the custody of the Magistrates" (item 178).

60. H.O. 40/15/199. See the similar item from Northallerton (H.O. 40/16/167).

61. Cf. the deposition of a Derbyshire prisoner (a sure stimulus to thoughts of revolution seemed to be the opportunity to confess them to jailors) (H.O. 40/15/202). See also H.O. 40/15/110, and Lean, *The Napoleonists*.

62. Wrote Carlile: "We have just been thinking, that the best way to settle this dispute, will be for the King to sit on the Hanoverian throne and the Queen on that of Great Britain and Ireland" (*The Republican*, 30 June 1820). The issue of the Hanoverian succession, still evidently unsettled in the popular consciousness, keeps cropping up throughout the Caroline affair.

63. *Political Register*, 7 October 1820, p. 798. A distinction is being drawn between the lawyer Brougham's self-serving defense of the queen and the defense offered by people and press. A striking analogy is suggested with the American populist movement, which had its Brougham in William Jennings Bryan, and also its grass-roots organizations and popular press which were full of distrust for the party leaders. See Goodwyn, *Democratic Promise*, chaps. 14, 15. See also H.O. 40/15/230 in which a correspondent draws a distinction (and suggests a split) between "partisans" and "radicals."

64. Place thought this "demystification" the major gain (Wallas, *Life of Place*, p. 151).

65. *The Republican*, 16 June 1820, p. 276; many more than one week was devoted wholly to the affairs of the queen.

66. H.O. 40/15/279; dated "24th Day, 2nd Month, 2nd Year, Manchester Massacre, without enquiry."

67. *The Republican*, 30 June 1820, p. 335.

68. Ibid., 25 August 1820.

69. *The Black Dwarf*, 14 June 1820.

70. Ibid., 28 June 1820.

71. The funeral provided the only serious violence of the affair. London was closed to the hearse, which the government intended to have proceed by a less prominent route. The crowd attempted to force its way into the City, troops charged the crowd and opened fire, killing two men; eventually the crowd had its way. There is a concise account in Stevenson, "The Queen Caroline Affair," pp. 136–37; see also Prothero, *Artisans and Politics*, pp. 151–53, and a contemporary pamphlet, *An Authentic and Detailed Account of the Funeral of Her Late Most Gracious Majesty*.

72. This was a classic form of protecting the kingship; see Gluckman, "The Frailty of Authority," chap. 2 of *Custom and Conflict in Africa*, and Weber, *Economy and Society*, p. 1147. This contradicts the views of Prothero, *Artisans and Politics*, p. 141, and Cole, *Life of Cobbett*, p. 248. Republicanism faded rather easily in nineteenth-century England, though it never disappeared.

73. Prothero, *Artisans and Politics*, p. 141.

74. Thompson, "The Very Type of the 'Respectable Artisan'."

75. We may liken the Caroline agitation to Gluckman's notion of "rituals of rebellion" (*Order and Rebellion in Tribal Africa*, chap. 3). The fit is somewhat loose, however, as the Caroline agitation only partially reaffirmed the existing order and was only partially sanctioned by that order.

76. Prothero, *Artisans and Politics*, pp. 141–42.

77. See chap. 8 for a further discussion of this transition.

78. Hodgskin, *Labour Defended against the Claims of Capital;* W. Thompson, *Inquiry into the Principles of the Distribution of Wealth* and *Labour Rewarded.* These arguments were given wide circulation in the *Mechanics' Magazine* and the *Poor Man's Guardian,* though they were mixed there with other less sophisticated views.

79. Samuel, "Workshop of the World," emphasizes the continuing importance of artisan production throughout the nineteenth century.

80. On the shifting grounds of negotiations between unions and employers, particularly in the cotton industry, see Turner, *Trade Union Growth, Structure, and Policy.* The importance of the contrast between piece rates and time-based wages has been emphasized by William Reddy in an unpublished work. I am also indebted to him for personal conversations on the issue.

81. It should not be thought that the transition has been complete in any country today. Populism is still central to the political claims of workers and others; various traditional notions of justice and fair play still often take precedence over arguments based on the notion of exploitation.

82. 11 April 1831.

83. *Poor Man's Guardian,* 12 October 1833, O'Brien editor, Hetherington publisher.

84. Ibid., 19 October 1833; see also the two articles on trade unions, 14 and 21 December 1833.

85. Ibid., 19 October 1833, among several.

86. Prothero, *Artisans and Politics,* p. 336.

87. Prothero's *Artisans and Politics* focuses on Gast, and through him on the shipwrights.

88. See Prothero, *Artisans and Politics,* pp. 250–51; Postgate, *The Builder's History.*

89. See the discussion above of production vs. consumption orientations, pp. 43–46, and of the emerging theory of exploitation as critical to the development of a differentiation of class from popular action, pp. 115–19.

90. The preceding four sentences use singular nouns to refer to what manifestly are usually groupings of workers, and also assume that alternative sources of supply (of labor or product) are constant.

91. Degraded crafts like that of the framework knitters provide interesting evidence, since they pushed the traditional artisan view to its limits. In them, the ease of entry or introduction of machinery reduced prices and glutted markets so that only production of an extremely large volume could keep a worker going: he had to "sweat" himself and often his family. Nonetheless the knitters' labor was not completely interchangeable—they had few other options for employment. Their statements stressed again and again the fact that they depended on their skill as well as on the sheer volume of their labor. In general, the knitters' demands were for a fair market for the goods they produced (cf. Felkin, *An Account of the Machine-Wrought Hosiery and Lace Manufactures*). Their claims were sometimes presented, however, as claims on wages; it is important to bear in mind that these were piece rates. Even so, some advocates such as Robert Hall held that the issue was the price at which the knitters sold their labor and skill. Hall's pamphlets present an admixture of the defense of the traditional position of the mechanic and a "modern" treatment of wages determined by market pressures (cf. his "An Appeal to the Public, on the Subject of the Framework-Knitters' Fund" and "A Reply to the Principal Objections Advanced by Cobbett and Others against the Framework-Knitters'

Friendly Relief Society"). Not coincidentally, these pamphlets were products of the early 1820s.

92. This was prominently the argument of Hodgskin's *Labour Defended*. Note that recognition of the division of labor did not necessarily imply an endorsement of the concentration of production in a factory.

93. See *Labour Defended*, pp. 86–91, making the important distinction between capitalist as manager and as mere "middleman." The term "middleman" is itself instructive, for it suggests how strongly even Hodgskin's account of exploitation continued to be influenced by traditional categories of thought.

94. Hall, the framework-knitters' advocate, took occasion to point out that it was wealth in general, not merely property in the means of production which caused the transfer of property from those who labor to those who do not. Depressed wages lead to depressed prices which benefit all those who have the wealth with which to purchase. Hall was in the process of taking Cobbett to task for failing to apply his general principles to the case of the knitters ("A Reply, p. 24).

Chapter Five

1. E. Jones, "Trades' Grievances," *Notes to the People*, 1:342.

2. G. J. Harney, "Dedication," *Democratic Review*, n.p.; Louis Blanc, "Social Reform," *Democratic Review*, pp. 207–13; F. Engels, "The Ten Hours Question," *Democratic Review*, pp. 371–77. The *Democratic Review* (1849–50) was never strongly committed to one view within the Chartist/socialist camp. As Saville has noted, Harney himself was more an "internationally minded Jacobin" than either a social investigator or Chartist or socialist leader (Introduction to *The Red Republican*, p. xv). See also Schoyen, *The Chartist Challenge*.

3. Lovett and Collins, Preface, *Chartism: A New Organization of the People*.

4. On this point I might note that the language of status and hierarchy developed initially as an exclusionary language, that is as a language for describing relative upper-classness. The use of "class" as an inclusionary term came later. Briggs has dated it essentially to the close of the eighteenth century ("The language of 'Class' in Early Nineteenth Century England"). Note that the very semantics of class point to polarization. It is a unidimensional hierarchy; it implicitly groups smaller units of population—trades, for example—together into larger ones.

5. As Foster would suggest, *Class Struggle*, p. 5.

6. It may well be that the elites of England saw class struggle more often in progress than did workers in the early nineteenth century, just as right-wing politicians are more apt than workers to see communism in trade-union activity today.

7. Probable exceptions are his endless advocacy of hard currency and his two-year devotion to the cause of Queen Caroline.

8. This paragraph crudely follows an important scenario developed in *The Making*.

9. I hesitate to call it a "society," for the population had only a limited autonomy from members of the middle and upper classes. Very roughly, this is analogous to the situation of peoples under foreign domination, especially if this has gone on for a long time and it is difficult to decide whether one can reasonably speak of a "native" society as distinct from the larger system which

includes members of the foreign group and various rulers and pressures which they may impose.

10. Though, once again, in the case of African tribal groupings the boundaries are vague at best and tend to shade both in indigenous labelings and analytical categorizations from one into the other across a sociogeographic region. See Fortes, *The Dynamics of Clanship among the Tallensi*, p. 241, and Goody, *The Social Organization of the LoWiili*, chap. 1.

11. These years were also crucial to determining what ideological content the memory of Peterloo would carry. As Thompson notes, in 1819 the loyalists still had their supporters, in and out of government; by 1829, "it was an event to be remembered, even among the gentry, with guilt" (*The Making*, p. 779).

12. Ibid., p. 774.

13. Ibid., p. 782.

14. London, with its artisan-dominated unions, is an exception to this assertion.

15. To the extent that one can lay out the forms of consciousness in temporal order for Oldham, that order would appear to be political–trade-union–political, not simply a transition from the second to the third, primitive to mature, as Foster implies.

16. *The Making*, p. 799. Thompson perhaps slightly overstates the change. See also Prothero, *Artisans and Politics*, parts three and four.

17. This is suggested in *The Making*, pp. 797–98, but see the better account in Hollis, *The Pauper Press*, pp. 206–13, 218.

18. This is suggested by Thompson in *The Making*, pp. 798 and 805. It should not be thought that I am arguing that individualism was at any point a substitute for organized action, only that its implications varied with the context.

19. Not all the freedoms indicated must be equally as "individual" as the epithet might suggest.

20. *The Making*, pp. 874, 863, 868.

21. Ibid., pp. 872, 884. See also Harrison, *Robert Owen and the Owenites*.

22. That is, the only way in which "class" can cope with these issues is to subsume within the term an entire theory of the necessary connections between objective or external classification and subjective or internal organization and action. See chap. 8, above.

23. The two are thus similar regardless of whether the latter took over when the former was defeated, as Thompson argues, or the two advanced at the same time, as Hobsbawm suggests (Hobsbawm, "Methodism and the Threat of Revolution"; *The Making*, pp. 405, 427–28, and 920–22). See also Calhoun, "The Social Function of Experiences of Altered Perception."

24. *The Making*, pp. 813, 816.

25. See Turner, *The Ritual Process* and *Schism and Continuity in an African Society*.

26. *The Making*, pp. 887–89.

27. Ibid., p. 888; he puts the date of the reversal at 1832.

28. "The Peculiarities." Thompson too has a French example in mind.

29. This view is concisely presented in Cobban, *Social Interpretation of the French Revolution*.

30. Marx, "The Class Struggles in France: 1848–50," pt. 1. See also Marx's "Eighteenth Brumaire of Louis Napoleon."

31. *The Making*, p. 889.

32. Ibid., p. 890. This radicalization within the revolution has, of course, been the prevalent pattern in modern history.

33. See ibid., chap. 16 generally, pp. 892–93 in particular; Hollis, *The Pauper Press*, chap. 8, and Tholfson, *Working Class Radicalism in Mid-Victorian England*, chap. 3.

34. *The Making*, p. 888.

35. Ibid., p. 939.

36. Engels began the labor aristocracy argument; it has become widespread but also widely debated. For citations to the relevant literature, as well as for important original contributions, see the three articles recently discussing the subject in *Social History*: Musson, "Class Struggle and the Labour Aristocracy 1830–60"; Moorhouse, "The Marxist Theory of the Labour Aristocracy"; and Reid, "Politics and Economics in the Formation of the British Working Class: A Response to H. F. Moorhouse." The present discussion does not attempt to summarize the complexities of debate on the labor aristocracy but only to indicate some of the relevance of my arguments concerning the early nineteenth century for this argument concerning the mid-nineteenth century.

37. Foster, *Class Struggle*, p. 3; in chap. 7, where Foster discusses liberalization in detail, he tends continually to refer to the action of the "ruling-class" with no specification of membership, or the bourgeoisie with no consideration of divergences within elite groups. This is largely a further result of his focus on the local level.

38. In *Class Struggle* there is an ambiguity in Foster's treatment between his acceptance of the Leninist position that trade-unionism and reform are the normal maxima of working-class action (pp. 123–24) and his implicit assumption that revolution ought "naturally" to occur and that the ruling class must have acted to prevent it (throughout chap. 7). The ambiguity is partially resolved by noting that the presence and acceptance of radical leaders, and of bearers of the "correct line," is his main indicator of class radicalism, despite his intention to examine characteristics of the class itself.

39. Ibid., p. 204.

40. It is also doubtful whether local capitalists rather than Conservatives on a national scale accomplished this stabilization. See Moore, *The Politics of Deference*.

41. Reid, "Politics and Economics," p. 361. By "defeat" one should read failure to secure fundamental political or social reorganization. Obviously workers win concessions, though how much this is due to "class" as opposed to "trade union" or other more local forms of action is open to question.

42. Thus Foster: "While mass movements often have radical leaderships few become socially radical themselves. The reasons are obvious. Struggles on purely immediate issues demand no direct challenge to existing sectional identities (and indeed usually develop in their material defence). On the other hand, for a movement to become radical, for dialectically new (and socially incompatible) ideas to be injected into it, those sectional identities have—however imperceptibly—to be broken down.... If, therefore, radicals are able to enter a group and express certain immediate aspirations in terms which (though themselves acceptable) ultimately become incompatible with the system itself, the overall fight for a wider consciousness will be that much easier" (*Class Struggle*, pp. 123–24).

43. E. P. Thompson, "Eighteenth-Century English Society," sects. IV and V, especially pp. 149, 156. See also Thompson's reply to Anderson's and Nairn's

use of Gramsci, *Poverty of Theory*, pp. 282–84 (revised version of "The Peculiarities").

44. The most important representative of this treatment is Poulantzas, *Political Power and Social Class*, and *Classes in Contemporary Capitalism*; see also the work of Wright, who disagrees with Poulantzas concerning the membership and structuration of the working class in advanced capitalist societies, *Class Structure and Income Inequality*, and *Class, Crisis, and State*. Note especially Wright's concept of classes in contradictory positions, not merely in indeterminate "gray" areas of definition (*Class, Crisis*, pp. 74–97).

45. I make no attempt to summarize this large and varied literature. See, for several perspectives: Amin, *Unequal Development*; Emmanuel, *Unequal Exchange*; Frank, *Towards a Theory of Underdevelopment*; Mandel, *Late Capitalism*, especially chap. 11; Meyer and Hannan, eds., *National Development and the World System*; and Wallerstein, *The Modern World System*.

46. The boundary line is indistinct, and obviously many of the key divisions remained important for generations. The times to which I refer are not definitive but rather illustrate the critical emergence of the split.

47. Weber, *Economy and Society*, p. 41.

48. Discussed, for example, by Perkin, *The Origins of Modern English Society*, esp. chap. 7.

Chapter Six

1. *Political Register*, 12 July 1817.

2. Macfarlane, "History, Anthropology and the Study of Communities"; see also Calhoun, "History, Anthropology and the Study of Communities: Some Problems in Macfarlane's Proposal."

3. For a more detailed discussion of the concept of community, see my "Community: Toward a Variable Conceptualization for Comparative Research."

4. Cobbett, *Rural Rides*, pp. 66–67.

5. See Polanyi, *The Great Transformation*, chap. 10; Myrdal, *The Political Element in the Development of Economic Theory*; and Reisman, *Adam Smith's Sociological Economics*.

6. See Zaret, "An Analysis of the Development and Content of the Covenant Theology of Pre-Revolutionary Puritanism"; Hill, *Society and Puritanism in Pre-Revolutionary England*; and Hanson, *From Kingdom to Commonwealth*.

7. Williams, *The Country and the City*, offers a good discussion from literary sources.

8. See Moffit, *England on the Eve of the Industrial Revolution*, chap. 2; Wadsworth and Mann, *The Cotton Trade and Industrial Lancashire, 1600–1780*, pp. 314–23. On the varying strength of the greater gentry (and other categories of landowners), see F. M. L. Thompson, *English Landed Society in the Nineteenth Century*, chap. 5, especially p. 114.

9. See Calhoun, "History, Anthropology and the Study of Communities: Some Problems in Macfarlane's Proposal."

10. Howitt, *The Rural Life of England*, pp. 201–2.

11. Thomis has commented on the tendency of historians to remind us of the separation of the two phenomena without themselves bearing in mind that contemporaries saw them as closely linked (*Responses to Industrialization*, p. 58). He does not, however, analyze the linkage.

12. Kay-Shuttleworth, *The Moral and Physical Condition of the Working Classes Employed in the Cotton Manufacture in Manchester.*

13. Taylor, *Notes of a Tour in the Manufacturing Districts of Lancashire,* p. 14.

14. See especially the chapter on "The Great Towns" (for example, pp. 78–79). See also Inglis, *Poverty and the Industrial Revolution* for a broad consideration of contemporary and historical accounts of a subject on which I can barely touch. His chap. 6 offers some considerations on the awakening consciousness of the urban poor in the 1830s.

15. The former was a question which led Carlyle to the church and Engels and Marx to a more socialized notion of alienation and to visions of the creation of a more effectively social man. The latter was a question which the *Manchester Guardian* could hold to be obvious by 1831: commerce means cycles of distress and prosperity (11 June); Engels, in *The Condition of the Working Class* could see this question as central, for crises resulting from competition would not only undermine the capitalist system but reorganize the society as the crises furthered the polarization of the population and the levelling of distinctions amongst its majority.

16. These are experiences of "communitas," if one does not accept Turner's wilder assertions of its maintenance over long periods of time. See his *The Ritual Process,* chaps. 3 and 4.

17. Simmel, "How is Society Possible?" p. 7.

18. Nadel, *The Foundations of Social Anthropology,* p. 154.

19. Multiplex bonds are those with many strands, so that actors linked in one context or through one institution are also linked in and through others. This makes it more difficult for an actor to cross another in any one context than it would be if there were only one strand to the link. The term is Gluckman's.

20. This is in contrast to Weber's use of the term which assumes that real continuity with the past is critical ("The Social Psychology of World Religions," p. 296). Sociologists who devote much attention to tradition have generally followed Weber on this (cf. Shils, "Tradition"). For the contrary view, see Yalman, "Some Observations on Secularism in Islam," p. 139, and Colson, *Tradition and Contract: The Problem of Order,* p. 76.

21. See further discussion in chap. 8.

22. Compare this with the entirely short-term and individualistic criteria of social interaction considered, for example, by exchange theory and rational-choice models of social structure. A good discussion of the long-term importance of kinship relations, in particular as they are morally sanctioned, is to be found in Bloch, "The Long Term and the Short Term: The Economic and Political Significance of the Morality of Kinship"; see also Calhoun, "The Authority of Ancestors."

23. Discussed in greater detail above, pp. 175–79.

24. Peel, "Old Cleckheaton," cited by Thompson, *The Making,* p. 274.

25. Corporations are "publics" in Smith's sense. Each is "an enduring, presumably perpetual group with determinate boundaries and membership, having an internal organization and a unitary set of external relations, and exclusive body of common affairs, and autonomy and procedures adequate to regulate them" ("A Structural Approach to Comparative Politics," p. 94).

26. Moore, "Legal Liability and Evolutionary Interpretation," p. 74.

27. Gluckman, "Les Rites de Passage," p. 28.

28. Ibid., p. 43.

29. Thus it is an illusion to think as some modern social scientists and planners have done, that it is equally plausible to create community with or without propinquity (cf. Webber, "Order in Diversity: Community without Propinquity"). These writers neglect the importance of multiplexity and focus their attention entirely on single-purpose relationships.

30. Colson, *Tradition and Contract*, p. 52.

31. This is not to suggest that the ancestors are necessarily very democratic—elders may have a greater ability to shape public opinion. They are, after all, apt to be at the center of networks of social relations, and it is such relations out of which community is made and therefore through which the authority of the community is exercised. See Calhoun, "The Authority of Ancestors."

32. See discussion above, pp. 42–48.

33. Thompson, "The Moral Economy of the English Crowd in the Eighteenth Century," p. 78. The reader should be aware that Thompson is unclear to the point of contradiction when he considers this moral economy in temporal perspective. On the one hand, he wants to show it developing; on the other hand, he feels it being stolen from traditional workers' communities by the onset of capitalist relations of production and consumption. The passage quoted in the text is a description of the eighteenth-century crowd given in protest against those who would call it a "mob." Among this latter number we must count an earlier Edward Thompson: "It is, indeed, this collective self-consciousness, with its corresponding theory, institutions, discipline and community values which distinguishes the nineteenth-century working class from the eighteenth-century mob" (*The Making*, p. 463). Generally, I think one is safer to follow Thompson's developmental assertions—though not to the end—than his romantic belief in the virtues of the past. See also R. Williams, *The Country and the City*, p. 131, on the active community of workers' protest movements as opposed to the mutuality of the oppressed.

34. See Nisbet, *The Quest for Community*, p. xii. During the industrial revolution, as Thompson has observed, the new ascendant social order was based on force and the "cash nexus" (though see above, chap. 3, n. 76). On the other hand, "ruling class control in the eighteenth century was located primarily in a cultural hegemony, and only secondarily in an expression of economic or physical (military) power" ("Patrician Society, Plebeian Culture," p. 387).

35. See F. M. L. Thompson, *English Landed Society in the Nineteenth Century*, and Mingay, *English Landed Society in the Eighteenth Century* and *The Gentry*. Throughout the period under consideration, tenant farmers grew in number and importance. They remained somewhat anomolous in the hierarchy.

36. A great deal of discussion was devoted to the question of who in fact was "gentle." See Thompson, *English Landed Society*, pp. 111–12, on the amounts of income and acreage considered vital. MacKinnon, in 1828, constructed a three-class model, with the ability to support one hundred laborers as the criterion for admittance to the highest level (*On Public Opinion*, p. 3). Where wealth was lacking or uncertain in adequacy, a variety of symbols were important, perhaps none more so than participation in field sports.

37. Redford, *Labour Migration in England, 1800–1850*; see also Chambers, "Enclosure and Labour Supply in the Industrial Revolution."

38. F. M. L. Thompson, *English Landed Society*, pp. 184–85.

39. Laslett, *The World We Have Lost*, p. 188.

40. Foster, *Class Struggle*, p. 27; note Foster's characteristic treatment of the issue as cultural rather than social. It may also be observed that his stress on the Puritan household is rather an overstatement.

41. Mingay notes: "Of necessity the great majority of politically ambitious gentry had to restrict their activities to local affairs. When they entered the lists a parliamentary career could spell financial ruin." (*The Gentry*, p. 75). It should also be noted, conversely, that launching a member of the family on a parliamentary career was a means of beginning to effect advancement from the gentry into the aristocracy. If the new member was fortunate enough to gain the favor of the government or the crown, he might be rewarded with various perquisites which made his efforts financially, as well as socially, worthwhile.

42. F. M. L. Thompson, *English Landed Society*, pp. 110–11 and 287–88, on qualifications for the magistracy and the determination of the landed interest not to relinquish control of it. See Mingay, *The Gentry*, pp. 124–34, on the JPs. He suggests that "The growing popularity of the Commission of the Peace was connected with its prestige and, one suspects, with the voluntary nature of the duties: in practice most of the work was done by an active minority, usually about a quarter of the whole bench" (p. 128).

43. On the latter, see Hay, "Property, Authority and the Criminal Law."

44. J. L. and B. Hammond, *The Village Labourer*, pp. 205–23.

45. Radzinowicz, *A History of English Criminal Law*, vol. 1.

46. Hay, "Property, Authority and the Criminal Law," p. 55.

47. F. M. L. Thompson, *English Landed Society*, p. 183; Mingay, *The Gentry*, p. 177.

48. Mingay, *The Gentry*, p. 10.

49. Spring, "English Landowners and Nineteenth-Century Industrialism," gives an account of the involvement of the great families in industrialization. On the weakness of smaller estates, see F. M. L. Thompson, *English Landed Society*, p. 225; Mingay, *The Gentry*, p. 168. The latter also indicates the greater tendency for MPs from the law or trade to be associated with the great Whig families rather than with the gentry (p. 75). See also Chambers and Mingay, *The Agricultural Revolution, 1750–1880*.

50. Mingay, *The Gentry*, p. 76.

51. F. M. L. Thompson, *English Landed Society*, p. 183.

52. Ibid., pp. 16–17.

53. Thornton, *The Habit of Authority*, p. 208.

54. Howitt, *Rural Life of England*, pp. 99–106. We may pity poor Cobbett for having this reputation, in view of all the people who learned to read from the pages of the *Political Register* and the *Two-Penny Trash*.

55. Watson, *The Reign of George III*, pp. 42–43.

56. Magistrates, for example, objected to "being used" by the Stamp Office to prosecute vendors of the unstamped press, especially when preventative action was not taken (Hollis, *Pauper Press*, pp. 169–70).

57. See Stevenson, "Social Control and the Prevention of Riots in England, 1789–1829," and Radzinowicz, *History of English Criminal Law*, vol. 2.

58. For general information on local government, see S. and B. Webb, *English Local Government: The Parish and the County*, and *English Poor Law History*, pt. 1; Redlich and Hirst, *The History of Local Government in England*. Regrettably there is no more recent or more authoritative general history of English local government.

59. Halévy, *England in 1815*, p. 38. Thornton suggests that in the 1790s

"Decisions at quarter sessions continued to mean more to more people than did sessions of the House of Commons" (*Habit of Authority*, p. 79).

60. Such feudal institutions as the court leet survived with at least some effectiveness into the nineteenth century, but they were more concerned with "civic improvements" than public order. See Vigier, *Change and Apathy: Liverpool and Manchester during the Industrial Revolution*, p. 5, n. 2, and Axon, *Annuals of Manchester*.

61. The Webbs, *English Local Government*, 1:557; see also pp. 309–10. 1835 was the year of the Municipal Corporations Act, which did a fair amount of rationalization and centralization of local government for the areas it covered. Among other things it separated justice from municipal administration. See Redlich and Hirst, *The History of Local Government*, pp. 129–30.

62. The Webbs, *English Local Government*, pp. 605–7.

63. See H.O. 40 and 42; "disturbed areas" could be widespread, depending on the nature of the disturbance. Agricultural villages were, for example, prominent in the Caroline agitation of 1820–21; see chap. 4 above.

64. 5 Geo. II, c. 18. F. M. L. Thompson, *English Landed Society*, p. 111, discusses practices, but, I believe erroneously, puts the enactment of the £100 criterion in 1745.

65. The clerical justices began to take a significant part in the Commission of the Peace during the course of the seventeenth century. Halévy estimates that by the early nineteenth century over half the justices sitting at sessions were clergymen (*England in 1815*, p. 41). See also Mingay, *The Gentry*, p. 127, and Evans, "Some Reasons for the Growth of English Rural Anti-Clericalism c. 1750–c. 1830." The significance of clerical justices was not lost on the popular radicals.

66. See Foster, *Class Struggle*, chap. 3, "Labour and State Power," which is really about labor and local government.

67. Watson, *The Reign of George III*, p. 44.

68. Vigier, *Change and Apathy*, pp. 214–15. Vigier's book contains a useful general account of the struggles to bring efficient local government to Manchester from the point of view of a public planner (with little interest in most of the issues discussed in the present work).

69. Axon, *Annals of Manchester*, p. 118.

70. Witness Arthur Onslow, considered by many the greatest speaker of the eighteenth-century Commons: "It was characteristic of Onslow to deplore the taking of divisions because votes in the house emphasized differences and the object of debate should be to induce ministers to follow a course universally felt to be right" (Watson, *The Reign of George III*, p. 64). Of course such a demand for consensus resulted in an inability to take much action at all. But then, although increasingly necessary from the 1790s, activity remained suspect. See above on the conservatism of authority.

71. See Vigier, *Change and Apathy*, p. 211.

72. Axon, *Annals of Manchester*, p. 151; *Manchester Herald*, 15 December 1818.

73. The shrievality, on the other hand, did not offer comparable social rewards and cost enough more that it was avoided by the greater gentry and became associated with those somewhat lower in social standing. Among other differences, the Commission of the Peace was voluntary whereas the duties of the sheriff were mandatory. See Mingay, *The Gentry*, p. 128.

74. "That the country in fact needed the services of any such *genus* as the

professional politician the country gentry took leave to doubt" (Thornton, *Habit of Authority*, p. 66).

75. Mingay, *The Gentry*, p. 118.

76. Perkin, *The Origins of Modern English Society*, discusses this contrast quite extensively.

77. Johnson distinguishes three stages in *The Disappearance of the Small Landowner* (chap. 8): the eighteenth century down to 1785 saw a decrease; there was perhaps a slight increase outside of Lancashire where the cotton industry attracted yeomen between 1785 and 1802; and there was decrease thereafter until 1832. Halévy disagrees with the second turning point, arguing that 1815, not 1802, was the turning point (*England in 1815*, p. 220). It is not at all clear that Toynbee's famous assertions on the decline of the yeomanry have to be as categorically rejected as Ashton has recently suggested (Toynbee, *Lectures on the Industrial Revolution in England*, chap. 5; Ashton, Introduction to Toynbee's *Industrial Revolution*. See also Chambers and Mingay, *The Agricultural Revolution, 1750–1880*, pp. 88–94; Mingay, *Enclosure and the Small Farmer in the Age of the Industrial Revolution*; and Clapham, *Economic History of Modern Britain*, 1: chap. 4, and 2: chap. 7.

78. These had not the capital either to profit greatly from innovations such as enclosure or to weather various cyclical crises of both production and demand. They had relatively small and often encumbered estates, and little means or opportunity for diversifying. The efficient professional management of agriculture benefited the larger owners, who had to depend on the growth of independent land agents. See Mingay, *English Landed Society in the Eighteenth Century*, chaps. 2–4, and *The Gentry*, p. 168; F. M. L. Thompson, *English Landed Society*, pp. 177–78.

79. Thompson, *The Making*, p. 68.

80. Smith, "A Structural Approach to Comparative Politics," p. 104.

81. This ambivalence also characterized African village headmen under British colonial rule. Generally headmen were less likely to have inherited wealth which set them and their families apart as a social class than British landowners were. Nonetheless, it is interesting to speculate as to the extent to which the British government followed a less explicit policy of indirect rule over its domestic population well before it formulated its approach to colonial governance. See Gluckman, "Interhierarchical Roles."

82. Indeed, people did not feel compelled to obey the law for authority's sake in all circumstances. But they were surprisingly willing to grant the authorities the right to punish them if they were caught. Thus, popular literature's frequent contrasts between "French Tyranny" and "British Liberties" suggested that a fault of the former system was its attempt at preventative action. The Englishman had the liberty of stealing game and getting hanged if he were caught.

83. Simultaneously, magistrates found that they had little if any ability to take recourse against employers who refused to obey the injunctions of the bench: they had no power to bring to bear. See Halévy, *England in 1815*, p. 336.

84. See Hay's illuminating article, "Property, Authority and the Criminal Law"; Radzinowicz's *A History of English Criminal Law* remains the most important general work; see vol. 1, chap. 4 on commutation of the death penalty.

85. Workers certainly tried to make the old system work at least as often as they pushed for anything new. Petition after petition flowed into Parliament expressing their grievances. Parliament seldom considered these petitions, let

alone took positive action. On a few occasions, workers had statute law on their side (such as the Statute of Artificers, 42 Eliz., cap. 63); Parliament then suspended or repealed the laws.

86. As Foster notes, "The effective practice of illegal unionism demanded more than just the elaboration of a mass of institutional supports. It compelled the formation of a labour *community*" (*Class Struggle*, p. 48; original emphasis). It is one of the merits of Foster's book to give serious attention to this issue (although see pp. 25–32 on particular problems in Foster's argument, especially the location and the preexistence or development of "labour community").

87. Craft and workplace could only exceed propinquity in impact within limits. Thus, sharing a craft might be more important than sharing a neighborhood, provided one's workmates were within walking distance.

88. See Prothero, *Artisans and Politics*, pp. 274–75 and 285.

89. Of course, in early nineteenth-century England as in all other historical cases, such complaints were not equal, either in the estimation of principals or outside analysts. I ignore the fact that weavers were much poorer than shipwrights, for example, in order to bring out the formal argument. Moreover, there does not appear to be any direct relationship between material well-being and radicalism differentiating among English working people during the industrial revolution.

90. See above, chap. 8.

91. The most important source for the argument from size is Blau, *Inequality and Heterogeneity*. Parts of the argument are at least as old as Montesquieu; they are prominent in the work of Michels and Simmel.

92. See Calhoun, "Democracy, Autocracy and Intermediate Associations in Organizations."

93. For a recent argument that Luddism was political, which is cast almost entirely in terms of motives, see Dinwiddy, "Luddism and Politics in the Northern Counties." See also chap. 3 above.

94. Mayhew and Levinger, "On the Emergence of Oligarchy in Human Interaction," p. 1025.

95. Blau, *Inequality and Heterogeneity*, pp. 70–71.

96. See above, chap. 8.

97. Michels, *Political Parties*.

98. See Olson, *Logic of Collective Action*, and above, chap. 8.

99. It may be worth noting again that both craft and locality may be foundations of community by my definition; I am not opposing community to craft but emphasizing the commonality between the largely propinquity-based small-town and village communities of, for example, northern outworkers, and the largely craft-based communities of London artisans.

100. See above, chap. 7.

Chapter Seven

1. Baines, *Lancashire* (a contemporary directory).

2. Blackley: 2,361 to 3,020; Burnage: 383 to 507; Moss-side: 150 to 208 (this was to become a classic Victorian working-class district); Moston township actually declined from 618 to 615. All figures from *Parliamentary Papers*, 1831, vol. XVIII, Census summaries.

3. Aspin, *Haslingden, 1800–1900*, p. 7.

4. See discussion above, in chap. 8.

5. Again, see discussion in chap. 8.

6. Tables 7.1 and 7.2 and figure 7.1 are all based on census reports in the *Parliamentary Papers*.

7. See above, pp. 197–203; also, Mitchell and Deane, *Abstract of British Historical Statistics*, p. 188.

8. "The workmen of the towns knew that in case of unemployment they could find work on farms in the neighborhood of the great manufacturing centres. Hence the price of labour rose or fell in the country as industry prospered or languished in the towns" (Halévy, *England in 1815*, p. 242). Anthropological studies have shown the prevalence of this sort of repeated migration in connection with both seasonal and economic cycles in peasant societies with developing urban centers. See, for example, Hart, "Entrepreneurs and Migrants: A Study of Modernization among the Frafras of Ghana."

9. Deane and Cole, *British Economic Growth*, p. 113. The high annual rate of growth suggests the preponderance of migration over natural increase, especially in towns where women most outnumber men.

10. Especially since they were, as Redford has shown, likely to be quite nearby (*Labour Migration in England*, pp. 63–67, and map E, following p. 192).

11. Anderson suggests something of this for Preston later in the century (*Family Structure in Nineteenth-Century Lancashire*, pp. 145–55).

12. Pinchbeck, *Women Workers in the Industrial Revolution*, p. 185. Later, of course, the Poor Law of 1834 would accentuate this process by moving families consisting primarily of women and children from the southern counties to the textile districts (First Report of the Commissioners under the Poor Law Amendment Act, *Parliamentary Papers*, 1835, XXXV, p. 55).

13. It could be objected that the Napoleonic wars themselves were the source of the 1811 imbalance of the sexes, but this seems unlikely. In the neighbouring West Riding, for instance, the ratio of women to men in 1811 was less than 1.03 to 1; it was still closer to being even for England as a whole.

14. See above, tables 7.3 and 7.4. It is likely that Rochdale would show at least as high or higher a proportion of weavers as Stockport, if data were available.

15. A weakness in this argument is the lack of any correlation between the rates of population increase and the peak of sexual imbalance in 1811; it is impossible to tell whether this is significant, or even whether that peak is perhaps an artificial result of census enumeration procedures. In general, it is important to note that all the statistical considerations in this chapter are intended to be more suggestive than conclusive. I draw some limited inferences, but no propositions are solidly demonstrated beyond the level of simple description.

16. Smelser, *Social Change in the Industrial Revolution*, p. 193.

17. Ibid., p. 202.

18. Ibid., pp. 190, 220–24. Further, factory managers advertised and sent agents into the countryside to seek child labor. See Pinchbeck, *Women Workers in the Industrial Revolution*, p. 185, and Redford, *Labour Migration*, p. 23.

19. Edwards and Lloyd-Jones, "N. J. Smelser and the Cotton Factory Family: A Reassessment," p. 302.

20. Ibid., p. 310. The same source also contains a reanalysis of some of the records examined by Smelser and points out that, while a number of operatives employed the children of other operatives, relatively few employed their own

children—their practice was not necessarily an abuse, but it was not a corrective to weakening of family bonds either (pp. 312–13).

21. Anderson, "Sociological History and the Working-Class Family," p. 325. Foster also challenges Smelser from census data (*Class Struggle*, pp. 302–3).

22. This argument is summarized by Smelser, "Sociological History: the Industrial Revolution and the British Working-Class Family," esp. pp. 83–86.

23. See Anderson's criticism, "Sociological History and the Working Class Family," p. 327.

24. Smelser, "Sociological History," p. 85. As I suggested above, this may be largely due to the growth in number and proportion of factory workers at this time; they were absent as much as they were quiescent before 1820. Note also that factory workers were much less against "progress" in industrialization than were craft workers like handloom weavers. The former were against specific features or for the addition of other features—like higher wages.

25. See discussion, pp. 196–203, especially tables 7.3 and 7.4.

26. Smelser, "Sociological History," p. 85.

27. Bythell, *The Handloom Weavers*, p. 40.

28. Wood's estimates, in Mitchell and Deane, *Abstract of British Historical Statistics*, p. 187.

29. For general description, see the Hammonds, *The Skilled Labourer*, chaps. 4 and 5; Thompson, *The Making*, chap. 9.

30. Anderson makes a similar point against Smelser, "Sociological History and the Working-Class Family," p. 326. See also Marshall, "The Lancashire Rural Labourer in the Early Nineteenth Century"; Redford, *Labour Migration*; Pinchbeck, *Women Workers*, pp. 184–85; and Collier, *The Family Economy of the Working Classes in the Cotton Industry*, pp. 15–16. There is, however, some evidence of the wives and daughters of distressed handloom weavers entering factories in the 1830s and 1840s (*S.C. on Handloom Weavers, Parliamentary Papers*, 1834 X, pp. 80–81).

31. See above, pp. 196–202.

32. "N. J. Smelser and the Cotton Factory Family," pp. 314–15. The figures are 11.6 percent employed by relatives in Preston, 24.5 percent in the district.

33. Curiously, an 1833 survey showed male children as much more likely to be sent into those occupations in which children were employed by operatives (mule-spinning, principally). For girls 6,091 were employed directly by manufacturers, 3,541 by operatives. For boys the figures are 3,585 and 6,557, respectively (Stanway's survey reported in Ure, *The Cotton Manufacture of Great Britain*, pp. 398–99).

34. Smelser, *Social Change*, pp. 194–95.

35. Ibid.

36. Smelser does not cite any factory workers who objected to it on the ground that it changed their relationships with their children.

37. For example, Smelser writes: "When the Factory Act of 1833 was passed, limiting children's hours to eight and suggesting a relay system for young children, the operatives were not satisfied. . . . For, indeed, the Factory Act of 1833, with its relay system and its eight hour limitation, worked to further weaken the link between parents' and children's labor. . . . With the Factory Act of 1833, Parliament opted in favor of pushing the family toward the future" ("Sociological History," pp. 86–87). The workers, of course, could not be anything but irrational to resist this push toward the future, and if it should mean,

as it did, that adults' work would be increased to as much as sixteen hours a day, well, such was the future.

38. Artisans in relatively prosperous crafts, of course, differed considerably from their poorer brethren such as the outworkers. See above, pp. 44−47, 54−59, and 119−26.

39. Remarkably, in this connection, Smelser never considers that the repeal of the Combination Acts in 1825 might have been an important stimulus to this new outburst of "disturbances." He does, elsewhere, allow that while in existence the Acts may have "retarded the development of trade unions," though he considers the evidence equivocal (*Social Change*, pp. 320−21). In line with my general argument, the Combination Acts were far more of an impediment in urban factory areas where new formal organizations were necessary to concerted collective actions among workers, than they were in artisan villages which could more readily act on informal lines of organization and could, in any case, better keep combinations secret.

40. The evidence is insufficient, but Rochdale might come fairly close on this dimension.

41. This is true with the possible exception of Stockport's relatively large factories (though these were still smaller than those of Manchester and Bolton).

42. On the variance in political activity, see Bamford, *Passages in the Life of a Radical*, pp. 8−9; Thompson, *The Making*, pp. 705−8; Read, *Peterloo: The "Massacre" and Its Background*, pp. 49−50; the Hammonds, *The Skilled Labourer*, pp. 92−121; Foster is not greatly concerned with local comparison but suggests at one point much the same breakdown of which towns were most active. Characteristically, he interprets one dimension of variance at a time—in this case arguing that higher wage rates were caused by "the breakdown in law and order" (*Class Struggle*, p. 49). It should be borne in mind that this ranking of towns would not necessarily apply to the Chartist period, when, for example, factory workers were more important and Ashton became a center under the leadership of McDougall.

43. See above, pp. 176−81.

44. Smelser, *Social Change*, pp. 232, 299. This was particularly true in machine spinning, a fact which reinforces the divergence of Oldham and Stockport, since they had proportionately more weavers, which ought, on the surface, to have increased the proportion of women factory workers.

45. Although there is little information as to how Stanway's "sample" was constituted (and thus how representative it is), there is no reason to believe that it was systematically biased. Apparently, Mr. Stanway issued forms widely, and the results are simply from those which were returned completed. The proportion must have been substantial, however. Foster, for example, reports the existence of eleven power-weaving factories in 1832, the Stanway survey thirteen (although the latter factories apparently do not include all of the former).

46. There were also thirteen small-ware manufacturers, all in Manchester, mean size 127.08; and sixty-one factories working cotton waste. Forty-seven of the latter were in Oldham, mean size 22.23; and fourteen in Manchester, Bolton, Dean, and Whalley, not differentiated by Mr. Horner, mean size 17.29. Oldham and Rochdale were the only towns with factories working wool full-time. The mean sizes were 11.29 and 63.31, respectively. Ashton had fourteen on short-time, mean size 12.14; Rochdale had seven such, mean size 11.29.

Rochdale had eight not at work, mean size 25.25; Oldham four, mean size 239.25. Insolvency of firms in wool was frequently of long-standing, not merely a phase between proprietors. One, in Oldham, had employed 725 persons before its demise three years previously.

47. See Prothero, *Artisans and Politics*, p. 35, on the mechanics' advantages over those subject to such objectionable features of factory work.

48. This is evidenced by the continued production and popularity of such works as Ure's treatises on textiles; see Pollard, *The Genesis of Modern Management*; Hartwell, "Business Management in England during the Period of Early Industrialization: Inducements and Obstacles"; Hunt, *The Development of the Corporation in Britain, 1800–1867*; Landes, *The Unbound Prometheus*; Payne, "The Emergence of the Large-Scale Company in Great Britain." British firms continued for most of the nineteenth century to grow by the accretion of similar units; as far as scanty evidence can show, there was little specialization within these units. It should be borne in mind that Taylorism waited for the twentieth century.

49. Blau and Schoenherr, *The Structure of Organizations*, pp. 297–329, and Blau, *Inequality and Heterogeneity*, pp. 203–8.

50. This aspect of the differentiation issue is somewhat neglected by Blau's treatment in *Inequality and Heterogeneity*, since that lacks any conception similar to "multiplexity," partly because it eschews consideration of the content of social relations in order to focus on structure. Multiplexity is a structural concept, but one which is founded on recognition of the different content given to interpersonal relations by different social contexts.

51. This does not necessarily follow formally, since population size also varied.

52. See discussion above, pp. 174–82.

53. It should be noted that studies finding a higher "propensity to strike" among workers in large factories or metropolitan areas do not disprove, or necessarily challenge, these conclusions. In the first place, such studies do not establish the independence of those factors which they have studied from the others discussed here. In the second place, strikes are only one form of collective action, one particularly suited to workers who can expect, and benefit from, ameliorative material improvements. The connections between propensity, to strike, riot, petition, sabotage, revolt, or elect specific sorts of officials are not clearly spelled out in the literature, and in any case are probably partial at most. Kerr and Siegel, "The Inter-Industry Propensity to Strike," is the often-cited basic work in this tradition. Shorter and Tilly found none of Kerr and Siegel's conclusions borne out by further research, *Strikes in France*, pp. 287–95; see also Snyder and Kelly, "Industrial Violence in Italy," Tilly, *From Mobilization to Revolution*, chap. 3, and the recent studies by Aminzade, "French Strike Development and Class Struggle," and Montgomery, "Strikes in Nineteenth-Century America."

54. Small communities, as I have defined the term socially, need not be small population centers. Villages are such, to be sure, but relatively strongly demarcated urban artisan populations may also be.

55. "The women in nine cases out of ten have only themselves to support,—while the men, generally have families," wrote a union official to the *Manchester Guardian*, 27 November 1824. A Manchester mill census taken twenty years later (reported by McCulloch, *A Descriptive and Statistical Account of the British Empire*, 1:702) showed nearly as great a proportion of

single women: 50,377 out of 61,098 or 82 percent. See also Smelser, *Social Change*, pp. 203, 232.

56. Collier, *The Family Economy of the Working Classes*, pp. 16–17. Smelser, incidentally, uses the intermittent nature of women's employment as an indication that the traditional family was surviving, and that, therefore, no "disturbance" would be likely to ensue (*Social Change*, p. 186). Anderson's data for Preston at mid-century suggest that women's employment was still intermittent, especially viewed over the life cycle; women worked most frequently when their domestic situations were most auspicious (and when their economic situations were least so) (*Family Structure*, pp. 71–74). Rushton's work also bears this out, and considers casual labor, especially in the 1850s–1870s, in more detail ("Housing Conditions and the Family Economy in the Victorian Slum," chap. 7).

57. The extent to which this was equally true in each town is uncertain; it is possible that the additional proportion of males in Oldham, for example, held jobs as unskilled as their female counterparts in Manchester. Stanway's survey, in Ure, *The Cotton Manufacture*, 1:400–407 would seem to bear out that the employment of more men was, at least in part, the employment of more skilled workers.

58. See ibid., for example, and Pinchbeck, *Women Workers*, pp. 190–94.

59. The men could either leave for the countryside (cf. Halévy, *England in 1815*, p. 242) or could tramp to another town in search of work in a similar trade. The latter practice declined in significance through the period of the industrial revolution, both because work of a given sort became more regionally concentrated (especially in textiles) and because, as Hobsbawm notes, tramping systems were "entirely adapted to single men.... Had they been originally designed to meet unemployment they could hardly have failed to bear the married workman in mind" ("The Tramping Artisan," p. 37). Tramping applied more to hand weavers than to factory workers, in any case.

60. See Edwards and Lloyd-Jones's comment on the highly casual nature of work at the country mills (which weighs against Smelser's suggestion of their communality, and, less directly, against his suggestion of their benevolence) ("N. J. Smelser and the Cotton Factory Family," p. 309).

61. See the local notes to the census returns, especially for 1831. See also Engels's *The Condition of the Working Class*, chap. 3, for descriptions.

62. Chorlton-Row grew from 675 in 1801 to 20,569 in 1831. On Ancoats, one of these areas soon to be swallowed up by Manchester, see Rushton, "Housing Conditions and the Family Economy in the Victorian Slum."

63. This is not, of course, to ignore the importance of the artisans' and the spinners' greater position of strength due to relative scarcity of their skills.

64. It must be borne in mind regarding the preceding discussion of differing levels of activity that the least active of these Lancashire towns was more active (and more proletarian) than most towns in England. Further, an important characteristic of each of these towns was its proximity to the others; they did not exist in relative isolation but could stimulate and reinforce each other.

Chapter Eight

1. This is the implicit position, for example, of Cole's *Short History of the British Working Class Movement*, the Webbs' *History of Trade Unionism*, and Cole and Postgate, *The Common People*.

2. See Calhoun, "Community."

3. In 1820, Canning thought that public meetings of a corporate character were legitimate, because "ancient habits, preconceived attachments, that mutual respect which makes the eye of a neighbour a security for each man's good conduct" made their opinions "authentic." But where the individual members of a mass were brought together "having no permanent relation to each other, no common tie but what arises from their concurrence as members of that meeting, "the result would likely be political mischief" (Jephson, The Platform, 1:508–10, quoted by Hollis, The Pauper Press, p. 4). Note the similarity to the ideas of community set out in chap. 6, above.

4. See Hay, "Property, Authority and the Criminal Law," and Rudé, The Crowd in History, on eighteenth-century mobs and ruling-class attitudes toward them. Note especially the fluctuation and overall changes in such attitudes, dependent in part on the particular interests affected by "mob action."

5. Le Bon, The Crowd: A Study of the Popular Mind and La Révolution Française et la Psychologie des Révolutions.

6. For example, McDougall, The Group Mind; Lévy-Bruhl, Primitive Mentality and Le Surnaturel et la Nature. Evans-Pritchard has related the latter to more recent thought in Theories of Primitive Religion, and Lévi-Strauss has attempted to rehabilitate the intellectual standing of "savage thought" in The Savage Mind.

7. See, for example, Horton, "African Traditional Thought and Western Science," although he is a bit too sanguine in his appreciation of modern "openness."

8. Freud, Group Psychology and the Analysis of the Ego, p. 88.

9. See Sherif and Harvey, "A Study in Ego Functioning: Elimination of Stable Anchorages in Individual and Group Situations."

10. See Calhoun, "Education and the Problem of Continuity," sec. II.

11. See Durkheim, Suicide, bk. 2, chap. 5.

12. Thus, conflicting maternal demands predispose offspring to schizophrenia (Bateson et al., "Toward a Theory of Schizophrenia").

13. The conflicting demands of the members of an individual's role-set, for example, may provoke or exacerbate a crisis. See Merton, Social Theory and Social Structure, chaps. 8 and 9, and Goode, "A Theory of Role Strain."

14. This is frequently observed in connection with millenarian sects, for example. See Worsley, The Trumpet Shall Sound; Cohn, The Pursuit of the Millennium; and Hobsbawm, Primitive Rebels.

15. Smelser, Theory of Collective Behavior, p. 73.

16. Other examples include Johnson, Revolutionary Change, and Gurr, Why Men Rebel.

17. This is a consideration which is of considerable importance for Smelser's analysis of popular protest during the industrial revolution. It leads him, for example, to seek reasons only in disturbances to communal, particularly family, organization. See discussion above, pp. 191–96.

18. Smelser's conception of the social order fits into the general system of social action described by Parsons (see The Social System and Smelser's own summary in relation to social change in Social Change in the Industrial Revolution, chaps. 1–3).

19. By way of clarification, there is both a value-added chain detailing the steps of "normal" social action, and one suggesting the series of conditions necessary to collective behavior. See Smelser's Theory of Collective Behavior,

p. 44, for a chart summarizing the various levels of specificity/generality of the components of social action, and p. 124 for a representation of the points of short-circuiting in the value-added series.

20. "Once the generalization has taken place, attempts are made to reconstitute the meaning of the high-level component. At this point, however, the critical feature of collective behavior appears. Having redefined the high-level component, people do not proceed to respecify, step by step, down the line to reconstruct social action. Rather, they develop a belief which 'short-circuits' from a very specialized component *directly* to the focus of the strain. The accompanying expectation is that the strain can be relieved by a direct application of a generalized component" (*Theory of Collective Behavior*, p. 71). Obviously, this argument contains a number of psychological propositions, but these are nowhere given much of a treatment by Smelser, even in the article he devotes specifically to psychological issues, "Social and Psychological Dimensions of Collective Behavior."

21. Smelser, "Two Critics in Search of a Bias: A Response to Currie and Skolnick," p. 48.

22. Specifically Currie and Skolnick, "A Critical Note on Conceptions of Collective Behavior."

23. Smelser's statement of order is strikingly similar to that of John Foster, who holds without evidence that it is more plausible to assume that nineteenth-century Oldham workers had a relatively high rate of intermarriage among crafts and trades because they were class conscious than to assume the reverse. See his *Class Struggle and the Industrial Revolution*, p. 128, and discussion in chap. 1, above.

24. Smelser, *Theory of Collective Behavior*, p. 72.

25. Ibid., p. 70.

26. This is very similar, as we shall see, to the problem with those Marxist considerations which stress the interests of workers to the exclusion of their social organization, their existence as a class for itself.

27. Berk, *Collective Behavior*, lists numerous social science efforts of both varieties. There have also been attempts to construct purely formal models of collective action, but these have not been extensively worked out for crowds or popular mobilizations.

28. G. Marx, "Issueless Riots," p. 23.

29. Berk, "A Gaming Approach to Crowd Behavior"; Weller and Quarantelli, "Neglected Characteristics of Collective Behavior."

30. In addition to Smelser, the "normative theorists" whom Berk criticizes include Turner and Killian; their approach is less sophisticated than Smelser's, and is less theoretical, more devoted to taxonomy. See Turner and Killian, *Collective Behavior*, and Turner, "Collective Behavior."

31. This is important because most social-choice theories postulate complete rationality, variously defined. See Arrow, *Social Choice and Individual Values*; Sen, *Collective Choice and Social Welfare*; and Olson, *The Logic of Collective Action*. See also Coleman's sociological application, *The Mathematics of Collective Action*.

32. Rationality may be defined simply as the process of defining options for actions, viewing them as (with various probabilities) associated with various outcomes, and choosing among them as (often implicitly) different measures of some common value. Rationality is unfortunately not taken as a variable by these writers, as, for example, Simon's conception of "satisficing"—limited

bureaucratic rationality—would have suggested (*Administrative Behavior*, especially Introduction to 1957 ed.).

33. Coleman, *Mathematics of Collective Action*, p. 65.

34. See Miller and Rice, *Systems of Organization*, chaps. 2 and 21, on "sentient groups."

35. Wolf, *Peasant Wars of the Twentieth Century*, p. 292, on the radical political importance of a "culturally conservative stratum" of the peasantry.

36. Notably the pioneering work of Soboul, *Les San-Culottes Parisiens en l'An II*. See also Rudé, *The Crowd in the French Revolution*, and Tilly, *The Vendée*, on the interesting counterrevolutionary mobilization.

37. C. Tilly, L. Tilly, and R. Tilly, *The Rebellious Century*, p. 269.

38. *Social Conflict and Social Movements*. This dimension has been most widely used in the study of more formally organized trade-union and political activity. See, in general, Tilly, *From Mobilization to Revolution*, chap. 3.

39. See above, pp. 115–19.

40. See, for example, the discussion in Marx, "The Class Struggles in France," sec. 1. See also Giddens, *The Class Structure of the Advanced Societies*, pp. 92–93, for a clear, concise statement.

41. Marx, *The Poverty of Philosophy*, p. 211.

42. Marx, "Contribution to the Critique of Hegel's Philosophy of Law," p. 185.

43. Perhaps this is spelled out as concisely in the "Manifesto of the Communist Party," pt. 1, and *Capital*, vol. 1, chap. 32, as anywhere. But note that the three ideas are not identical.

44. See the somewhat similar set of questions in Lukács's *History and Class Consciousness*, p. 46, and the different approach to answering them in his famous chapter on "class consciousness."

45. See the brief discussion in Poulantzas, *State, Power, and Socialism*, pp. 63–69.

46. See H. Lefebvre, *The Sociology of Marx*, chap. 2, also p. 7.

47. In my opinion, this is not a fair judgment of Hegel.

48. Marx, *The Holy Family*, p. 37. See discussion above, pp. 231–33.

49. Marx, *Poverty of Philosophy*, p. 211; *Capital*, vol. 1, chap. 14; "Class Struggles in France"; "Eighteenth Brumaire"; Engels, "Socialism: Utopian and Scientific," sec. II.

50. Marx and Engels, "Manifesto of the Communist Party"; Marx, *Capital*, chaps. 23 and 32.

51. See *The German Ideology*, p. 47; also Lenin, *The State and Revolution*, sec. 1, pp. 7–11.

52. More precisely, Feuerbachian materialism was passive; idealism treated activity but only in a disembodied way which rendered it impotent. See Marx, "Theses on Feuerbach" and the first part of *The German Ideology*.

53. Marx, "Contribution to the Critique of Hegel's Philosophy of Law," p. 186.

54. Weber, *Economy and Society*, p. 930; the "talented author" is presumably Georg Lukács; see Roth's and Wittich's introduction.

55. Perhaps an older strain of scientism as well is involved; see Habermas, *Communication and the Evolution of Societies*, chap. 2.

56. Market position is not only Weber's defining characteristic of class but, curiously, John Foster's as well. Weber rather more rigorously follows up the implications of his usage. See the discussion of Foster's *Class Struggle and the*

Industrial Revolution, above chap. 1. See also, on Weber and Marx, Therbörn, *What Does the Ruling Class Do When It Rules?* pp. 138–43.

57. Collective goods are simply those goods which cannot be consumed by any members of a collectivity without becoming available to all. See discussion in the next section of this chapter.

58. It is worth stressing, contrary to Therbörn, that Marx did not conceptualize the necessity of class action in terms of individual members. He did not ask of the individual proletarian "What does he do?" let alone "What is he likely to do?" but rather he asked what the class as the largest unifying social actor must do. For all the ambiguous individualism in his conceptualization, Marx consistently struggled against making class an additive property of individual opinion or action. See Therbörn, *What Does the Ruling Class Do When It Rules?* pp. 190–91; Marx, *The Holy Family,* p. 37. See also Poulantzas's appropriate stress on political action in class definition (*Political Power and Social Classes,* pp. 73–79, especially p. 78).

59. One may identify this contrast between class as an objective category and class as a subjective collective actor with Smith's distinction of corporate categories from corporate groups: "A corporate category is a clearly bounded, identifiable, and permanent aggregate which differs from the corporate group in lacking exclusive common affairs autonomy, procedures adequate for their regulation, and the internal organization which constitutes the group" ("A Structural Approach to Comparative Politics," p. 100).

60. Poulantzas, *Classes in Contemporary Capitalism,* p. 14. Thompson, in "The Peculiarities of the English," and "Eighteenth-Century English Society: Class Struggle without Class?" offers similar repudiations, though in earlier works, particularly in *The Making,* his language is ambiguous. Foster, in *Class Struggle,* tends toward a cruder duality, especially in his general pronouncements (as opposed to his particular analyses).

61. As Gramsci, most importantly among Marx's followers, held, class struggle can be understood as the process of creating class. It is in this sense, I believe, that Thompson has argued against structuralist interpretations of class. See, in addition to the essays cited in the previous note, *The Poverty of Theory.*

62. Thelwall, *The Rights of Nature,* 1:21–24; see also, *The Making,* p. 207. On Marx's and Engels's position, see Engels, *Socialism Utopian and Scientific,* esp. sec. II, and Marx, *Capital,* 1: chap. xiv.

63. The tendency to reduce subjectivity to what people think, has been most marked in French social history where, of late, the focus on consciousness or "mentalités" threatens to displace social relations in research and analysis. On occasion one can find E. P. Thompson's treatment of English workers tending in the same direction. See chap. 1 above.

64. One might phrase this, less dichotomously, as the extent to which individuals' self-consciousness and activity are determined by their membership in a class.

65. One could rephrase "e" as the anticipated cost/benefit ratio. It is my suggestion, however, that the potential costs of radical class action—revolution—are always enormous, and the potential benefits always quite uncertain.

66. Capitalism was able to offer significant concessions to the newer industrial workers emergent during the industrial revolution, but not for the most part to the older groupings of artisans and outworkers. This was in part because of the nature of the "goods" which the latter sought. The protection of tradi-

tional craft communities was more in contradiction to capitalism than the granting of higher wages to employees.

67. They have been seen as such by G. D. H. Cole and E. P. Thompson in the former instance and by John Foster and D. C. Moore in the latter.

68. Implicit in this is the notion that the universalization and intensification of class struggle is progressive, and therefore that the mature classes at the end of capitalist development will be the ones locked in revolutionary struggle. It is my suggestion that internal concessions may more readily be made to such workers in mature capitalist economies than to various (especially skilled nonfactory) workers in early capitalism. See also Giddens, *The Class Structure of the Advanced Societies*, p. 153; and Mills, "The New Left," p. 256.

69. Marx did sometimes doubt himself, generally in private communications, and thus gave a field day to those who wonder what he *might* have said.

70. It is necessary to assume also that this productivity can be stably maintained. As Michael Harrington has recently stressed in *The Twilight of Capitalism*, one of Marx's most brilliant insights was to focus on crises not of dearth but of overproduction, the distinctive creation of capitalism. It could well be various social or ecological problems produced by affluence which present the greatest threats to capitalism, not simply lack of productive capacity.

71. Principally, as it turns out, capitalism can give material goods.

72. By "scientific" understanding, I refer to positivist and especially verificationist notions or ideologies of science, rather than to what scientists in fact do. For a discussion of reflectionism, and an (unsuccessful) defense, see Ruben, *Marxism and Materialism*; also, Timpanaro, *On Materialism*.

73. See discussion in chap. 1, above; of Thompson's work, see especially *Poverty of Theory*. Anderson, *Arguments within English Marxism*, chap. 2, contains a good discussion of Thompson's notion of agency.

74. Bear in mind that I have already argued, in consonance with Tilly, Oberschall, and Wolf, that preexisting social bonds, particularly those of community, make mobilization easier and more likely.

75. Lenin, *What Is to Be Done?* p. 24.

76. This is precisely the Hegelian Marx followed up by Lukács in *History and Class Consciousness*; see also Avineri, *Hegel's Theory of the Modern State*.

77. Lenin's claim to avoid the pitfalls of contemporary ideologies of science is dubious. See his *Materialism and Empirio-Criticism*, pp. 136–42.

78. Lenin, *What Is to Be Done?* sec. 1.

79. Wright, *Class, Crisis, and the State*, p. 89.

80. This is critical to the significance of the notion of practice in Marx's third and eighth "Theses on Feuerbach." The original Hegelian assertion of the identity of the rational and the actual is from the Preface to Hegel's *Philosophy of Right*, p. 10. See Marx's comment on p. 63 of the "Contribution to the Critique of Hegel's Philosophy of Law."

81. Cf. Marx's famous contrast between bees and human architects (*Capital*, 1:174).

82. See Polanyi, *Personal Knowledge*, pt. II.

83. The development of such apparatuses was the later nineteenth- and early twentieth-century contribution of the partially interwoven lineages of phenomenology, neo-Kantianism, psychoanalysis, and part of sociology (Weber and Pareto).

84. Second thesis on Feuerbach.

85. He had the notion, however, that people were being progressively freed of the determination by their needs, that consciousness was gaining more (though not nearly complete) autonomy.

86. Marx, "Class Struggles in France," p. 146. The rest of the sentence is: "They do not make it under circumstances chosen by themselves, but under circumstances directly encountered, given and transmitted from the past."

87. It is in this connection that Marx eschewed universal abstractions in favor of historically determinate ones. In the *Poverty of Theory* Thompson brilliantly defends Marx on this against Althusser (though sometimes overstating his case). See also the good discussion of the related difference between Weber on the one hand and Schutz and Parsons on the other in Zaret, "From Weber to Parsons and Schutz: The Eclipse of History in Modern Social Theory."

88. Gadamer, *Philosophical Hermeneutics*, p. 9; see also the fuller discussion of Gadamer's views in his earlier *Truth and Method*.

89. Thompson, *Poverty of Theory*; Anderson (*Arguments*, chaps. 1 and 2) does not give this part of Thompson's argument its due, though the category of "experience," as Thompson introduces it, is markedly vague.

90. Anthropologists have long recognized the malleability of tradition, and known that it is only in attitude, not in reality, Weber's "that which has always been" (*Economy and Society*, p. 36). Of course, societies may be more or less traditional, and more or less rapidly changing. See Colson, *Tradition and Contract*; and Bourdieu, *Outline of a Theory of Practice*, chap. 2. The tendency has been for anthropologists to see the present-day manipulation of tradition as more or less self-conscious and somewhat hypocritical. It is taken as evidence for the primacy of self-interested individualism over any notion of social determination or cultural rules. See Worsley, "The Kinship System of the Tallensi," and Peters, "The Proliferation of Segments in the Lineage of the Bedouin in Cyrenaica," who are respectively arguing against the superior ethnographers and theorists Fortes and Evans-Pritchard. See particularly Fortes's arguments that such traditional forms as the reckoning of lineage descent are based on, as well as regulative of, present-day social relations (*The Web of Kinship among the Tallensi*, p. 33; "Oedipus and Job in West African Religion," p. 40; and "Some Reflections on Ancestor Worship in Africa," p. 129).

91. Thus, even in a relatively stable, segmentary, lineage-based society, the specific content of tradition must be flexible in order to provide for the continual readjustment of small-scale processes within the larger social organization. In addition to the works cited in the previous note, see Calhoun, "The Authority of Ancestors."

92. As can easily be seen in the ebbs and flows of various kinds of Christianity. It is not the traditions or biblical texts which change, as fundamentalism spreads and retreats; rather, it is the uses made of them. Similarly, during the early years of industrialization, the efficacy of some traditions in shaping workers' attitudes was redoubled—the idea of the Englishman's liberties, for example, took on new strength because of its relevance to practical affairs. The equally ancient tradition of deference to rank went into some abeyance, as practice showed that elites did not reciprocate. Yet, it was still present to be drawn upon in the Victorian era as a new politics of deference was instated.

93. Accounts entirely in terms of the consciousness of contemporaries are likely to lack the awareness of structural constraints or possibilities which ought to be the historian's advantage over the original actors. As Simmel noted,

even though the connections which constitute society (in the larger, structural sense) may be matters of consciousness, "this does not mean, of course, that each member of a society is conscious of such an abstract notion of unity. It means that he is absorbed in innumerable, specific relations and in the feeling and the knowledge of determining others and of being determined by them" ("Conflict," p. 77). Anderson has usefully called attention to Thompson's failure to recognize the limits of contemporaneous accounts (*Arguments*, p. 98).

94. That is, British political economists had failed to recognize the problem. Storch, and with greater sophistication, Say, had both developed the distinction between a collective good and an individual benefit. See discussion in Baumol, *Welfare Economics and the Theory of the State*, chap. 12.

95. Marx, "Eighteenth Brumaire," esp. sec. VII. This view is suggested, in somewhat different specific character, by Poulantzas in *State, Power, and Socialism*, pp. 127–39.

96. The formal basis of this discussion of collective action is drawn largely from Mancur Olson's *The Logic of Collective Action*. I have, however, put considerably more stress on the internal organization of collectivities than he does.

97. Notably Dahrendorf, in *Class and Class Conflict in Industrial Society*; Giddens points out some of the problems in Dahrendorf's over-valued work in *The Class Structure of the Advanced Societies*, pp. 70–74.

98. See Olson's thin, but provocative, comments on this point in *The Logic of Collective Action*, pp. 102–10. It must be obvious that the point just made calls the notion of "false consciousness" into serious question.

99. *The Making*, p. 537.

100. Lenin, *What Is to Be Done?* p. 24.

101. See, for example, his detailed quotation from and endorsement of Kautsky's criticism of revisionism, *What Is to Be Done?* pp. 27–28.

102. The extent to which Marx changed his mind about this, or especially the extent to which the later works of Engels suggest another view, is problematic. See discussion in Lichtheim, *Marxism*, pt. 5; Harrington, *The Twilight of Capitalism*, chap. 2. The issue, of course, remains politically current; see Claudin's historical review in *The Communist Movement*, chap. 2 and chap. 4, especially pt. 2, and, following up his suggestions regarding the relationship of trade unions and the Communists, "La Vía al Socialismo en Europa."

103. These brief characterizations probably fit the German political divisions and groupings most precisely, but with some variation they had referents in most European countries and in Russia. It should perhaps be pointed out that I am not specifically concerned here with the question of whether Lenin's argument was formulated to deal with such "backward" nations as Russia. Lenin's work on party organization during the first decade of the twentieth century does not seem to be founded on the notions of imperialism and unequal development as he later elaborated them.

104. Rosa Luxemburg, together with the "Spartacists," was the most important voice on the left. Her position, though not identical to it, had a good deal in common with that of the anarcho-syndicalists of the Latin countries.

105. Bernstein was the theoretician of the revisionists, to whatever extent he can be justly considered a theoretician. Though of different ideological background, and still less theoretical, the French parliamentary socialists reached similar conclusions. English laborism gave the revisionists possibly their

greatest case in point—but then English socialism never really had a substantial revolutionary wing.

106. A distinction between fundamental and transient features of personality organization is developed formally by Heise in *Understanding Events*. The social psychology being developed here is in the tradition of Lewin as developed by Festinger. See the latter's *A Theory of Cognitive Dissonance*, and *Conflict, Decision and Dissonance*.

107. Marx, *The Holy Family*, p. 37. Notice the Rousseauian difference between the way Marx in the first sentence refers to the whole proletariat as merely the sum, it would seem, of individual proletarians' opinions (the will of all), while the proletariat predicated in the second and third sentences appears to be a transcendental ego, or completely structurally determined so that only one course of action is, in the long run, possible (as with the general will).

108. Festinger, *A Theory of Cognitive Dissonance* is the best general treatment of this perspective on social psychology. See also Festinger, et al., *When Prophecy Fails*, for a germane discussion of millennialism. Heise, *Understanding Events*, attempts to balance Festinger's stress on psychical readjustment with more attention to the dynamics of social action.

109. Bourdieu, *Outline of a Theory of Practice*, pp. 79–87.

110. See the discussion of cumulative change in history, in which Engels is taken as a point of departure, in both Thompson, *The Poverty of Theory*, sec. xii, and Anderson, *Arguments*, chaps. 1 and 3. Thompson is concerned, in part, to reject Althusser's notion of history as a process without a subject.

111. C. Wright Mills twenty years ago complained that "what I do not quite understand about some New-Left writers is why they cling so mightily to 'the working class' of the advanced capitalist societies as the historic agency, or even as the most important agency, in the face of the really impressive historical evidence that now stands against this expectation" ("The New Left," p. 256). I have tried to show some of the stretching and twisting of the concept of class which has resulted from this determination to save it. Thompson is not yet ready to give in to Mills's suggestion that "only at certain (earlier) stages of industrialization, and in a political context of autocracy, etc., do wage-workers tend to become a class-for-themselves" (ibid.). (And Mills's statement does confuse old and new varieties of workers.) But, Thompson does think that "a certain climactic moment is passed" (*The Poverty of Theory*, p. 281; revised version of "The Peculiarities").

112. Attention, in other words, is a scarce resource; we cannot afford to try to devote it equally to all possible objects of decision. See Csikszentmihalyi, "Attention and the Holistic Approach to Behavior," and Simon, *Models of Man*, chap. 14.

113. See chap. 6 above, especially pp. 157–59, and Calhoun, "Community."

114. I use the more general term "ideas" to allow for the possibility of commitment to values or beliefs not simply learned from tradition. It is my contention, however, that most of our deepest commitments derive from social and cultural roots, not novel individual creation.

Bibliography

Manuscript Sources

British Library, London
  Place, Additional Manuscripts, 27808
Manchester Central Reference Library, Manchester
  The Linen and Cotton Broad-Ware Weavers' Apology, 1758
Public Record Office, London
  Home Office Papers, vols. 40 and 42

Primary Printed Sources*

1. Parliamentary Papers

1817, VI, *First Report of the Committee of Secrecy*
1824, V, *First Report from the Select Committee on Artisans and Machinery*
1831, XVIII, *Census Summary*
1834, X, *Report of the Select Committee on Handloom Weavers*
1835, XXXV, *First Report of the Commissioners under the Poor Law Amendment Act*
1842, XXII, *Reports of the Inspectors of Factories*

2. Other Contemporary Sources

An Authentic and Detailed Account of the Funeral of Her Late Most Gracious Majesty, Queen Caroline, from the Departure of the Procession from Hammersmith, to the Interment at Brunswick. London: Dean and Munday, n.d. (c. 1821).

---

*The distinction of primary from secondary sources is at best vague in a work of this kind. Works by authors such as Marx and Engels who were nearly contemporaneous with the events I study and in whom my interest is largely theoretical I treat by arbitrary convention as secondary sources. Compilations of works by contemporary authors have been treated as primary sources; more general anthologies as secondary.

Bamford, S. *Passages in the Life of a Radical*. London: Cass, 1967 (orig. 1839–41).

Blanc, L. "Social Reform." *Democratic Review*:207–13. London: Merlin, 1968 (orig. 1849).

Brougham. *Life and Times of Henry, Lord Brougham*. 3 vols. New York: Harper and Brothers, 1871.

Cartwright, J. *The Life and Correspondence of Major Cartwright*. F. D. Cartwright, ed. 2 vols. New York: Burt Franklin, 1969 (orig. date unknown).

Cobbett, W. *Rural Rides*. Harmondsworth: Penguin, 1967 (orig. 1830).

———. *Cobbett's Political Works*. J. M. and J. P. Cobbett, eds. 6 vols. London: Anne Cobbett, n.d. (c. 1840).

———. *The Opinions of William Cobbett*. G. D. H. and M. Cole, eds. London: The Cobbett Publishing Company, 1944.

Felkin, W. *History of the Machine-wrought Hosiery and Lace Manufacturers*. Newton Abbot: David and Charles, 1967 (orig. 1867).

Gammage, R. G. *History of the Chartist Movement*. London: Merlin Press, 1969 (orig. 1894).

George IV, Rex. *The Letters of George IV 1812–1830*. A. Aspinall, ed. 3 vols. London: Cambridge University Press, 1938.

Hall, R. "An Appeal to the Public, on the Subject of the Framework-Knitters' Fund." New York: Arno Press, 1972 (orig. 1820).

———. "A Reply to the Principal Objections Advanced by Cobbett and Others against the Framework-Knitters' Friendly Relief Society." New York: Arno Press, 1972 (orig. 1821).

Harney, G. J. "Dedication." *Democratic Review*, no page nos. London: Merlin, 1968 (orig. 1849).

Henson, G. *History of the Framework Knitters*. Newton Abbot: David and Charles, 1970 (orig. 1831).

Hodgskin, T. *Labour Defended against the Claims of Capital*. New York: Kelley, 1963 (orig. 1825).

Howitt, W. *The Rural Life of England*. Shannon: Irish University Press, 1971 (orig. 1838).

Huish, R. *Memoirs of Caroline, Queen Consort of England*. London, 1820–21.

Hunt, H. *Autobiography*. New York: Kelley, n.d. (orig. 1820).

———. *Memoirs of Henry Hunt, Esq*. 3 vols. London: T. Dolby, 1822.

An Impartial and Authentic Memoir of the Life of Her Late Most Gracious Majesty Queen Caroline, Consort of Geo. IV, from her First Introduction to This Country to Her Death and Funeral. London: Dean and Munday, n.d. (c. 1821).

Jones, E. "Trades grievances." *Notes to the People*, 1:341–44. London: Merlin Press, 1967 (orig. 1851).

Kay-Shuttleworth, J. P. *The Moral and Physical Condition of the Working Classes Employed in the Cotton Manufacture in Manchester*. Shannon: Irish University Press, 1971 (orig. 1832).

Lovett, W. *The Life and Struggles of William Lovett, in His Pursuit of Bread, Knowledge, and Freedom*. London: Trubner, 1876.

———, and J. Collins. *Chartism: A New Organization of the People*. Leicester:

Leicester University Press, 1969 (orig. 1840).

MacKinnon, W. A., *On the Rise, Progress and Present State of Public Opinion in Great Britain and Other Parts of the World*. Shannon: Irish University Press, 1971 (orig. 1828).

Martineau, H. *History of England during the Peace, 1815–1846*. London: Chambers, 1858 (orig. 1849).

Peel, F. *The Risings of the Luddites*. New York: Kelley, 1968 (orig. 1880).

Taylor, W. C. *Notes of a Tour in the Manufacturing Districts of Lancashire*. London: Cass, 1968 (orig. 1841).

Thelwall J. *The Rights of Nature against the Usurpations of Establishments, Being Letters to the People of Britain in Answer to the Recent Effusions of the Right Honourable E. Burke*. London: published by the author, 1796.

Thompson, W. *An Inquiry into the Principles of the Distribution of Wealth Most Conducive to Human Happiness*. London: Hunt and Clarke, 1824.

————. *Labour Rewarded. The Claims of Labour and Capital Conciliated: or How to Secure to Labour the Whole Product of Its Exertions*. London: Hunt and Clarke, 1827.

Ure, A. *The Cotton Manufacture of Great Britain*. 2 vols. London: H. G. Bohn, 1861.

The Whole Proceedings before the Coroner's Inquest at Oldham, Etc., on the Body of John Lees. London: Dowling, n.d. (c. 1820).

3. Periodicals

The Black Dwarf
Democratic Review
The Gorgon
Manchester Guardian
Manchester Herald
Manchester Observer
Mechanics Magazine
Notes to the People
Political Register
Poor Man's Guardian
The Red Republican
The Republican
Sherwin's Political Register
The Times
Two-Penny Trash
The White Dwarf

4. Statistical Compilations

Gayer, A. D., W. W. Rostow and A. J. Schwartz. *The Growth and Fluctuation of the British Economy, 1790–1860*. 2 vols. Hassocks, Sussex: Harvester, 1975.

McCulloch, J. R. *A Descriptive and Statistical Account of the British Empire*. London: Longmans, 1847.

Mitchell, B. R., and P. Deane. *Abstract of British Historical Statistics*. Vol. 1. Cambridge: Cambridge University Press, 1962.

Secondary Printed Sources and General Works

Abarbanel, J. "The Dilemma of Economic Competition in an Israeli Moshav." In S. F. Moore and B. G. Myerhoff, eds., *Symbol and Politics in Communal Ideology*, pp. 144–65. Ithaca, NY: Cornell University Press, 1975.

Althusser, L. *For Marx*. London: New Left Books, 1970 (orig. 1965).

―――, and E. Balibar. *Reading Capital*. London: New Left Books, 1970 (orig. 1968).

Amin, S. *Unequal Development*. New York: Monthly Review Press, 1976 (orig. 1972).

Aminzade, R. "French Strike Development and Class Struggle." *Social Science History* 4 (1980):57–79.

Anderson, M. *Family Structure in Nineteenth-Century Lancashire*. Cambridge: Cambridge University Press, 1971.

―――. "Sociological History and the Working-Class Family: Smelser Revisited." *Social History* no. 6 (1976):317–34.

Anderson, P. "Socialism and Pseudo-Empiricism." *New Left Review*, no. 35 (1966).

―――. *Arguments within English Marxism*. London: New Left Review Books, 1980.

Arrow, K. *Social Choice and Individual Values*. New York: John Wiley, 1951.

Ashton, T. S. *An Economic History of England: The Eighteenth Century*. London: Methuen, 1955.

Aspin, C. *Haslingden, 1800–1900*. Haslingden: Haslingden Printing Works, 1962.

Aspinall, A. *Lord Brougham and the Whig Party*. Manchester: Manchester University Press, 1939.

―――. *Politics and the Press, 1780–1850*. New York: Barnes and Noble, 1974.

Avineri, S. *Hegel's Theory of the Modern State*. Cambridge: Cambridge University Press, 1972.

Axon, W. E. A. *The Annals of Manchester*. Manchester, 1886.

Baines, E. *Baine's Lancashire*; reprint of *History, Directory and Gazetteer of the County Palatine of Lancaster*. 2 vols. Newton Abbot: David and Charles, 1968 (orig. 1824).

Bateson, G., D. D. Jackson, J. Haley, and J. H. Weakland. "Toward a Theory of Schizophrenia." In Bateson, *Steps to an Ecology of Mind*. New York: Ballantine, 1972 (orig. 1956).

Baumol, W. J. *Welfare Economics and the Theory of the State*. Cambridge, MA: Harvard University Press, 1952.

Berk, R. A. "A Gaming Approach to Crowd Behavior." *American Sociological Review* 39 (1974):355–73.

―――. *Collective Behavior*. Dubuque, IA: W. C. Brown, 1974.

Bion, W. *Experiences in Groups*. London: Tavistock, 1961.

Blau, P. M. *Inequality and Heterogeneity*. New York: Free Press, 1977.

―――, and R. A. Schoenherr. *The Structure of Organizations*. New York: Basic Books, 1974.

Bloch, M. "The Long Term and the Short Term: The Economic and Political

Significance of the Morality of Kinship." In J. Goody, ed., *The Character of Kinship*. Cambridge: Cambridge University Press, 1973.

Bourdieu, P. *Outline of a Theory of Practice*. Trans. R. Nice. Cambridge: Cambridge University Press, 1977 (orig. 1972).

Bowman, W. D. *The Divorce Case of Queen Caroline*. London: Routledge, 1930.

Briggs, A. "Middle Class Consciousness in English Politics, 1780–1846." *Past and Present* 9 (1956):65–74.

———. "The Language of 'Class' in Early Nineteenth-Century England." In A. Briggs and J. Saville, eds., *Essays in Labour History*. Rev. ed. London: Papermac, 1967 (orig. 1960).

Buckle, H. T. *History of Civilization in England*. 3 vols. London: Longmans, 1885.

Bythell, D. *The Handloom Weavers*. Cambridge: Cambridge University Press, 1969.

Calhoun, C. J. "The Social Function of Experiences of Altered Perception." In T. R. Williams, ed., *Socialization and Communication in Primary Groups*. The Hague: Mouton, 1975.

———. "Education and the Problem of Continuity." In C. J. Calhoun and F. A. J. Ianni, eds., *The Anthropological Study of Education*. The Hague: Mouton, 1976.

———. "History, Anthropology and the Study of Communities: Some Problems in Macfarlane's Proposal." *Social History* 3, no. 3 (1978):363–73.

———. " 'Community': toward a Variable Conceptualization for Comparative Research." *Social History* 5, no. 1 (1980):105–29.

———. "Democracy, Autocracy and Intermediate Associations in Organizations." *Sociology* 14, no. 3 (1980):345–64.

———. "The Authority of Ancestors," *MAN* 15, no. 2 (1980):304–19.

Chambers, J. D., and G. E. Mingay, *The Agricultural Revolution, 1750–1880*. London: Batsford, 1966.

Chambers, J. D. "Enclosure and the Labour Supply in the Industrial Revolution." *Economic History Review*, 2d ser., 5 (1952–53):318–43.

Chapman, S. D. *The Early Factory Masters: The Transition to the Factory System in the Midlands Textile Industry*. Newton Abbot: David and Charles, 1967.

Clapham, J. H. "The Transference of the Worsted Industry from Norfolk to the West Riding." *Economics Journal* 20 (1910):195–210.

———. *An Economic History of Modern Britain*, 2 vols. Cambridge: Cambridge University Press, 1926.

Claudin, F. *The Communist Movement*. Harmondsworth: Penguin, 1975 (orig. 1970).

———. "La Vía al Socialismo en Europa." *Systema*, no. 15 (1976):33–44.

Cobban, A. *The Social Interpretation of the French Revolution*. Cambridge: Cambridge University Press, 1969.

Cohn, N. *The Pursuit of the Millenium*. New York: Oxford University Press, 1970.

Cole, G. D. H. *Short History of the British Working Class Movement, 1789–1937*. London: Allen and Unwin, 1932.

————. The Life of William Cobbett. London: Allen and Unwin, 1947.

————. Attempts at General Union, 1818–1834. London: Macmillan, 1953.

————, and M. Cole, Introduction, The Opinions of William Cobbett. London: The Cobbett Publishing Company, 1944.

————, and A. W. Filson, eds. British Working Class Movements: Selected Documents, 1789–1875. London: Macmillan, 1965.

————, and R Postgate. The Common People. London: Methuen, 1942.

Coleman, J. S. The Mathematics of Collective Action. Chicago: Aldine, 1976.

Collier, F. The Family Economy of the Working Classes in the Cotton Industry, 1784–1833. Manchester: Manchester University Press, 1964.

Colson, E. Tradition and Contract: The Problem of Order. London: Heinemann, 1974.

Cookson, J. E. Lord Liverpool's Administration, 1815–1822. Edinburgh: Scottish Academic Press, 1975.

Csikszentmihalyi, M. "Attention and the Holistic Approach to Behavior." In J. K. Pope and J. L. Singer, eds., The Stream of Consciousness. New York: Plenum, 1978.

Currie, E., and J. H. Skolnick. "A Critical Note on Conceptions of Collective Behavior." The Annals of the American Academy of Political and Social Science, no. 391, 1970 pp. 34–45.

Currie, R., and R. M. Hartwell. "The Making of the English Working Class?" Economic History Review. 2d ser., 18, pp. 633–43.

Dahrendorf, R. Class and Class Conflict in Industrial Society. London: Routledge and Kegan Paul, 1959.

Darvall, F. O. Popular Disturbances and Public Order in Regency England. Oxford: Oxford University Press, 1934.

Davis, N. Z. Society and Culture in Early Modern France. Stanford: Stanford University Press, 1975.

Deane, P., and W. A. Cole, British Economic Growth, 1688–1959. Cambridge: Cambridge University Press, 1969.

Dinwiddy, J. "Luddism and Politics in the Northern Counties." Social History 4 no. 1 (1979):33–63.

Donnelly, F. K. "Ideology and Early English Working-Class History: Edward Thompson and His Critics." Social History, no. 2 (1976):219–38.

Durkheim, E. Suicide: A Study in Sociology. New York: The Free Press, 1951 (orig. 1897).

————. The Elementary Forms of the Religious Life. New York: The Free Press, 1915.

Edwards, M. M., and R. Lloyd-Jones. "N. J. Smelser and the Cotton Factory Family: A Reassessment." In N. B. Harte and K. G. Pointing, eds., Textile History and Economic History. Manchester: Manchester University Press, 1973.

Emmanuel, A. Unequal Exchange: A Study of the Imperialism of Trade. New York: Monthly Review Press, 1972.

Engles, F. The Conditions of the Working Class in England in 1844. In Collected Works, 4:297–596. London: Lawrence and Wishart, 1975 (orig. 1844).

————. "The Ten Hours Question." *Democratic Review*, pp. 371–97. London: Merlin, 1968 (orig. 1850).

————. "Socialism: Utopian and Scientific." In L. Feuer, ed., *Marx and Engels: Basic Writings in Politics and Philosophy*. New York: Doubleday Anchor, 1959 (orig. 1880).

Evans, E. J. "Some Reasons for the Growth of English Rural Anti-Clericalism, c. 1750–c. 1830," *Past and Present* 66 (1975):84–109.

Evans-Pritchard, E. E. *Theories of Primitive Religion*. London: Oxford University Press, 1965.

Festinger, L. *A Theory of Cognitive Dissonance*. Stanford: Stanford University Press, 1962.

————. *Conflict, Decision, and Dissonance*. Stanford: Stanford University Press, 1964.

————, H. W. Riecker and S. Schachter. *When Prophecy Fails*. New York: Harper, 1956.

Fortes, M. *The Dynamics of Clanship among the Tallensi*. London: Oxford University Press, for the International African Institute, 1945.

————. *The Web of Kinship among the Tallensi*. London: Oxford University Press, for the International African Institute, 1949.

————. "Oedipus and Job in West African Religion." In C. Leslie, ed., *Anthropology of Folk Religion*. New York: Doubleday, 1959.

————. "Some Reflections on Ancestor Worship in Africa." In Fortes and Dieterlen, eds., *African Systems of Thought*. Oxford: Oxford University Press, 1965.

Foster, J. "Oldham." Ph.D. thesis, Cambridge University, 1967.

————. *Class Struggle and the Industrial Revolution*. London: Weidenfeld and Nicolson, 1974.

Frank, A. G. *Lumpenbourgeoisie and Lumpendevelopment*. New York: Monthly Review Press, 1972.

Fremantle, A. "The Truth about Oliver the Spy." *English Historical Review* 47 (1932):601–16.

Freud, S., *Group Psychology and the Analysis of the Ego*. The Standard Edition, 18:65–143. London: Hogarth Press, 1976 (orig. 1921).

Fulford, R. *The Trial of Queen Caroline*. New York: Stein and Day, 1968.

Gadamer, H-G. *Truth and Method*. New York: Seabury, 1975 (orig. 1960).

————. *Philosophical Hermeneutics*. Trans. D. E. Linge. Berkeley: University of California Press, 1976.

Gauldie, E. *Cruel Habitations*. London: Allen and Unwin, 1974.

George, M. D. *London Life in the Eighteenth Century*. Harmondsworth: Penguin, 1965.

Gerth, H. H., and C. W. Mills, eds. *From Max Weber*. London: Routledge and Kegan Paul, 1948.

Gibbard, G. S., J. J. Hartman, and R. D. Mann, eds. *Analysis of Groups*. San Francisco: Jossey-Bass, 1974.

Giddens, A. *The Class Structure of the Advanced Societies*. New York: Harper and Row, 1973.

Gluckman, M. Custom and Conflict in Africa. Oxford: Blackwell, 1956.

————. "Rituals of Rebellion in South-East Africa." In Order and Rebellion in Tribal Africa. London: Cohen and West, 1963 (orig. 1954).

————. "Les Rites de Passage" In Gluckman, ed., Essays on the Ritual of Social Relations. Manchester: Manchester University Press, 1962.

————. Order and Rebellion in Africa. London: Cohen and West, 1963.

————. Politics, Law and Ritual in Tribal Society. New York: New American Library. 1965.

————. "Interhierarchical Roles." In M. J. Swartz, ed., Local-Level Politics. Chicago: Aldine, 1968.

Godelier, M. Rationality and Irrationality in Economics. London: New Left Books, 1972 (orig. 1966).

Goode, W. J. "A Theory of Role Strain." American Sociological Review 25 (1960):483–96.

Goodwyn, L. Democratic Promise: The Populist Movement in America. New York: Oxford University Press, 1976.

Goody, J. The Social Organization of the LoWiili. Rev. ed. London: Oxford University Press, for the International African Institute, 1967 (orig. 1956).

Gurr, T. R. Why Men Rebel. Princeton: Princeton University Press, 1969.

Habermas, J. Communications and the Evolution of Societies. Trans. T. McCarthy. Boston: Beacon Press, 1979 (orig. 1976).

Halévy, E. England in 1815. London: Benn, 1961 (orig. 1913).

————. The Liberal Awakening. London: Benn, 1961 (orig. 1923).

Hammond, J. L., and B. Hammond, The Village Labourer. London: Longmans, 1966 (orig. 1911).

————. The Skilled Labourer. New York: Kelley, 1967 (orig. 1919).

Hanson, D. W. From Kingdom to Commonwealth: The Development of Civic Consciousness in English Political Thought. Cambridge, MA: Harvard University Press, 1970.

Harland, J. Ballads and Songs of Lancashire. Manchester: Heywood, 1882.

Harrington, M. Fragments of the Century. New York: Simon and Schuster, 1972.

————. The Twilight of Capitalism. New York: Simon and Schuster, 1976.

Harrison, J. F. C. Robert Owen and the Owenites in Britain and America. London: Routledge and Kegan Paul, 1969.

Hart, J. K. "Entrepreneurs and Migrants: A Study of Modernization among the Frafras of Ghana." Ph.D. thesis, Cambridge University, 1969.

Hartwell, R. M. "Business Management in England during the Period of Early Industrialization: Inducements and Obstacles." In Hartwell, ed., The Industrial Revolution. Oxford: Blackwell, 1970.

Hay, D. "Property, Authority and the Criminal Law." In D. Hay, P. Linebaugh, and E. P. Thompson, eds., Albion's Fatal Tree. London: Allen Lane, 1975.

Hegel, G. W. F. Philosophy of Right. Trans. T. M. Knox. Oxford: Oxford University Press, 1967 (orig. 1821).

Heise, D. Understanding Events. New York: Cambridge University Press, 1979.

Hill, C. Society and Puritanism in Pre-Revolutionary England. New York: Schocken, 1967.

Hobsbawm, E. J. "The Machine Breakers." In *Labouring Men*. London: Weidenfeld and Nicolson, 1968 (orig. 1952).

———. "Methodism and the Threat of Revolution in Britain." In *Labouring Men*. London: Weidenfeld and Nicolson, 1968 (orig. 1964).

———"The Tramping Artisan." In *Labouring Men*. London: Weidenfeld and Nicolson, 1968 (orig. 1964).

———. "The Labour Aristocracy in Nineteenth-Century Britain." In *Labouring Men*. London: Weidenfeld and Nicolson, 1968, pp. 272–315 (orig. 1964).

———. *Primitive Rebels*. Manchester: Manchester University Press, 1959.

———. "Should the Poor Organize?" *New York Review of Books*, March 23, 1978, pp. 44–49.

———, and G. Rudé, *Captain Swing*. Harmondsworth: Penguin, 1973 (orig. 1969).

Hollis, P. *The Pauper Press. A Study in Working-Class Radicalism in the 1830s*. Oxford: Oxford University Press, 1970.

Horton, R. "African Traditional Thought and Western Science." *Africa* 27 (1967):50–71, 155–87.

Hunt, B. C. *The Development of the Business Corporation in Britain 1800–1867*. Cambridge, MA: Harvard University Press, 1936.

Inglis, B. *Poverty and the Industrial Revolution*. London: Panther, 1971.

Jephson, H. *The Platform*. London: Macmillan, 1892.

Johnson, A. H. *The Disappearance of the Small Landowner*. Oxford: Oxford University Press, 1963.

Johnson, C. *Revolutionary Change*. Boston: Little, Brown, 1966.

Johnson, R. "Edward Thompson, Eugene Genovese, and Socialist-Humanist History." *History Workshop* 6 (1978):79–106.

Kerr, C. and A. Siegel "The Interindustry Propensity to Strike—an International Comparison." In A. Kornhauser, ed. *Industrial Conflict*. New York: McGraw-Hill, 1954.

Kinsey, W. W. "Some Aspects of Lancashire Radicalism 1816–21." M. A. thesis, Manchester University, 1927.

Kirby, R. G., and A. E. Musson, *The Voice of the People: John Doherty, 1789–1854*. Manchester: Manchester University Press, 1975.

Laqueur, T. W. *Religion and Respectability*. New Haven and London: Yale University Press, 1976.

Landes, D. S. *The Unbound Prometheus*. Cambridge: Cambridge University Press, 1969.

Laslett, P. *The World We Have Lost*. London: Methuen, 1971.

Lean, E. T. *The Napoleonists: A Study in Political Disaffection, 1760–1960*. Oxford: Oxford University Press, 1970.

Le Bon, G. *The Crowd: A Study of the Popular Mind*. New York: Viking, 1960 (orig. 1909).

———. *La Révolution Française et la Psychologie des Révolutions*. Paris: Flammarion, 1912.

Leeson, R. A. *Travelling Brothers: The Six Centuries' Road from Craft-Fellowship to Trade Unionism*. London: Allen and Unwin, 1979.

Lefebvre, H. *The Sociology of Marx*. London: Allen Lane, 1968 (orig. 1966).

Lenin, V. I. *What Is to Be Done?* In R. Tucker, ed., *The Lenin Anthology*. New York: Norton, 1975 (orig. 1902).

———. *Materialism and Empirio-Criticism*. New York: International Publishers, 1970 (orig. 1908).

———. *The State and Revolution*. Peking: Foreign Languages Press, 1976 (orig. 1917).

Lévi-Strauss, C. *The Savage Mind*. Chicago: University of Chicago Press, 1962.

Lévy-Bryhl. *Primitive Mentality*. New York: Macmillan, 1923 (orig. 1922).

———. *Le Surnaturel et la Nature dans la Mentalité Primitive*. Paris: Alcan, 1931.

Lichtheim, G. *Marxism*. London: Routledge and Kegan Paul, 1967 (orig. 1961).

"The Luddites in the Period 1779–1830." In L. M. Munby, ed., *The Luddites and Other Essays*. Edgware, Middx.: Katanka, 1971.

Lukács, G. *History and Class Consciousness*. London: Merlin Press, 1971 (orig. 1924).

Maccoby, S. *English Radicalism, 1786–1832*. London: Allen and Unwin, 1955.

Macfarlane, A. "History, Anthropology and the Study of Communities." *Social History* 5 (1977):631–52.

McDougall, W. *The Group Mind*. Cambridge: Cambridge University Press, 1920.

Macrae, D. "Populism as an Ideology." In G. Ionescu and E. Gellner, eds., *Populism: Its Meanings and National Characteristics*. London: Weidenfeld and Nicolson, 1969.

Marshall, J. D. "The Lancashire Rural Labourer in the Early Nineteenth Century." *Transactions of the Lancashire and Cheshire Antiquarian Society* 71 (1961).

Marx, G. "Issueless Riots." *Annals of the American Academy of Political and Social Science*, 391:21–23.

Marx, K. "Contribution to the Critique of Hegel's Philosophy of Law." In *Collected Works*, 3:3–129. London: Lawrence and Wishart, 1975 (orig. 1927).

———. *The Holy Family*. In *Collected Works*, 4:5–211. London: Lawrence and Wishart, 1975 (orig. 1845).

———. "Theses on Feuerbach." In *Collected Works*, 5:3–8. London: Lawrence and Wishart, 1976 (orig. 1845).

———. *The Poverty of Philosophy*. In *Collected Works*, 6:105–212. London: Lawrence and Wishart, 1976 (orig. 1847).

———. "The Class Struggles in France: 1848–1850." In *Surveys from Exile*. Harmondsworth: Penguin, 1973 (orig. 1850).

———. "The Eighteenth Brumaire of Louis Bonaparte." In *Surveys from Exile*, pp. 143–249. Harmondsworth: Penguin, 1973 (orig. 1852).

———. *A Contribution to the Critique of Political Economy*. London: Lawrence and Wishart, 1971 (orig. 1859).

———. *Capital*. Vol. I. Harmondsworth: Penguin, 1976 (orig. 1867).

———. *Capital*. 3 vols. London: Lawrence and Wishart, 1970 (orig. 1867–84).

———. "The Civil War in France." In R. Tucker, ed., *The Marx-Engels Reader*. New York: Norton, 1972 (orig. 1871).

————, and F. Engels, "Manifesto of the Communist Party." In *Collected Works*, 6:477–519. London: Lawrence and Wishart, 1976 (orig. 1848).

————. *The German Ideology*. In *Collected Works*, 5:19–539. London: Lawrence and Wishart, 1976 (orig. 1932).

————, and F. Engels. *On Britain*. Moscow: Foreign Languages Publishing House, 1953.

Mather, F. C. "The General Strike of 1842: A Study in Leadership, Organization and the Threat of Revolution during the Plug Plot Disturbances." In J. Stevenson and R. Quinault, eds., *Popular Protest and Public Order*. London: Allen and Unwin, 1974.

Mayhew, B. H., and T. Levinger. "On the Emergence of Oligarchy in Human Interaction." *American Journal of Sociology* 81 (1976):1017–49.

Merton, R. K. *Social Theory and Social Structure*. New York: The Free Press, 1957.

Meyer, J., and M. Hannan, eds. *National Development and the World System*. Chicago: University of Chicago Press, 1979.

Michels, R. *Political Parties*. Glencoe, IL: The Free Press, 1949.

Miller, E. J., and A. K. Rice. *Systems of Organization*. London: Tavistock, 1967.

Mills, C. W. "The New Left." In I. L. Horowitz, ed., *Power Politics, and People: The Collected Essays of C. Wright Mills*. New York: Oxford, 1963.

Mingay, G. E. *English Landed Society in the Eighteenth Century*. London: Routledge and Kegan Paul, 1963.

————. *Enclosure and the Small Farmer in the Age of the Industrial Revolution*. London: Macmillan, 1973.

————. *The Gentry: The Rise and Fall of the Ruling Class*. London: Longmans, 1976,

Moffit, L. *England on the Eve of the Industrial Revolution*. New York: Barnes and Noble, 1925.

Montgomery, D. "Strikes in Nineteenth-Century America," *Social Science History* 4 (1980):81–104.

Moore, D. C. "Concession or Cure: The Sociological Premises of the First Reform Act." *Historical Journal* 9 (1966):39–59.

————. *The Politics of Deference*. Hassocks, Sussex: Harvester, 1976.

Moore, S. F. "Legal Liability and Evolutionary Interpretation: Some Aspects of Strict Liability, Self-Help and Collective Responsibility." In M. Gluckman, ed., *The Allocation of Responsibility*. Manchester: Manchester University Press, 1972.

Moorhouse, H. F. "The Marxist Theory of the Labour Aristocracy." *Social History* 3, no. 1 (1978):61–82.

Musson, A. E. "Class Struggle and the Labour Aristocracy. 1830–1860." *Social History* 1 (1976):335–56.

Myrdal, G. *The Political Element in the Development of Economic Theory*. London: Routledge and Kegan Paul, 1953.

Nadel, S. F. *The Foundations of Social Anthropology*. London: Cohen and West, 1951.

Nairn, T. *The Break-Up of Britain*. London: New Left Books, 1977.

Nisbet, R. A. *The Quest for Community* (also published as *Community and Power*). New York: Oxford University Press, 1951.

Oberschall, A. *Social Conflict and Social Movements*. Englewood Cliffs, NJ: Prentice-Hall, 1973.

Olson, M. *The Logic of Collective Action*. Rev. ed. New York: Schocken, 1971 (orig. 1965).

Orwell, G. *1984*. New York: Harcourt Brace, 1949.

Osborne, J. W. *John Cartwright*. Cambridge: Cambridge University Press, 1972.

Pälm, G. *The Flight from Work*. Cambridge: Cambridge University Press, 1977 (orig. 1972, 1974).

Parkin, F. "Strategies of Social Closure in Class Formation." In F. Parkin, ed., *The Social Analysis of Class Structure*. London: Tavistock, 1974.

Parsons, T. *The Social System*. New York: The Free Press, 1952.

Payne, P. L. "The Emergence of the Large-Scale Company in Great Britain." *Economic History Review*, 2d ser., vol. 20 (1967).

Perkin, H. *The Origins of Modern English Society, 1780–1880*. London: Routledge and Kegan Paul, 1969.

Peters, E. L. "The Proliferation of Segments in the Lineage of the Bedouin in Cyrenaica." *Journal of the Royal Anthropological Institute* 90 (1960):29–53.

——. "Aspects of the Control of Moral Ambiguities: A Comparative Analysis of Two Culturally Disparate Modes of Social Control." In M. Gluckman, ed., *The Allocation of Responsibility*. Manchester: Manchester University Press, 1972.

Pinchbeck, I. *Women and the Industrial Revolution, 1750–1850*. London: Cass, 1930.

Piven, F. F., and R. A. Cloward. *Poor People's Movements*. New York: Vintage, 1977.

Polanyi, K. *The Great Transformation*. Boston: Beacon, 1944.

Polanyi, M. *Personal Knowledge*. Chicago: University of Chicago Press, 1962.

Pollard, S. *The Genesis of Modern Management*. London: Edward Arnold, 1965.

——, and J. Salt, eds. *Robert Owen: Prophet of the Poor*. London: Macmillan, 1971.

Postgate, R. W. *The Builders' History*. London: National Foundation of Building Trade Operatives, 1923.

Poulantzas, N. *Political Power and Social Classes*. London: New Left Books, 1973 (orig. 1968).

——. *Classes in Contemporary Capitalism*. London: New Left Books, 1975 (orig. 1974).

——. *State, Power, and Socialism*. London: New Left Books, 1979.

Prothero, I. *Artisans and Politics in Early Nineteenth-Century London*. Folkestone, Kent: Dawson, 1979.

Radzinowicz, L. *A History of English Criminal Law*. Vol. 1, *The Movement for Reform*. Vol. 2: *The Enforcement of the Law*. London: Stevens, 1948.

Read, D. *Peterloo: The "Massacre" and Its Background*. Manchester: Manchester University Press, 1958.

Redford, A. *Labour Migration in England, 1800–1850*. Manchester: Manchester University Press, 1976 (orig. 1926).

Redlich, J., and F. W. Hirst, *The History of Local Government in England*. 2d ed. With epilogue by B. Keith-Lucas. London: Macmillan, 1970.

Reid, A. "Politics and Economics in the Formation of the British Working Class: A Response to H. F. Moorhouse," *Social History* 3 (1978):347–61.

Reisman, D. A. *Adam Smith's Sociological Economics*. London: Croom Helm, 1976.

Richardson, J. *The Disastrous Marriage: A Study of George IV and Caroline of Brunswick*. London: Jonathan Cape, 1960.

Rose, A. G. "The Plug Plot Riots of 1842 in Lancashire and Cheshire." *Transactions of the Lancashire and Cheshire Antiquarian Society* 67 (1957):75–112.

Rose, R. B. "Eighteenth-Century Price Riots and Public Policy in England." *International Review of Social History* 6 (1961):277–82.

Ruben, D. H. *Marxism and Materialism: A Study in Marxist Theory of Knowledge*. Atlantic Highlands, NJ: Humanitites Press, 1977.

Rudé, G. *The Crowd in the French Revolution*. Oxford: Oxford University Press, 1959.

———. *Wilkes and Liberty*. Oxford: Oxford University Press, 1962.

———. *The Crowd in History: A Study of Popular Disturbances in France and England, 1730–1848*. New York: John Wiley, 1964.

Rudkin, O. *Thomas Spence and His Connections*. London: Allen and Unwin, 1927.

Rushton, P. "Housing Conditions and the Family Economy in the Victorian Slum: A Study of a Manchester District, 1790–1871." Ph.D. thesis, Manchester University, 1977.

Samuel, R. "Workshop of the World: Steam Power and Hand Technology in Mid-Victorian Britain." *History Workshop* 3 (1977):6–72.

Saville, J. Introduction *The Red Republican*. London: Merlin, 1966.

———. "Class Struggle and the Industrial Revolution." In *The Socialist Register, 1974*. London: Merlin.

Schoyen, A. R. *The Chartist Challenge: A Portrait of George Julian Harney*. London: Heinemann, 1958.

Seldon, A., ed. *The Long Debate on Poverty*. Rev. ed. London: Institute of Economic Affairs, 1974 (orig. 1972).

Sen, A. K. *Collective Choice and Social Welfare*. Edinburgh: Oliver and Boyd, 1971.

Sennett, R. *The Uses of Disorder*. New York: Vintage, 1970.

———. *The Fall of Public Man*. New York: Knopf, 1976.

Sherif, M., and O. J. Harvey. "A Study in Ego Functioning: Elimination of Stable Anchorages in Individual and Group Situations." *Sociometry* 15 (1952):272–305.

Shils, E. A. "Tradition." *Comparative Studies in Society and History* 13, no. 2 (1971):122–59.

Shorter, E., and C. Tilly, *Strikes in France, 1830–1968*. Cambridge: Cambridge University Press, 1974.

Simmel, G. "How Is Society Possible?" In D. N. Levine, ed., *Georg Simmel on Individuality and Social Forms*. Chicago: University of Chicago Press, 1971 (orig. 1908).

————. "Conflict." Trans. K. Wolff. In D. Levine, ed., *Georg Simmel on Individuality and Social Forms*. Chicago: University of Chicago Press, 1971 (1908).

Simon, H. A. *Administrative Behavior*. Glencoe, IL: The Free Press, 1957 (orig. 1949).

————. *Models of Man*. New York: John Wiley, 1957.

Slater, P. *Microcosm*. New York: John Wiley, 1967.

Smelser, N. J. *Social Change in the Industrial Revolution*. London: Routledge and Kegan Paul, 1959.

————. *Theory of Collective Behavior*. New York: The Free Press, 1962.

————. "Sociological History: The Industrial Revolution and the British Working-Class Family." In *Essays in Sociological Explanation*. Englewood Cliffs, NJ: Prentice-Hall, 1968.

————."Social and Psychological Dimensions of Collective Behavior." In *Essays in Sociological Explanation*. Englewood Cliffs, NJ: Prentice-Hall, 1968.

————. "Two Critics in Search of a Bias: A Response to Currie and Skolnick." *Annals of the American Academy of Political and Social Science*, no. 391 (1970):46–55.

Smith, M. G. "A Structural Approach to Comparative Politics." In *Corporations and Society*. London: Duckworth, 1974 (orig. 1966).

Snyder, D., and W. R. Kelly, "Industrial Violence in Italy, 1878–1903." *American Journal of Sociology* 82 (1976):131–62.

Soboul, A. *Les Sans-Culottes Parisiens en l'An II*. La Roche-sur-Yon: Potier, 1958.

Spring, D. "English Landowners and Nineteenth-Century Industrialism." In J. T. Ward and R. G. Wilson, eds., *Land and Industry*. Newton Abbot: David and Charles, 1971, pp. 16–62.

Stevenson, J. "Food Riots in England, 1792–1818." In J. Stevenson and R. Quinault, eds., *Popular Protest and Public Order*. London: Allen and Unwin, 1974.

————. "Social Control and the Prevention of Riots in England, 1789–1829." In A. P. Donajgrodski, ed., *Social Control in Nineteenth-Century Britain*. London: Croom Helm, 1977.

————. "The Queen Caroline Affair." In J. Stevenson, ed., *London in the Age of Reform*. Oxford: Blackwell, 1978.

Stinchcombe, A. *Theoretical Models in Social History*. New York: Academic Press, 1978.

Taylor, A. J., ed. *The Standard of Living in the Industrial Revolution*. London: Methuen, 1975.

Therbörn, G. *What Does the Ruling Class Do When It Rules?* London: New Left Books, 1978.

Tholfson, T. *Working Class Radicalism in Mid-Victorian England*. London: Croom Helm, 1976.

Thomis, M. I. *The Luddites*. Newton Abbot: David and Charles, 1970.

———. *Responses to Industrialization.* Newton Abbot: David and Charles, 1976.

Thompson, D. K. G. *The Early Chartists.* Columbia: University of South Carolina Press, 1971.

Thompson, E. P. *The Making of the English Working Class.* Rev. ed. Harmondsworth: Penguin, 1968 (orig. 1963).

———. "The Peculiarities of the English." In R. Miliband and J. Saville, eds., *The Socialist Register, 1965.* London: Merlin.

———. "Time, Work-Discipline and Industrial Capitalism." In M. W. Flinn and T. C. Smout, eds., *Essays in Social History.* London: Oxford University Press, 1974 (orig. 1967).

———. "The Moral Economy of the English Crowd in the Eighteenth Century." *Past and Present* 50 (1971):76–136.

———. "Rough Music: Le Charivari Anglais." *Annales ESC* 27 (1972):285–313.

———. "Patrician Society, Plebeian Culture." *Journal of Social History* 7 (1974):382–405.

———. "The Crime of Anonymity." In D. Hay, P. Linebaugh, and E. P. Thompson, eds., *Albion's Fatal Tree.* London: Allen Lane, 1975.

———. *Whigs and Hunters: The Origins of the Black Act.* London: Allen Lane, 1975.

———. "Eighteenth-century English Society: Structure, Field-of-Force, Dialectic." Paper presented to the Groupe de Travail Internationale de l'Histoire Sociale et Contemporaine. University of Constance (FRG) 1977.

———. "Eighteenth-century English Society: Class Struggle without Class?" *Social History* 4 (1979):133–66.

———. *The Poverty of Theory and Other Essays.* New York: Monthly Review Press, 1979.

———"The Very Type of the 'Respectable Artisan'." *New Society,* 3 May 1979, pp. 275–77.

Thompson, F. M. L. *English Landed Society in the Nineteenth Century.* London: Routledge and Kegan Paul, 1963.

Thornton, A. P. *The Habit of Authority: Paternalism in British History.* London: Allen and Unwin, 1965.

Tilly, C. *The Vendée.* Cambridge, MA: Harvard University Press, 1964.

———. "Food Supply and Public Order in Modern Europe." In C. Tilly, ed., *The Formation of National States in Western Europe.* Princeton: Princeton University Press, 1975.

———. *From Mobilization to Revolution.* Reading, MA: Addison-Wesley, 1978.

———, L. Tilly, and R. Tilly. *The Rebellious Century.* Cambridge, MA: Harvard University Press, 1975.

Timpanaro, S. *On Materialism.* London: New Left Books, 1976.

Toynbee, A. *Lectures on the Industrial Revolution in England, Popular Addresses, Notes and Other Fragments.* Newton Abbot: David and Charles, 1969 (orig. 1884).

Tucker, R. S. "Real Wages of Artisans in London, 1729–1935." In A. J. Taylor, ed., *The Standard of Living in Britain in the Industrial Revolution.* London: Methuen, 1975 (orig. 1936).

Turner, H. A. *Trade Union Growth, Structure, and Policy.* London: Oxford University Press, 1962.

Turner, R. H. "Collective Behavior." In R. E. L. Faris, ed., *Handbook of Modern Sociology.* Chicago: Rand-McNally, 1964.

———, and L. M. Killian. *Collective Behavior.* Englewood-Cliffs, NJ: Prentice-Hall, 1957.

Turner, V. W. *Schism and Continuity in an African Society.* Manchester: Manchester University Press, 1957.

———. *The Forest of Symbols.* Ithaca, NY: Cornell University Press, 1967.

———. *The Ritual Process.* Chicago: Aldine, 1969.

Unwin, G. *Industrial Organization in the Sixteenth and Seventeenth Centuries.* Oxford: The Clarendon Press, 1904.

Vigier, F. *Change and Apathy: Liverpool and Manchester during the Industrial Revolution.* Cambridge, MA: The MIT Press, 1970.

Wadsworth, A. P., and J. de L. Mann. *The Cotton Trade and Industrial Lancashire, 1600–1780.* Manchester: Manchester University Press, 1931.

Wallas, G. *The Life of Francis Place, 1771–1854.* London: Allen and Unwin, 1925.

Walmsley, R. *Peterloo: The Case Re-Opened.* Manchester: University Press, 1969.

Watson, J. S. *The Reign of George III, 1760–1815.* Oxford: Oxford University Press, 1960.

Wearmouth, R. F. *Some Working-Class Movements of the Nineteenth Century.* London: Epworth, 1948.

Webb, R. K. *The British Working-Class Reader, 1790–1848.* London: Allen and Unwin, 1955.

Webb, S., and B. Webb. *English Local Government: The Parish and the County.* London: Longmans, 1906.

———. *History of Trade Unionism.* London: Longmans, 1920.

———. *English Poor Law History: The Old Poor Law.* London: Longmans, 1927.

Webber, M. M. "Order in Diversity: Community without Propinquity." In L. Wirigo, ed., *Cities and Space.* Baltimore: The Johns Hopkins University Press, 1963.

Weber, M. "The Social Psychology of World Religions." In H. H. Gerth and C. W. Mills, eds., *From Max Weber.* London: Routledge and Kegan Paul, 1948 (orig. 1915).

———. *Economy and Society.* Trans. by G. Roth and K. Wittich. Berkeley: University of California Press, 1968 (orig. 1925).

Weller, J. M., and E. L. Quarantelli. "Neglected Characteristics of Collective Behavior." *American Journal of Sociology* 9 (1973):665–85.

Wertheim, W. F. *Evolution and Revolution.* Harmondsworth: Penguin, 1974.

White, R. J. *From Waterloo to Peterloo.* London: Mercury Books, 1957.

Wickwar, W. H. *The Struggle for the Freedom of the Press, 1819–1832.* London: Allen and Unwin, 1928.

Williams, G. *Artisans and Sans-Culottes.* London: Edward Arnold, 1968.

Williams, R. *Culture and Society, 1780–1950.* Harmondsworth: Penguin, 1963 (orig. 1958).

————. *The Country and the City*. St Albans, Herts.: Paladin, 1973.

Wolf, E. R. *Peasant Wars of the Twentieth Century*. New York: Harper and Row, 1969.

Woodward, L. *The Age of Reform*. Oxford: The Clarendon Press, 1962.

Worsley, P. "The Kinship System of the Tallensi: A Revaluation." *Journal of the Royal Anthropological Institute* 86, pt. 1 (1956):37–75.

Worsley, P. *The Trumpet Shall Sound: A Study of Cargo Cults in Melanesia*. New York: Shocken, 1957.

Wright, E. O. *Class, Crisis, and State*. London: New Left Books, 1978.

————. *Class Structure and Income Inequality*. New York: Academic Press, 1979.

Yalman, N. "Some Observations on Secularism in Islam: The Cultural Revolution in Turkey." *Daedalus* 102, no. 1 (1973):139–68.

Yonge, C. *The Life and Administration of Robert Banks, Second Earl of Liverpool*. 3 vols. London: Macmillan, 1868.

Zaret, D. "An Analysis of the Development and Content of the Covenant Theology of Pre-Revolutionary Puritanism." D.Phil. thesis, Oxford University, 1977.

————. "From Weber to Parsons and Schutz: The Eclipse of History in Modern Social Theory." *American Journal of Sociology* 85 (1980):1180–1201.

Index